THE ROUGH GUIDE TO
BANGKOK

Written and researched by
Paul Gray and Lucy R

This eighth edition updated by
Paul Gray

Contents

INTRODUCTION — 4

What to see	5	Author picks	13
When to go	10	Things not to miss	14

BASICS — 22

Getting there	23	The media	36
Arrival and departure	25	Festivals	37
City transport	28	Crime, safety and the law	38
Information and maps	34	Culture and etiquette	40
Health	34	Travel essentials	42

THE GUIDE — 49

1 Ratanakosin	49	5 Dusit	88
2 Banglamphu and the Democracy Monument area	65	6 Downtown Bangkok	91
3 Chinatown and Pahurat	75	7 Chatuchak Weekend Market and the outskirts	105
4 Thonburi	81	8 Excursions from Bangkok	111

LISTINGS — 149

9 Accommodation	149	13 Entertainment	176
10 Eating	157	14 Mind and body	180
11 Drinking and nightlife	169	15 Shopping	183
12 LGBTQ+ Bangkok	174	16 Kids' Bangkok	190

CONTEXTS — 193

History	194	Books	221
Religion: Thai Buddhism	206	Language	224
Art and architecture	212	Glossary	229

SMALL PRINT & INDEX — 231

CITY PLAN — 239

Introduction to
Bangkok

The headlong pace and flawed modernity of Bangkok match few people's visions of the capital of exotic Siam. Spiked with scores of high-rise buildings of concrete and glass, it's a vast flatness that holds an estimated population of nearly fifteen million, and feels even bigger. But under the shadow of the skyscrapers you'll find a heady mix of chaos and refinement, of frenetic markets and hushed golden temples, of early-morning alms-giving ceremonies and ultra-hip designer bars.

Bangkok is a relatively young capital, established in 1782 after the Burmese sacked Ayutthaya, its predecessor. A temporary base was set up on the western bank of the Chao Phraya River, in what is now Thonburi, before work started on the more defensible east bank, where the first king of the new dynasty, Rama I, built his fabulously ornate palace within a protective ring of canals. Around the temples and palaces of this "royal island", there spread an amphibious city of shops and houses built on bamboo rafts moored on the river and canals.

Ever since its foundation, but with breakneck acceleration in recent years, Bangkok has attracted internal migration from all over Thailand, pushing the city's boundaries

RAT OR RAJA?

There's no standard system of transliterating Thai script into Roman, so you're sure to find that the Thai words in this book don't always match the versions you'll see elsewhere. Maps and street signs are the biggest sources of confusion, so we've generally gone for the **transliteration** that's most common on the spot; where it's a toss-up between two equally popular versions, we've used the one that helps best with pronunciation. However, sometimes you'll need to do a bit of lateral thinking, bearing in mind that a classic variant for the town of Ayutthaya is Ayudhia, while among street names, Thanon Rajavithi could come out as Thanon Ratwithi – and it's not unheard of to find one spelling posted at one end of a road, with another at the opposite end. See the Language section of this book for an introduction to Thai.

DAMNOEN SADUAK FLOATING MARKET

ever outwards in an explosion of modernization that has seen the canals on the east side of the river concreted over and left the city without an obvious centre. The capital now sprawls over 330 square kilometres and, with a population forty times that of the second city, Chiang Mai, and four-fifths of the nation's automobiles, it's far and away the country's dominant metropolis. In the make-up of its population, however, Thailand's capital supports world trends – over half of its inhabitants are under thirty, a fact that helps to consolidate Bangkok's position as one of the liveliest and most fashionable cities in Asia.

What to see

Rama I named his royal island **Ratanakosin**, and this remains the city's spiritual heart, not to mention its culturally most rewarding quarter. No visit to the capital would be complete without seeing the star attractions here – if necessary, the dazzling ostentation of **Wat Phra Kaeo** and the **Grand Palace**, lively and grandiose **Wat Pho** and the **National Museum**'s hoard of exquisite works of art can all be crammed into a single action-packed day.

One of the other great pleasures of the city is a ride on its remaining waterways; the majestic **Chao Phraya River** is served by frequent ferries and longtail boats, and is the backbone of a network of old canals, stilted houses and lovely waterside temples

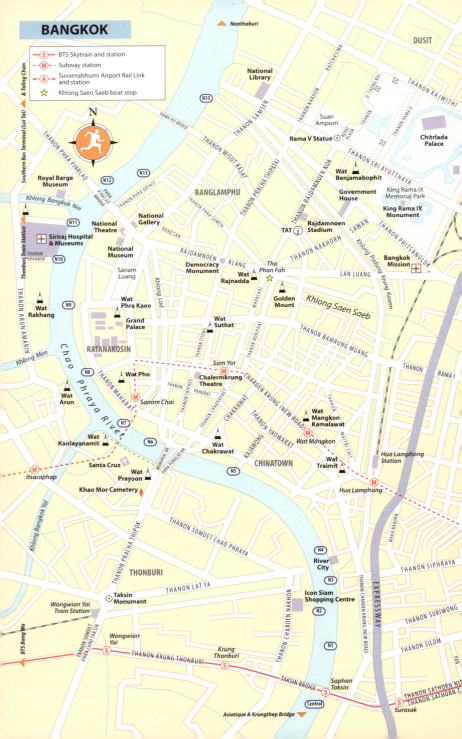

FACT FILE

- Bangkok (**Krung Thep** in Thai) is the capital of Thailand, which was known as **Siam** until 1939 (and again from 1945 to 1949); some academics feel changing the name back again would better reflect the country's Thai and non-Thai diversity.
- Buddhism is the national **religion**, Islam the largest minority religion, but nearly all Thais also practise some form of animism (spirit worship).
- Since 1932 the country has been a **constitutional monarchy**. At the time of his death in 2016, King Bhumibol, also known as Rama IX (being the ninth ruler of the Chakri dynasty), was the world's longest-ruling head of state, having been on the throne since 1946. He was succeeded by his son, who became King Vajiralongkorn (Rama X).
- **Tourism** is the country's main industry, and its biggest **exports** are computers and components, vehicles and vehicle parts, textiles and rubber.
- Bangkok has only around three square metres of public space per inhabitant, one of the lowest figures in the world, compared, for example, to London's 38 square metres per person. Meanwhile, over two million of the city's inhabitants live in two thousand areas of the city that are classified by the Bangkok Metropolitan Administration as slums.

– including the striking five-towered **Wat Arun** – that remains fundamentally intact in the west-bank **Thonburi** district. Inevitably the waterways have earned Bangkok the title of "Venice of the East", a tag that seems all too apt when you're wading through flooded streets in the rainy season.

Bangkok began to assume its modern guise at the end of the nineteenth century, when the forward-looking Rama V relocated the royal family to a neighbourhood north of Ratanakosin called **Dusit**. Here he commissioned grand European-style boulevards, built the new Chitrlada Palace (still used by the royal family today), had a charming summer palace constructed nearby, and capped it all with the erection of a sumptuous new temple, **Wat Benjamabophit**, which was built from Italian marble. When political modernization followed in 1932, Dusit was the obvious choice of home for Thailand's new parliament, where it remains, though in a new location overlooking the river.

Bangkok's commercial heart lies to the southeast of Dusit, where sleek glass towers and cool marble malls lend an air of energy and big-city drama to the districts of **Silom**, **Siam Square** and **Sukhumvit**. These areas shelter a few noteworthy tourist sights, too, best of which is **Jim Thompson's House**, a small, elegant and very personal museum of Thai design. **Shopping** downtown varies from touristic outlets selling Thai silks and handicrafts to international fashion emporia and boutiques showcasing the country's home-grown contemporary designs. For livelier scenes, explore the dark alleys of the bazaars in **Chinatown** or the Indian district, **Pahurat**, or head out to the enormous, open-air **Chatuchak Weekend Market**. Similarly, the city offers wildly varied entertainment, ranging from traditional dancing and the orchestrated bedlam of Thai boxing, through cool bars and clubs both downtown and in the backpackers' enclave of **Banglamphu**, to the farang-only sex bars of the notorious Patpong district.

North and west of the city, the unwieldy urban mass of Greater Bangkok peters out into the vast, well-watered central plains, a region that for centuries has grown the

> **CITY OF ANGELS**
>
> When Rama I was crowned in 1782, he gave his new capital a grand 43-syllable name to match his ambitious plans for the building of the city. Since then 21 more syllables have been added.
>
> Krungthepmahanakhornboworn-ratanakosinmahintarayutthayamahadilokpopnoppa ratratchathaniburiromudomratchaniwetmahasathanamornpimanavatarnsathitsakkath attiyavisnukarprasit is Guinness-certified as the longest place name in the world and roughly translates as "Great city of angels, the supreme repository of divine jewels, the great land unconquerable, the grand and prominent realm, the royal and delightful capital city full of nine noble gems, the highest royal dwelling and grand palace, the divine shelter and living place of the reincarnated spirits". Fortunately, all Thais refer to the city simply as Krung Thep ("City of Angels"), though plenty can recite the full name at the drop of a hat. Bangkok – "Riverside Village of the Plum Olive" – was the name of the original village on the Thonburi side of the Chao Phraya; with remarkable persistence, it has remained in use by foreigners since the 1660s, when the French built a short-lived garrison fort in the area.

bulk of the nation's food. The atmospheric ruins of Thailand's fourteenth-century capital **Ayutthaya** lie here, ninety minutes' train ride to the north of Bangkok and, together with the ornate palace at nearby **Bang Pa-In**, make a rewarding excursion from the modern metropolis. Further west, the massive stupa at **Nakhon Pathom** and the floating markets of **Damnoen Saduak** are also easily manageable as a day-trip, and combine well with a visit to the historic town of **Phetchaburi**, famous for its charming old temples. Riverside **Amphawa** is similarly evocative and makes a perfect escape from the bustle of the city, with its genuine floating markets and traditional canalside neighbourhoods. An overnight stay at **Kanchanaburi** is also well worth the effort: impressively sited on the River Kwai, it holds several moving World War II memorials, including the notorious Death Railway.

When to go

Bangkok's climate is governed by three seasons, though in reality the city sits firmly within the tropics and so enjoys warm days and nights year-round. The so-called **cool season**, which runs from November to February, is the most pleasant time of year to visit; days are invariably bright and clear, and temperatures average a manageable 27ºC (though they can still reach a broiling 31ºC at noon). This is high season for the tourist industry, so rooms and flights are at a premium and well worth booking in advance; prices shoot up further for the Christmas and New Year period.

> **AVERAGE DAILY TEMPERATURES AND RAINFALL IN BANGKOK**
>
> | | Jan | Feb | Mar | Apr | May | Jun | Jul | Aug | Sep | Oct | Nov | Dec |
> |---|---|---|---|---|---|---|---|---|---|---|---|---|
> | Max/min (ºC) | 28/21 | 28/21 | 29/21 | 30/22 | 31/23 | 31/23 | 30/23 | 31/23 | 31/23 | 30/23 | 29/23 | 28/22 |
> | Max/min (ºF) | 82/70 | 82/70 | 84/70 | 86/72 | 88/73 | 88/73 | 86/73 | 88/73 | 88/73 | 86/73 | 84/73 | 82/72 |
> | Rainfall (mm) | 11 | 28 | 31 | 72 | 190 | 152 | 158 | 187 | 320 | 231 | 57 | 9 |

March sees the beginning of the **hot season**, when temperatures hit 35ºC and higher, and continue to do so beyond the end of April. During these sweltering months you may find yourself spending more money than at other times, simply in order to secure the benefits of air-conditioning, whether in hotel rooms, restaurants, taxis or buses. Come in mid-April and you'll also find the city in full swing as it celebrates Songkhran, the Thai New Year (see page 37), filling the streets with raucous waterfights.

The downpours that characterize the **rainy season** can come as a welcome relief, though being hot and wet is a sensation that doesn't necessarily appeal to everyone. The rainy season varies in length and intensity from year to year, but usually starts with a bang in May, gathers force between June and August, and comes to a peak in September and October, when whole districts of the capital are flooded. Rain rarely lasts all day however, so as long as you're armed with an umbrella there's no reason to reschedule your trip – come during the rainy season and you'll get more for your money, too, as many hotels and airlines drop their prices right down at this time of year.

WOMAN PRAYING INSIDE WAT BENCHAMABOPHIT

Author picks

Having finally settled down in Thailand after twenty years of toing and froing, our author, Paul, has plenty to write home about. Here are some of his personal favourites:

Aroy aroy "Delicious, delicious" food is always at hand in the city of fifty thousand restaurants. Try the house deep-fried fish salad at *Taling Pling* (see page 168) or sample the meticulously authentic dishes at *Bolan* (see page 167). The area south of Democracy Monument is a fruitful hunting ground for traditional restaurants such as *Krua Apsorn* (see page 162).

Oishi aroy Perhaps surprisingly, Bangkok is a great place for delicious Japanese food, too, at lower prices than in Japan or the West. The sushi at *Hinata* (see page 165) is superb while the miso ramen at *Ramentei* (see page 168) and just about anything at all-rounder *Aoi* (see page 167) always hit the spot.

Bangkok de luxe The Thai capital's hotels do luxury extremely well so, if you can, push the boat out at the resort-like *Siam Kempinski* (see page 154), the elegant *Sukhothai* (see page 156) or the graceful *Anantara Siam* (see page 154).

Kneads must A good pummelling at the massage pavilions amid the historic, kaleidoscopic architecture of Wat Pho is one of Bangkok's unbeatable experiences (see page 57).

Khon Soak up the haunting music, beautiful costumes and exquisite gestures of Thailand's highest dramatic art (see page 178).

On the river Catch one of the express boats on the Chao Phraya whenever you can (see page 29): they're cheap, faster than road transport and open a window on the river's teeming life, set against a backdrop of temples, skyscrapers and colonial-style villas.

MONKEY KHON MASK
THE CHAO PHRAYA RIVER

Our author recommendations don't end here. We've flagged up our favourite places – a perfectly sited hotel, an atmospheric café, a special restaurant – throughout the Guide, highlighted with the ★ symbol.

20 things not to miss

It's not possible to see everything Bangkok has to offer on a short trip – and we don't suggest you try. What follows is a selective taste of the city's highlights, from extravagant palaces and frenetic markets to tranquil neighbourhoods and cutting-edge shopping, plus great day-trip destinations out of the city. All entries have a page reference to take you straight into the guide, where you can find out more.

1 WAT ARUN
See page 85
The Temple of Dawn looks great from the river – and even better close up.

2 THAI COOKERY CLASSES
See page 164
Insider tips on everything from five-star cuisine to fruit-carving and vegetarian curries.

3 WAT PHO
See page 57
This lavish and lively temple is home to the awesome Reclining Buddha and a great massage school.

4 CHATUCHAK WEEKEND MARKET
See page 106
Bangkok's top shopping experience features over ten thousand stalls selling everything from hill-tribe jewellery to designer lamps.

5 CYCLING
See page 30
Venture beyond the downtown gloss on a bicycle tour through the capital's rural fringes.

6 JIM THOMPSON'S HOUSE
See page 94
A very personal museum of Thai crafts and architecture.

7 SONGKHRAN
See page 37
Thai New Year is the excuse for a national water fight – don't plan on getting much done if you come in mid-April, just join in the fun.

8 THANON KHAO SAN
See page 66
Legendary hub for Southeast Asian backpackers: the place for cheap sleeps, baggy trousers and tall tales.

9 THAI BOXING
See page 178
Nightly bouts at the national stadia are accompanied by live music and frenetic betting.

10 TRADITIONAL MASSAGE
See page 181
Combining elements of acupressure and yoga, a pleasantly brutal way to help shed jet lag or to end the day.

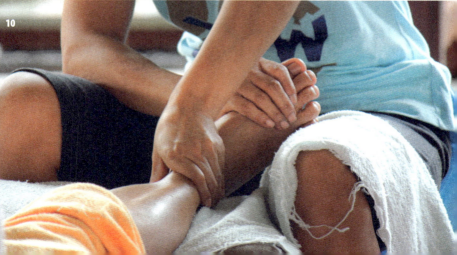

11 NATIONAL MUSEUM
See page 61
The cornucopia of Thailand's artistic heritage, ranging from sculptural treasures to royal funeral chariots.

12 MUANG BORAN ANCIENT CITY
See page 112
Escape from the city to this attractively landscaped open-air museum, which features beautiful replicas of Thailand's finest monuments.

13 A BOAT TRIP ON THE THONBURI CANALS
See page 82
The best way to explore the city's waterside communities.

14 WAT BENJAMABOPHIT
See page 89
A striking hybrid, Wat Ben fuses revered Buddha images with Italian marble and stained glass.

15 AYUTTHAYA
See page 116
Razed by the Burmese, the old capital is a brooding graveyard of temples, an hour-and-a-half away by train.

16 CONTEMPORARY DESIGN
See page 185
Shop for design pieces that fuse traditional East and minimalist West.

17 LOY KRATHONG
See page 37
At this festival in honour of the water spirits, Thais float baskets of flowers and lighted candles on rivers, ponds and seashores.

18 ERAWAN SHRINE
See page 97
The spiritual full monty: Buddhism, Hinduism and animism, dancing, lottery tickets, jasmine and gold.

19 63RD-FLOOR SUNDOWNER
See page 173
Fine cocktails and jaw-dropping views at *The Sky Bar* and *Distil*.

20 THE GRAND PALACE
See page 50
Sheltering Thailand's holiest temple, Wat Phra Kaeo, and its most sacred image, the Emerald Buddha, this huge complex is a kaleidoscope of colours and shapes.

TALING CHAN FLOATING MARKET

Basics

- **23** Getting there
- **25** Arrival and departure
- **28** City transport
- **34** Information and maps
- **34** Health
- **36** The media
- **37** Festivals
- **38** Crime, safety and the law
- **40** Culture and etiquette
- **42** Travel essentials

Getting there

Nearly all international flights into Bangkok use Suvarnabhumi Airport (see page 25); a few flights from other Asian countries, low-cost flights, and many domestic services, use the old Don Muang Airport (see page 26).

Air fares to Bangkok generally depend on the **season**, with the highest being from approximately mid-November to mid-February, when the weather is best (with premium rates charged for flights between mid-December and New Year), and in July and August to coincide with school holidays. You will need to book several months in advance to get reasonably priced tickets during these peak periods.

Flights from the UK and Ireland

The fastest and most comfortable way of reaching Thailand **from the UK** is to fly nonstop from London to Bangkok with Thai Airways (Wthaiairways.com), British Airways (Wba.com) or Eva Airways (Wevaair.com), a journey of about eleven and a half hours. These airlines sometimes have special promotions, but a typical fare in high season might come in at around £900. Fares on indirect scheduled flights to Bangkok are always cheaper than nonstop flights – starting at about £600 in high season if booked many months in advance – though these journeys can take anything from two to twelve hours longer.

There are no nonstop flights from any **regional airports** in Britain or from any **Irish airports**, but rather than routing via London, you may find it convenient to fly to another hub such as Frankfurt (with Lufthansa; Wlufthansa.com), Doha (Qatar Airways), Abu Dhabi (with Etihad; Wetihadairways.com) or Istanbul (with Turkish Airlines; Wturkishairlines.com), and take a connecting flight from there.

Flights from the US and Canada

At the moment, Thai Airways is no longer offering non-stop flights from the West Coast to Bangkok, though it's considering restarting them, either from Seattle or, possibly, San Francisco. Plenty of other airlines run to Bangkok from East and West Coast cities with one stop en route; it's generally easier to find a reasonable fare on flights via Asia than via Europe, even if you're departing from the East Coast – if you book far in advance, you can get a flight from LA or New York for as little as US$900–1000 return in high season, including taxes. Air Canada (Waircanada.com) has the most convenient service to Bangkok from the largest number of Canadian cities; from Vancouver, expect to pay around Can$1500 in high season if booked in advance. Cheaper rates are often available if you're prepared to make two or three stops and take more time.

Minimum **flying times** are around twenty hours from New York or Toronto (westbound or eastbound), including stopovers, twenty hours from LA, and eighteen hours from Vancouver.

Flights from Australia and New Zealand

There's no shortage of **scheduled flights** to Bangkok **from Australia**, with direct services from major cities operated by Thai Airways (Wthaiairways.com), Qantas (Wqantas.com) and half a dozen others (around 9hr from Sydney, Melbourne and Perth), and plenty of indirect flights via Asian hubs, which take at least eleven and a half hours. There's often not much difference between the fares on nonstop and indirect flights with the major carriers, nor between the fares from the major eastern cities. From Melbourne, if you book far in advance, you can get a ticket to Bangkok in high season for as little as Aus$700, on a low-cost carrier such as Jetstar; nonstop flights with the major airlines from the east coast more typically cost from Aus$1000–1100 if booked ahead. Fares from Perth and Darwin can be up to Aus$200 cheaper.

From **New Zealand**, Thai Airways has discontinued its nonstop flights between Auckland and Bangkok. Fares for indirect flights, with a total flight time of around fifteen hours or more, can start as low as NZ$1000 in high season, if booked far in advance.

A BETTER KIND OF TRAVEL

At Rough Guides we are passionately committed to travel. We believe it helps us understand the world we live in and the people we share it with – and of course tourism is vital to many developing economies. But the scale of modern tourism has also damaged some places irreparably, and climate change is accelerated by most forms of transport, especially flying. We encourage all our authors to consider the carbon footprint of the journeys they make in the course of researching our guides.

Flights from South Africa

Thai Airways' nonstop code-sharing flights with South African Airways (W flysaa.com) from Johannesburg to Bangkok have been discontinued, so you'll be making a stop in East Africa, the Middle East, Singapore or Hong Kong, with fares starting at around ZAR10,000 for an advance booking in high season, and a journey time of fourteen hours (via Singapore) or more.

TRAVEL AGENTS AND TOUR OPERATORS

Grasshopper Adventures W grasshopperadventures.com. Cycling trips around Bangkok with self-guiding and e-bike options.

Hivesters Thailand W facebook.com/profile.php?id=61554835254320. This social enterprise and sustainable travel company offers interesting tours in and around Bangkok.

Local Alike Thailand W localalike.com. Online marketplace that gives access to responsible tourism activities in communities.

North South Travel W northsouthtravel.co.uk. Friendly, competitive travel agency, offering discounted fares worldwide. Profits are used to support grassroots projects in the developing world, especially the promotion of sustainable tourism.

Nutty's Adventures Thailand W nutty-adventures.com. Fascinating, multi-day, community-based-tourism trips going off the beaten track all over the country, including Bangkok city tours and trips to Kanchanaburi and Ayutthaya.

Origin Asia Thailand W alex-kerr.com. Cultural programmes lasting from a day to a week that teach and explain living Thai arts such as dance, music, martial arts, textiles, flower offerings and cooking.

Responsible Travel W responsibletravel.com. One-stop shop for scores of fair-trade, ethically inclined holidays in Thailand.

Spice Roads W spiceroads.com. Escorted multi-day bike tours that include trips to Kanchanaburi and Ayutthaya.

TakeMeTour Thailand W takemetour.com. Online marketplace for one-day tours with local guides all over Thailand.

Trailfinders W trailfinders.com. One of the best-informed and most efficient agents for independent travellers in the UK and Ireland.

Travelling via neighbouring countries

Sharing land borders with Myanmar, Laos, Cambodia and Malaysia, Thailand works well as part of many overland itineraries, both across Asia and between Europe and Australia. Bangkok is also one of the major regional flight hubs for Southeast Asia, with flights to and from all her neighbouring countries. Cross-border links in Southeast Asia have improved considerably in the last couple of decades and are likely to continue to do so in the next few years.

The main restrictions on overland routes in and out of Thailand are determined by where the permitted land crossings lie and by **visas** – all **Asian embassies** are located in Bangkok (see page 45). Many Khao San tour agents offer to get your visa for you, but beware: some are reportedly **faking the stamps**, which could get you into pretty serious trouble, so it's safer to go to the embassy yourself.

Looking beyond the country's immediate borders, it's possible to get **from Vietnam** into Thailand, via Savannakhet on the Lao–Thai border, in a matter of hours; you'll need to use Vietnam's Lao Bao border crossing, west of Dong Ha, where you can catch a bus to Savannakhet and then another bus across the Mekong bridge to Mukdahan. Coming **from China**, the much-improved Route 3 and the Fourth Thai–Lao Friendship Bridge over the Mekong at Chiang Khong now form a popular link between Yunnan and northern Thailand, just as the high-speed rail line to Vientiane is now a major link between Yunnan and northeastern Thailand.

Myanmar

Before the brutal military coup in 2021, there were four overland access points between **Myanmar (Burma)** and Thailand that were open to non-Thais: at Thachileik opposite Mae Sai; at Myawaddy near Mae Sot; at remote Htee Khee opposite Phu Nam Ron in Kanchanaburi province, a crossing that's being developed to facilitate transport between the major new port at Dawei on the Bay of Bengal and Bangkok; and at Kaw Thaung (Victoria Point) near Ranong. In normal times, Western tourists forearmed with a Burmese **tourist visa** can enter Myanmar at these borders, and at most of them can get a temporary US$10 (or B500) **border pass**, which allows limited-distance trips into Myanmar, usually just for the day. (The crossings at Three Pagodas Pass near Kanchanaburi and at Dan Singkhon near Prachuap Khiri Khan are only for Thais.)

Cambodia

At the time of writing, six overland crossings on the **Thai-Cambodian border** were open to Westerners. The most commonly used land crossing is at **Poipet**, which lies just across the border from the Thai town of **Aranyaprathet** and has public-transport connections with Sisophon, Siem Reap and Phnom Penh. There are now direct public buses that run all the way between Bangkok's Northern Terminal (Mo Chit) and Siem Reap and between Mo Chit and Phnom Penh, which should help you dodge the scams and touts at this frontier post. The second most popular route is from Sihanoukville in Cambodia via Koh Kong (Cham Yeam) and Hat Lek to Trat, which is near Ko Chang on Thailand's east coast.

The crossings in northeast Thailand include the Chong Chom – O'Smach border pass, near Kap

Choeng in Thailand's Surin province, and the Chong Sa Ngam – Choam border in Thailand's Si Saket province; from both these borders there's transport to Anlong Veng and on to Siem Reap. There are also two little-used crossings in Chanthaburi province, with transport to and from Pailin in Cambodia.

Tourist **visas** for Cambodia are issued to travellers **on arrival** at all the overland border crossings. If you want to buy an **advance** thirty-day visa, you can do so online at W evisa.gov.kh, which should help you to avoid the more excessive scams at Poipet and Koh Kong.

Laos

There are seven main points along the **Lao border** where tourists can cross into Thailand: Houayxai (for Chiang Khong); between Nam Ngeun and Huai Kon in Thailand's Nan province; on the Nam Heuang River at the Thai settlement of Tha Li (Loei province); Vientiane (for Nong Khai); Khammouan (aka Thakhek, for Nakhon Phanom); Savannakhet (for Mukdahan); and Pakse (for Chong Mek). Increasing numbers of direct, long-distance public buses, such as those between Bangkok's Northern (Mo Chit) Bus Terminal and Vientiane and between Bangkok and Pakse, use these crossings to link major towns in the two countries; most of the Thai border towns mentioned above also have direct bus connections with Bangkok. All these borders can also be used as exits into Laos; tourist **visas** are available **on arrival** at all of the above-listed land borders, or you can buy one in **advance** from the Lao Embassy in Bangkok or online at W laoevisa.org.

Malaysia

Travelling between Thailand and **Malaysia** has in the past been a straightforward and very commonly used overland route, with plentiful connections by bus, minibus, share-taxi and train, most of them routed through the southern Thai city and transport hub of Hat Yai. However, because of the ongoing **violence in Thailand's deep south** (see page 203), all major Western governments are currently advising people not to travel to or through Songkhla, Pattani, Yala and Narathiwat provinces, unless essential (and consequently most insurance companies are not covering travel there). This encompasses Hat Yai and the following border crossings to and from Malaysia: at Padang Besar, on the main rail line connecting Malaysia (and, ultimately, Singapore) with Hat Yai and Bangkok; at Sungai Kolok, terminus of a railway line from Hat Yai and Bangkok, and at adjacent Ban Taba, both of which are connected by road to nearby Kota Bharu in Malaysia; and at the road crossings at Sadao, south of Hat Yai, and at Betong, south of Yala. (The routes towards Kota Bharu and Betong pass through particularly volatile territory, with martial law declared in Pattani, Yala and Narathiwat provinces; however, martial law is not in effect in Hat Yai itself.)

Nevertheless, the provinces of Trang and Satun on the west coast are not affected, and it's still perfectly possible to travel **overland via Satun**: by ferry between Satun's Thammalang pier and the island of Langkawi, or overland between Satun and Kangar; or by boat between Ko Lipe and Langkawi. For up-to-the-minute advice, consult your government travel advisory (see page 40).

Most Western tourists can spend thirty days in Malaysia without having bought a visa beforehand, and there are Thai embassies or consulates in Kuala Lumpur, Kota Bharu and Penang.

Arrival and departure

Unless you arrive in Bangkok by train, be prepared for a long trip into the city centre. Suvarnabhumi Airport and Don Muang airports are both 25km out, and the three long-distance bus stations are not much closer in, though at least the Northern Terminal is fairly near the Skytrain and subway, while the Eastern Terminal is close to a Skytrain station.

By plane

When departing from Bangkok, leave plenty of time to get to Suvarnabhumi or Don Muang, as getting there by road can be severely hampered by traffic jams.

Suvarnabhumi airport

Bangkok's main airport (coded "BKK" and pronounced "soo-wanna-poom"; W airportthai.co.th) is situated 25km east of central Bangkok between highways 7 and 34. The large airport is well stocked with 24hr exchange booths, ATMs, places to eat, pharmacies, a medical centre and a post office. In the arrivals hall on Floor 2, TAT operates an official tourist information counter and the tourist police have an office; left-luggage depots can be found near arrivals on Floor 2 and in the departures hall on Floor 4. There are a number of accommodation options near Suvarnabhumi (see page 156).

Airport transport

The **Suvarnabhumi Airport Rail Link** (SARL; W bangkokairporttrain.com; daily 5.30am–midnight) from the basement of the Suvarnabhumi terminal is generally the quickest means of getting downtown, though it also serves as an important link for commuters and can get very crowded. There's only one set of elevated tracks, ending at Phaya Thai station, with trains running roughly every 15min (26min), stopping at Makkasan, Ratchaprarop and four other stations. Makkasan is handy for Phetchaburi subway station and for Khlong Saen Saeb canal boats to Banglamphu (see page 31) at Tha Asoke (Phetchaburi) pier, while Phaya Thai is an interchange with the Skytrain system, and is served by #59 buses (heading south on Thanon Phrayathai) to Thanon Rajadamnoen Klang, for Banglamphu.

Taxis to the centre are comfortable, a/c and reasonably priced, although the driving can be hairy. Walk past the pricey taxis and limousines on offer within the baggage hall and arrivals hall, and ignore any tout who may offer a cheap ride in an unlicensed and unmetered vehicle, as newly arrived travellers are seen as easy prey for robbery and the cabs are untraceable. Licensed and metered public taxis are operated from clearly signposted and well-regulated counters, outside on Floor 1. On top of the fare on the meter, you'll be charged a B70 airport pick-up fee and around B70 tolls for the overhead expressways. Heading back to the airport, drivers will nearly always try to leave their meters off and agree an inflated price with you – say *"poet meter, dai mai khrap/kha?"* to get them to switch the meter on. If you leave the downtown areas before roughly 7am or after 9pm you can get to the airport in half an hour, but at other times it's best to set off at least an hour and a half before you have to check in.

The Bangkok Mass Transit Authority (BMTA) operates the S1 **bus** service to Thanon Khao San and Sanam Luang from outside Arrivals roughly every 45min. Operating between every 20min and every hour, an a/c shuttle bus that's free to passengers runs between Suvarnabhumi and Don Muang airports. At Suvarnabhumi, it picks up outside Floor 2, and drops off outside Floor 4; allow at least 50min for the journey. The BMTA also runs other public a/c buses and minibuses out of the Public Transportation Center on the other side of the huge airport complex from the terminal building (linked by shuttle bus), but they're really designed for airport staff. On departure, many travellers opt for one of the private minibus services to Suvarnabhumi organized through guesthouses and travel agents in Banglamphu and elsewhere around the city.

The **car-rental** companies, most of which can be found in the arrivals hall (Floor 2), include Avis and Budget (see page 33).

Don Muang airport

The old Don Muang Airport (coded "DMK"; W airportthai.co.th), 25km north of the city, is now Bangkok's main base for low-cost airlines (though some still use Suvarnabhumi – check your booking carefully). Don Muang's two interconnected buildings effectively form one very long terminal, sheltering currency exchange booths, ATMs, car-rental outlets, a left-luggage depot, a post office and plenty of places to eat.

Airport transport

Just across the main highway and the railway line from the south end of Don Muang's terminal building, SRT Dark Red Line elevated trains run from Don Muang station every 12–20 minutes north to Rangsit and south, via Chatuchak, to Krungthep Aphiwat (Bang Sue). Now, Bangkok's main railway station, Krungthep Aphiwat is on the MRT subway line and the Light Red Line (across to Taling Chan in Thonburi).

The easiest way to get into the city centre is usually by licensed, metered **taxis**, which are organized

---

BANGKOK ADDRESSES

Thai **addresses** can be immensely confusing, mainly because property is often numbered twice, first to show which real-estate lot it stands in, and then to distinguish where it is on that lot. Thus 154/7–10 Thanon Rajdamnoen means the building is on lot 154 and occupies numbers 7–10. However, neither of these numbers will necessarily help you to find a particular building on a long street; when asking for directions or talking to taxi drivers, it's best to be able to quote a nearby temple, big hotel or other landmark. There's an additional idiosyncrasy in the way Thai roads are sometimes named: in large cities a minor road running off a major road is often numbered as a soi ("lane" or "alley", though it may be a sizeable thoroughfare), rather than given its own street name. Thanon Sukhumvit for example – Bangkok's longest – has minor roads numbered Soi 1 to Soi 103, with odd numbers on one side of the road and even on the other; so a Thanon Sukhumvit address could read something like 27/9–11 Soi 15, Thanon Sukhumvit, which would mean the property occupies numbers 9–11 on lot 27 on minor road number 15 running off Thanon Sukhumvit.

ORIENTATION

Bangkok ("Krung Thep" in Thai) can be a tricky place to get your bearings as it's huge and ridiculously congested, with largely featureless modern buildings and no obvious centre. The boldest line on the map is the **Chao Phraya River**, which divides the city into Bangkok proper on the east bank, and **Thonburi**, part of Greater Bangkok, on the west.

The historical core of Bangkok proper, site of the original royal palace, is **Ratanakosin**, cradled in a bend in the river. Three concentric canals radiate eastwards around Ratanakosin: the southern part of the area between the canals is the old-style trading enclave of **Chinatown** and Indian **Pahurat**, connected to the old palace by Thanon Charoen Krung (aka New Road); the northern part is characterized by old temples and the **Democracy Monument**, west of which is the backpackers' ghetto of **Banglamphu**. Beyond the canals to the north, **Dusit** is the site of many government buildings and royal palaces, and is linked to Ratanakosin by the three stately avenues, Thanon Rajdamnoen Nok, Thanon Rajdamnoen Klang and Thanon Rajdamnoen Nai.

"New" Bangkok begins to the east of the canals and beyond the main rail line and Hualamphong Station, and stretches as far as the eye can see to the east and north. The main business district is south of **Thanon Rama IV**, with the port of Khlong Toey at its eastern edge. The diverse area north of Thanon Rama IV includes the sprawling campus of Chulalongkorn University and huge shopping centres around **Siam Square**. To the east lies the swish residential quarter of **Thanon Sukhumvit**.

---

from a large waiting room on Floor 1 at the south end of the terminal buildings. On top of the fare on the meter, you'll be charged a B50 airport fee and expressway fees (B110 to Banglamphu, for instance).

The Bangkok Mass Transit Authority offers several special **bus** services from outside the arrivals hall (all a/c), including the A1 (every 5min) to Mo Chit Skytrain station, though it's unclear whether these services will continue now that the Dark Red Line serves Don Muang. Operating between every 20min and every hour, an a/c shuttle bus that's free to passengers runs between Suvarnabhumi and Don Muang airports. At Don Muang, it can be found outside arrivals on Floor 1; allow at least 50min for the journey.

On departure, many travellers opt for one of the private minibus services to Don Muang organized through guesthouses and travel agents in Banglamphu and elsewhere around the city.

By train

Nearly all long-distance trains now arrive at the new main terminal, **Krungthep Aphiwat Station**, to the north of the centre in Bang Sue, near the Northern Bus Terminal. Krungthep Aphiwat is served by the MRT subway and by the SRT Dark Red Line to Don Muang Airport. Many shorter-distance and slower trains still arrive at the old main terminal, **Hualamphong Station,** which is centrally located at the edge of Chinatown and on the subway line. Trains to Hualamphong also stop at Bang Sue Junction station, which is just to the west of Krungthep Aphiwat. (At the moment, there are free shuttle buses between Krungthep Aphiwat and Hualamphong.) The other main routes are the slow services from south of Bangkok and from Kanchanaburi and Nam Tok via Nakhon Pathom, which arrive at **Thonburi Station** (sometimes still referred to by its former name, Bangkok Noi Station), across the river from Banglamphu in Thonburi. The station is about a 750m walk east of Bang Khun Non subway station and an 850m walk west of the Thonburi Railway Station N11 express boat stop.

By bus

Bangkok's three main bus terminals, all of which have left-luggage facilities of some kind, are distributed around the outskirts of town. On many shorter routes, buses have been wholly or partly replaced by *rot tuu* (a/c minibuses), which now use the same three terminals. If you happen to need to buy a ticket out of Bangkok, seats on the most popular long-distance a/c bus services should be reserved online ahead of time, on the official website of Baw Khaw Saw (The Transport Company; ⓦtransport.co.th). On departure, leave plenty of time to reach the terminals, especially if setting off from Banglamphu, from where you should allow at least 1hr 30min (outside rush hour) to get to the Eastern Bus Terminal, and a good hour to get to the Northern or Southern terminals.

All services from the north and northeast terminate at the **Northern and Northeastern Bus Terminal**

(**Mo Chit**) on Thanon Kamphaeng Phet 2; some east-coast buses and a few from the south also use Mo Chit (plans have been mooted to move Mo Chit to another site that's closer to the Skytrain and subway within the next few years). The quickest way to get into the city centre from Mo Chit is to hop onto the Skytrain at Mo Chit Station on Thanon Phaholyothin, or the subway at the adjacent Chatuchak Park Station or at Kamphaeng Phet Station (at the bottom of Thanon Kamphaeng Phet 2), all of which are about a 15min walk from the bus terminal, and then change onto a city bus or taxi if necessary.

Most buses to and from east-coast destinations such as Pattaya, Ban Phe (for Ko Samet) and Trat (for Ko Chang) use the **Eastern Bus Terminal** (Ekamai) between sois 40 and 42 on Thanon Sukhumvit. This bus station is right beside the Ekamai Skytrain stop. Alternatively, you can use the Khlong Saen Saeb canal-boat service, which runs westwards almost as far as Banglamphu (see page 66); there's a pier called Tha Charn Issara, near the northern end of Sukhumvit Soi 63 (Soi Ekamai), which is easiest reached from the bus station by taxi. Otherwise, you could get off the Khlong Saen Saeb canal boat at Saphan Hua Chang, walk round to Ratchathevi Station and catch the Skytrain to Ekamai Station.

The huge, airport-like **Southern Bus Terminal**, or Sathaanii Sai Tai, handles transport to and from Malaysia and all points south of the capital, including Hua Hin, Chumphon (for Ko Tao), Surat Thani (for Ko Samui), Phuket and Krabi, as well as buses for destinations west of Bangkok, such as Nakhon Pathom and Kanchanaburi. The terminal lies at the junction of Thanon Borom Ratchonani and Thanon Phuttham-onthon Sai 1 in Taling Chan, an interminable 11km west of the Chao Phraya River and Banglamphu, so access to and from accommodation can take an age, even in a taxi. Note that when arriving in Bangkok most long-distance bus services make a more convenient stop before reaching the terminus (via a time-consuming U-turn), towards the eastern end of Thanon Borom Ratchonani, much nearer Phra Pinklao Bridge and the river; the majority of passengers get off here, as it's a faster and cheaper place to grab a taxi into town, and it's highly recommended to do the same rather than continue to the terminus.

City transport

Transport can undoubtedly be a headache in a city where it's not unusual for residents to spend three hours getting to work – and these are people who know where they're going.

Bangkok's main form of transport is **buses**, with a labyrinth of routes that reaches every part of the city, albeit slowly. Catching the various kinds of **taxi** is more expensive – though a/c metered taxis are surprisingly good value – and you'll still get held up by the daytime traffic jams. **Boats** are obviously more limited in their range, but they're regular and as cheap as buses, and you'll save a lot of time by using them whenever possible – a journey between Banglamphu and Saphan Taksin, for instance, will take around 30min by water, half what it would usually take on land. The **Skytrain** and **subway** each have a similarly limited range but are also worth using whenever suitable for all or part of your journey. Their networks roughly coincide with each other at the east end of Thanon Silom; at the corner of Soi Asoke and Thanon Sukhumvit; on Thanon Phaholyothin (BTS Mo Chit–MRT Chatuchak Park and BTS Ha Yaek Lat Phrao–MRT Phahon Yothin); and at Bang Wa in Thonburi. The Skytrain joins up with the Chao Phraya River express boats at the vital hub of Sathorn/Saphan Taksin (Taksin Bridge). At each Skytrain and subway station, you'll find a useful map of the immediate neighbourhood. Several other urban rail lines have recently opened in the suburbs, of which the only one likely to be useful to visitors is the **SRT Dark Red Line** in the north of the city, from Krungthep Aphiwat train station (Bang Sue; to connect with the subway), stopping at Don Muang airport on its way to Rangsit. **Walking** might often be quicker than travelling by road, but the heat can be unbearable, pavements are poorly maintained and the engine fumes are stifling.

Buses

Bangkok has reputedly the world's largest bus network, on which operate two main types of bus service. Ordinary (non-a/c) buses are mostly red and white or blue and white; most routes operate from about 5am to 11pm, but some maintain a 24hr service. Air-conditioned buses are mostly either blue, orange or yellow; most stop in the late evening, but a few of the more popular routes run 24hr services. As buses can only go as fast as the car in front, which at the moment is averaging 4km/h, you'll probably be spending a long time on each journey, so you'd be well advised to pay the extra for cool air – and the a/c buses are usually less crowded, too. For information on Bangkok's buses, try the Bangkok Mass Transit Authority website's (W bmta.co.th), though the route descriptions can be difficult to follow. Easier-to-use maps are available in bookshops – Thinknet's *Bangkok Bus Guide* – and online on W transitbangkok.com, but are not as up to date. There's also an app, designed

USEFUL BUS ROUTES

In addition to those listed below, there are also bus routes from Suvarnabhumi Airport (see page 25) and Don Muang (see page 26). In Banglamphu, finding the right bus stop can sometimes be tricky (see page 66).

#3 (ordinary)
Northern Bus Terminal–Chatuchak Weekend Market–Thanon Phaholyothin–Thanon Samsen–Thanon Chakrabongse/Thanon Phra Arthit (for Banglamphu guesthouses)–Thanon Sanam Chai (for Museum of Siam)– Memorial Bridge–Taksin Monument (for Wongwian Yai) –Krung Thonburi Skytrain station.

#15 (ordinary)
Sanam Luang–Thanon Phra Arthit–Thanon Chakrabongse (for Banglamphu guesthouses)–Democracy Monument–Siam Square–Thanon Rajdamri–Thanon Silom–Thanon Charoen Krung (for Saphan Taksin and Asiatique).

#16 (ordinary and a/c)
Northern Bus Terminal–Chatuchak Weekend Market–Thanon Samsen–Thewet (for guesthouses)–Thanon Phitsanulok–Thanon Phrayathai–Siam Square–Thanon Suriwong.

#25 (ordinary)
Pak Nam (for Ancient City buses)–Thanon Sukhumvit–Eastern Bus Terminal–Siam Square–Hualamphong Station–Thanon Yaowarat (for Chinatown)–Pahurat–Wat Pho–Tha Chang (for the Grand Palace).

#53 circular (also anticlockwise; ordinary)
Thewet–Thanon Krung Kasem– Hualamphong Station–Thanon Yaowarat (for Chinatown)–Pahurat–Thanon Maharat (for Wat Pho and the Grand Palace)–Sanam Luang (for National Museum)–Thanon Phra Arthit and Thanon Samsen (for Banglamphu guesthouses)–Thewet.

#503 (a/c)
Sanam Luang–Democracy Monument (for Banglamphu guesthouses)–Thanon Rajdamnoen Nok (for TAT and boxing stadium)–Wat Benjamabophit–Thanon Sri Ayutthaya–Victory Monument–Chatuchak Weekend Market–Rangsit.

#508 (ordinary and a/c)
Sanam Luang–Grand Palace–Siam Square–Thanon Sukhumvit–Eastern Bus Terminal–Pak Nam (for Ancient City buses).

#509 (a/c)
Northern Bus Terminal–Chatuchak Weekend Market–Victory Monument–Thanon Rajdamnoen Nok (for TAT and boxing stadium)–Democracy Monument–Thanon Rajdamnoen Klang (for Banglamphu guesthouses)–Phra Pinklao Bridge–Thonburi.

#511 (a/c)
Southern Bus Terminal–Phra Pinklao Bridge (for Banglamphu guesthouses)–Democracy Monument–Thanon Sukhumvit–Eastern Bus Terminal–Pak Nam (for Ancient City buses).

by Chulalongkorn University, Via Bus, which will plan your route for you and show bus arrival times.

Boats

Bangkok was built as an amphibious city around a network of canals – or **khlongs** – and the first streets were constructed only in the second half of the nineteenth century. Many canals remain on the Thonburi side of the river, but most of those on the Bangkok side have been turned into roads. Longtail boats (*reua hang yao*) ply the canals of Thonburi like commuter buses, stopping at designated shelters, and are available for individual rental on the river (see page 82). The Chao Phraya River itself is still a major transport route for residents and non-residents alike, forming more of a link than a barrier between the two halves of the city.

Express boats

The Chao Phraya Express Boat Company operates the vital express-boat (*reua duan*; Ⓦ chaophrayaexpress-boat.com) services, using large water buses to plough up and down the river, between clearly signed piers (*tha*), which appear on all Bangkok maps. Tha Sathorn, which gives access to the Skytrain network, nas been

TOURS OF THE CITY

Unlikely as it sounds, the most popular organized **tours** in Bangkok for independent travellers are by bicycle, heading to the city's outer neighbourhoods and beyond; these are an excellent way to gain a different perspective on Thai life and offer a unique chance to see traditional communities close up. In addition to those listed below, other tour options include Thonburi canal tours (see page 82), Chao Phraya Express tourist boats (see below), and breakfast and dinner cruises along the Chao Phraya River (see page 162).

ABC Amazing Bangkok Cyclist Tours 10/6–7 Soi Aree, Soi 26, Thanon Sukhumvit ⓦrealasia.net. ABC's popular, long-running and child-friendly bicycle tours last half a day or a full day, starting in the Sukhumvit area and taking you across the river to surprisingly rural khlong- and riverside communities (including a floating market at weekends); they also offer cycle-and-dine tours in the evening. Tours operate every day year-round, cover up to 24km depending on the itinerary, and need to be reserved in advance. Bike rental also available.

Bangkok Vanguards 4/4 Trok Sin, Thanon Tanao ⓦbangkokvanguards.com. Fun, educational and unconventional tours, with a focus on social entrepreneurism, including walking tours of Chinatown and evening bike tours.

Velo Thailand Soi 4, Thanon Samsen ⓦvelothailand.com. Velo Thailand runs half a dozen different bike tours of the capital (and further afield) out of its cycle shop on the edge of Banglamphu, including an after-dark tour that takes in floodlit sights including Wat Pho and Wat Arun. Bike rental also available.

---

designated "Central Pier", with piers to the south of here numbered S1, S2, etc, those to the north N1, N2 and so on (see page 31). Boats do not necessarily stop at every landing – they only pull in if people want to get on or off, and when they do stop, it's not for long – so when you want to get off, be ready at the back of the boat in good time for your pier.

Orange-flag, local-line boats call at every pier between Nonthaburi and Wat Rajsingkorn, 90min away to the south beyond Sathorn. They operate all day on Saturdays and Sundays (every 20–40min), but from Monday to Friday they take a long midday break (departures roughly 6–9.40/10.40am & 2.40/3–6.10pm). Limited-stop services include those flying a yellow flag (Mon–Fri only): during rush hours they run an express service for commuters with just a few stops between Nonthaburi and Tha Sathorn; in the middle of the day, they stop at most piers between Nonthaburi and Wat Rajsingkorn. Weekday boats with yellow-and-green flags (Pakkred–Sathorn in the morning rush hour, Sathorn–Pakkred in the evening rush hour) or red flags (Nonthaburi–Sathorn in the morning rush hour, Sathorn–Nonthaburi in the evening rush hour) are designed for commuters.

Tickets can be bought on board; don't discard your ticket until you're off the boat, as the staff at some piers impose a B1 fine on anyone disembarking without one.

Chao Phraya Tourist Boats

The Chao Phraya Express Boat Company also runs Tourist Boats (ⓦchaophrayatouristboat.com), distinguished by their light-blue flags, between Sathorn (departing roughly every 30min, 9am–7.15pm) and Phra Arthit piers (departing roughly every 30min, 8.30am–6.30pm). In between (in both directions), these boats call in at Icon Siam shopping centre, Rachawongse, Ratchinee, Wat Arun, Chang (for the Grand Palace), Maharat (near Wat Mahathat and the National Museum) and Wang Lang/Prannok pier. Boats departing Phra Arthit between 3.30pm and 6.30pm extend their journey southwards beyond Sathorn to Asiatique. On-board guides provide running commentaries, and you can either buy a one-day pass for unlimited trips or a single-journey ticket.

Thai Smile Boats

This new rival to the Chao Phraya Express Boat Company operates large, electric-powered catamarans with an enclosed a/c cabin (ⓦthaismilegroup.com). Two routes are in operation, using express-boat piers for the most part: the City Line with just six stops between Phra Pinklao Bridge and Tha Sathorn; and the Urban Line with fourteen stops between Phra Nang Klao Bridge (just north of Nonthaburi pier) and Tha Sathorn. The City Line operates daily throughout the day (every 15–30min), while the Urban Line takes an extended midday break every day (schedules in English on ⓦthaiest.com/thailand/bangkok/thai-smile-boattheir website).

Cross-river ferries

Smaller than express boats are the slow cross-river ferries (*reua kham fak*), which shuttle back and forth between the same two points. Found at or beside every express-boat stop and plenty of other piers

CENTRAL STOPS FOR THE CHAO PHRAYA EXPRESS BOATS

N15 Thewet (all boats) – for Thewet guesthouses.
N13 Phra Arthit (orange flag and weekday midday yellow flag) – for Thanon Phra Arthit, Thanon Khao San and Banglamphu guesthouses.
N12 Phra Pinklao Bridge (all boats except red flag) – for Royal Barge Museum.
N11 Thonburi Railway Station (or Bangkok Noi; all boats except red flag) – for the Siriraj museums and trains to Kanchanaburi.
N10 Wang Lang (aka Siriraj or Prannok; all boats) – for Wat Rakhang.
N9 Chang (all boats except red flag) – for the Grand Palace, Sanam Luang and the National Museum.
N8 Thien (orange flag and weekday midday yellow flag) – for Wat Pho, and the cross-river ferry to Wat Arun
N7 Ratchini (aka Rajinee; all boats) – for Sanam Chai subway station and the Museum of Siam.
N6 Saphan Phut (Memorial Bridge; orange flag; boats sometimes stop at the adjacent Yodpiman pier, N6/1, instead) – for Pahurat and Wat Prayoon.
N5 Rachawongse (aka Rajawong; all boats) – for Chinatown.
N4 Harbour (Marine) Department (all boats except red flag).
N3 Si Phraya (all boats except red flag) – walk north past the *Sheraton Royal Orchid Hotel* for River City shopping complex; also for Thailand Creative & Design Center (TCDC).
N2 Icon Siam shopping centre (orange flag, weekday midday yellow flag and red flag).
N1 Oriental (orange flag, but currently closed for renovation) – for Thanon Silom.
Central Sathorn (Saphan Taksin; all boats) – for the Skytrain and Thanon Sathorn.

in between, they are especially useful for exploring Thonburi. Fares are payable at the entrance to the pier.

Khlong Saen Saeb boats

On the Bangkok side, Khlong Saen Saeb is well served by passenger boats, which run at least every 20min during daylight hours (eastbound services start and end a little later; Ⓦ transitbangkok.com/khlong_boats.html). They start from the Phan Fah pier (Panfa Leelard) at the Golden Mount (handy for Banglamphu, Ratanakosin and Chinatown), and head way out east via Wat Sribunruang to Minburi, with useful stops at Thanon Phrayathai, aka Saphan Hua Chang (for Jim Thompson's House and Ratchathevi Skytrain stop); Pratunam (for the Erawan Shrine); Soi Chitlom; Thanon Witthayu (Wireless Road); and Soi Nana Nua (Soi 3), Thanon Asok Montri (Soi 21, for TAT headquarters and Phetchaburi subway stop), Soi Thonglor (Soi 55) and Charn Issara, near Soi Ekamai (Soi 63), all off Thanon Sukhumvit. This is your quickest and most interesting way of getting between the west and east parts of town, if you can stand the stench of the canal. You may have trouble actually locating the piers as few are signed in English and they all look very unassuming and rickety; keep your eyes peeled for a plain wooden jetty – most jetties serve boats running in both directions. Once you've jumped on the boat, state your destination to the conductor when they collect your fare. Due to the construction of some low bridges, all passengers change onto a different boat at Tha Pratunam – just follow the crowd – and it's "all change" again at Wat Sribunruang, as the final leg to Minburi is covered by new electric-powered boats.

Khlong Padung Krung Kasem boats

This little-publicized service (boats depart from each terminus every 30min on the hour and half-hour: Mon–Fri 6–8.30am & 3.30–7pm; Sat & Sun 8–9.30am, noon–12.30pm, 3–4pm & 6–7pm; free) runs along the canal between Hualamphong Station and the pier at Talat Dhevaraj, which is a 10min walk from the Thewet guesthouses and the express-boat pier at Tha Thewet. The only intermediate stops that may be of interest to visitors are at Thanon Nakhorn Sawan and Thanon Rajdamnoen Nok, while the pier at Thanon Lan Luang (Tha Reua Yaek Lan Luang) is walkable from the Khlong Saen Saeb boat pier at Talat Bobe (Bobe Market).

The Skytrain

Although its network is limited, the BTS Skytrain, or ***rot fai faa*** (Ⓦ bts.co.th), provides a much faster alternative to the bus, and is clean, efficient and over-vigorously air-conditioned. There are only two Skytrain lines, which interconnect at Siam Square (Central Station), both running every few minutes from around 6am to midnight. Most of the ticket machines accept only coins, but you can change notes or buy tickets at staffed counters. The Sukhumvit Line runs from Ku Kot (N24) in the northern part of the city, running along the back of Don Muang Airport, down Thanon Phaholyothin, and via Mo Chit (stop N8) and the interchange at Phayathai (N2) with the airport rail link, to Kheha way to the south in Samut Prakan (E23) in around 90min. The Silom Line runs from the National Stadium (W1) via Saphan Taksin (Taksin, or Sathorn, Bridge; S6), to link up with the full gamut of express boats on the Chao Phraya River, passing Krung Thonburi (S7), which has a monorail link (the "Gold Line") to Icon Siam shopping centre, and on to Bang Wa (S12) in Thonburi (on Thanon Phetkasem, Highway 4, with a link to Bang Wa subway station).

The subway

Bangkok's underground rail system, the MRT subway (in Thai, *rot fai tai din*; Ⓦ mrta.co.th), has similar advantages to the Skytrain, though its main Blue Line goes to fewer places of interest for visitors (its other lines connect nothing of touristic interest, unless you happen to be taking the Purple Line and Pink Line to Pakkred for the ferry to Ko Kred – see page 109). The Blue Line runs every few minutes between around 6am and midnight on a circuit from Tha Phra station up through Thonburi, before crossing the Chao Phraya River to Krungthep Aphiwat (Bang Sue) train station (connecting with the SRT Dark Red Line to Don Muang Airport) and Chatuchak Park, turning

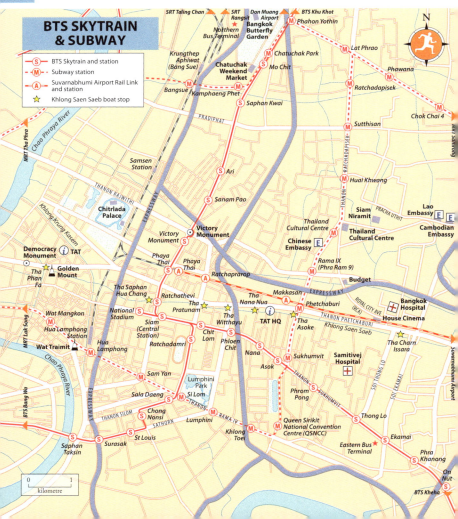

south to Phetchaburi (near Makkasan station on the Suvarnabhumi Airport Rail Link) and Sukhumvit, then heading west through Silom, Hualamphong train station, Chinatown and Sanam Chai in Ratanakosin to Tha Phra again, with a continuation westwards into Thonburi to Lak Song. Pay your fare at a staffed counter or machine, where you'll receive a token to tap on the entrance gate and insert into your exit gate (the various stored-value cards available are unlikely to be worthwhile for visitors).

Taxis

Bangkok taxis come in three main forms, and are so plentiful that you rarely have to wait more than a couple of minutes before spotting an empty one of some description. Neither tuk-tuks nor motorbike taxis have meters, so you should agree on a price before setting off, and expect to do a fair amount of haggling. App-based taxi services have now come to Bangkok, of which the most popular are Grab (who bought up Uber's Southeast Asian operations) and, in association with the Siam Taxi Co-operative, Line Man (Line is East Asia's equivalent to WhatsApp).

Metered taxis

For nearly all journeys, the best and most comfortable option is to flag down one of Bangkok's metered, a/c taxi cabs; look out for the "TAXI METER" sign on the roof, and a red light in the windscreen in front of the passenger seat, which means the cab is available for hire. Starting at B40, fares are displayed on a clearly visible meter that the driver should reset at the start of each trip (say *"poet meter, dai mai khrap/kha?"* to ask him to switch it on), and increase in stages on a combined distance/time formula. Try to have change with you as cabs tend not to carry a lot of money; tipping of up to ten percent is common, though occasionally a cabbie will round down the fare on the meter. If a driver tries to quote a flat fare (often the case with taxis that park outside tourist hotels waiting for business, or with any taxi for journeys to the airports) rather than using the meter, let him go, and avoid the now-rare unmetered cabs (denoted by a "TAXI" sign on the roof). Getting a metered taxi in the middle of the afternoon when the cars return to base for a change of drivers can sometimes be a problem.

Tuk-tuks

Somewhat less stable though typically Thai, tuk-tuks in Bangkok have very little to recommend them. These noisy, three-wheeled, open-sided buggies, which can carry three medium-sized passengers comfortably, fully expose you to the worst of Bangkok's pollution and weather.

Fares are usually at least double what you would pay in a metered taxi, even with some hard bargaining. Be aware, also, that tuk-tuk drivers tend to speak less English than taxi drivers – and there have been cases of robberies and attacks on women passengers late at night.

During the day it's quite common for tuk-tuk drivers to try and con their passengers into visiting a jewellery, tailor's or expensive souvenir shop with them (see page 39).

Motorbike taxis

Motorbike taxis generally congregate at the entrances to long sois – pick the riders out by their numbered, coloured vests – and charge from B10 for short trips down into the side streets. If you're short on time and have nerves of steel, it's also possible to charter them for hairy journeys out on the main roads. Crash helmets are compulsory on all main roads in the capital (traffic police fine non-wearers on the spot), though they're rarely worn on trips down the sois.

Car and bike rental

You'd need to be a bit mad to rent a self-drive car for getting around Bangkok, especially as taxis are so cheap. Theoretically, foreigners need an international driver's licence to rent a car, but most companies accept national licences.

Prices for a small car start at about B1000 per day; for **petrol**, most Thais use gasohol, which can generally be used in rental cars (though it's worth checking). Thais drive on the left, and the speed limit is generally 60km per hour within built-up areas and 90km per hour outside them.

CAR AND BIKE RENTAL AGENCIES

Avis Branches are at 259 Soi 19, Thanon Sukhumvit, as well as Suvarnabhumi and Don Muang airports (☏ 02 251 1131–2, ⓦ avisthailand.com).
Budget Branches can be found at the following locations: 19/23 Building A, Royal City Avenue, Thanon Phetchaburi Mai; Suvarnabhumi Airport; and Don Muang Airport (☏ 02 203 9222, ⓦ budget.co.th).
Rent A Scooter Bangkok 39/4 Soi Atthakrawi 1, Soi 26, Thanon Sukhumvit ⓦ rentascooterbangkok.com. Not recommended unless you know the Bangkok road system inside out. And even then, accidents are frequent.
Velo Thailand Soi 4, Thanon Samsen (☏ 02 628 8628, ⓦ velothailand.com). Offers good-quality bikes to brave/foolhardy souls.

Information and maps

The Tourism Authority of Thailand, or TAT (Ⓦ www.tourismthailand.org), maintains offices in several cities abroad, where you can pick up a few glossy brochures and get answers to pre-trip questions. More comprehensive local information is given at the TAT offices in Bangkok and at booths run by the city's Bangkok Tourism Division. You can also contact the helpful TAT tourist assistance phoneline from within Thailand for free on ☏ 1672 (daily 8am–8pm), with social media and "live chat" options available, including on Line (the most popular equivalent to WhatsApp in East Asia).

Part of the Bangkok Metropolitan Administration, the **Bangkok Tourism Division** is the official source of information on the capital, with its head office next to Phra Pinklao Bridge at 17/1 Thanon Phra Arthit in Banglamphu (☏ 02 225 7612–3, Ⓦ visitbangkok. go.th). The head office is supported by about twenty strategically placed satellite booths around the capital, including on Thanon Maharat near Tha Chang and the Grand Palace, at Paragon and Mah Boon Krong shopping centres, and in front of Banglamphu's Wat Bowoniwes.

The head office of the nationwide **Tourism Authority of Thailand** is rather inconveniently located at 1600 Thanon Phetchaburi Mai (Phetchaburi subway station), but it does maintain useful local offices in Amphawa, Ayutthaya and Kanchanaburi.

It's worth noting, however, that the many travel agents, shops and private offices across the capital displaying signs announcing "TAT Tourist Information" or similar are **not official Tourism Authority of Thailand information centres** and will not be dispensing impartial advice (they may be licensed by TAT to run their business, but that doesn't make them government information offices).

The Tourism Authority of Thailand never uses the acronym "TAT" on its office-fronts or in its logo and none of its offices offers accommodation, tour or transport booking.

TAT OFFICES ABROAD

Australia and New Zealand Suite 2002, Level 20, 56 Pitt St, Sydney, NSW 2000 ☏ 02 9247 7549, ✉ info@thailand.net.au.
South Africa Contact the UK office.
UK and Ireland 4th Floor, 12 Conduit St, London W11 2XH ☏ 020 7925 2511, ✉ info@tourismthailand.co.uk.
US and Canada 61 Broadway, Suite 2810, New York, NY 10006 ☏ 212 432 0433, ✉ info@tatny.com; 611 North Larchmont Blvd, 1st Floor, Los Angeles, CA 90004 ☏ 323 461 9814, Etatla@tat.or.th; 700 N Rush St, Chicago 60016 ✉ tatchicago@tat.or.th.

Maps and listings magazines

For a personal guide to Bangkok's most interesting shops, markets, restaurants and backstreets, look out for the famously idiosyncratic hand-drawn *Nancy Chandler's Map of Bangkok*, which carries a mass of annotated recommendations. It hasn't been updated since 2019, but should still be available in most tourist areas.

Listings media rise and fall with confusing rapidity in Bangkok; the best of the current crop is *BK* (Ⓦ bk. asia-city.com), which gives a decent rundown of events, live music and club nights.

Health

Although Thailand's climate, wildlife and cuisine present Western travellers with fewer health worries than in many Asian destinations, it's still good to know in advance what the risks might be, and what preventive or curative measures you should take.

For a start, there's no need to bring huge supplies of non-prescription medicines with you, as Thai **pharmacies** (*raan khai yaa*; typically open daily 8.30am–8pm) are well stocked with local and international branded medicaments, and of course they are generally much less expensive than at home. Nearly all pharmacies – including the city-wide branches of the British chain, Boots (see page 185) – are run by trained English-speaking pharmacists, who are usually the best people to talk to if your symptoms aren't acute enough to warrant seeing a doctor.

MEDICAL RESOURCES

Canadian Society for International Health ☏ 613 241 5785, Ⓦ csih.org. Extensive list of travel health centres.
CDC ☏ 800 232 4636, Ⓦ cdc.gov/travel. Official US government travel health site.
Hospital for Tropical Diseases Travel Clinic UK Ⓦ www.thehtd. org/travelclinic.aspx.
International Society for Travel Medicine US ☏ 404 373 8282, Ⓦ istm.org. Has a full list of travel health clinics.
MASTA (Medical Advisory Service for Travellers Abroad) UK Ⓦ masta-travel-health.com.
The Travel Doctor Ⓦ traveldoctor.com.au. Lists travel clinics in Australia, New Zealand and South Africa.

Tropical Medical Bureau Ireland ☎ 01 271 5200, Ⓦ tmb.ie.

Inoculations

There are no compulsory **inoculation** requirements for people travelling to Thailand from the West, but you should consult a doctor or other health professional, preferably at least four weeks in advance of your trip, for the latest information on recommended immunizations. In addition to making sure that your recommended immunizations for life in your home country are up to date, most doctors strongly advise vaccinations or boosters against tetanus, diphtheria, hepatitis A and, in many cases, typhoid, and in some cases they might also recommend protecting yourself against Japanese encephalitis, rabies and hepatitis B. If you forget to have all your inoculations before leaving home, or don't leave yourself sufficient time, you can get them in Bangkok at, for example, the Thai Red Cross Society's Queen Saovabha Institute or Global Doctor (see page 36).

Mosquito-borne diseases

Only certain regions of Thailand are now considered malarial, and **Bangkok is malaria-free**, so if you are restricting yourself to the capital you do not have to take malaria prophylactics. Bangkok does however have its fair share of **mosquitoes**; though nearly all the city's hotels and guesthouses have screened windows, you will probably need to have mosquito repellent containing the chemical compound DEET. Supermarkets and pharmacies in Bangkok stock it, but if you want the highest-strength repellent, or convenient roll-ons or sprays, it's probably best to do your shopping before you leave home – or at a branch of Boots in Bangkok (see page 185). DEET is strong stuff, and if you have sensitive skin, a natural alternative is citronella (available in the UK as Mosi-guard), made from a blend of eucalyptus oils; the Thai version is made with lemon grass. Plug-in insecticide vaporizers, insect room sprays and mosquito coils – also widely available in Thailand – help keep the insects at bay; electronic "buzzers" are useless. If you are bitten, applying locally made "yellow oil" is effective at reducing the itch.

A further reason to protect yourself is the possibility of contracting **dengue fever**, a debilitating and occasionally fatal viral disease that is particularly prevalent during and just after the rainy season. It's on the increase throughout tropical Asia, and is endemic to many areas of Thailand (including Bangkok), with around 200,000 reported cases a year. Unlike malaria, dengue fever is spread by mosquitoes that can bite during daylight hours, so you should also use mosquito repellent during the day. Symptoms may include fever, headaches, fierce joint and muscle pain ("breakbone fever" is another name for dengue), and possibly a rash, and usually develop between five and eight days after being bitten.

If you think you may have contracted the disease, you should see a doctor: the treatment is lots of rest, liquids and paracetamol (or any other acetaminophen painkiller, not aspirin or ibuprofen), and more serious cases may require hospitalization. Similar to dengue, both chikungunya fever and Zika virus are also in the ascendant in Thailand.

Digestive problems

By far the most common travellers' complaint in Thailand, **digestive troubles** are often caused by contaminated food and water, or sometimes just by an overdose of unfamiliar foodstuffs.

Stomach trouble usually manifests itself as simple **diarrhoea**, which should clear up without medical treatment within three to seven days and is best combated by drinking lots of fluids. If this doesn't work, you're in danger of getting **dehydrated** and should take some kind of rehydration solution, either a commercial sachet of ORS (oral rehydration solution), sold in all Thai pharmacies, or a do-it-yourself version, which can be made by adding a handful of sugar and a pinch of salt to every litre of boiled or bottled water (soft drinks are not a viable alternative). If you can eat, avoid fatty foods.

Anti-diarrhoeal agents such as Imodium are useful for blocking you up on long bus journeys, but only attack the symptoms and may prolong infections; an antibiotic such as ciprofloxacin, however, can often reduce a typical attack of traveller's diarrhoea to one day. If the diarrhoea persists for a week or more, or if you have blood or mucus in your stools, or an accompanying fever, go to a doctor or hospital.

Other diseases

Rabies is endemic in Thailand, mainly carried by dogs (between four and seven percent of stray dogs in Bangkok are reported to be rabid), but also cats and monkeys. It is transmitted by bites, scratches or even occasionally licks. Dogs are everywhere in Thailand and even if kept as pets they're often not very well cared for; hopefully their mangy appearance will discourage the urge to pat them, as you should steer well clear of them. Rabies is invariably fatal if the patient waits until symptoms begin, though modern vaccines and treatments are very effective and deaths are rare. The important thing is, if you are bitten, licked or scratched by an animal, to vigorously clean the wound with soap and disinfect it, preferably with something containing iodine, and to seek medical advice regarding treatment, at the Thai Red Cross Society, for example (see below), right away.

Sexually transmitted diseases are widespread in Thailand, primarily because of the sex trade. **Condoms** (*meechai*) are sold in pharmacies, convenience stores, department stores, hairdressers and even street markets. Due to rigorous screening methods, Thailand's medical blood supply is now considered safe from HIV/AIDS infection.

Worms can be picked up through the soles of your feet, so avoid going barefoot outside. They can also be ingested by eating undercooked meat, and liver **flukes** by eating raw or undercooked freshwater fish.

Medical and dental treatment

Hospital (*rong phayaabahn*) cleanliness and efficiency vary, but generally hygiene and healthcare standards are good, the ratio of medical staff to patients is considerably higher than in most parts of the West, and the doctors speak English. For emergency numbers in Thailand, see page 39. In the event of a major health crisis, get someone to contact your embassy (see page 45) and insurance company.

HOSPITALS AND CLINICS

Bangkok Hospital 2 Soi Soonvijai 7, Thanon Phetchaburi Mai ☎ 02 310 3000 or ☎ 1719, W bangkokhospital.com.
BNH (Bangkok Nursing Home) Hospital 9 Thanon Convent ☎ 02 022 0700, emergency ☎ 02 632 1000, W bnhhospital.com.
Bumrungrad International Hospital 33 Sukhumvit Soi 3 ☎ 02 066 8888 or freephone 1378, W bumrungrad.com. Most expats rate this private hospital as the best and most comfortable in the city.
Global Doctor Ground Floor, Holiday Inn Hotel, 981 Thanon Silom (corner of Thanon Surasak) ☎ 02 236 8444, W globaldoctorclinic.com. General clinic.
Thai Red Cross Society's Queen Saovabha Memorial Institute (QSMI) and Snake Farm Corner of Thanon Rama IV and Thanon Henri Dunant; ☎ 02 252 0161–4, W saovabha.org. A good place to get travel vaccinations, as well as rabies advice and treatment.

DENTISTS

Bumrungrad Hospital (see above) dental department ☎ 02 011 4100.
Dental Hospital 7 Sukhumvit Soi 77 ☎ 02 092 2000, W dentalhospitalbangkok.com.
Siam Family Dental Clinic Soi 3, Siam Square ☎ 081 987 7700, W siamfamilydental.com.

The media

To keep you abreast of world affairs, there are several English-language newspapers in Thailand, though various forms of censorship (and self-censorship) affect all newspapers and the predominantly state-controlled broadcast media.

Newspapers and magazines

Of the hundreds of **Thai-language newspapers and magazines** published every week, the sensationalist daily tabloid *Thai Rath* attracts the widest readership, while the moderately progressive *Matichon* is the leading quality daily.

Alongside these, the two main daily **English-language papers** are the *Bangkok Post* (W bangkokpost.com) and the *Nation* (W nationthailand.com), but you'll get a more balanced idea of what's going on in Thailand at W khaosodenglish.com, which is owned by *Matichon*. The *Post* is still sold at many newsstands in the capital.

Television

There are six government-controlled, terrestrial **TV channels** in Thailand: channels 3, 5 (owned and operated by the army), 7 (operated under license from the army) and 9 transmit a blend of news, soaps, sports, talk, quiz, reality and game shows, while the more serious-minded public-service channels are NBT, owned and operated by the government's public relations department, and the state-funded but more independent PBS. **Cable** networks – available in many guesthouse and hotel rooms, alongside streaming services such as Netflix – carry channels from all around the world, including CNN from the US, BBC World News from the UK and sometimes ABC from Australia, as well as English-language movie channels and various sports, music and documentary channels.

Radio

Thailand boasts over five hundred **radio stations**, mostly music-oriented, ranging from Eazy (105.5 FM; W eazyfm.teroradio.com), which serves up Western pop, through *luk thung* on Rak Thai (90FM; W 90rakthai.com), to Cat (formerly Fat) Radio, which streams Thai indie sounds 24hr on its website (W thisiscat.com) and app. Met 107 on 107 FM (W met107.fm) is one of several stations that include English-language news bulletins.

By going **online**, you can listen to the BBC World Service (W bbc.co.uk/worldserviceradio), Radio Australia

(W radioaustralia.net.au), Voice of America (W voanews.com) and Radio Canada (W rcinet.ca).

Festivals

Nearly all Thai festivals have a religious aspect. The most theatrical are generally Brahmin (Hindu) or animistic in origin, honouring elemental spirits with ancient rites and ceremonial costumed parades. In Buddhist celebrations, merit-making plays an important role and events are usually staged at the local temple, but a light-hearted atmosphere prevails, as the wat grounds are swamped with food- and trinket-vendors and makeshift stages are set up to show likay folk theatre, singing stars and beauty contests; there may even be funfair rides as well.

Many of the **secular festivals** – like the World Heritage Site *son et lumière* in Ayutthaya (see page 117), the Bridge over the River Kwai spectacle (see page 138) and the Phra Nakhon Khiri Fair in Phetchaburi (see page 135) – are outdoor local culture shows, geared specifically towards Thai and farang tourists.

Few of the dates for religious festivals are fixed, so check with TAT for specifics (W tourismthailand.org). Some of the festivals below are designated as national holidays (see page 47).

JANUARY– APRIL

Chinese New Year (Truut Jiin) New moon of the first lunar month, some time between mid-Jan and late Feb. Even more food stalls than usual in Chinatown (Thanon Yaowarat and Charoen Krung) and plenty to feast your eyes on too, including Chinese opera shows and jaunty parades led by traditional Chinese dragons and lions.

Maha Puja On the day of full moon in Feb. A day of merit-making marks the occasion when 1250 disciples gathered spontaneously to hear the Buddha preach. Best experienced at Wat Benjamabophit, where the festival culminates with a candlelit procession round the temple.

Cat Expo In Bangkok over a weekend in March; details on Facebook near the time. Formerly Fat Festival, this is Thailand's biggest indie music event, featuring over a hundred established and emerging bands on several stages, meet-the-bands booths and film screenings.

Songkran: Thai New Year April 13–15. The Thai New Year is welcomed in with massive waterfights, and no one, least of all foreign tourists, escapes a good-natured soaking. Trucks roam the streets spraying passers-by with hosepipes and half the population carry huge water pistols for the duration. Don't wear your favourite outfit as water is sometimes laced with dye. Celebrated throughout the city but famously raucous on Thanon Silom and, particularly, on Thanon Khao San, which also stages special organized entertainments.

MAY–AUGUST

Raek Na (Royal Ploughing Ceremony) Early in May. To mark the beginning of the rice-planting season, ceremonially clad Brahmin leaders parade sacred oxen and the royal plough across Sanam Luang, interpreting omens to forecast the year's rice yield (see also page 60).

Visakha Puja May/June; on the day of full moon of the sixth lunar month. Temples across the city are the focus of this holiest day of the Buddhist calendar, which commemorates the birth, enlightenment and death of the Buddha. The most photogenic event is the candlelit evening procession around the wat, particularly at Wat Benjamabophit in Dusit.

SEPTEMBER–DECEMBER

Chulalongkorn Day October 23. The city marks the anniversary of the death of the widely loved Rama V, King Chulalongkorn (1868–1910), by laying offerings around the famous equestrian statue of the king, at the Thanon U-Thong–Thanon Sri Ayutthaya crossroads in Dusit.

Awk Pansa On the day of full moon usually in Oct. Devotees at temples across the city make offerings to monks and there's general merrymaking to celebrate the Buddha's descent to Earth from Tavatimsa heaven and the end of the Khao Pansa retreat.

Thawt Kathin Oct–Nov; the month between Awk Pansa and Loy Krathong. During the month following the end of the monks' rainy-season retreat, it's traditional for the laity to donate new robes to the monkhood. Occasionally, when it coincides with a kingly anniversary, this is celebrated with a spectacular Royal Barge Procession down the Chao Phraya River in Bangkok.

Loy Krathong On the full moon day of the twelfth lunar month, in late Oct or Nov. Wishes and prayers wrapped up in banana-leaf baskets full of flowers and lighted candles are released on to the Chao Phraya River and Thonburi canals in this charming festival that both honours the water spirits and celebrates the end of the rainy season.

Ngan Wat Saket Nine days around Loy Krathong, usually Nov. Probably Thailand's biggest temple fair, held around Wat Saket (near Democracy Monument) and the Golden Mount, with funfairs, folk theatre, music and tons of food.

Vegetarian Festival (Ngan Kin Jeh) Oct/Nov; held over nine days during the ninth lunar month in the Chinese calendar. Many Chinese people become vegetarian for this annual nine-day Taoist detox, so most food vendors and restaurants in Chinatown, and many outlets in other parts of the city, turn veggie too, displaying a yellow pennant to alert their customers (see page 161).

Trooping the Colour Dec 2. An extraordinary array of sumptuous uniforms makes this annual marshalling of the Royal Guards a sight worth stopping for. Head to Suan Amporn in Dusit.

> ### LOY KRATHONG
>
> Every year on the evening of the full moon of the twelfth lunar month (usually in November), Thais all over the country celebrate the end of the rainy season with **Loy Krathong**, also known as the Festival of Light. One of Thailand's most beautiful festivals, it's held to honour and appease the spirits of the water at a time when all the fields are flooded and the canals and rivers are overflowing their banks. The festival is said to have originated seven hundred years ago, when **Nang Noppamas**, the consort of a Sukhothai king, adapted an ancient Brahmin tradition of paying homage to the water goddess.
>
> At this time, nearly everyone makes or buys a **krathong** and sets it afloat (*loy*) on the nearest body of water, to cast adrift any bad luck that may have accrued over the past year. *Krathongs* are miniature basket-boats made of banana leaves that have been elegantly folded and pinned, origami style, and then filled with flowers, three sticks of incense and a lighted candle; the traditional base is a slice of banana tree trunk, but it's increasingly popular to buy your *krathong* ready-made from the market, sometimes with an eco-unfriendly polystyrene bottom. Some people slip locks of hair and fingernail clippings between the flowers, to represent sinful deeds that will then be symbolically released along with the *krathong*; others add a coin or two to persuade the spirits to take away their bad luck (swiftly raided by opportunist young boys looking for small change). It's traditional to make a wish or prayer as you launch your *krathong* and to watch until it disappears from view: if your candle burns strong, your wishes will be granted and you will live long.

Western New Year's Eve Dec 31. The new year is greeted with fireworks along the river and at Sanam Luang, and huge crowds gather for a mass countdown around the Central World and Siam Square area, which is usually pedestrianized for the night.

Crime, safety and the law

As long as you keep your wits about you, you shouldn't encounter much trouble in Bangkok. Pickpocketing and bag-snatching are two of the main problems – not surprising, considering that a huge percentage of the local population scrape by on under US$10 per day – but the most common cause for concern is the number of con-artists who dupe gullible tourists into parting with their cash. There are various Thai laws that tourists need to be aware of, particularly regarding passports, the age of consent and smoking in public.

Theft

To **prevent theft**, most travellers prefer to carry their valuables with them at all times, but it's often possible to use a safe in a hotel or a locker in a guesthouse – the safest lockers are those that require your own padlock, as there are occasional reports of valuables being stolen by guesthouse staff. **Padlock your luggage** when leaving it in storage or taking it on public transport. Padlocks also come in handy as extra security on your room.

Personal safety

Be wary of accepting food and drink from strangers, especially on public transport, as it may be drugged. This might sound paranoid, but there have been enough **drug-muggings** for TAT to publish a specific warning about the problem. Drinks are sometimes spiked in bars and clubs, especially by sex-workers who later steal from their victim's room.

Violent crime against tourists is not common, but it does occur, and there have been several serious attacks on travellers in the last few years. However, bearing in mind that thirty million foreigners visit Thailand every year, the statistical likelihood of becoming a victim is extremely small. **Obvious precautions** for travellers of either sex include locking accessible windows and doors at night (with your own padlock in the simpler guesthouses), taking care at night, especially around bars, and not travelling alone at night in a taxi or tuk-tuk. Nor should you risk jumping into an unlicensed taxi at the airport in Bangkok at any time of day: there have been some very violent robberies in these, so take the well-marked licensed, metered taxis instead.

Unfortunately, it is also necessary for female tourists to think twice about spending time alone with a **monk**, as not all men of the cloth uphold the Buddhist precepts and there have been rapes and murders committed by men wearing the saffron robes of the monkhood.

Though unpalatable and distressing, Thailand's high-profile **sex industry** is relatively unthreatening for Western women, with its energy focused exclusively on farang men; it's also quite easily avoided, being contained within certain pockets of the capital. As for **harassment** from men, it's hard to generalize, but most Western women find it less of a problem in Thailand than they do back home. Outside the main tourist spots, you're more likely to be of interest as a foreigner rather than a woman and, if travelling alone, as an object of concern rather than of sexual aggression.

For advice on safe travelling in Thailand, consult your government's travel advisory (see page 40).

Scams

Despite the best efforts of guidebook writers, TAT and the Thai tourist police, countless travellers to Thailand get scammed every year. Nearly all **scams** are easily avoided if you're on your guard against anyone who makes an unnatural effort to befriend you. We have outlined the main scams in the relevant sections of this Guide, but con-artists are nothing if not creative, so if in doubt walk away at the earliest opportunity.

Many Bangkok **tuk-tuk drivers** earn most of their living through securing **commissions** from tourist-oriented shops and will do their damnedest to get you to go to a gem shop (see page 188). The most common tactic is for drivers to pretend that the Grand Palace or other major sight you intended to visit is closed for the day – they usually invent a plausible reason, such as a festival or royal occasion (see page 50) – and then offer to take you on a round-city tour instead, perhaps even for free. The tour will invariably include a visit to a gem shop. The easiest way to avoid all this is to take a **metered taxi**; if you're fixed on taking a tuk-tuk, ignore any tuk-tuk that is parked up or loitering and be firm about where you want to go.

Self-styled **tourist guides**, **touts** and anyone else who might introduce themselves as **students** or **businesspeople** and offer to take you somewhere of interest, or invite you to meet their family, are often the first piece of bait in a well-honed chain of con-artists. If you bite, chances are you'll end up either at a gem shop or in a gambling den, or, at best, at a tour operator or hotel that you had not planned to patronize. This is not to say that you should never accept an invitation from a local person, but be extremely wary of doing so following a street encounter in Bangkok. Tourist guides' ID cards are easily faked.

For many of these characters, the goal is to get you inside a dodgy **gem shop** (see page 188), but the bottom line is that if you are not experienced at buying and trading in valuable gems you will definitely be ripped off, possibly even to the tune of several thousand dollars.

A less common, but potentially more frightening, scam involves a similar cast of warm-up artists leading tourists into a **gambling** game. The scammers invite their victim home on an innocent-sounding pretext, get out a pack of cards, and then set about fleecing the incomer in any number of subtle or unsubtle ways. Often this can be especially scary as the venue is likely to be far from hotels or recognizable landmarks, and there have been stories of visitors being forced to withdraw large amounts of money from ATMs. You're unlikely to get any sympathy from police, as gambling is **illegal** in Thailand.

Age restrictions and other laws

Thai law requires that tourists **carry their original passports** at all times, though sometimes it's more

> ### REPORTING A CRIME OR EMERGENCY
>
> In the event of a crime, contact the English-speaking **tourist police**, who maintain a 24-hour toll-free nationwide line (☏ 1155) and are based on the grounds of Suvarnabhumi Airport (⊛ touristpolice.go.th); getting in touch with the tourist police first is invariably more efficient than directly contacting the local police. The tourist police's job is to offer advice and tell you what to do next, but they do not file crime reports, which must be done at the nearest police station, such as the Chana Songkhram Police Station at the west end of Thanon Khao San in Banglamphu (☏ 02 282 2323).
>
> In a medical emergency, call either the tourist police or the nationwide ambulance hotline (☏ 1669), which is likely to be quicker than calling an individual hospital for an ambulance.

> **GOVERNMENTAL TRAVEL ADVISORIES**
>
> **Australian Department of Foreign Affairs** W smartraveller.gov.au.
> **British Foreign & Commonwealth Office** W gov.uk/foreign-travel-advice/Thailand.
> **Canadian Department of Foreign Affairs** W travel.gc.ca.
> **Irish Department of Foreign Affairs** W dfa.ie/travel.
> **New Zealand Ministry of Foreign Affairs** W safetravel.govt.nz.
> **South African Department of Foreign Affairs** W dirco.gov.za.
> **US State Department** W travel.state.gov.

practical to carry a photocopy and keep the original locked in a safety deposit. The **age of consent** is 15, but the law allows anyone under the age of 18, or their parents, to file charges in retrospect even if they consented to sex at the time. It is against the law to have sex with a prostitute who is under 18. It is illegal for **under-18s** to buy cigarettes or to drive and you must be 20 or over to **buy alcohol** or be allowed into a **bar or club** (ID checks are sometimes enforced in Bangkok). It is illegal for anyone to **gamble** in Thailand (though many do).

Smoking in public is widely prohibited. The ban covers all public buildings (including restaurants, bars and clubs) and trains, buses and planes and can even be extended to parks and the street; violators may be subject to a B2000–5000 fine. Possession of e-cigarettes is currently illegal, and several foreign nationals have been arrested. Dropping cigarette butts, **littering** and spitting in public places can also earn you a B2000–5000 fine. There are fines for **overstaying your visa** (see page 45), **working without a permit**, **not wearing a motorcycle helmet** and violating other **traffic laws**.

Drugs

The medicinal use of **cannabis** has recently been legalized in Thailand but recreational use has been left in a grey area of the law. Small high-street shops selling *gancha* have sprung up in many places, but the authorities seem to have drawn the line at cannabis cafés and bars. Smoking in public places remains illegal, as does dealing, export and import. The current Pheu Thai government have indicated that they would like to tighten up the law again to make recreational use illegal, but their main coalition partner, Bhumjaithai, objects – watch this space.

Drug-smuggling carries a maximum penalty in Thailand of death, and **dealing drugs** will get you anything from four years to life in a Thai prison; penalties depend on the drug and the amount involved.

Travellers caught with even the smallest amount of drugs at airports and international borders are prosecuted for trafficking, and no one charged with trafficking offences gets bail. Heroin, amphetamines, LSD and ecstasy are classed as Category 1 drugs and carry the most severe penalties: even **possession** of Category 1 drugs for personal use can result in a **life sentence**.

Despite occasional royal pardons, don't expect special treatment as a farang: you only need to read one of the first-hand accounts by foreign former prisoners (see page 221) to get the picture. The **police** actively look for tourists doing drugs, reportedly searching people randomly on Thanon Khao San, for example. They have the power to order a urine test if they have reasonable grounds for suspicion. Be wary also of **being shopped** by a farang or local dealer keen to earn a financial reward for a successful bust, or having substances slipped into your luggage (simple enough to perpetrate unless all fastenings are secured with padlocks).

If you are arrested, ask for your embassy to be contacted immediately (see page 45), which is your right under Thai law, and embassy staff will talk you through procedures; the website of the British government even includes a Prisoner Pack for Thailand (W gov.uk/government/publications/thailand-prisoner-pack). The British charity Prisoners Abroad (W prisonersabroad.org.uk) carries lots of useful information on its website, and may be able to offer direct support to a British citizen (and their family) facing imprisonment in a Thai jail.

Culture and etiquette

Tourist literature has marketed Thailand as the "Land of Smiles" so successfully that a lot of farangs arrive in the country expecting to be forgiven any outrageous behaviour. This is just not the case: there are some things so universally sacred in Thailand that even a hint of disrespect will cause deep offence.

The monarchy

It is both socially unacceptable to many Thais and a criminal offence to make critical or defamatory remarks about the **royal family**. Thailand's monarchy is technically a constitutional one, but pictures of King Vajiralongkorn, who acceded to the throne on the death of his much-loved father King Bhumibol in 2016, are displayed in many public places and submissive crowds mass whenever the royals make a public appearance. When addressing or speaking about royalty, Thais use a special language full of deference, called *rajasap* (literally translates as "royal language").

Thailand's **lèse majesté laws** are among the most strictly applied in the world and have been increasingly invoked since the 2014 coup. Accusations of lèse majesté can be levelled by and against anyone, Thai national or farang, and must be investigated by the police. As a few high-profile cases involving foreigners have demonstrated, they can be raised for seemingly minor infractions, such as defacing a poster or being less than respectful in a work of fiction.

Article 112 of the Thai criminal code specifies insults to the king, the queen, the heir apparent and the regent, but the law has been wielded against supposed slights to the king's dog and to kings who have been dead for four centuries. Transgressions are met with jail sentences of up to fifteen years for each offence. We have had to take into account the lèse majesté laws in writing this guidebook.

Aside from keeping any anti-monarchy sentiments to yourself, you should be prepared to stand when the **king's anthem** is played at the beginning of every cinema programme – though more and more locals now remain in their seats. A less obvious point: as the king's head features on all Thai currency, you should never step on a coin or banknote, which is tantamount to kicking the king in the face.

Religion

Almost equally insensitive would be to disregard certain **religious** precepts. **Buddhism** plays a fundamental role in Thai culture, and Buddhist monuments should be treated with respect – which basically means wearing long trousers or knee-length skirts, covering your arms and removing your shoes whenever you visit one.

All **Buddha images** are sacred, however small, tacky or ruined, and should never be used as a backdrop for a portrait photo, clambered over, placed in a position of inferiority or treated in any manner that could be construed as disrespectful. In an attempt to prevent foreigners from committing any kind of transgression the government requires a special licence for all Buddha statues exported from the country (see page 44).

Monks come only a little beneath the monarchy in the social hierarchy, and they too are addressed and discussed in a special language. If there's a monk around, he'll always get a seat on the bus, usually right at the back. Theoretically, monks are forbidden to have any close contact with women, which means that, as a female, you mustn't sit or stand next to a monk, or even brush against his robes; if it's essential to pass him something, put the object down so that he can then pick it up – never hand it over directly. Nuns, however, get treated like ordinary women.

See "Contexts" for more on religious practices in Thailand (see page 206).

The body

The Western liberalism embraced by the Thai sex industry is very unrepresentative of the majority Thai attitude to the body. **Clothing** – or the lack of it – is what bothers Thais most about tourist behaviour. You need to dress modestly when entering temples (see page 52), but the same also applies to other important buildings and all public places. Stuffy and sweaty as it sounds, you should keep short shorts and vests for the real tourist resorts, and be especially diligent about covering up. Baring your flesh on beaches is very much a Western practice: when Thais go swimming they often do so fully clothed, and they find topless and nude bathing offensive.

According to ancient Hindu belief, the **head** is the most sacred part of the body and the **feet** are the most unclean. This belief, imported into Thailand, means that it's very rude to touch another person's head or to point your feet either at a human being or at a sacred image – when sitting on a temple floor, for example, you should **tuck your legs beneath you** rather than stretch them out towards the Buddha. These hierarchies also forbid people from wearing **shoes** (which are even more unclean than feet) inside temples and most private homes, and – by extension – Thais take offence when they see someone sitting on the "head", or prow, of a boat. **Putting your feet up** on a table, a chair or a pillow is also considered very uncouth, and Thais will always take their shoes off if they need to stand on a train or bus seat to get to the luggage rack, for example. On a more practical note, the **left hand** is used for washing after going to the toilet, so Thais never use it to put food in their mouth, pass things or shake hands – as a farang, though, you'll be assumed to have different customs, so left-handers shouldn't worry unduly.

Social conventions

Thais rarely shake hands, instead using the **wai** to greet and say goodbye and to acknowledge respect, gratitude or apology. A prayer-like gesture made with raised hands, the *wai* changes according to the relative status of the two people involved: Thais can instantaneously assess which *wai* to use, but as a farang your safest bet is to raise your hands close to your chest, bow your head and place your fingertips just below your nose. If someone makes a *wai* at you, you should generally *wai* back, but it's safer not to initiate.

Public displays of **physical affection** in Thailand are more common between friends of the same sex than between lovers, whether hetero- or homosexual. Holding hands and hugging is as common among male friends as with females, so if you're caressed by a Thai acquaintance of the same sex, don't necessarily assume you're being propositioned.

Finally, there are three specifically Thai **concepts** you're bound to come across, which may help you comprehend a sometimes laissez-faire attitude to delayed buses and other inconveniences. The first, **jai yen**, translates literally as "cool heart" and is something everyone tries to maintain: most Thais hate raised voices, visible irritation and confrontations of any kind, so losing one's cool can have a much more inflammatory effect than in more combative cultures. Related to this is the oft-quoted response to a difficulty, **mai pen rai** – "never mind", "no problem" or "it can't be helped" – the verbal equivalent of an open-handed shoulder shrug, which has its basis in the Buddhist notion of karma (see page 207). And then there's **sanuk**, the wide-reaching philosophy of "fun", which, crass as it sounds, Thais do their best to inject into any situation, even work. Hence the crowds of inebriated Thais who congregate at waterfalls and other beauty spots on public holidays (travelling solo is definitely not *sanuk*), the reluctance to do almost anything without high-volume musical accompaniment, and the national waterfight which takes place during Songkran every April on streets right across Thailand.

Thai names

Although all Thais have a first **name** and a family name, everyone is addressed by their first name – even when meeting strangers – prefixed by the title "**Khun**" (Mr/Ms); no one is ever addressed as Khun Surname, and even the phone book lists people by their given name. In Thailand you will often be addressed in an anglicized version of this convention, as "Mr Paul" or "Miss Lucy" for example. Bear in mind, though, that when a man is introduced to you as Khun Pirom, his wife will definitely not be Khun Pirom as well (that would be like calling them, for instance, "Mr and Mrs Paul"). Among friends and relatives, **Phii** ("older brother/sister") is often used instead of Khun when addressing older familiars (though as a tourist you're on surer ground with Khun), and **Nong** ("younger brother/sister") is used for younger ones.

Many Thai **first names** come from ancient Sanskrit and have an auspicious meaning; for example, Boon means good deeds, Porn means blessings, Siri means glory and Thawee means to increase. However, Thais of all ages are commonly known by the **nickname** given them soon after birth rather than by their official first name. This tradition arises out of a deep-rooted superstition that once a child has been officially named the spirits will begin to take an unhealthy interest in them, so a nickname is used instead to confuse the spirits. Common nicknames – which often bear no resemblance to the adult's personality or physique – include Yai (Big), Uan (Fat) and Muu (Pig); Lek or Noi (Little), Nok (Bird), Nuu (Mouse) and Kung (Shrimp); and English nicknames like Apple, Joy or even Pepsi.

Family names were only introduced in 1913 (by Rama VI, who invented many of the aristocracy's surnames himself), and are used only in very formal situations, always in conjunction with the first name. It's quite usual for good friends never to know each other's surname. Ethnic Thais generally have short surnames like Somboon or Srisai, while the long, convoluted family names – such as Sonthanasumpun – usually indicate Chinese origin, not because they are phonetically Chinese but because many Chinese immigrants have chosen to adopt Thai surnames and Thai law states that every newly created surname must be unique. Thus anyone who wants to change their surname must submit a shortlist of five unique Thai names – each to a maximum length of ten Thai characters – to be checked against a database of existing names. As more and more names are taken, Chinese family names get increasingly unwieldy, and more easily distinguishable from the pithy old Thai names.

Travel essentials

Accessible travel

Thailand makes few provisions for its disabled citizens and this obviously affects **travellers with disabilities**, but taxis, comfortable hotels and personal tour guides are all more affordable than in the West and most travellers with disabilities find Thais only too happy to offer assistance where they can. (Note that most taxis run on natural gas, with a gas tank in the boot if it's a sedan car, so there may not be room there for a wheelchair – you might have to hire a larger taxi.) Hiring a local tour guide to accompany you on a day's sightseeing is particularly recommended: government-licensed tour guides can be arranged through any TAT office.

Most **wheelchair-users** end up driving on the roads because it's too hard to negotiate the uneven pavements, which are high to allow for flooding, poorly maintained and invariably lack dropped kerbs. Crossing the road can be a trial in Bangkok, where it's usually a question of climbing steps up to a bridge rather than taking a ramped underpass. Few buildings, buses and trains have ramps, but in Bangkok some Skytrain stations and all subway stations have lifts (though you might have to ask someone to unlock them). Facilities at Suvarnabhumi Airport (and on the airport rail link) are fairly good, and modern shopping centres have lifts and disabled toilets.

Several **tour companies** in Thailand specialize in organizing trips featuring adapted facilities, accessible transport and escorts. The Bangkok-based Help and Care Travel Company (W wheelchairtours.com) designs **accessible holidays** and tours in Thailand for slow walkers and wheelchair-users, as well as offering accessible taxis, vans and hotels, personal assistants and other services. Accessible Thailand Tours (accessible-thailandtours.com) by Nutty's Adventures (see page 24) provides tours for the blind and for wheelchair travellers.

Charities and volunteer projects

Reassured by the plethora of well-stocked shopping plazas, efficient services and abundance of bars and restaurants, it is easy to forget that life is extremely hard for many people in Bangkok. Countless **charities** work with Thailand's many poor and disadvantaged communities: listed below are a few that would welcome help in some way from visitors.

CHARITABLE AND VOLUNTEER ORGANIZATIONS

Human Development Foundation Mercy Centre Klong Toey, Bangkok W mercycentre.org. Founded in 1973, Father Joe Maier's organization provides education and support for Bangkok's street kids and slum-dwellers. It now runs two dozen kindergartens in the slums, as well as one in Ranong for sea-gypsy children, among many other projects. Check the centre's website for information about donations, sponsoring and volunteering. Father Joe's books, *Welcome to the Bangkok Slaughterhouse* and *The Open Gate of Mercy*, give eye-opening insights into this often invisible side of Thai life.

The Mirror Foundation W themirrorfoundation.org. NGO working mainly with the hill tribes in northern Thailand, with a branch in Bangkok dealing with urban problems; volunteers and donations sought.

The Students' Education Trust (SET) W thaistudentcharity.org. High-school and further education in Thailand is a luxury that the poorest kids cannot afford so many are sent to live in temples instead. The SET helps such kids pursue their education and escape from the poverty trap. Some of their stories are told in *Little Angels: The Real-Life Stories of Twelve Thai Novice Monks* (see page 221). SET welcomes donations.

Costs

Bangkok can be a very cheap place to visit. At the bottom of the scale, you can just about manage on a **daily budget** of around B750 (about £18/US$25) if you're willing to opt for basic accommodation and eat, drink and travel as the locals do. With extras like air conditioning, taxis and a meal and beer in a more touristy restaurant, a day's outlay would be at least B1000 (about £23/US$32). Staying in well-equipped, mid-range hotels and eating in the more upmarket restaurants, you should be able to live comfortably for around B2000 a day (about £46/US$64).

Bargaining is expected practice for a lot of commercial transactions, particularly at markets and when hiring tuk-tuks and motorbike taxis (though not in supermarkets or department stores). It's a delicate art that requires humour, tact and patience. If your price is way out of line, the vendor's vehement refusal should be enough to make you increase your offer: never forget that the few pennies or cents you're making such a fuss over will go a lot further in a Thai person's hands than in your own.

It's rare that foreigners can bargain a price down as low as a Thai could, anyway, while **two-tier pricing** has been made official at government-run sights, as a kind of informal tourist tax. A number of privately owned tourist attractions follow a similar two-tier system, posting an inflated price in English for foreigners and a lower price in Thai for locals.

Shoppers who are departing via an international airport can save some money by claiming a **Value Added Tax refund** (W rd.go.th), though it's a bit of a palaver for seven percent (the current rate of VAT, though this may increase to ten percent). The total amount of your purchases from participating shops needs to be at least B2000 per person. You'll need to show your passport and fill in an application form (to which original tax invoices need to be attached) at the shop. At the relevant airport, you'll need to show your form and purchases to customs officers before checking in, then make your claim from VAT refund officers – from which fees of at least B60 are deducted.

Customs regulations

The **duty-free** allowance on entry to Thailand is 200 cigarettes (or 250g of tobacco or cigars) and a litre of spirits or wine (see W customs.go.th for more information).

To **export antiques** or newly cast **Buddha images** from Thailand, you need to have a licence granted by the Fine Arts Department (the export of religious antiques, especially Buddha images, is forbidden; W thailandntr.com). Licences can be obtained for example through the Office of Archeology and National Museums, 81/1 Thanon Si Ayutthaya (near the National Library), Bangkok (T 02 126 6252). Applications take at least three working days and need to be accompanied by the object itself, some evidence of its rightful possession, two postcard-sized colour photos of it, taken face-on and against a white background, and photocopies of the applicant's passport; furthermore, if the object is a Buddha image, the passport photocopies need to be certified by your embassy in Bangkok. Some antiques shops can organize all this for you.

Electricity

Mains **electricity** is supplied at 220 volts AC. If you're packing phone and camera chargers, a laptop or other appliance, you'll need to take a set of travel-plug adaptors as several plug types are commonly in use, most usually with two round pins, but also with two flat-blade pins, and sometimes with both options.

Entry requirements

There are three main entry categories for visitors to Thailand; for all of them, your passport should be valid for at least six months. As visa requirements are subject to frequent change, you should always consult before departure a Thai embassy or consulate, a reliable travel agent, or the Thai Ministry of Foreign Affairs' website at W mfa.go.th. For further, unofficial but usually reliable, details on all visa matters – especially as the rules are not consistently enforced across all Thai border checkpoints and immigration offices – go to the moderated forums on W aseannow.com (formerly W thaivisa.com).

Most Western passport holders (that includes citizens of the UK, Ireland, the US, Canada, Australia, New Zealand and South Africa) are allowed to enter the country without having to apply for a visa – officially termed the **tourist visa exemption** (not to be confused with "visas on arrival", another category of entry that's not available to citizens of the countries listed above).

For a long time, the period of stay, which is stamped into your passport by immigration officials upon entry, was 30 days. In July 2024, this was increased to 60 days, though the change may be temporary. You're supposed to be able to show proof of means of living while in the country (B10,000 per person, B20,000 per family), and you're also required to show proof of tickets to leave Thailand again within the allotted time, and, in theory, you may be put back on the next plane or sent back to get a sixty-day tourist visa from the nearest Thai embassy. However, the Thai immigration authorities do not appear to be consistent about checking these requirements (it seems to be more likely at land borders, especially Aranyaprathet).

If you have a one-way air ticket to Thailand and no evidence of onward travel arrangements, it's best to buy a tourist visa in advance: many airlines will stop you boarding the plane without one, as they would be liable for flying you back to your point of origin if you did happen to be stopped.

You can apply for a **sixty-day tourist visa** through the Ministry of Foreign Affairs' e-visa site (W thaievisa.go.th). The visa currently costs B1000 or very rough equivalent; multiple-entry versions are available, with more stringent requirements. Ordinary tourist visas are valid for three months; ie you must enter Thailand within three months of the visa being issued by the Thai embassy or consulate.

The Ministry of Foreign Affairs also considers applications on W thaievisa.go.th for **ninety-day non-immigrant visas** (B2000 or rough equivalent for single entry, B5000 for multiple-entry) as long as you can offer a reason for your visit, such as study, business or visiting family (there are different categories of non-immigrant visa for which different levels of proof are needed).

As it can be a hassle to organize a ninety-day visa, it's generally easier to apply for a thirty-day extension to your sixty-day visa or tourist visa exemption once inside Thai borders.

It's not a good idea to **overstay** your visa limits. Once you're at the airport or the border, you'll have to pay a fine of B500 per day before you can leave Thailand. More importantly, however, if you're in the country with an expired visa and you get involved with police or immigration officials for any reason, however trivial, they are obliged to take you to court, possibly imprison you, and deport you.

Extensions, border runs and re-entry permits

Tourist visa exemptions, as well as sixty-day tourist visas, can be **extended** within Thailand for a further thirty days, at the discretion of immigration officials; extensions cost B1900 and are issued over the counter at immigration offices (*kaan khao muang* or *taw maw*; ☎1178 for information, ⓦimmigration.go.th). You'll need to bring one or two photos, one or two photocopies of the main pages of your passport including your arrival stamp and visa (if applicable); you may be asked for proof of tickets to leave Thailand again within the proposed time and evidence of where you're staying, and it's possible that you'll be asked for proof of means of living while in Thailand.

Many Khao San tour agents offer to get your visa extension for you, but beware: some are reportedly faking the stamps, which could get you into serious trouble.

The Thai immigration authorities have recently made it more difficult for foreigners to stay in Thailand long-term by doing back-to-back **border runs** for tourist visa exemptions, **repeatedly** hopping **across** into a neighbouring country and back again. The limit seems to be two tourist visa exemptions using a land border within a year, but at the time of writing, it was not clear how the increase in the tourist visa exemption from 30 to 60 days would affect this.

Immigration offices and Immigration Bureau desks at international airports also issue **re-entry permits** (B1000 single re-entry, B3800 multiple) if you want to leave the country and come back again while maintaining the validity of your existing visa.

Bangkok immigration office

The **immigration office** is north of the centre off Thanon Wiphawadi Rangsit at Floor 2, B Building, Government Complex, Soi 7, Thanon Chaengwattana (ⓦbangkok.immigration.go.th, which includes a map), which is within walking distance of Government Complex station on the MRT Pink Line (catch the Skytrain to Wat Phra Sri Mahathat (N17) station to change onto the Pink Line). It also has a nearby tourist service centre on Floor 3, IT Square, Laksi Plaza, Thanon Chaengwattana (next to Lak Si Dark Red Line and MRT Pink Line stations), which handles, for example, extensions of tourist visa exemptions.

THAI EMBASSIES AND CONSULATES ABROAD

For a full listing of Thai diplomatic missions abroad, consult the Thai Ministry of Foreign Affairs' website at ⓦmfa.go.th; its other site, ⓦthaiembassy.org, has links to the websites of most of the offices below.

Australia 111 Empire Circuit, Yarralumla, Canberra ACT 2600 ☎02 6206 0100; plus consulate at 131 Macquarrie St, Sydney, NSW 2000 ☎02 9241 2542–3.
Canada 180 Island Park Drive, Ottawa, ON, K1Y 0A2 ☎613 722 4444; plus consulate at 1040 Burrard St, Vancouver, BC, V6Z 2R9 ☎604 687 1143.
New Zealand 110 Molesworth St, Thorndon, Wellington ☎04 496 2900.
South Africa 248 Pretorius/Hill St, Arcadia, Pretoria 0083 ☎012 342 5470.
UK and Ireland 29–30 Queens Gate, London SW7 5JB ☎020 7589 2944.
US 1024 Wisconsin Ave NW, Suite 401, Washington, DC 20007 ☎202 944 3600; plus consulates at 700 North Rush St, Chicago, IL 60611 ☎312 664 3129; 611 North Larchmont Blvd, 2nd Floor, Los Angeles, CA 90004 ☎323 962 9574; and 351 E 52nd St, New York, NY 10022 ☎212 754 1770.

FOREIGN EMBASSIES AND CONSULATES IN BANGKOK

For further details about Bangkok's diplomatic corps, go to ⓦmfa.go.th/en/page/diplomatic-and-consular-list on the Thai Ministry of Foreign Affairs' website.

Australia 181 Thanon Witthayu ☎02 344 6300, ⓦthailand.embassy.gov.au.
Cambodia 518/4 Thanon Pracha Uthit (Soi Ramkamhaeng 39) ☎02 957 5851–2.
Canada 15th floor, Abdulrahim Place, 990 Thanon Rama IV ☎02 646 4300, ⓦthailand.gc.ca.
Ireland Floor 12, 208 Thanon Witthayu ☎02 016 1360.
Laos 502/1–3 Soi Sahakarnpramoon, Thanon Pracha Uthit ☎02 539 4018, ⓦlaoembassybangkok.gov.la.
Malaysia 3 Level 17, Kronos Sathorn Tower, 46 Thanon Sathorn Nua ☎02 340 5720, ⓦkln.gov.my/web/tha_bangkok/home.
Myanmar (Burma) 110 Thanon Sathorn Nua ☎02 234 4698.
New Zealand 14th Floor, M Thai Tower, All Seasons Place, 87 Thanon Witthayu ☎02 254 2530, ⓦnzembassy.com/thailand.
South Africa Floor 12A, M Thai Tower, All Seasons Place, 87 Thanon Witthayu ☎02 092 2900, ⓦwww.dirco.gov.za/Bangkok.
UK Floor 12A, AIA Sathorn Tower, 11/1 Thanon Sathorn Tai ☎02 305 8333.
US 120 Thanon Witthayu ☎02 205 4000.
Vietnam 83/1 Thanon Witthayu ☎02 650 8979, ⓦvnembassybangkok.mofa.gov.vn.

Internet

Internet access is now almost ubiquitous in Thailand. As well as broadband mobile phone networks (see page 47), there's free wi-fi in nearly all hotels and guesthouses (though in cheaper places, the signal may not stretch to all bedrooms) and most shopping centres, cafés, restaurants and bars in Bangkok. Internet cafés are now generally only found in the suburbs, full of schoolkids playing games, but most hotels and guesthouses will have computers and printers for printing out boarding passes and the like.

Laundry

In luxury hotels, laundry will cost an arm and a leg, but guesthouses and cheap hotels run low-cost, same- or next-day services. In some places you pay per item, in others you're charged by the kilo (generally around B50/kg); ironing is often included in the price. There are also several self-service laundries around Thanon Khao San.

Left luggage

Luggage can be left at the airports, the bus terminals and most hotels and guesthouses.

Living in Bangkok

The most common source of **employment** in Bangkok is **teaching English**. You can search for openings at schools on Ⓦajarn.com (*ajarn* means "teacher"), which also features extensive general advice on teaching and living in Bangkok. Another useful resource is the excellent Ⓦaseannow.com, whose scores of well-used forums focus on specific topics that range from employment in Thailand to legal issues and cultural and practical topics. Guesthouse noticeboards occasionally carry adverts for more unusual jobs, such as playing extras in Thai movies.

A tourist visa does not entitle you to work in Thailand, so, legally, you'll need to apply for a **work permit**.

Thai language classes

The most popular place to **study Thai** is Bangkok, and there's plenty of choice, including private and group lessons for both tourists and expats; note, however, that some schools' main reason for existence is to provide educational visas for long-staying foreigners. The longest-running and best-regarded courses and private lessons are provided by AUA (American University Alumni; Ⓦauathailand.org).

Mail

Overseas airmail usually takes around seven days from Bangkok (it's worth asking at the post office about its express EMS services, which can cut this down to three days and aren't prohibitively expensive). **Post offices** in Thailand (Ⓦthailandpost.com) have recently been quite successfully privatized, and many now offer money-wiring facilities (in association with Western Union), parcel boxes, amulets, whitening cream, you name it. They're generally open Monday to Friday 8.30am to 4.30pm, Saturday 9am to noon; some close Monday to Friday noon to 1pm and may stay open until 6pm, and a few open 9am to noon on Sundays and public holidays. Post offices are the best places to buy **stamps**, though hotels and guesthouses often sell them too.

Almost all post offices operate a **poste restante** service and will hold letters for one to three months. Mail should be addressed: *Name* (family name underlined or capitalized), Poste Restante, GPO, *Town or City*, Thailand. It will be filed by surname, though it's always wise to check under your first and middle names as well; you need to show your passport.

If you're staying in Banglamphu, it's probably most convenient to use the local postal, packing and poste restante services at Banglamphubon PO, Soi Sibsam Hang, Bangkok 10203. Downtown, Nana PO, between sois 4 and 6, Thanon Sukhumvit, Bangkok 10112, is handy for the BTS.

Money and banks

Thailand's unit of currency is the **baht** (abbreviated in this guide to "B"), divided into 100 satang – which are rarely seen these days. Coins come in B1 (silver), B2 (golden), B5 (silver) and B10 (mostly golden, encircled by a silver ring) denominations, notes in B20, B50, B100, B500 and B1000 denominations, inscribed with Western as well as Thai numerals, and generally increasing in size according to value.

At the time of writing, **exchange rates** were around B34 to US$1 and B43 to £1. A good site for current exchange rates is Ⓦxe.com. Note that Thailand has no black market in foreign currency.

Banking hours are generally Monday to Friday from 8.30am to 3.30 or 4.30pm, though branches in shopping centres and supermarkets are often open longer hours and at weekends. Streetside exchange kiosks run by the banks in the main tourist areas are always open till at least 5pm, sometimes 10pm, and upmarket hotels change money (at poor rates) 24 hours a day. The Suvarnabhumi Airport exchange counters also operate 24 hours, while exchange kiosks at overseas airports with flights to Thailand usually keep Thai currency. Note that Scottish and Northern Irish sterling notes may not be accepted in some places.

Visa and MasterCard **credit and debit cards** are accepted at upmarket guesthouses and hotels as well as in upscale restaurants, department stores, tourist shops and travel agents; American Express is less widely accepted. It's common for smaller businesses to add on a surcharge of three percent, which amounts to the fee that Visa and Mastercard charge them for the privilege. Beware theft and forgery – try not to let the card out of your sight, and never leave cards in baggage storage.

With a debit or credit card and personal identification number (PIN), you can also withdraw cash from hundreds of 24hr **ATMs** around the city, including a huge number of standalone ATMs in shopping malls and on the streets, often outside supermarkets and post offices. However, Thai banks now levy a charge of B200–250 per ATM withdrawal (on top of whatever your bank at home will be charging you); the same goes for getting a cash advance inside the bank. Check with your bank before you come to Thailand – some overseas banks will not pass on to customers this levy.

Opening hours and public holidays

Most **shops** open at least Monday to Saturday from about 8am to 8pm, while department stores and shopping malls operate daily from around 10am to 9pm. Private office hours are generally Monday to Friday 8am to 5pm, plus perhaps Saturday 8am to noon, though in tourist areas these hours are longer, with weekends worked like any other day. Government offices work Monday to Friday 8.30am to 4.30pm (often closing for lunch between noon and 1pm). Temples generally open their gates every day from dawn to dusk.

Many tourists only register **national holidays** because trains and buses suddenly get extraordinarily crowded, especially if the holiday is moved from a Saturday or a Sunday to a Monday or a Friday as a substitution day, thus creating a long weekend: although government offices shut on these days, most shops and tourist-oriented businesses carry on regardless, and TAT branches continue to hand out free maps. (Bank holidays vary slightly from the government office holidays given below: banks close on May 1 for Labour Day, but not for the Royal Ploughing Ceremony, Khao Pansa and New Year's Eve.) Some national holidays are celebrated with theatrical festivals (see page 37). The only time an inconvenient number of shops, restaurants and hotels do close is during **Chinese New Year**, which, though not marked as an official national holiday, brings many businesses to a standstill for several days in late January or February.

Thais use both the Western Gregorian **calendar** and a Buddhist calendar – the Buddha is said to have died

> ## INTERNATIONAL DIALLING CODES
>
> Calling from abroad, the international **country code** for Thailand is **66**, after which you leave off the initial zero of the Thai number.
>
> Calling from Thailand, you'll need the relevant country code:
> **Australia** 61
> **Canada** 1
> **Ireland** 353
> **New Zealand** 64
> **South Africa** 27
> **UK** 44
> **US** 1

(or entered Nirvana) in the year 543 BC, so Thai dates start from that point: thus 2019 AD becomes 2562 BE (Buddhist Era).

NATIONAL HOLIDAYS

Jan 1 Western New Year's Day.
Feb (day of full moon) Makha Puja. Commemorates the Buddha preaching to a spontaneously assembled crowd of 1250.
April 6 Chakri Day. The founding of the Chakri dynasty, the current royal family.
April (usually 13–15) Songkran. Thai New Year.
May 4 Coronation Day.
May (early in the month) Royal Ploughing Ceremony. Marks the traditional start of the rice-planting season.
May (day of full moon) Visakha Puja. The holiest of all Buddhist holidays, which celebrates the birth, enlightenment and death of the Buddha.
June 3 Queen Suthida's birthday.
July (day of full moon) Asanha Puja. The anniversary of the Buddha's first sermon.
July (day after Asanha Puja) Khao Pansa. The start of the annual three-month Buddhist rains retreat, when new monks are ordained.
July 28 King Vajiralongkorn's birthday.
Aug 12 Queen Mother's birthday and Mothers' Day.
Oct 13 The anniversary of Rama IX's death.
Oct 23 Chulalongkorn Day. The anniversary of Rama V's death.
Dec 5 The late King Bhumibol's birthday and Fathers' Day. Also now celebrated as National Day (instead of Constitution Day).
Dec 10 Constitution Day.
Dec 31 Western New Year's Eve.

Phones

Most foreign **mobile-phone** networks have links with Thai networks but you need to check on roaming rates, which are often exorbitant, before you leave home. To get round this, most travellers either rely on wi-fi coverage, which is fairly widespread in Thailand, especially in Bangkok, or purchase a Thai pre-paid SIM card (providers include AIS, DTAC and True Move) usually for an old mobile phone (*moe thoe*) brought from home or for a new set cheaply purchased in Thailand (which can most easily be done in a shopping centre, especially Mah Boon Krong opposite Siam Square – see page 187). Available for as little as B50 (sometimes free at airports) and refillable at 7-Elevens around the country, Thai SIM cards offer very cheap calls, both domestically and internationally (especially if you use low-cost international prefixes such as 009, rather than the standard 001 prefix). They also offer data packages (5G is now available in most places), very cheap texting and are, of course, free of charge for all incoming calls.

When **dialling** any number in Thailand, you must now always preface it with what used to be the area code, even when dialling from the same area. Where we've given several line numbers – eg ❶02 431 1802–9 – you can substitute the last digit, 2, with any digit between 3 and 9.

Mobile-phone numbers in Thailand have ten digits, beginning "06", "08" or "09". Note, however, that Thais tend to change mobile-phone providers – and therefore numbers – comparatively frequently, in search of a better deal.

One final local idiosyncrasy: Thai phone books list people by their first name, not their family name.

Time

Thailand is in the same time zone year-round, with no daylight savings period. Bangkok is five hours ahead of South Africa, seven hours ahead of GMT, twelve hours ahead of US Eastern Standard Time, three hours behind Australian Eastern Standard Time and five hours behind New Zealand Standard Time.

Tipping

It is usual to **tip** hotel bellboys and porters B20–40, and to round up taxi fares to the nearest B10. Most guides, drivers, masseurs, waiters and maids also depend on tips. Some upmarket hotels and restaurants will add an automatic ten percent service charge to your bill, though this is not always shared out.

WAT PHRA KAEO

Ratanakosin

The only place to start your exploration of Bangkok is Ratanakosin, the royal island where the city's most important sights are located. When Rama I developed Ratanakosin for his new capital in 1782, after the sacking of Ayutthaya and a stay in Thonburi, he paid tribute to its precursor by imitating Ayutthaya's layout and architecture. Like Ayutthaya, Ratanakosin was sited beside a river and turned into an artificial island by the construction of defensive canals, with a central Grand Palace and adjoining royal temple, Wat Phra Kaeo, fronted by an open field. Wat Pho, which predates the capital's founding, was further embellished by Rama I's successors, who also built several European-style palaces, as well as Wat Mahathat, the National Theatre, the National Gallery, and Thammasat and Silpakorn universities.

Bangkok has expanded eastwards away from the river, leaving the Grand Palace a good 5km from the city's commercial heart, and the royal family has long since moved its residence to Dusit, but Ratanakosin remains the ceremonial centre of the whole kingdom – so much so that it feels as if it might sink into the boggy ground under the weight of its own mighty edifices. The heavy, stately feel is lightened by traditional shophouses selling herbal medicines, pavement amulet-sellers and studenty canteens along the riverside road, **Thanon Maharat**; and by Sanam Luang, which is still used for cremations and royal ceremonies. Despite containing several of the country's main sights, the area is busy enough in its own right not to have become a swarming tourist zone, and strikes a neat balance between liveliness and grandeur.

ARRIVAL AND DEPARTURE   RATANAKOSIN

Ratanakosin is within easy walking distance of Banglamphu, but is best approached from the river, via the **express-boat piers** of Tha Chang (the former bathing place of the royal elephants, which gives access to the Grand Palace) or Tha Thien (for Wat Pho). The **subway** line stops at Sanam Chai, at the Museum of Siam, 5min walk from Wat Pho, 10min from Tha Thien express boat pier and 15min from the entrance to the Grand Palace.

Wat Phra Kaeo and the Grand Palace

Thanon Na Phra Lan • Charge, including admission to a *khon* show at Sala Chalermkrung Theatre (see page 89); 2hr personal audioguide available (charge), with passport or credit card as deposit • ⓦ palaces.thai.net

Hanging together in a precarious harmony of strangely beautiful colours and shapes, **Wat Phra Kaeo** is the apogee of Thai religious art and the holiest Buddhist site in the country, housing the most important image, the **Emerald Buddha**. Built as the private royal temple, Wat Phra Kaeo occupies the northeast corner of the huge **Grand Palace**, whose official opening in 1785 marked the founding of the new capital and the rebirth of the Thai nation after the Burmese invasion. Successive kings have all left their mark here, and the palace complex now covers 2 acres, though very little apart from the wat is open to tourists.

The only **entrance** to the complex in 2km of crenellated walls is on the north side, from Sanam Luang and the east end of Thanon Na Phra Lan, which brings you straight into Wat Phra Kaeo. The complex's exit is at the west end of Thanon Phra Lan, which will take you past a driveway with a much-photographed view of the temple's glittering spires behind a manicured lawn, as well as the dowdy buildings of the Offices of the Royal Household: this is the powerhouse of the kingdom's ceremonial life, providing everything down to chairs and catering, even lending an urn when someone of rank dies. Among these buildings, the hagiographic Queen Sirikit Museum of Textiles, which claims to show how she invented the Thai national dress in the 1960s,

> **A WORD OF WARNING**
>
> When you're heading for the Grand Palace or Wat Pho, you may well be approached by someone, possibly pretending to be a student or an official, who will tell you that the sight is closed when it's not, or some other lies to try to lead you away from the entrance, because they want to take you on a shopping trip for souvenirs, tailored clothes or, if you seem really gullible, gems (see page 188). The opening hours of the Grand Palace – but not Wat Pho – are indeed sometimes erratic because of state occasions, and the palace does close quite early: last ticket sales are at 3.30pm, though you can look round Wat Phra Kaeo until 4pm and the palace buildings until 4.30pm. You can check out the details of closures for state occasions on the website, ⓦ palaces.thai.net (click on "Schedules") – and even if it's closed on the day you want to visit, that's no reason to throw yourself at the mercy of these shysters.

is included in the admission ticket but well worth missing, though you might want to check out the museum shop (see page 185).

As this is Thailand's most sacred site, you have to **dress in smart clothes**: no vests or see-through clothes; no flip-flops or open-back sandals; men must wear full-length trousers, women trousers or over-the-knee skirts. If you come up short of the stringent requirements (detailed on Ⓦpalaces.thai.net), suitable garments can be borrowed near the entrance.

Wat Phra Kaeo

It makes you laugh with delight to think that anything so fantastic could exist on this sombre earth.
W. Somerset Maugham, The Gentlemen in the Parlour

Entering the temple is like stepping onto a lavishly detailed stage set, from the immaculate flagstones right up to the gaudy roofs. Reinforcing the sense of unreality, the whole compound is surrounded by arcaded walls, decorated with extraordinary murals of scenes from the *Ramayana*. Although it receives hundreds of foreign sightseers and at least as many Thai pilgrims every day, the temple, which has no monks in residence, maintains an unnervingly sanitized look, as if it were built only yesterday.

The approach to the bot

Inside the arcaded walls, you're confronted by 6m-tall **yaksha**, gaudy demons from the *Ramayana*, who watch over the Emerald Buddha from every gate of the temple and ward off evil spirits; the king of the demons, green, ten-faced Totsagan (labelled "Tosakanth"), stands by the southwest corner of the golden Phra Si Ratana Chedi. Less threatening is the toothless old codger, cast in bronze and sitting on a plinth by the back wall of the bot, who represents a Hindu **hermit** credited with inventing yoga and herbal medicine. In front of him is a large grinding stone where previously herbal practitioners could come to grind their ingredients – with enhanced powers, of course. The bot's **main entrance** is on the eastern side, in front of which stands a cluster of grey **statues** that have a strong Chinese feel: next to Kuan Im, the Chinese *bodhisattva* of mercy shown holding a bottle of *amritsa* (sacred elixir), are a sturdy pillar topped by a lotus flower, which Bangkok's Chinese community presented to Rama IV during his 27 years as a monk, and two handsome cows which commemorate Rama I's birth in the Year of the Cow. Worshippers make their offerings to the Emerald Buddha at two small, stand-in Buddhas here, where they can look at the main image through the open doors of the bot without messing up its pristine interior with gold leaf, candle wax and joss-stick ash.

The bot and the Emerald Buddha

The **bot**, the largest building of the temple, is one of the few original structures left at Wat Phra Kaeo, though it has been augmented so often it looks like the work of a wildly inspired child. Eight *sema* stones mark the boundary of the consecrated area around the bot, each sheltering in a psychedelic fairy castle, joined by a low wall decorated with Chinese porcelain tiles, which depict delicate landscapes. The walls of the bot itself, sparkling with gilt and coloured glass, are supported by 112 golden garudas (birdmen) holding nagas (serpents), representing the god Indra saving the world by slaying the serpent-cloud that had swallowed up all the water. The symbolism reflects the king's traditional role as a rainmaker.

Of the bot's three doorways, the largest, in the middle, is reserved for the king himself. Inside, a 9m-high pedestal supports the tiny **Emerald Buddha**, a figure whose mystique draws pilgrims from all over Thailand – as well as politicians accused of corruption, who traditionally come here to publicly swear their innocence. Here especially you must act with respect, sitting with your feet pointing away from the

Main entrance		Porcelain viharn	7	Exit from Wat Phra Kaeo	14
Entrance to Queen Sirikit		Supplementary library	8	Phra Thinang Amarin Winichai	15
Museum of Textiles and Shop	2	Prangs	9	Chakri Maha Prasat	16
Royal Decorations and Coins Pavilion	3	Royal Pantheon	10	Weapons museum	17
The bot and Emerald Buddha	4	Phra Mondop	11	Dusit Maha Prasat	18
Chapel of the Gandhara Buddha	5	Angkor Wat model	12	Mount Krailas model	19
Royal mausoleum	6	Phra Si Ratana Chedi	13	Wat Phra Kaeo museum	20

Buddha. The spiritual power of the 60cm jadeite image derives from its legendary past. Reputed to have been created by the gods in India, it was discovered when lightning cracked open an ancient chedi in Chiang Rai in the early fifteenth century. The image was then moved around the north, dispensing miracles wherever it went, before being taken to Laos for two hundred years. As it was believed to bring great fortune to its possessor, the future Rama I snatched it back when he captured Vientiane in 1779, installing it at the heart of his new capital as a talisman for king and country.

Seated in the *Dhyana Mudra* (meditation), the Emerald Buddha has three **costumes**, one for each season: the crown and ornaments of an Ayutthayan king for the hot season; a gilt monastic robe for the rainy season, when the monks retreat into the temples; this is augmented with a full-length gold shawl in the cool season. To this day it's the job of the king himself to ceremonially change the Buddha's costumes. The Buddha was granted a new set of these three costumes in 1997: the old set is now in the Wat Phra Kaeo Museum (see page 57) while the two costumes of the new set that are not in use are on display among the blinding glitter of crowns and jewels in the Royal Decorations and Coins Pavilion, which lies between the ticket office and the entrance to Wat Phra Kaeo.

Among the paraphernalia in front of the pedestal sits the tiny, silver **Phra Chai Lang Chang** (Victory Buddha), which Rama I always carried into battle on the back of his elephant for luck and which still plays an important part in coronation ceremonies. Recently covered in gold, it occupies a prestigious spot dead centre, but is obscured by the umbrella of a larger gold Buddha in front. The tallest pair of a dozen standing Buddha images, all made of bronze but encased in gold and raising both hands to dispel fear, are at the front: Rama III dedicated the one on the Emerald Buddha's left to Rama I, the one on his right to Rama II, and Rama IV enshrined relics of the Buddha in their crowns.

The Chapel of the Gandhara Buddha

Near the entrance to the bot, in the southeastern corner of the temple precinct, look out for the exquisite scenes of rice sheaves, fish and turtles painted in gold on blue glass on the doors and windows of the **Chapel of the Gandhara Buddha** (labelled "Hor Phra Kanthara Rat"). The decorations allude to the fertility of the rice fields, as this building was crucial to the old royal rainmaking ritual and is still used during the Royal Ploughing Ceremony (see page 60). Adorning the roof are thousands of nagas, symbolizing water; inside the locked chapel, among the paraphernalia used in the ritual, is kept the Gandhara Buddha, a bronze image in the gesture of calling down the rain with its right hand, while cupping the left to catch it. In times of drought the king would order a week-long rainmaking ceremony to be conducted, during which he was bathed regularly and kept away from the opposite sex while Buddhist monks and Hindu Brahmins chanted continuously.

The Royal Pantheon and minor buildings

On the north side of the bot, the eastern end of the **upper terrace** is taken up with the **Prasat Phra Thep Bidorn**, known as the **Royal Pantheon**, a splendid hash of styles. The pantheon has its roots in the Khmer concept of *devaraja*, or the divinity of kings: inside are bronze and gold statues, precisely life-size, of all the kings since Bangkok became the Thai capital. Constructed by Rama IV, the building is open only on special occasions, such as Chakri Day (April 6), when the dynasty is commemorated, and Coronation Day (May 5).

From here you get the best view of the **royal mausoleum**, the **porcelain viharn** and the **supplementary library** to the north (all of which are closed to tourists, though you can sometimes glimpse Thai Buddhists worshipping in the library), and, running along the east side of the temple, a row of eight bullet-like **prangs**, each of which has a different nasty ceramic colour. Described as "monstrous vegetables" by Somerset Maugham, they represent, from north to south, the Buddha, Buddhist scripture, the monkhood, the nunhood, the Buddhas who attained enlightenment but did not preach, previous emperors, the Buddha in his previous lives and the future Buddha.

The Phra Mondop and Phra Si Ratana Chedi

In the middle of the terrace, dressed in deep-green glass mosaics, the **Phra Mondop** was built by Rama I to house the *Tripitaka*, or Buddhist scripture, which the king had rewritten at Wat Mahathat in 1788, the previous versions having all been lost in the sacking of Ayutthaya. It's famous for the mother-of-pearl cabinet and solid-silver mats inside, but is never open. Four tiny **memorials** at each corner of the mondop show the symbols of each of the nine Chakri kings, from the ancient crown representing Rama I to the present king's discus, while the bronze statues surrounding the memorials portray each king's lucky white elephants, labelled by name and pedigree. A contribution of Rama IV, on the north side of the mondop, is a **scale model of Angkor Wat**, the prodigious Cambodian temple, which during his reign (1851–68) was under Thai rule (apparently, the king had wanted to shift a whole Khmer temple to Bangkok but, fortunately, was dissuaded by his officials). At the western end of the terrace, you can't miss the golden dazzle of the **Phra Si Ratana Chedi**, which Rama IV erected, in imitation of the famous bell-shaped chedis at Ayutthaya's Wat Phra Si Sanphet (see page 120), to enshrine a piece of the Buddha's breastbone.

The murals

Extending for about a kilometre in the arcades that run inside the wat walls, the **murals of the Ramayana** depict every blow of this ancient story of the triumph of good over evil, using the vibrant buildings of the temple itself as backdrops, and setting them off against the subdued colours of richly detailed landscapes. Because of the damaging humidity, none of the original work of Rama I's time survives: maintenance is a never-ending process, so you'll always find an artist working on one of the scenes. The story is told in 178 panels, labelled and numbered in Thai only, starting in the middle of the northern side opposite the porcelain viharn: in the first episode, a hermit, while out ploughing, finds the baby Sita, the heroine, floating in a gold urn on a lotus leaf and brings her to the city. Panel 109 near the gate leading to the palace buildings shows the climax of the story, when Rama, the hero, kills the ten-headed demon Totsagan (Ravana), and the ladies of the enemy city weep at the demon's death. Panel 110 depicts his elaborate funeral procession, and in 113 you can see the funeral fair, with acrobats, sword-jugglers and tightrope-walkers. In between, Sita – Rama's wife – has to walk on fire to prove that she has been faithful during her fourteen years of imprisonment by Totsagan. If you haven't the stamina for the long walk round, you could sneak a look at the end of the story, to the left of the first panel, where Rama holds a victory parade and distributes thank-you gifts.

The palace buildings

The exit in the southwest corner of Wat Phra Kaeo brings you to the palace proper, a vast area of buildings and gardens, of which only the northern edge is on show to the

THE RAMAYANA/RAMAKIEN

The **Ramayana** is generally thought to have originated as an oral epic in India, where it appears in numerous dialects. The most famous version is that of the sage Valmiki, who is said to have drawn together the collection of stories as a tribute to his king over two thousand years ago. From India, the *Ramayana* spread to all the Hindu-influenced countries of Southeast Asia and was passed down through the Khmers to Thailand, where as the **Ramakien** it has become the national epic, acting as an affirmation of the Thai monarchy and its divine Hindu links. As a source of inspiration for literature, painting, sculpture and dance-drama, it has acquired the authority of holy writ, providing Thais with moral and practical lessons, while its appearance in the form of films and comic strips shows its huge popular appeal. The version current in Thailand was composed by a committee of poets sponsored by Rama I (all previous Thai texts were lost in the sacking of Ayutthaya in 1767), and runs to three thousand pages – available in an abridged English translation by M.L. Manich Jumsai (see page 222).

The central story of the *Ramayana* concerns **Rama** (in Thai, Phra Ram), son of the king of Ayodhya, and his beautiful wife **Sita**, whose hand he wins by lifting, stringing – and breaking – a magic bow. The couple's adventures begin when they are exiled to the forest, along with Rama's good brother, **Lakshaman** (Phra Lak), by the hero's father under the influence of his evil stepmother. Meanwhile, in the city of Lanka (Longka), the demon king **Ravana** (Totsagan) has conceived a passionate desire for Sita and, disguised as a hermit, sets out to kidnap her. By transforming one of his demon subjects into a beautiful deer, which Rama and Lakshaman go off to hunt, Ravana catches Sita alone and takes her back to Lanka. Rama then wages a long war against the demons of Lanka, into which are woven many battles, spy scenes and diversionary episodes, and eventually kills Ravana and rescues Sita.

The Thai version shows some characteristic differences from the Indian, emphasizing the typically Buddhist virtues of filial obedience and willing renunciation. In addition, Hanuman, the loyal monkey general, is given a much more playful role in the *Ramakien*, with the addition of many episodes which display his cunning and talent for mischief, not to mention his promiscuity. However, the major alteration comes at the end of the story, when Phra Ram doubts Sita's faithfulness after rescuing her from Totsagan. In the Indian story, this ends with Sita being swallowed up by the earth so that she doesn't have to suffer Rama's doubts any more; in the *Ramakien* the ending is a happy one, with Phra Ram and Sita living together happily ever after.

public. Though the king now lives in the Chitrlada Palace in Dusit, the **Grand Palace** is still used for state receptions and official ceremonies, during which there is no public access to any part of the palace.

Phra Maha Monthien

Coming out of the temple compound, you'll first of all see to your right a beautiful Chinese gate covered in innumerable tiny porcelain tiles. Extending in a straight line behind the gate is the **Phra Maha Monthien**, which was the grand residential complex of earlier kings.

Only the **Phra Thinang Amarin Winichai**, the main audience hall at the front of the complex, is open to the public. The supreme court in the era of the absolute monarchy, it nowadays serves as the venue for ceremonies such as the king's birthday speech. Dominating the hall are two gleaming, intricately carved thrones that date from the reign of Rama I: a white umbrella with the full nine tiers owing to a king shelters the front seat, while the unusual *busbok* behind is topped with a spired roof and floats on a boat-shaped base. The rear buildings are still used for the most important part of the elaborate coronation ceremony, and each new king is supposed to spend a night there to show solidarity with his forefathers.

Chakri Maha Prasat

Next door you can admire the facade of the "farang with a Thai crown", as the **Chakri Maha Prasat** is nicknamed. Rama V, whose portrait you can see over its entrance, employed an English architect to design a purely Neoclassical residence, but other members of the royal family prevailed on the king to add the three Thai spires. This used to be the site of the elephant stables: the large red tethering posts are still there and the bronze elephants were installed as a reminder. The building displays the emblem of the Chakri dynasty on its gable, which has a trident (*ri*) coming out of a *chak* (a discus with a sharpened rim). The only part of the Chakri Maha Prasat open to the public is the ground-floor **weapons museum**, which houses a forgettable display of hooks, pikes and guns.

The Inner Palace

The **Inner Palace** (closed to the public), which used to be the king's harem, lies behind the gate on the left-hand side of the Chakri Maha Prasat. Vividly described in M.R. Kukrit Pramoj's *Si Phaendin* (see page 223), the harem was a town in itself, with shops, law courts and an all-female police force for the huge population: as well as the current queens, the minor wives and their children (including pre-pubescent boys) and servants, this was home to the daughters and consorts of former kings, and the daughters of the aristocracy who attended the harem's finishing school. Today, the Inner Palace houses a school of cooking, fruit-carving and other domestic sciences for well-bred young Thais.

Dusit Maha Prasat

On the western side of the courtyard, the delicately proportioned **Dusit Maha Prasat**, an audience hall built by Rama I, epitomizes traditional Thai architecture. Outside, the soaring tiers of its red, gold and green roof culminate in a gilded *mongkut*, a spire shaped like the king's crown, which symbolizes the 33 Buddhist levels of perfection. Each tier of the roof bears a typical *chofa*, a slender, stylized bird's-head finial, and several *hang hong* (swans' tails), which represent three-headed nagas. Inside, you can still see the original throne, the **Phra Ratcha Banlang Pradap Muk**, a masterpiece of mother-of-pearl inlaid work. When a senior member of the royal family dies, the hall is used for the lying-in-state: the body, embalmed and seated in a huge sealed urn, is placed in the west transept, waiting up to two years for an auspicious day to be cremated.

THE ROYAL TONSURE CEREMONY

To the right and behind the Dusit Maha Prasat rises a strange model mountain, decorated with fabulous animals and topped by a castle and prang. It represents **Mount Krailas**, the Himalayan home of the Hindu god Shiva (Phra Isuan in Thai), and was built by Rama IV as the site of the **royal tonsure ceremony**, last held here in 1932, just three months before the end of the absolute monarchy. In former times, Thai children generally had shaved heads, except for a tuft or topknot on the crown, which, between the age of eleven and thirteen, was cut in a Hindu initiation rite to welcome adolescence. For the royal children, the rite was an elaborate ceremony that sometimes lasted seven days, culminating with the king's cutting of the hair knot, which was then floated away on the Chao Phraya River. The child was then bathed at the model Krailas, in water representing the original river of the universe flowing down the central mountain.

The Wat Phra Kaeo Museum

In the nineteenth-century Royal Mint in front of the Dusit Maha Prasat, the **Wat Phra Kaeo Museum** houses a mildly interesting collection of artefacts donated to the Emerald Buddha, along with architectural elements rescued from the Grand Palace grounds during restoration in the 1980s. Highlights include the bones of various kings' white elephants, and upstairs, the Emerald Buddha's original costumes and two useful scale models of the Grand Palace, one as it is now, the other as it was when first built. Also on the first floor stands the grey stone slab of the Manangsila Seat, where Ramkhamhaeng, the great thirteenth-century king of Sukhothai, is said to have sat and taught his subjects. It was discovered in 1833 by Rama IV during his monkhood and brought to Bangkok, where Rama VI used it as the throne for his coronation.

Wat Pho (Wat Phra Chetuphon)

Soi Chetuphon, to the south of the Grand Palace • Charge • ⓦ watpho.com

Where Wat Phra Kaeo may seem too perfect and shrink-wrapped for some, **Wat Pho** is lively and shambolic, a complex arrangement of lavish structures which jostle with classrooms, basketball courts and a turtle pond. Busloads of tourists shuffle in and out

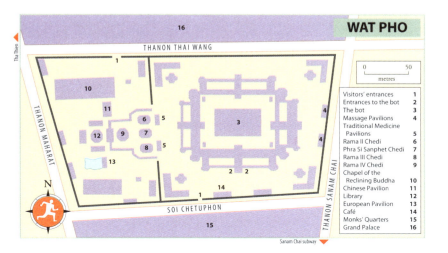

THE ROYAL WHITE ELEPHANTS

In Thailand, the most revered of all elephants are the so-called **white elephants** – actually tawny brown albinos – which are considered so sacred that they all, whether wild or captive, belong to the king by law. Their special status originates from Buddhist mythology, which tells how the previously barren Queen Maya became pregnant with the future Buddha after dreaming one night that a white elephant had entered her womb. The thirteenth-century King Ramkhamhaeng of Sukhothai adopted the beast as a symbol of the great and the divine, decreeing that a Thai king's greatness should be measured by the number of white elephants he owns. A white elephant appeared on the Thai national flag until 1917, and the last king, Rama IX, had eleven of the creatures, the largest royal collection to date.

Before an elephant can be granted official "white elephant" status, it has to pass a stringent assessment of its physical and behavioural **characteristics**. Key qualities include a paleness of seven crucial areas – eyes, nails, palate, hair, outer edges of the ears, tail and testicles – and an all-round genteel demeanour, manifested, for instance, in the way in which it cleans its food before eating, or in a tendency to sleep in a kneeling position. Tradition holds that an elaborate ceremony should take place every time a new white elephant is presented to the king, with the animal paraded with great pomp from its place of capture to Bangkok, before being anointed with holy water in front of an audience of priests and dignitaries. Rama IX, however, called time on this exorbitantly expensive ritual, and the royal white elephants now live in less luxurious, rural accommodation under the care of the Thai Elephant Conservation Centre.

The expression "white elephant" probably derives from the legend that the kings used to present certain troublesome noblemen with one of these exotic creatures. The animal required expensive attention but, being royal, could not be put to work in order to pay for its upkeep.

---

of the **north entrance**, stopping only to gawp at the colossal Reclining Buddha, but you can avoid the worst of the crowds by using the **main entrance** on Soi Chetuphon to explore the huge compound.

Wat Pho is the oldest temple in Bangkok and is older than the city itself, having been founded in the seventeenth century under the name Wat Photaram. Foreigners have stuck to the contraction of this old name, even though Rama I, after enlarging the temple, changed the name in 1801 to **Wat Phra Chetuphon**, which is how it is generally known to Thais. The temple had another major overhaul in 1832, when Rama III built the chapel of the Reclining Buddha, and turned the temple into a public centre of learning by decorating the walls and pillars with inscriptions and diagrams on subjects such as history, literature, animal husbandry and astrology. Dubbed Thailand's first university, the wat is still an important centre for traditional medicine, notably **Thai massage** (see page 181), which is used against all kinds of illnesses, from backaches to viruses.

The eastern courtyard

The main entrance on Soi Chetuphon is one of a series of sixteen monumental gates around the main compound, each guarded by stone **giants**, many of them comic Westerners in wide-brimmed hats – ships that exported rice to China would bring these statues back as ballast.

The entrance brings you into the eastern half of the main complex, where a courtyard of structures radiates from the bot in a disorientating symmetry. To get to the **bot**, the principal congregation and ordination hall, turn right and cut through the two surrounding cloisters, which are lined with hundreds of Buddha images. The elegant bot has beautiful teak doors decorated with mother-of-pearl, showing stories from the *Ramayana* (see page 55) in minute detail. Look out also for the stone bas-reliefs around the base of the bot, which narrate the story of the capture and rescue of Sita from the *Ramayana* in 152 action-packed panels. The plush interior has a well-proportioned altar on which ten statues of disciples frame a graceful, Ayutthayan Buddha image containing the remains of Rama I, the founder of Bangkok (Rama IV placed them there so that the public could worship him at the same time as the Buddha).

Back outside the entrance to the double cloister, keep your eyes open for a miniature mountain covered in statues of naked men in tall hats who appear to be gesturing rudely: they are *rishis* (hermits), demonstrating various positions of healing massage. Skirting the southwestern corner of the cloisters, you'll come to two pavilions between the eastern and western courtyards, which display plaques inscribed with the precepts of traditional medicine, as well as anatomical pictures showing the different pressure points and the illnesses that can be cured by massaging them.

The western courtyard

Among the 99 chedis strewn about the grounds, the four **great chedis** in the western courtyard stand out as much for their covering of garish tiles as for their size. The central chedi is the oldest, erected by Rama I to hold the remains of the most sacred Buddha image of Ayutthaya, the Phra Si Sanphet. Later, Rama III built the chedi to the north for the ashes of Rama II and the chedi to the south to hold his own remains; Rama IV built the fourth, with bright blue tiles, though its purpose is uncertain.

In the northwest corner of the courtyard stands the chapel of the **Reclining Buddha**, a 45m-long gilded statue of plaster-covered brick which depicts the Buddha entering Nirvana, a common motif in Buddhist iconography. The chapel is only slightly bigger than the statue – you can't get far enough away to take in anything but a surreal close-up view of the beaming 5m smile. As for the feet, the vast black soles are beautifully inlaid with delicate mother-of-pearl showing the 108 *lakshana*, or auspicious signs, which distinguish the true Buddha. Along one side of the statue are 108 bowls: putting a coin in each will bring you good luck and a long life.

Museum of Siam

Thanon Sanam Chai • Charge • museumsiam.org

The excellent **Museum of Siam** is a high-tech, mostly bilingual attraction that occupies the century-old, European-style, former Ministry of Commerce. It looks at what it is to be Thai, with lots of humorous short films and imaginative touches such as shadow-puppet cartoons and war video games. In addition, the museum stages playful temporary exhibitions, which in the past have, for example, let visitors have a go at rice-growing, or explored the minds of Thai inventors. Generally, it's great fun for adults and kids, and there's a lovely indoor-outdoor **café-bakery-restaurant** in the grounds.

The museum exhibition kicks off with the prehistory of Southeast Asia, or Suvarnabhumi (Land of Gold) as ancient Indian documents refer to it, and the legendary arrival of Buddhism via missionaries sent by the Indian emperor, Ashoka (Asoke). Much space is devoted to Ayutthaya, where we learn that during that kingdom's four-hundred-year history, there were no fewer than twenty outbreaks of war with the Burmese states, before the final annihilation in 1767. Beyond this, look out for a fascinating map of Thonburi, King Taksin's new capital between 1768 and 1782, as drawn by a Burmese spy. In the Bangkok period, under the banner of westernization, visitors can wind up cartoon peep-shows and dress up in colonial-style uniform shirts.

Sanam Luang

Sprawling across 30 acres north of the Grand Palace, **Sanam Luang** is one of the largest open spaces in central Bangkok. Residents of the capital traditionally gather on this

> ### KITE FLYING
>
> Flying intricate and colourful **kites** is now done mostly for fun in Thailand, but it has its roots in more serious activities. Filled with gunpowder and fitted with long fuses, kites were deployed in the first Thai kingdom at Sukhothai (1240–1438) as machines of war. In the same era, special *ngao* kites, with heads in the shape of bamboo bows, were used in Brahmin rituals: the string of the bow would vibrate in the wind and make a noise to frighten away evil spirits (nowadays noisy kites are still used, though only by farmers, to scare the birds). By the height of the Ayutthayan period (1351–1767) kites had become largely decorative: royal ceremonies were enhanced by fantastically shaped kites, adorned with jingling bells and ornamental lamps.
>
> In the nineteenth century, Rama V, by his enthusiastic lead, popularized kite flying as a wholesome and fashionable recreation. **Contests** are now held all over the country between February and April, when winds are strong enough and farmers traditionally have free time after harvesting the rice. These contests fall into two broad categories: those involving manoeuvrable flat kites, often in the shapes of animals; and those in which the beauty of static display kites is judged. The most popular contest of all, which comes under the first category, matches two teams, one flying star-shaped *chulas*, 2m-high "male" kites, the other flying the smaller, more agile *pakpaos*, diamond-shaped "females". Each team uses its skill and teamwork to ensnare the other's kites and drag them back across a dividing line.

bare field in the early evening to eat, play and, in and around March, stage **kite-fighting** contests (see box), but unfortunately it's currently closed to visitors. On its western side, spreading around Thammasat University and Wat Mahathat, especially on Sundays, scores of small-time hawkers sell amulets (see page 72), taking advantage of the spiritually auspicious location.

The field is also the venue for national ceremonies, such as **royal cremations**, when huge, intricate, wooden *meru* or *phra mane* (funeral pyres) are constructed, representing Mount Meru, the Himalayan centre of the Hindu-Buddhist universe; and the **Ploughing Ceremony**, held in May at a time selected by astrologers to bring good fortune and rain to the coming rice harvest. Revived in 1960 to boost the status of the monarchy during the Cold War, the elaborate Brahmin ceremony is led by an official from the Ministry of Agriculture, who stands in for the king in case the royal power were to be reduced by any failure in the ritual. At the designated time, the official cuts a series of circular furrows with a plough drawn by two white oxen, and scatters rice from the king's experimental crop station at Chitrlada Palace, which has been sprinkled with lustral water by the Brahmin priests of the court. When the ritual is over, spectators rush in to grab handfuls of the rice, which they then plant in their own paddies for good luck.

The lak muang

Thanon Rajdamnoen Nai, southeast corner of Sanam Luang

At 6.54am on April 21, 1782 – the astrologically determined time for the auspicious founding of Bangkok – a pillar containing the city's horoscope was ceremonially driven into the ground opposite the northeast corner of the Grand Palace. This phallic pillar, the **lak muang** – most Thai cities have one, to provide a home for their guardian spirits – was made from a 4m tree trunk carved with a lotus-shaped crown. In the nineteenth century, Rama IV had a new, shorter *lak muang* made, and the two pillars now amicably cohabit in an elegant shrine surrounded by immaculate gardens.

Hundreds of worshippers come every day to pray and offer flowers, particularly childless couples seeking the gift of fertility. In one corner of the gardens you can often see short performances of **classical dancing**, paid for by well-off families when they have a piece of good fortune to celebrate.

Silpakorn University Art Centre

Thanon Na Phra Lan, directly across the road from the entrance to the Grand Palace • Free • Ⓦ www.art-centre.su.ac.th

Housed partly in the throne hall of a palace built during the reign of Rama I, the **Silpakorn University Art Centre** stages regular exhibitions of contemporary art, mostly by former students, teachers, artists-in-residence and national artists. The country's first art school, Silpakorn was founded in 1935 by Professor Silpa Bhirasri, the much-revered, naturalized Italian sculptor; a charming, shady garden along the east wall of the art centre is dotted with his sculptures.

Wat Mahathat

Main entrance on Thanon Maharat, plus a back entrance on Thanon Na Phra That on Sanam Luang

Eighteenth-century **Wat Mahathat** provides a welcome respite from the surrounding tourist hype, and a chance to engage with the eager monks studying at **Mahachulalongkorn Buddhist University** here. The wat buzzes with purpose; it's the most important centre of Buddhist learning in Southeast Asia, the nation's centre for the Mahanikai monastic sect (where Rama IV spent many years as a monk before becoming king in 1851), and houses one of the two Buddhist universities in Bangkok. It's this activity, and the chance of interaction and participation, rather than any special architectural features, that make a visit so rewarding. The many university-attending monks at the wat are friendly and keen to practise their English, and are more than likely to approach you: diverting topics might range from the poetry of Dylan Thomas to English football results.

Vipassana Meditation Centre

Section Five, Wat Mahathat • Donations welcome • ☎ 02 222 6011 or ☎ 02 222 4981

At the wat's **Vipassana Meditation Centre**, where the monk teachers speak some English, sitting and walking meditation practice, with chanting and dhamma talks, is available to drop-in visitors.

The National Museum

Thanon Na Phra That, northwest corner of Sanam Luang • Charge • Ⓦ thai-heritage.org

The **National Museum** houses a colossal hoard of Thailand's chief artistic riches, ranging from sculptural treasures in the north and south wings, through outlandish funeral chariots, to the exquisite Buddhaisawan chapel, as well as sometimes staging worthwhile temporary exhibitions (often in the Gallery of Thai History).

   It's well worth while taking one of the free guided tours run by the National Museum Volunteers: they're generally entertaining and their explication of the choicest exhibits provides a good introduction to Thai religion and culture (the NMV organize interesting lectures and excursions, too; Ⓦ mynmv.com). There's also a museum shop and a café by the ticket office, as well as a simple outdoor restaurant inside the museum grounds, near the west end of the main collection's northern building, which dishes up decent, inexpensive Thai food.

Gallery of Thai History

The first building you'll come to near the ticket office houses an overview of the authorized history of Thailand, illustrated by some choice artworks plucked from the main collection. Among them is the most famous piece of Srivijaya art, a bronze **Bodhisattva Padmapani** from around the twelfth century found at Chaiya (according to Mahayana Buddhism, a *bodhisattva* is a saint who has postponed his passage into Nirvana to help ordinary believers gain enlightenment). With its pouting face and lithe torso, this image has become the ubiquitous emblem of southern Thailand. Look out also for an elaborate eighth-century **lintel** from Ku Suan Tang, Buriram, which depicts Vishnu (aka Narayana) reclining on the dragon Ananta in the sea of eternity, dreaming up a new universe after the old one has been annihilated in the Hindu cycle of creation and destruction. Out of his navel comes a lotus, and out of this emerges four-headed Brahma, who will put the dream into practice.

This gallery houses a fascinating little archeological gem, too: a black stone **inscription**, credited to King Ramkhamhaeng of Sukhothai, which became the first capital of the Thai nation (c.1278–99) under his rule. Discovered in 1833 by the future Rama IV, Mongkut, it's the oldest extant inscription using the Thai alphabet. This, combined with the description it records of prosperity and piety in Sukhothai's Golden Age, has made the stone a symbol of Thai nationhood. There's recently been much controversy over the stone's origins, arising from the suggestion that it was a fake made by Mongkut, but it seems most likely that it is indeed genuine, and was written partly as a kind of prospectus for Sukhothai, to attract traders and settlers to the underpopulated kingdom.

The main collection: southern building

At the back of the compound, two large modern buildings, flanking an old converted palace, house the museum's **main collection**, kicking off on the ground floor of the **southern building**. Look out here for some historic sculptures from the rest of Asia (Room 401), including one of the earliest representations of the Buddha, in the Gandhara style (first to fourth centuries AD). Alexander the Great left a garrison at Gandhara (in modern-day Pakistan), which explains why the image is in the style of Classical Greek sculpture: for example, the *ushnisha*, the supernatural bump on the top of the head, which symbolizes the Buddha's intellectual and spiritual power, is rationalized into a bun of thick, wavy hair.

Upstairs, the **prehistory** room (402) displays axe heads and spear points from Ban Chiang in the northeast of Thailand, one of the earliest Bronze Age cultures ever discovered. Alongside are many roughly contemporaneous metal artefacts from Kanchanaburi province, as well as some excellent examples of the developments of Ban Chiang's famous pottery. In the adjacent **Dvaravati** room (403; sixth to eleventh centuries), there are several fine dharmachakras (see page 207), while the pick of the stone and terracotta Buddhas is a small head in smooth, pink clay from Wat Phra Ngam, Nakhon Pathom, whose downcast eyes and faintly smiling full lips typify the serene look of this era. At the far end of the first floor, you can't miss a voluptuous Javanese statue of elephant-headed Ganesh, Hindu god of wisdom and the arts, which, being the symbol of the Fine Arts Department, is always freshly garlanded. As Ganesh is known as the clearer of obstacles, Hindus always worship him before other gods, so by tradition he has grown fat through getting first choice of the offerings – witness his trunk jammed into a bowl of food in this sculpture.

Room 405 next door is devoted to **Srivijaya** art (roughly seventh to thirteenth centuries), including an interesting *ekamukhalinga* from Nong Wai, Chaiya, a phallic stone lingam (see page 215), carved with a sweet, almost plaintive bust of Shiva. The rough chronological order of the collection continues back downstairs with an exhibition of **Khmer** and **Lopburi** sculpture (Room 406; seventh to fourteenth centuries), most notably some dynamic bronze statuettes and stone lintels. Look out for an elaborate eleventh- or twelfth-century lintel from Phanom Rung, which depicts Krishna subduing the poisonous serpent Galiya.

The main collection: northern building

The second half of the survey, in the northern building, begins upstairs with the **Sukhothai** collection (thirteenth to fifteenth centuries; room 502), which features some typically elegant and sinuous Buddha images, as well as chunky bronzes of Hindu gods and a wide range of ceramics. An ungainly but serene Buddha head, carved from grainy, pink sandstone, represents the **Ayutthaya** style of sculpture (fourteenth to eighteenth centuries; room 503): the faintest incision of a moustache above the lips betrays the Khmer influences that came to Ayutthaya after its conquest of Angkor. A sumptuous scripture cabinet, showing a cityscape of old Ayutthaya, is a more unusual piece, one of a surviving handful of such carved and painted items of furniture.

Downstairs in the section on **Bangkok** or **Ratanakosin** art (eighteenth century onwards; room 505), a small, stiffly realistic standing bronze in the posture of calling down the rain brings you full circle. In his zeal for Western naturalism, Rama V had the statue made in the Gandhara style of the earliest Buddha image displayed in the first room of the museum.

The funeral chariots

To the east of the northern building stands a large garage containing the royal family's fantastically elaborate **funeral chariots**, which are constructed of teak and decorated with lacquer, gold leaf and mirrored glass. Pre-eminent among these is Phra Maha Pichai Ratcharot (the Royal Chariot of Great Victory), built by Rama I in 1796 for carrying the urn at his father's funeral. The 11m-high structure symbolizes heaven on Mount Meru, while the dragons and divinities around the sides – piled in five golden tiers to suggest the flames of the cremation – represent the mythological inhabitants of the mountain's forests. Weighing fourteen tonnes and requiring the pulling power of over two hundred soldiers, the chariot last had an outing in 2017, for the funeral of King Bhumibol (Rama IX).

Wang Na (Palace of the Second King)

The sprawling central building of the compound was originally part of the **Wang Na**, a huge palace stretching across Sanam Luang to Khlong Lod, which housed the "second king", appointed by the reigning monarch as his heir and deputy. When Rama V did away with the office in 1887, he turned the palace into a museum, which now contains a fascinating array of Thai objets d'art and richly decorated musical instruments. The display of sumptuous rare gold pieces includes a well-preserved armlet taken from the ruined prang of fifteenth-century Wat Ratburana in Ayutthaya, while an intricately carved ivory seat turns out, with gruesome irony, to be a *howdah*, for use on an elephant's back. Among the masks worn by *khon* actors, look out especially for a fierce Hanuman, the white monkey-warrior in the *Ramayana* epic, gleaming with mother-of-pearl. The huge and varied ceramic collection includes some sophisticated pieces from Sukhothai, and nearby there's a riot of mother-of-pearl items, whose flaming rainbow of colours comes from the shell of the turbo snail from the Gulf of Thailand.

The Buddhaisawan chapel

The second-holiest image in Thailand, after the Emerald Buddha, is housed in the **Buddhaisawan chapel**, the vast hall in front of the eastern entrance to the Wang Na. Inside, the fine proportions of the hall, with its ornate coffered ceiling and lacquered window shutters, are enhanced by painted rows of divinities and converted demons, all turned to face the chubby, glowing **Phra Sihing Buddha**, which according to legend was magically created in Sri Lanka in the second century and sent to Sukhothai in the thirteenth century. Like the Emerald Buddha, the image was believed to bring good luck to its owner and was frequently snatched from one northern town to another, until Rama I brought it down from Chiang Mai in 1795 and installed it here in the second king's private chapel. Two other images (in Nakhon Si Thammarat and Chiang Mai) now claim to be the authentic Phra Sihing Buddha, but all three are in fact derived from a lost original – this one is in a fifteenth-century Sukhothai style. It's still much loved by ordinary people and at Thai New Year in April is carried out to the nearby City Hall, where it sits for three days while worshippers sprinkle it with water as a merit-making gesture.

The careful detail and rich, soothing colours of the surrounding two-hundred-year-old **murals** are surprisingly well preserved; the bottom row between the windows narrates the life of the Buddha, beginning in the far right-hand corner with his parents' wedding.

Tamnak Daeng

On the south side of the Buddhaisawan chapel, the gaudily restored **Tamnak Daeng** (Red House) stands out, a large, airy Ayutthaya-style house made of rare golden teak, surmounted by a multi-tiered roof decorated with swan's-tail finials. Originally part of the private quarters of Princess Sri Sudarak, elder sister of Rama I, it was moved from the Grand Palace to the old palace in Thonburi for Queen Sri Suriyen, wife of Rama II; when her son became second king to Rama IV, he dismantled the edifice again and shipped it here to the Wang Na compound. Inside, it's furnished in the style of the early Bangkok period, with some of the beautiful objects that once belonged to Sri Suriyen, a huge, ornately carved box-bed, and the uncommon luxury of an indoor bathroom.

The National Gallery

4 Thanon Chao Fa, across from the National Theatre on the north side of Sanam Luang • Charge • ⓦ facebook.com/thenationalgallerythailand

If wandering around Bangkok's National Museum doesn't finish you off, the **National Gallery** nearby probably will. In its upstairs gallery, it displays some rather beautiful early twentieth-century temple banners depicting Buddhist subjects, but the permanent collection of modern Thai art downstairs is largely uninspiring and derivative. Its temporary exhibitions can be pretty good, however. The fine old building that houses the gallery is also worth more than a cursory glance – it was constructed in typical early twentieth-century, Neoclassical style, by Carlo Allegri, Rama V's court architect, as the Royal Mint.

THANON KHAO SAN, BANGLAMPHU

Banglamphu and the Democracy Monument area

Best known as the site of the travellers' hub Thanon Khao San, the Banglamphu district, immediately north of Ratanakosin, has some noteworthy temples and still boasts a number of wooden shophouses and narrow alleyways alongside the purpose-built guesthouses, travel agents and jewellery shops. But the most interesting sights in this part of the city are found in the charmingly old-fashioned neighbourhoods to the south and east of the huge stone Democracy Monument, which forms the centrepiece of an enormous roundabout that siphons traffic from the Rajdamnoen Klang artery.

Most of these old neighbourhoods are within walking distance of the Khao San guesthouses and equally accessible from the Grand Palace; their proximity to the royal district means they retain a traditional flavour, unsullied by high-rise architecture. The string of temple-supply shops around Wat Suthat and Sao Ching Cha makes Thanon Bamrung Muang a rewarding area to explore, there are some great traditional food shops along Thanon Tanao, and the amulet market in the grounds of Wat Rajnadda is also worth seeking out.

ARRIVAL AND DEPARTURE   BANGLAMPHU & THE DEMOCRACY MONUMENT AREA

By boat This is the fastest and least stressful way of getting here. The Chao Phraya express-boat stops in the area are: N13 (Phra Arthit), a few hundred metres west of Thanon Khao San; and N15 (Thewet), at the west end of Thanon Krung Kasem. The area is also served by public boats along Khlong Saen Saeb to and from their Phan Fah terminus near the Golden Mount; their Tha Saphan Hua Chang stop, which is a few minutes' walk from Siam Square and the Ratchathewi and Siam Skytrain stops, is especially useful. Thewet to the north is connected by boat along Khlong Phadung Krung Kasem to Hualamphong Station.

By subway and Skytrain The south side of this area is within walking distance of Sam Yot and Sanam Chai subway stations (Sam Yot is just a 5min walk southeast of Wat Suthat). In addition to connecting to the Skytrain via Khlong Saen Saeb boat, the other fast way to get on to the BTS system is to take a taxi from Banglamphu to BTS National Stadium.

By bus For access from anywhere else you can make use of the city bus network: Democracy Monument is served by buses from all parts of the city and is a landmark hard to miss; if you're coming from eastern or northern parts of the city (such as Hualamphong Station, Siam Square or Sukhumvit), get off the bus as soon as you see it rather than waiting for Rajdamnoen Klang's more westerly stop outside the *Royal Ratanakosin Hotel*, where it's almost impossible to cross the multiple lanes of traffic.

Banglamphu

Banglamphu's primary attraction is the legendary "Khao San Road", **Thanon Khao San**, a tiny sliver of a road no more than 400m long, which was built over a canal in 1892 and is now established as *the* backpackers' hub of Southeast Asia. Crammed with guest-houses and restaurants serving yoghurt shakes and muesli, its sidewalks lined with tattooists and hair-braiders, it's a lively, high-energy place that's fun to visit even if you're not staying here – the area is a cultural curiosity in its own right,

BANGLAMPHU'S BUS STOPS AND ROUTES

The main bus stops serving Banglamphu are on Thanon Rajdamnoen Klang: with nearly thirty westbound and eastbound routes, you can get just about anywhere in the city from here. But there are some other useful pick-up points in Banglamphu for routes running out of the area. To make things simpler, we've assigned numbers to these **bus stops** on our Banglamphu map (see page 68), though they are not numbered this way on the ground. Where there are two stops served by the same buses they share a number.

Bus stop 1: Thanon Krung Kasem, north side
#53 (clockwise) to Hualamphong train station
Bus stop 2: Thanon Phra Sumen, south side; and Thanon Phra Arthit, east side
#53 (anticlockwise) to the Grand Palace and Chinatown
Bus stop 3: Thanon Phra Arthit, west side; and Thanon Phra Sumen, north side
#3 to Chatuchak Weekend Market and Northern Bus Terminal
#15 to Jim Thompson's House, Siam Square and Thanon Silom
#53 (clockwise) to Hualamphong train station (change at Bus Stop 1, but same ticket)
Bus stop 4: Thanon Chakrabongse
#3 to Wat Pho, the Museum of Siam and Wongwian Yai train station
#15 to Jim Thompson's House, Siam Square and Thanon Silom

a unique and continually evolving expression of global youth culture fuelled by Thai entrepreneurship. Cheap clothes, jewellery and handicrafts are all great buys here (little is top quality on Khao San, but vendors are quick to pick up on global trends) and it's also a good spot to organize onward travel – bearing in mind the innumerable Khao San scams (see page 39).

Though ultra budget-conscious world travellers are still Khao San's main customers, Banglamphu attracts higher-spending sophisticates to its growing number of **stylish restaurants** and **lively bars and clubs**. At night, young Thais from all over the city gather here to browse the fashion stalls and pavement displays set up by local art students, mingling with the crowds of foreigners and squashing into the trendy bars and clubs that have made Khao San one of the city's most happening places to party (see page 170).

Banglamphu boasts a surprising range of eating places too, from bohemian Thai restaurants located on Thanon Phra Athit to famous traditional shophouses on Thanon Tanao (see page 161). Sadly, the stately lamphu trees (*duabanga grandiflora*) after which the area is named – Banglamphu means "the place beside the river with lamphu trees" – have all but disappeared now.

Wat Chana Songkhram

Thanon Chakrabongse

Sandwiched between Thanon Khao San and the Chao Phraya River, at the heart of the Banglamphu backpackers' ghetto, stands the lusciously renovated eighteenth-century **Wat Chana Songkhram**. As with temples throughout the country, the compound doubles as general-purpose neighbourhood yard; beside a knot of stalls selling secondhand books and travellers' clothes, a stream of tourists cuts through the wat en route between the river and Khao San.

It's worth slowing down for a closer look, though: the bot's roof gables are beautifully ornate, embossed with a golden relief of Vishnu astride Garuda, enmeshed in an intricate design of red and blue glass mosaics, and the golden finials are shaped like nagas. Peeking over the compound walls onto the guesthouses and bars of Soi Ram Bhuttri is a row of *kuti*, or monks' quarters: simple, elegant wooden cabins on stilts with steeply pitched roofs.

Thanon Phra Athit

Thanon Phra Athit, the Banglamphu road that runs alongside the (mostly obscured) Chao Phraya River, is known for its arty atmosphere and numerous little bar-restaurants that draw crowds of students from nearby Thammasat University. Many of these places open only at night, but some serve passing tourists during the day. There are also a few shops selling unusual Thai crafts and art-photocards towards the northern end of the road.

This northern stretch of Thanon Phra Athit is dominated by the crenellated whitewashed tower of **Phra Sumen Fortress** (also known as Phra Sumeru), a renovated corner of the original eighteenth-century city walls that stands beside the river and its juncture with Khlong Banglamphu. The fortress was the northernmost of fourteen octagonal towers built by Rama I in 1783 to protect the royal island of Ratanakosin – the only other surviving tower, also renovated, is Phra Mahakhan Fortress, next to the Golden Mount (see page 74).

The Phra Sumen Fortress originally contained 38 rooms for storing ammunition but now there's nothing to see inside the tower. However, it makes a striking landmark and the area around it has been turned into a pleasant grassy riverside recreation area, **Santichaiprakarn Park**, with English-language signs describing the history of the fortifications.

The riverside walkway

Phra Sumen Fortress marks the northernmost limit of a **riverside walkway** that runs down to Phra Pinklao Bridge (plans have been mooted to extend the walkway northwards for 6km to the Rama VII Bridge, with a parallel promenade along the Thonburi bank). The walkway provides a good view of the boats and barges on the Chao Phraya and takes you past the front entrances of two very grand and beautifully restored buildings, both currently occupied by international organizations. The United Nations' Food and Agriculture Organization (FAO) uses the early twentieth-century mansion known as **Baan Maliwan** as its library (closed to casual visitors), while the nearby UNICEF office is housed in the late nineteenth-century palace of one of the wives of Rama IV, which also served as the headquarters of the clandestine Seri Thai resistance movement during World War II. Both mansions show their most elegant faces to the river as visitors would have arrived by boat. On the eastern side of Thanon Phra Athit, there's another fine early twentieth-century mansion, **Baan Phra Athit**, at number 201/1, which now houses an Italian restaurant.

Wat Indraviharn

Thanon Wisut Kasat, about 20min walk north of Khao San • 10min walk from Chao Phraya express-boat stop N15

Though it can't match the graceful serenity of Ratanakosin's enormous Reclining Buddha at Wat Pho, Banglamphu has its own super-sized Standing Buddha at **Wat Indraviharn** (also spelt Wat Intharawihan or Wat In), a glittering 32m-high mirror-plated statue of the Buddha bearing an alms bowl. Commissioned by Rama IV in the mid-nineteenth century to enshrine a Buddha relic from Sri Lanka (in the topknot), it's hardly the most elegant of images, but the 30cm-long toenails peep out beneath offertory garlands of fragrant jasmine, and you can get reasonable views of the neighbourhood by climbing the stairways of the supporting tower; when unlocked, the doorways in the upper tower give access to the statue's hollow interior, affording vistas from shoulder level. The rest of the temple compound features the usual amalgam of architectural and spiritual styles, including a Chinese shrine and statues of Ramas IV and V.

Unfortunately, Wat Indraviharn is an established hangout for **con-artists** offering tourists a tuk-tuk tour of Bangkok at a bargain price, which invariably features a hard-sell visit to a jewellery shop (see page 188). Avoid all these hassles by hailing a passing metered taxi instead, or catching a bus along Thanon Samsen.

Democracy Monument and around

The megalithic yellow-tinged wings of **Democracy Monument** (*Anu Sawari Pracha Thipphathai*) loom provocatively over Thanon Rajdamnoen Klang, the avenue that connects the Grand Palace and the new royal district of Dusit, and have since their erection in 1939 acted as a focus for pro-democracy rallies. Conceived as a testimony to the ideals that fuelled the 1932 revolution and the changeover to a constitutional monarchy, the monument's positioning between the royal residences is significant, as are its dimensions, which allude to June 24, 2475 BE (1932 AD), the date the system was changed. In the decades since, Thailand's leaders have promulgated numerous interim charters and constitutions, the more repressive and regressive of which have been vigorously challenged in demonstrations on these very streets.

Thanon Tanao

A stroll down **Thanon Tanao** brings you into some engagingly old-fashioned neighbourhoods of nineteenth-century wooden shophouses, which are especially famous for their specialist **traditional Thai foods**. Many of these places have been making their

> **THE OCTOBER 14 MEMORIAL**
>
> One of the biggest and most notorious demonstrations around the Democracy Monument was the fateful student-led protest of October 14, 1973, when half a million people gathered on Rajdamnoen Klang to demand an end to the autocratic regime of the so-called "Three Tyrants". It was savagely quashed and turned into a bloody riot that culminated in the death of several hundred protesters at the hands of the police and the military; the Three Tyrants were forced into exile and a new coalition government was soon formed. After three decades of procrastination, the events of this catastrophic day were finally commemorated with the erection of the **October 14 Memorial**, a small granite amphitheatre encircling an elegant modern chedi bearing the names of some of the dead; photographs and a bilingual account of the ten-day protest fill the back wall. The memorial stands in front of the former headquarters of Colonel Narong Kittikachorn, one of the Three Tyrants, 200m west of Democracy Monument, at the corner of Rajdamnoen Klang and Thanon Tanao.

specialities for generations, and there are all sorts of fun things to browse here, even if you're not inclined to taste, from beef noodles to pigs' brain soup, home-made ice cream to sticky rice with mango. If you are after some recommendations on what to eat, the *Good Eats Ratanakosin* map (published by Pan Siam Publishing and available in major bookshops) is an exhaustive survey, which is especially handy given that few of these places have English-language signs or shop numbers.

The area around the south end of Thanon Tanao is also sometimes referred to as **Sao Ching Cha** (see below), after the **Giant Swing**, which is easily reached either by following any of the eastbound lanes off Tanao to Thanon Dinso, or by browsing the Buddhist paraphernalia stalls that take you there via Thanon Bamrung Muang. Alternatively, if you continue to walk one block south along Tanao you'll reach the lovely little temple of Wat Rajabophit.

San Chao Poh Seua
Thanon Tanao

Not far south of Thanon Rajdamnoen Klang sits **San Chao Poh Seua**, the **Tiger God Shrine**, an atmospheric, incense-filled Taoist shrine built in 1834 to honour the Chinese tiger guardian spirit and the God of the North Stars, whose image graces the centre of the main altar. It's a favourite with Chinese-Thais who come here to pray for power, prestige and successful pregnancy and offer in return pork rashers, fresh eggs, sticky rice, bottles of oil and sugar tigers.

Wat Rajabophit
Thanon Rajabophit, one block south of the Tanao/Bamrung Muang intersection, just to the east of Khlong Lod (see page 51)

One of Bangkok's prettiest temples, **Wat Rajabophit** is another example of the Chinese influence in this neighbourhood. It was built by Rama V in 1869–70 and, typical of him, is unusual in its design, particularly the circular cloister that encloses a chedi and links the rectangular bot and viharn. Every external wall in the compound is covered in the pastel shades of Chinese *bencharong* ceramic tiles, creating a stunning overall effect. The interior of the bot, which enshrines some of the ashes of the Mahidols, the current royal family, looks like a tiny banqueting hall, with gilded Gothic vaults and intricate mother-of-pearl doors.

Thanon Bamrung Muang

Thanon Bamrung Muang, which runs east from Thanon Tanao to Sao Ching Cha and Wat Suthat, was an old elephant trail that, a hundred years ago, became one of the first paved streets in Bangkok. It's famous as the best place in Thailand to buy **Buddhist paraphernalia**, or *sanghapan*, and is well worth a browse. The road is lined with shops selling everything a good Buddhist might need, from household offertory tables to temple umbrellas and cellophane-wrapped Buddha images up to 2m high. They also sell special alms packs for donating to monks, which typically come in saffron-coloured plastic buckets (used by monks for washing their robes, or themselves), and include such necessities as soap, toothpaste, soap powder, toilet roll, candles and incense.

Sao Ching Cha
Midway along Thanon Bamrung Muang, just in front of Wat Suthat • Sam Yot subway

You can't miss the towering, red-painted teak posts of **Sao Ching Cha**, otherwise known as the **Giant Swing**. Built in 1784, this strange contraption used to be the focal point of a ceremony to honour the Hindu god Shiva's annual visit to earth at Brahmin New Year, in which teams of young men competed to swing up to a height of 25m and grab a suspended bag of gold with their teeth. The act of swinging probably symbolized the rising and setting of the sun, though legend also has it that Shiva and his consort Uma were banned from swinging in heaven because doing so caused cataclysmic floods on earth – prompting Shiva to demand that the practice be continued on earth to ensure moderate rains and bountiful harvests. Accidents were so common with the terrestrial version that it was outlawed in the 1930s.

AMULETS

To invite good fortune, ward off malevolent spirits and gain protection from physical harm, many Thais wear or carry at least one **amulet** at all times. The most popular images are copies of sacred statues from famous wats, while others show revered monks, kings (Rama V is a favourite) or healers. On the reverse side, a yantra is often inscribed, a combination of letters and figures also designed to deflect evil, sometimes of a very specific nature: protecting your durian orchards from gales, for example, or your tuk-tuk from oncoming traffic. Individually hand-crafted or mass-produced, amulets can be made from bronze, clay, plaster or gold, and some even have sacred ingredients added, such as special herbs, or the ashes of burnt holy texts. But what really determines an amulet's efficacy is its history: where and by whom it was made, who or what it represents and who consecrated it. Stories of miracle cures and lucky escapes also prompt a rush on whatever amulet the survivor was wearing. Monks are often involved in the making of the images and are always called upon to consecrate them – the more charismatic the monk, the more powerful the amulet. Religious authorities take a relaxed view of the amulet industry, despite its anomalous and commercial functions, and proceeds contribute to wat funds and good causes.

The **belief in amulets** is thought to have originated in India, where tiny images were sold to pilgrims who visited the four holy sites associated with the Buddha's life. But not all amulets are Buddhist-related; there's a whole range of other enchanted objects to wear for protection, including tigers' teeth, rose quartz, tamarind seeds, coloured threads and miniature phalluses. Worn around the waist rather than the neck, the phallus amulets provide protection for the genitals as well as being associated with fertility, and are of Hindu origin.

For some people, amulets are not only a vital form of spiritual protection, but valuable **collectors' items** as well. Amulet-collecting mania is something akin to stamp collecting and there are at least half a dozen Thai magazines for collectors, which give histories of certain types, tips on distinguishing between genuine items and fakes, and personal accounts of particularly powerful amulet experiences. The most rewarding places to watch the collectors and browse the wares yourself are at Wat Rajnadda Buddha Centre (see page 73), the biggest amulet market and probably the best place in Bangkok; along "Amulet Alley" on Trok Mahathat, between Wat Mahathat (see page 61) and the river, where streetside vendors will have cheaper examples; and at Chatuchak Weekend Market (see page 106). Prices start as low as B50 and rise into the thousands.

Wat Suthat
Thanon Bamrung Muang • Charge • Sam Yot subway

Wat Suthat is one of Thailand's six most important temples, built in the early nineteenth century to house the 8m-high statue of the meditating **Phra Sri Sakyamuni Buddha**, which is said to date from 1361 and was brought all the way down from Sukhothai by river. It now sits on a glittering mosaic dais, which contains some of the ashes of Rama VIII, the uncle of the current king, surrounded with surreal murals that depict the last 24 lives of the Buddha rather than the more usual ten. The encircling galleries contain 156 serenely posed Buddha images, making a nice contrast to the **Chinese statues** dotted around the temple courtyards, most of which were brought over from China during Rama I's reign, as ballast in rice boats; there are some fun character studies among them, including gormless Western sailors and pompous Chinese scholars.

Wat Rajnadda
5min walk east of Democracy Monument, at the point where Rajdamnoen Klang meets Thanon Mahachai • **Loha Prasat** Charge

Among the assortment of religious buildings known collectively as **Wat Rajnadda**, the most striking is the multi-tiered, castle-like, early nineteenth-century **Loha Prasat**, or "Iron Monastery", whose 37 golden spires represent the 37 virtues necessary for attaining enlightenment. Modelled on a Sri Lankan monastery, its tiers are pierced by passageways running north–south and east–west (fifteen in each direction at ground level), with small meditation cells at each point of intersection.

Wat Rajnadda Buddha Centre
In the southeast (Thanon Mahachai) corner of the temple compound, Bangkok's biggest **amulet market**, the **Wat Rajnadda Buddha Centre**, shelters dozens of stalls selling tiny Buddha images of all designs. Alongside these miniature charms are statues of Hindu deities, dolls and carved wooden phalluses, also bought to placate or ward off disgruntled spirits, as well as love potions.

Phra Mahakhan Fortress
Thanon Mahachai

The whitewashed crenellations of the renovated eighteenth-century **Phra Mahakhan Fortress** lie across the road from Wat Rajnadda. Inside the walls used to be a historic, working-class neighbourhood that operated as a living museum, where some of the fifty or so wooden houses, inhabited by about 300 people, dated from the early nineteenth century. However, after the community had campaigned for 26 years against a redevelopment plan by the Bangkok Metropolitan Administration, in 2018 the BMA sent in soldiers from the powerful ISOC (Internal Security Operations Command, the political arm and domestic surveillance agency of the military), to occupy the community, before knocking it down and replacing it with a park. The land here had been granted by Rama III to some of his servants, but as there were no accompanying title deeds, the BMA regarded the residents as illegal occupants.

In the block of shops on Thanon Mahachai, immediately south of the crenellations, is a famous shop selling *nam op*, a traditional wet-powder fragrance that originated in the royal palace.

Wat Saket
Easiest access is along Thanon Boriphat (the specialist street for custom-carved wooden doors), 5min walk south from the khlong bridge and Phan Fah canal-boat stop at the eastern end of Rajdamnoen Klang

Beautifully illuminated at night, when it seems to float unsupported above the neighbourhood, the gleaming gold chedi of late eighteenth-century **Wat Saket** actually sits atop a structure known as the Golden Mount. Being outside the capital's city walls, the wat initially served as a crematorium and then a dumping ground for sixty thousand plague victims left to the vultures because they couldn't afford funeral pyres. There's no sign of this grim episode at modern-day Wat Saket of course, which these days is a smart, buzzing hive of religious activity at the base of the golden hilltop chedi. Wat Saket hosts an enormous annual **temple fair** in the first week of November, when the mount is illuminated with lanterns and the compound seethes with funfair rides and travelling theatre shows.

The Golden Mount
Charge

The **Golden Mount**, or **Phu Khao Tong**, dates back to the early nineteenth century, when Rama III commissioned a huge chedi to be constructed here, using building materials from the ruined fortresses and walls of the former capital, Ayutthaya. However, the ground proved too soft to support the chedi. The whole thing collapsed into a hill of rubble, but as Buddhist law states that a religious building can never be destroyed, however tumbledown, fifty years later Rama V simply crowned it with the more sensibly sized chedi we see today, in which he placed some relics of the Buddha's teeth from India, donated by the British government. These days the old rubbly base is picturesquely planted with shrubs and shady trees and dotted with memorials and cooling waterfalls. Winding stairways take you up to the chedi terrace and a fine view over Banglamphu and Ratanakosin landmarks, including the golden spires of the Grand Palace, the finely proportioned prangs of Wat Arun across the river beyond and, further upriver, the striking superstructure of the Rama VIII bridge.

King Prajadhipok (Rama VII) Museum
Thanon Lan Luang • Free • W kingprajadhipokmuseum.com

Appropriately located just 400m east of Democracy Monument, the **King Prajadhipok Museum** exists to "promote democracy", though its mission is tinged with irony: it charts the life of **Rama VII**, a weak king who was in thrall to the old guard of courtiers, but was forced by the coup of 1932 to accept the end of his absolute monarchy and a transition to democratic constitutional monarchy. Situated within the elegant European-style walls of an early twentieth-century former shop, the museum is hardly an unmissable attraction, though its displays are accessible and easy to digest, and offer expansive English-language captions. The section explaining the background to the 1932 revolution is the most important, featuring browsable copies of early drafts of the Constitution and some insight into the exchanges between the king and the committed group of intellectuals behind this radical political change. When this group finally seized power in 1932, Rama VII took the compromise option, later presiding at a ceremony in which the Constitution was officially conferred. It wasn't long, however, before relations between Rama VII and Thailand's new leaders soured, leading to his abdication in 1935. Rama VII was a keen amateur film-maker and he commissioned the building of Thailand's first cinema, the Sala Chalermkrung Theatre (see page 177), in 1933; the museum contains a miniature replica of this movie theatre.

The Queen's Gallery
North across Rajdamnoen Klang from Wat Rajnadda, on the corner of Thanon Phra Sumen • Charge • W facebook.com/queengallerybkk

The privately funded, five-storey **Queen's Gallery**, named after Sirikit, the Queen Mother, hosts temporary shows of contemporary Thai art, plus the occasional exhibition by foreign artists. It makes a more stimulating alternative to the rather staid National Gallery down the other end of Rajdamnoen Klang, and houses a bookshop and café.

YAOWARAT ROAD

Chinatown and Pahurat

When the newly crowned Rama I decided to move his capital across to the east bank of the river in 1782, the Chinese community living on the proposed site of his palace was obliged to relocate downriver, to the Sampeng area. Two centuries on, Chinatown has grown into the country's largest Chinese district, a sprawl of narrow alleyways, temples and shophouses packed between Charoen Krung (New Road) and the river, separated from Ratanakosin by the Indian area of Pahurat – famous for its cloth and dressmakers' trimmings – and bordered to the east by Hualamphong train station.

The **Chinese influence** on Thai culture and commerce has been significant ever since the first Chinese merchants gained a toehold in Ayutthaya in the fourteenth century. Following centuries of immigration and intermarriage, there is now some Chinese blood in almost every Thai citizen, including the king, and Chinese-Thai business interests play an enormous role in the Thai economy. This is played out at its most frantic in Chinatown, whose real estate is said to be among the most valuable in the country; there are over a hundred gold and jewellery shops along Thanon Yaowarat alone.

For the tourist, Chinatown is chiefly interesting for its **markets**, shophouses, open-fronted warehouses and remnants of colonial-style architecture, though it also harbours a few noteworthy **temples**. A meander through its most interesting neighbourhoods could easily fill up a whole day, allowing for frequent breaks from the thundering traffic and choking fumes. For the most authentic Chinatown experience, it's best to come during the week, as some shops and stalls shut at weekends; on weekdays they begin closing around 5pm, after which time the neighbourhood's other big draw – its **food** – takes centre stage. Weekend evenings, however, see a "**walking street**" market of crafts and food (Fri, Sat & Sun eves) along the renovated canal banks of **Khlong Ong Ang**, between Sampeng Lane and Thanon Charoen Krung.

ARRIVAL AND GETTING AROUND   CHINATOWN AND PAHURAT

Arrival The easiest way to reach Chinatown is either by subway, with stations at Hualamphong (for Wat Traimit), Wat Mangkon Kamalawat and Sam Yot, or by Chao Phraya express boat to Tha Rachawongse (Rajawong; N5) at the southern end of Thanon Rajawong. This part of the city is also well served by buses, with Hualamphong a useful and easily recognized place to disembark. Be warned that buses and taxis may take an unexpectedly circuitous route due to the many and complex one-way systems in Chinatown.

Getting around Orientation in Chinatown can be tricky: the alleys (often known as trok rather than the more usual soi) are extremely narrow, their turn-offs and other road signs often obscured by mounds of merchandise and thronging crowds, and the longer ones can change their names several times. For a detailed tour of the alleys and markets, use *Nancy Chandler's Map of Bangkok* (see page 34); alternatively, ask for help at the BMA tourist information booth, just northwest of the Chinese Arch at the beginning of Thanon Yaowarat.

Wat Traimit

Thanon Mittaphap Thai-China, just west of Hualamphong train and subway stations (exit 1) • Charge

The obvious place to start a Chinatown tour is on its eastern perimeter, with **Wat Traimit** and its famous Golden Buddha. You can see the temple mondop's golden spire from quite a distance, a fitting beacon for the gleaming treasure housed on its third floor, the world's largest solid-gold Buddha. It's an apt attraction for a community so closely linked with the gold trade, even if the image has nothing to do with China's spiritual heritage. A recent attempt has been made to bridge this gap, with the installation of exhibitions of varying interest on the mondop's first and second floors, covering the history of Chinatown and of the iconic Buddha image.

The Golden Buddha

Over 3m tall and weighing five tonnes, the **Golden Buddha** gleams as if coated in liquid metal, seated on a white marble lotus-pad pedestal and surrounded with offerings of lotus flowers. It's a fine example of the curvaceous grace of Sukhothai art, slim-waisted and beautifully proportioned. Cast in the thirteenth century, the image was brought to Bangkok by Rama III, completely encased in stucco – a common ruse to conceal valuable statues from would-be thieves. The disguise was so good that no one guessed what was underneath until 1955 when the image was accidentally knocked in the process of being moved to Wat Traimit, and the stucco cracked to reveal a patch of gold. Just in time for Buddhism's 2500th anniversary, the discovery launched a

country-wide craze for tapping away at plaster Buddhas in search of hidden precious metals, but Wat Traimit's is still the most valuable – it is valued, by weight alone, at around US$250 million.

The exhibitions

The exhibition on the making and history of the Golden Buddha, on the second floor of the mondop, is fairly missable, but the **Yaowarat Chinatown Heritage Centre** on the floor below is rather more compelling. Interesting though sanitized, its display boards trace the rapid expansion of the Chinese presence in Bangkok from the late eighteenth century, first as junk traders, later as labourers and tax farmers. Enhancing the story are a diorama of life on board a junk, lots of interesting photos from the late nineteenth century onwards and a fascinating scale model of Thanon Yaowarat in its 1950s heyday, when it was Bangkok's business and entertainment hub.

Sampeng Lane

From Wat Traimit, walk northwest from the big China Gate roundabout along Thanon Yaowarat, and make a left turn onto Thanon Songsawat to reach Sampeng Lane

One of Chinatown's most enjoyable shopping alleys, **Sampeng Lane** (also signposted as Soi Wanit 1) is where the Chinese community first settled in the area, when they were moved from Ratanakosin in the late eighteenth century to make way for the Grand Palace. Stretching southeast–northwest for about 1km, it's a great place to browse, unfurling itself like a serpentine department store and selling everything from Chinese silk pyjama trousers to selfie sticks at bargain rates. Similar goods are more or less gathered in sections, so at the eastern end you'll find mostly cheap jewellery and hair accessories, for example, before passing through stalls specializing in Chinese lanterns, stationery, toys, then shoes, clothes (west of Thanon Rajawong) and, as you near Pahurat, fabrics, haberdashery and irresistibly girlie accessories.

Soi Issaranuphap

Taking a right turn about halfway down Sampeng Lane will bring you into **Soi Issaranuphap** (also signed along its course as Yaowarat Soi 11, then Soi 6, and later Charoen Krung sois 16 and 21). Packed with people from dawn till dusk, this long, dark alleyway, which also traverses Charoen Krung, is where locals come in search of ginseng roots (essential for good health), quivering fish heads, cubes of cockroach-killer chalk and a gastronome's choice of dried mushrooms and brine-pickled vegetables. Alleys branch off to florid Chinese temples and tiny squares before Soi Issaranuphap finally ends at the Thanon Plaplachai intersection amid a flurry of shops specializing in paper **funeral art**. Believing that the deceased should be well provided for in their afterlife, Chinese people buy miniature paper replicas of necessities to be burned with the body: especially popular are houses, cars, suits of clothing and, of course, money.

Wat Mangkon Kamalawat

Best approached via its dramatic multi-tiered gateway 10m up Thanon Charoen Krung from the Soi Issaranuphap junction • Wat Mangkon subway

If Soi Issaranuphap epitomizes age-old Chinatown commerce, then **Wat Mangkon Kamalawat** (also known as **Wat Leng Noei Yee** or, in English, "Dragon Flower Temple")

stands as a fine example of the community's spiritual practices. Built in 1871, it receives a constant stream of devotees, who come to leave offerings at the altars inside this important Mahayana Buddhist temple. As with the Theravada Buddhism espoused by the Thais, Mahayana Buddhism fuses with other ancient religious beliefs, notably Confucianism and Taoism, and the statues and shrines within Wat Mangkon cover the spectrum. As you pass through the secondary gateway, under the glazed ceramic gables topped with undulating Chinese dragons, you're greeted by a set of forbidding statues of four guardian kings (one for each point of the compass), each symbolically clasping either a parasol, a pagoda, a snake's head or a mandolin. Beyond them, a series of Chinese-style Buddha images swathed in saffron netting occupies the next chamber, a lovely open-sided room of gold paintwork, red-lacquered wood, lattice lanterns and pictorial wall panels inlaid with mother-of-pearl. Elsewhere in the compound are booths selling devotional paraphernalia, a Chinese medicine stall and a fortune-teller.

Wat Ga Buang Kim

From Thanon Rajawong, take a right turn into Thanon Anawong and a further right turn into the narrow, two-pronged Soi Krai

The typical neighbourhood temple of **Wat Ga Buang Kim** is set around a tiny, enclosed courtyard. This particular wat is remarkable for its exquisitely ornamented "vegetarian hall", a one-room shrine with altar centrepiece framed by intricately carved wooden tableaux of gold-painted miniatures arranged as if in sequence, with recognizable characters reappearing in new positions and in different moods. The hall's outer wall is adorned with small tableaux, too, the area around the doorway at the top of the stairs peopled with finely crafted ceramic figurines drawn from Chinese opera stories. The other building in the wat compound is a stage used for Chinese opera performances.

Wat Chakrawat

Thanon Chakrawat

Wat Chakrawat is home to several long-suffering crocodiles, not to mention monkeys, dogs and chess-playing local residents. **Crocodiles** have lived in the tiny pond behind the bot for about fifty years, ever since one was brought here after being hauled out of the Chao Phraya River, where it had been endangering the limbs of bathers. The original crocodile – stuffed – sits in a glass case overlooking the current generation in the pond.

Across the other side of the wat compound is a grotto housing two unusual Buddhist artefacts. The first is a black silhouette on the wall, decorated with squares of gold leaf and believed to be the Buddha's shadow. Nearby, the statue of a fat monk looks on. The story goes that this monk was so good-looking that he was forever being tempted by the attentions of women; the only way he could deter them was to make himself ugly, which he did by gorging himself into obesity.

Nakhon Kasem

Further along Thanon Chakrawat from Wat Chakrawat, away from the river, is the site of the old **Nakhon Kasem** (literally "City of Happiness"), bordered by Thanon Charoen Krung and Thanon Yaowarat to the north and south and Chakrawat and Boriphat roads to the east and west. This grid of lanes was originally famous as the Thieves' Market and was latterly known for its musical instrument shops, but the traders have been forced to move out and it's now undergoing a major redevelopment as a shopping centre.

Pahurat

Sam Yot subway

West of Khlong Ong Ang, in the small square south of the intersection of Chakraphet and Pahurat roads, is the area known as **Pahurat**, where Bangkok's sizeable Indian community congregates. Unless you're looking for *bidi* cigarettes or Punjabi sweets, curiosity-shopping is not as rewarding here as in Chinatown, but it's good for all sorts of **fabrics**, from shirting to curtain materials and saree lengths.

Also here, at the Charoen Krung/Thanon Triphet intersection, is **Old Siam Plaza**, a colonial-look shopping centre whose nostalgia theme continues in part inside, with its ground-floor concourse given over to stalls selling traditional, handmade Thai snacks, sweets and sticky desserts. The adjacent Sala Chalermkrung Theatre stages classical Thai drama for non-Thai speakers (see page 177).

Pak Khlong Talat

Chao Phraya express boat to Tha Saphan Phut (Memorial Bridge; N6)

A browse through the 24-hour flower and vegetable market, **Pak Khlong Talat**, is a fitting way to round off a day in Chinatown, though it's also a great place to come before dawn, when market gardeners from Thonburi and beyond boat and truck their freshly picked produce across the Chao Phraya ready for sale to shopkeepers, restaurateurs and hoteliers. The market has been operating from covered halls between the southern ends of Khlong Lod, Thanon Banmo, Thanon Chakraphet and the river bank since the nineteenth century. The flower stalls sell twenty different varieties of cut orchids and countless other tropical blooms and, though prices are lowest in the early morning, you can still get some good bargains in the afternoon.

For the most interesting approach to the flower market from the Old Siam Plaza, turn west across Thanon Triphet to reach Thanon Banmo, and then follow this road south down towavrds the Chao Phraya. As you near the river, notice the facing rows of traditional Chinese shophouses, still in use today, which retain their characteristic pastel-painted facades, shutters and stucco curlicues.

WAT ARUN

Thonburi

For fifteen years between the fall of Ayutthaya in 1767 and the founding of Bangkok in 1782, the west-bank town of Thonburi, across the Chao Phraya from modern-day Bangkok, stood in as the Thai capital, under the rule of General Phraya Taksin. Its time in the spotlight was too brief for the building of the fine monuments and grand temples like those that had graced the earlier capitals at Sukhothai and Ayutthaya, but some of its centuries-old canals (khlongs), which once transported everyone and everything, have endured. It is these ancient waterways and the fascinating ways of life that depend on them that still continue to constitute Thonburi's main attractions and draw visitors to the area.

In some quarters, life on this side of the river still revolves around these **canals**: vendors of food and household goods paddle their boats along the waterways that crisscross the residential areas, and canalside factories use them to ferry their wares to the Chao Phraya River artery. Venture onto the backroads just three or four kilometres west of the river and you find yourself surrounded by market gardens and rural homes, with no hint of the throbbing metropolis across on the other bank. The most popular way to explore these old neighbourhoods is by **boat**, but joining a bicycle tour of the older neighbourhoods is also very rewarding (see page 30). Most boat trips also encompass Thonburi's imposing riverside Temple of the Dawn, **Wat Arun**, and often the **Royal Barge Museum** as well, though both are easily visited independently, as are the small but historic temple of **Wat Rakhang** and the surprisingly intriguing and child-friendly cemetery at **Wat Prayoon**.

ARRIVAL AND GETTING AROUND THONBURI

Arrival Getting to Thonburi is generally just a matter of crossing the river. Use Phra Pinklao or Memorial/Phra Pokklao bridge, take a cross-river ferry, or hop on one of the express boats, which make several stops on the Thonburi bank. The wide expanse of Thonburi is now served by the subway and other urban rail lines, but the only station likely to be of use to visitors is Itsaraphap subway station, which is within walking distance of Wat Arun.

EXPLORING THONBURI BY BOAT

The most popular way to explore the sights of Thonburi is by **boat**, taking in Wat Arun and the Royal Barge Museum, then continuing along Thonburi's network of small canals. We've detailed some interesting, fixed-price tours below, but generally it's just a question of turning up at a pier on the Bangkok side of the Chao Phraya and chartering a longtail. The boatmen usually offer a choice between a kiss-me-quick hour-long ride and a two-hour trip, taking in an orchid farm deep among the Thonburi canals. You can charter your own longtail from Tha Phra Athit in Banglamphu, the pier underneath Phra Pinklao Bridge behind the Bangkok Tourism Division head office, Tha Chang, River City shopping centre, Tha Sathorn and other piers.

Many tours include visits to one of Thonburi's two main **floating markets**, both of which are heavily touristed and rather contrived. **Wat Sai** floating market is very small, very commercialized and worth avoiding; **Taling Chan** floating market is also fairly manufactured but more fun, though it only operates on Saturdays and Sundays (roughly 8am–4pm; accessible only on a two-hour longtail boat trip). Taling Chan market is held on Khlong Chak Phra, in front of Taling Chan District Office, a couple of kilometres west of Thonburi train station. For a more authentic floating-market experience, consider heading out of Bangkok to Amphawa, in Samut Songkhram province (see page 132).

Arguably more photogenic, and certainly a lot more genuine than the floating markets, are the individual **floating vendors** who continue to paddle from house to house in Thonburi, touting anything from hot food to plastic buckets. You've a good chance of seeing some of them in action on almost any longtail boat tour on any day of the week, particularly in the morning.

Mitchaopraya Travel Service Tha Chang – on the left at the start of the pier, as you walk in from Thanon Na Phra Lan w facebook.com/Mitchaopraya.travel. Licensed by TAT, offering fixed-price trips along the Thonburi canals of varying durations: in 1hr, you'll pass Wat Arun and the Royal Barge Museum without stopping; in 90min, you'd have time to stop at either; while in 2hr, you'll have time to go right down the back canals on the Thonburi side and visit an orchid farm. On Saturday and Sunday, the 90min and 2hr trips take in Taling Chan floating market. Weekend trips to the more authentic Lat Mayom floating market, far to the west in a leafy, more traditional part of Thonburi, were not available at the time of writing because of major works on the locks, but may reappear.

Pandan Tour 780/488 Thanon Charoen Krung w thaicanaltours.com. A selection of full-day tours of the Thonburi canals, the floating markets and beyond on an eco-friendly, natural-gas-powered teak boat, in small groups with an English-speaking guide.

Getting around If you're not exploring Thonburi on a boat tour (see box, page 82), getting around the district can be complicated as the lack of footbridges over canals means that walking between sights often involves using the heavily trafficked Thanon Arun Amarin. A more convoluted alternative would be to leapfrog your way up or down the river by boat, using the various cross-river ferries that connect the Thonburi bank with the Chao Phraya express-boat stops on the other side.

Royal Barge Museum

Soi Wat Dusitaram, north bank of Khlong Bangkok Noi • Charge, extra for a camera permit • ⓦ facebook.com/RoyalBargesNationalMuseum/ • Take the Chao Phraya express boat to Tha Phra Pinklao (N12), or cross-river ferry from under Pinklao Bridge in Banglamphu to Tha Phra Pinklao, then walk up the road 100m and take the first left down Soi Wat Dusitaram; if you are coming by road, you'll also need to walk from the mouth of Soi Wat Dusitaram — signs from Soi Wat Dusitaram lead you through a jumble of walkways and stilt-houses to the museum (10min)

Since the Ayutthaya era, kings of Thailand have been conveyed along their country's waterways in royal barges. For centuries, these slender, exquisitely elegant, black-and-gold wooden vessels were used on all important royal outings, and even up until 1967 the current king would process down the Chao Phraya to Wat Arun in a flotilla of royal barges at least once a year, on the occasion of Kathin, the annual donation of robes by the laity to the temple at the end of the rainy season. But the boats, some of which are a hundred years old, are becoming quite frail, so **royal barge processions** are now held only every few years to mark special anniversaries. However, if your trip happens to coincide with one of these magnificent events, you shouldn't miss it (see ⓦ tourismthailand.org). Fifty or more barges fill the width of the river and stretch for almost 1km, drifting slowly to the measured beat of a drum and the hypnotic strains of ancient boating hymns, chanted by over two thousand oarsmen dressed in luscious brocades.

The most important vessels at the heart of the ceremony are suspended above their docks in the **Royal Barge Museum**, which often features as part of longtail-boat tours. Up to 50m long and intricately lacquered and gilded all over, they taper at the prow into imposing mythical figures after a design first used by the kings of Ayutthaya. Rama I had the boats copied and, when those fell into disrepair, Rama VI commissioned exact reconstructions, some of which are still in use today. The most important is *Sri Suphanahongse*, which bears the king and is graced by a glittering 5m-high prow representing the golden swan Hamsa, mount of the Hindu god Brahma; constructed from a single piece of timber, it's said to be the largest dugout boat in the world. In front of it floats *Anantanagaraj*, fronted by a magnificent seven-headed naga and bearing a Buddha image. The newest addition to the fleet is *Narai Song Suban*, which was commissioned by the current king for his golden jubilee in 1996; it is a copy of the mid-nineteenth-century original and is crowned with a black Vishnu (Narai) astride a garuda figurehead. A display of miniaturized royal barges at the back of the museum re-creates the exact formation of a traditional procession.

The Siriraj museums

Siriraj Hospital • Charge • ⓦ facebook.com/siriraj.museum • Take an orange-, green- or yellow-flag Chao Phraya express boat to Tha Thonburi Railway Station/Bangkok Noi (N11)

The enormous Siriraj teaching hospital — where Rama IX spent his final years in the penthouse of one of the central buildings, before his death in 2016 — is home to no fewer than seven museums. Right in front of express-boat pier N11, the **Siriraj Bimuksthan Museum** shelters some engaging exhibits on the history of the neighbourhood. Scattered widely around the hospital compound, the other six museums are devoted mostly to medical curiosities, ranging from internal organs and liver flukes to the corpses of notorious murderers and foetuses of conjoined twins; poorly captioned and ghoulish, they're all rather forgettable.

The Siriraj Bimuksthan Museum

The **Siriraj Bimuksthan Museum** occupies the former Bangkok Noi Railway Station, a typical example of red-brick municipal architecture dating from 1950. It's given over largely to a history of medicine in Thailand, featuring a long roll call of members of the royal family – including Prince Siriraj, son of Rama V – taking credit for introducing Western medicine, and a room on traditional medicine. Probably more interesting, however, is the building that traces local history: at the mouth of the strategic Bangkok Noi canal, this area was around the turn of the nineteenth century the site of the Wang Lang (Rear Palace), home of the "third king", a deputy to the "second king" who lived across the river in the Wang Na (Front Palace; now part of the National Museum). The canal mouth was home to an important floating market and dockyards, over which, in 1890, a royal opium den was built. The dockyards, however, have yielded the museum's most impressive exhibit: a largely intact, 24m, nineteenth-century, wooden merchant ship that was excavated from the nearby mud in 2003.

Wat Rakhang

Take a cross-river ferry from Tha Chang express-boat pier (near the Grand Palace) to Wat Rakhang's pier, or walk 5min from the Tha Wang Lang/Prannok express-boat pier (N10), south (left) through the Prannok pierside market

The charming riverside temple of **Wat Rakhang** (Temple of the Bells) gets its name from the five large bells donated by King Rama I and is notable for the hundreds of smaller chimes that tinkle away under the eaves of the main bot and, more accessibly, in the temple courtyard, where devotees come to strike them and hope for a run of good luck. To be extra certain of having their wishes granted, visitors also buy loaves of bread from the temple stalls and feed the frenzy of fat fish in the Chao Phraya River below. Behind the bot stands an attractive eighteenth-century wooden *ho trai* (scripture library) that still boasts some original murals on the wooden panels inside, as well as exquisitely renovated gold-leaf paintwork on the window shutters and pillars.

Walking to Wat Rakhang from the Tha Wang Lang express-boat pier, you'll pass through the enjoyable **Prannok pierside market**, which is good for cheap clothes and tempting home-made snacks, especially sweet ones.

Wat Arun

Charge • ⓦ facebook.com/watarunofficial • Take a City Line Thai Smile boat direct to Wat Arun, or the cross-river ferry from the pier adjacent to the Chao Phraya express-boat pier at Tha Thien (N8)

Almost directly across the river from Wat Pho rises the enormous, gleamingly restored five-spired prang of **Wat Arun**, the Temple of Dawn, probably Bangkok's most memorable landmark and familiar as the silhouette used in the TAT logo. It looks particularly impressive from the river as you head downstream from the Grand Palace towards the *Oriental Hotel*, but is ornate enough to be well worth stopping off for a closer look.

A wat has occupied this site since the Ayutthaya period, but only in 1768 did it become known as the Temple of Dawn – when General Phraya Taksin reputedly reached his new capital at the break of day. The temple served as his royal chapel and housed the recaptured Emerald Buddha for several years until the image was moved to Wat Phra Kaeo in 1785. Despite losing its special status after the relocation, Wat Arun

ENG AND CHANG, THE SIAMESE TWINS

Eng (In) and Chang (Chan), the "original" **Siamese twins**, were born in Samut Songkhram in 1811, when Thailand was known as Siam. The boys' bodies were joined from breastbone to navel by a short fleshy ligament, but they shared no vital organs and eventually managed to stretch their connecting tissue so that they could stand almost side by side instead of permanently facing each other.

In 1824 the boys were spotted by entrepreneurial Scottish trader Robert Hunter, who returned five years later with an American sea merchant, Captain Abel Coffin, to convince the twins' mother to let them take her sons on a world tour. Hunter and Coffin anticipated a lucrative career as producer-managers of an exotic **freak show**, and were not disappointed. They launched the twins in Boston, advertising them as "the Monster" and charging the public 50 cents to watch the boys demonstrate how they walked and ran. Though shabbily treated and poorly paid, the twins soon developed a more theatrical show, enthralling their audiences with acrobatics and feats of strength, and earning the soubriquet "the eighth wonder of the world". At the age of 21, having split from their exploitative managers, the twins became self-employed, but continued to tour with other companies across the world. Wherever they went, they would always be given a thorough examination by local **medics**, partly to counter accusations of fakery, but also because this was the first time the world and its doctors had been introduced to conjoined twins. Such was the twins' international celebrity that the term "Siamese twins" has been used ever since. Chang and Eng also sought advice from these doctors on surgical separation – an issue they returned to repeatedly right until their deaths but never acted upon, despite plenty of gruesome suggestions.

By 1840 the twins had become quite wealthy and decided to settle down. They were granted American citizenship, assumed the family name Bunker, and became slave-owning **plantation farmers** in North Carolina. Three years later they married two local sisters, Addie and Sally Yates, and between them went on to father 21 children. The families lived in separate houses and the twins shuttled between the two, keeping to a strict timetable of three days in each household; for an intriguing imagined account of this bizarre state of affairs, read Darin Strauss's novel *Chang and Eng* (see page 223). Chang and Eng had quite different personalities, and relations between the two couples soured, leading to the division of their assets, with Chang's family getting most of the land, and Eng's most of the slaves. To support their dependants, the twins were obliged to take their show back on the road several times, on occasion working with the infamous showman P. T. Barnum. Their final tour was born out of financial desperation following the 1861–65 Civil War, which had wiped out most of the twins' riches and led to the liberation of all their slaves.

In 1874, Chang succumbed to bronchitis and died; Eng, who might have survived on his own if an operation had been performed immediately, died a few hours later, possibly of shock. They were 62. The twins are buried in White Plains in North Carolina, but there's a **statue** of them near their birthplace in Samut Songkhram, on an untended plot of land surrounded by local government buildings just south of Route 3092, aka Thanon Ekachai, about 4km northeast of town.

---

continued to be revered, and its corncob prang was reconstructed and enlarged to its present height of 81m by Rama II and Rama III.

The prang that you see today is classic Ayutthayan style, built as a representation of Mount Meru, the home of the gods in Khmer cosmology. Both the **central prang** and the four minor ones that encircle it are studded all over with bits of broken porcelain, ceramic shards and tiny bowls that have been fashioned into an amazing array of polychromatic flowers. The statues of mythical *yaksha* demons and half-bird, half-human *kinnari* that support the different levels are similarly decorated. The crockery probably came from China, possibly from commercial shipments that were damaged at sea or used as ballast, and the overall effect is highly decorative and far more subtle than the dazzling glass mosaics that clad most wat buildings. On the first terrace, the mondops at each cardinal point contain statues of the Buddha at birth (north), in meditation (east), preaching his first sermon (south) and entering Nirvana (west). The second platform surrounds the base of the prang proper, whose closed entranceways are guarded by four statues of the Hindu god Indra on his three-headed elephant Erawan. In the niches of the smaller prangs stand statues of Phra Pai, the god of the wind, on horseback.

Wat Prayoon

Off Thanon Pracha Thipok, 3min walk from Memorial Bridge; though on the Thonburi bank, it's easiest to reach from the Bangkok side, by walking over Memorial Bridge from the express-boat stop at Tha Saphan Phut (N6)

Just west of the Thonburi approach to Memorial Bridge, the unusual **Khao Mor cemetery** makes an unexpectedly enjoyable place to take the kids, with its miniaturized shrines and resident turtles. Its dollhouse-sized chedis and shrines are set on an artificial hillock, which was constructed by Rama III to replicate the pleasing shapes made by dripping candle wax; it's the most famous *khao mor* (miniature mountain) in Bangkok, an art form that's been practised in Thailand since the early eighteenth century. Wedged in among the grottoes, caverns and ledges of this uneven mass are numerous memorials to the departed, forming a not-at-all sombre gallery of different styles, from traditional Thai chedis, bots and prangs to more foreign designs like the tiny Wild West house complete with cacti at the front door. Turtles fill the pond surrounding the mound and you can feed them with the bags of fruit and bread sold nearby. The cemetery is part of **Wat Prayoon** (officially Wat Prayurawongsawat) but located in a separate compound on the southeast side of the wat.

Memorial Bridge

It wasn't until 1932 that Thonburi was linked to Bangkok proper by the **Memorial Bridge**, or **Saphan Phut**, constructed by English company Dorman Long who also built the Sydney Harbour Bridge and Newcastle upon Tyne's Tyne Bridge. It commemorates the hundred and fiftieth anniversary of the foundation of the Chakri dynasty and of Bangkok, and is dedicated to Rama I (or Phra Buddha Yodfa, to give him his official title), whose bronze statue sits at the Bangkok approach. It proved to be such a crucial river-crossing that the bridge has since been supplemented by the adjacent twin-track **Saphan Phra Pokklao**. A narrow sliver of real estate between the two carriageways of Saphan Phra Pokklao has been pleasantly landscaped along the length of the bridge and saddled with the moniker of **Chao Phraya Skypark**.

WAT BENJAMABOPHIT

Dusit

Connected to Ratanakosin via the boulevards of Rajdamnoen Klang and Rajdamnoen Nok, spacious, leafy Dusit has been a royal district since the reign of Rama V, King Chulalongkorn (1860–1910). The first Thai monarch to visit Europe, Rama V returned with plans for the modernization of his capital, the fruits of which are most visible in Dusit, notably at Wat Benjamabophit and Phya Thai Palace. Even now, Rama V still commands a loyal following, and his statue, which stands in Royal Plaza, is presented with offerings every week and is the focus of celebrations on Chulalongkorn Day (Oct 23). On December 2, Dusit is the venue for the spectacular annual Trooping the Colour, when hundreds of magnificently uniformed Royal Guards demonstrate their allegiance to the king by parading around Royal Plaza.

Today, the Dusit area retains its European feel, and much of the country's decision-making goes on behind the high fences and impressive facades along its tree-lined avenues: Government House (which shelters the prime minister's and cabinet ministers' offices) and the king's residence, Amporn Palace, while the Queen Mother's home, Chitrlada Palace, occupies the eastern edge of the area. Normally a calm, stately district, in both 2008 and 2013 Dusit became the focus of **mass anti-government protests** by royalist yellow-shirts, who occupied Thanon Rajdamnoen Nok for several months on both occasions, creating a heavily defended temporary village in this most refined of neighbourhoods.

ARRIVAL AND DEPARTURE   DUSIT

By bus From Banglamphu, you can get to Dusit by taking the #70 (non-expressway) bus from Rajdamnoen Klang and getting off near the Rama V statue for Wat Benjamabophit.
By Skytrain Phya Thai Palace is just a 10min walk from Victory Monument Station. From Phaya Thai Station, it's a 30min walk to Wat Benjamabophit, or there are plenty of buses along Thanon Sri Ayutthaya.
By boat From the express-boat pier at Tha Thewet, it's about a 30min walk to Wat Benjamabophit. There's also a pier near the Thanon Nakhon Sawan bridge on the Khlong Phadung Krung Kasem boat line that's handy for the temple.

Wat Benjamabophit

Corner of Thanon Sri Ayutthaya and Thanon Rama V • Charge • facebook.com/watbencha

Wat Benjamabophit (aka Wat Ben or Wat Benja) is a fascinating fusion of classical Thai and nineteenth-century European design, which features on the front of five-baht coins. The Carrara-marble walls of its bot – hence the tourist tag "**The Marble Temple**" – are pierced by unusual stained-glass windows, neo-Gothic in style but depicting figures from Thai mythology. Rama V commissioned the temple in 1899, at a time when he was keen to show the major regional powers, Britain and France, that Thailand was *siwilai* (civilized), in order to baulk their usual excuse for colonial aggression. The temple's sema stones are a telling example of the compromises involved: they're usually prominent markers of the bot's sacred area, but here they're hard to spot, decorative and almost apologetic – look for the two small, stone lotus buds at the front of the bot on top of the white, Italianate balustrade. Inside the unusually cruciform bot, a fine replica of the highly revered Phra Buddha Chinnarat image of Phitsanulok contains some of Rama V's bones. The courtyard behind the bot houses a gallery

of Buddha images from all over Asia, set up by Rama V as an overview of different representations of the Buddha.

Wat Benjamabophit is one of the best temples in Bangkok to see religious **festivals** and rituals. Whereas monks elsewhere tend to go out on the streets every morning in search of alms, at the Marble Temple the ritual is reversed, and merit-makers come to them. Between about 5.30 and 7 or 7.30am, the monks line up on Thanon Nakhon Pathom, their bowls ready to receive donations of curry and rice, lotus buds, incense, even toilet paper and Coca-Cola; the demure row of saffron-robed monks is a sight that's well worth getting up early for. The evening candlelight processions around the bot during the Buddhist festivals of Maha Puja (in Feb) and Visakha Puja (in May) are among the most entrancing in the country.

Phya Thai Palace

Thanon Rajwithi • Access by guided tours on Sat & Sun at 9.30am & 1.30pm • Charge • Visitors must dress in smart clothes (see page 41) • W facebook.com/phyathaipalace • About 10min walk west of Victory Monument and its Skytrain station

A grandiose and eccentric relic of the early twentieth century, the **Phya Thai Palace** was started by Rama V, but built mostly by **Vajiravudh**, Rama VI, who lived here from 1919 for the last six years of his reign. After his death, the palace initially became the most luxurious hotel in Southeast Asia (an attempt by Rama VII to recoup some of the vast fortune squandered by his predecessor), incorporating Thailand's first radio station, then, after the 1932 coup, it was turned into a military hospital. Parts of the airy, rambling complex have been splendidly restored by the Palace Fan Club, while others show nearly a century's worth of wear and tear, and one building is still used as offices by Phra Mongkutklao Army Hospital; you're quite likely to come across a musical performance or rehearsal as you're being guided round the otherwise empty rooms. It's well worth buying the excellent guidebook, not only to help the palace restoration fund, but also to read the extraordinary story of **Dusit Thani**: this miniature utopian city (now dismantled) was set up by King Vajiravudh on an acre of the palace grounds, as a political experiment complete with two daily newspapers, elections and a constitution – only a decade or so before a real constitution was forcibly imposed on the monarchy after the coup of 1932.

The palace buildings

Most of the central building, the **Phiman Chakri Hall**, is in a sumptuous, English, Art Nouveau style, featuring silk wallpaper, ornate murals, Italian marble – and an extravagant but unusable fireplace that reminded Vajiravudh of his schooling in England. The king's first bedroom, decorated in royal red and appointed with a huge, step-down, marble bath, later went for B120 a night as a hotel suite. Outside in the grounds, between a pond used for bathing and the canal which gave access to Khlong Samsen, Vajiravudh first constructed for himself a simple wooden house so that he could keep an eye on the builders, the **Mekhala Ruchi Pavilion**, which later became the king's barbers. In front of the Phiman Chakri Hall, the **Thewarat Sapharom Hall**, a neo-Byzantine teak audience hall built by Rama V, is still used for occasional **classical concerts**. Don't leave without sampling the lovely Art Nouveau **coffee shop**, a former waiting room covered in ornate teak carving.

JIM THOMPSON'S HOUSE

Downtown Bangkok

Extending east from Chinatown and south to Thanon Sathorn and beyond, downtown Bangkok is central to the colossal expanse of Bangkok as a whole, but rather peripheral in a sightseer's perception of the city. In this modern high-rise area, you'll find the main shopping centres around Siam Square, though don't come looking for an elegant commercial piazza here: the "square" is in fact a grid of small streets, sheltering trendy fashion shops, cinemas and inexpensive restaurants. It lies to the southeast of Pathumwan intersection, the junction of Thanon Rama I (in Thai, "Thanon Phra Ram Neung") and Thanon Phrayathai, and the name is applied freely to the surrounding area. Further east, you'll find yet more shopping malls around the noisy and glittering Erawan Shrine.

DOWNTOWN BANGKOK

The Erawan Shrine is located where Rama I becomes Thanon Ploenchit, an intersection known as Ratchaprasong. It was here that the opposition redshirts set up a fortified camp for several months in early 2010, before the Democrat Party government sent in the troops, leading to the deaths of 91 people. It's possible to stroll in peace above the cracked pavements, noise and fumes of Thanon Rama I, by using the elevated **walkway** that runs beneath the Skytrain lines all the way from the Siam Paragon shopping centre to the Erawan Shrine (further progress is blocked by Central and Chitlom Skytrain stations). East of Ratchaprasong, you pass under the expressway flyover and enter the farang hotel, shopping and entertainment quarter of **Thanon Sukhumvit**.

The area south of Thanon Rama I is dominated by Thailand's most prestigious centre of higher learning, Chulalongkorn University, and the green expanse of **Lumphini Park**. Thanon Rama IV (in Thai "Thanon Phra Ram Sii") then marks another change of character: downtown proper, centring around the high-rise, American-style boulevard of **Thanon Silom**, the heart of the financial district, extends from here to the river. Alongside the smoked-glass banks and offices, and opposite Convent Road, site of Bangkok's Carmelite nunnery, lies the dark heart of Bangkok nightlife, **Patpong**.

Surprisingly, among downtown's vast expanse of skyscraping concrete, the main attractions for visitors are four attractive museums housed in historic teak houses: **Jim Thompson's House**, the **Ban Kamthieng**, the **Suan Pakkad Palace Museum** and **M.R. Kukrit's Heritage Home**. The area's other tourist highlight is **Siam Ocean World**, a high-tech aquarium that both kids and adults can enjoy. You can survey the whole area and beyond from the top of 314-metre-high **Mahanakhon**, Bangkok's new tallest building on Thanon Narathiwat Ratchanakharin (wkingpowermahanakhon.co.th).

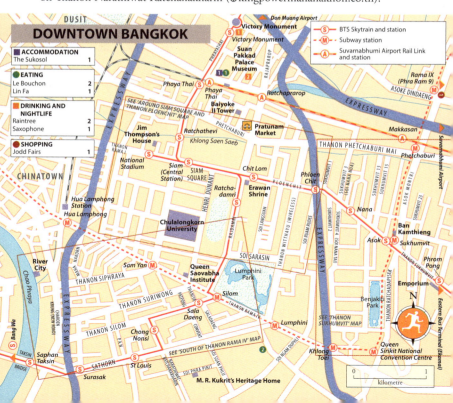

ARRIVAL AND DEPARTURE

By Skytrain and subway All of the sights reviewed here are within walking range of a Skytrain station; some of the sights are also served by the subway.
By boat The fastest way to head downtown from Banglamphu is by public boat along Khlong Saen Saeb, beginning near Democracy Monument. A slower but much more scenic route (and during rush hours, possibly quicker than a bus from Banglamphu downtown) is to take an express boat downriver, then change onto the Skytrain at BTS Saphan Taksin.

Victory Monument

Northern downtown is traversed by several major thoroughfares, including the original road to the north, Thanon Phaholyothin, which runs past the weekend market and doesn't stop until it gets to the border with Myanmar at Mae Sai, 1005km away – though it's now more commonly known as Highway 1, at least in between towns. The start of Phaholyothin is marked by the stone obelisk of **Victory Monument** (*Anu Sawari Chaisamoraphum*, or just *Anu Sawari*), which can be seen most spectacularly from Skytrains as they snake their way round it. It was erected after the Indo-Chinese War of 1940–41, when Thailand temporarily pinched some territory in Laos and Cambodia while the French government was otherwise occupied in World War II, but nowadays it commemorates all of Thailand's past military glories.

Suan Pakkad Palace Museum

352–4 Thanon Sri Ayutthaya • Closed for renovations at the time of writing • Charge • W suanpakkad.com • 5min walk from BTS Phaya Thai

The **Suan Pakkad Palace Museum** stands on what was once a cabbage patch (*suan pakkad*) but is now one of the finest gardens in Bangkok. Most of this private collection of beautiful Thai objects from all periods is displayed in lovely traditional wooden houses on stilts, which were transported to Bangkok from various parts of the country.

In House no. 5, as well as in the modern Chumbhot-Pantip Center of Arts in the palace grounds, you'll find a very good collection of elegant, whorled pottery and bronze jewellery, axe- and spearheads, which the former owner of Suan Pakkad Palace, Princess Chumbhot, excavated from tombs at Ban Chiang, the major Bronze Age settlement in the northeast. Scattered around the rest of the museum are some fine ceramics, notably celadon and bencharong; attractive Thai and Khmer religious sculptures; an extensive collection of colourful papier-mâché *khon* masks; beautiful betel-nut sets; an impressive display of traditional musical instruments, including beautiful xylophones (*ranat ek*) inlaid with mother-of-pearl and ivory; and monks' elegant ceremonial fans.

The Lacquer Pavilion

The highlight of Suan Pakkad is the **Lacquer Pavilion**, across the reedy pond at the back of the grounds. Set on stilts, the pavilion is actually an amalgam of two eighteenth- or late seventeenth-century teak temple buildings, a *ho trai* (library) and a *ho khien* (writing room), one inside the other, which were found between Ayutthaya and Bang Pa-In. The interior walls are beautifully decorated with gilt on black lacquer: the upper panels depict the life of the Buddha while the lower ones show scenes from the *Ramayana*. Look out especially for the grisly details in the tableau on the back wall of the inner building, showing the earth goddess drowning the evil forces of Mara. Underneath are depicted some European dandies on horseback, probably merchants, whose presence suggests that the work was executed before the fall of Ayutthaya in 1767. The carefully observed details of daily life and nature are skilful and lively, especially considering the restraints that the lacquering technique places on the artist, who has no opportunity for corrections or touching up.

Jim Thompson's House

Just off Siam Square at the north end of Soi Kasemsan 2, Thanon Rama I • Viewing on frequent 30–40min guided tours • Charge • ⓦ jimthompsonhouse.org • BTS National Stadium, or via a canalside path from the Khlong Saen Saeb pier at Saphan Hua Chang

Jim Thompson's House is a kind of Ideal Home in elegant Thai style, and a peaceful refuge from downtown chaos. The house was the residence of the legendary American adventurer, entrepreneur, art collector and all-round character whose mysterious disappearance in the jungles of Malaysia in 1967 has made him even more of a legend among Thailand's farang community.

Apart from putting together this beautiful home, completed in 1959, Thompson's most concrete contribution was to turn traditional silk-weaving in Thailand from a dying art into the highly successful international industry it is today. The complex now includes a **shop**, part of the Jim Thompson Thai Silk Company chain (see page 186), a café, a bar and an excellent **restaurant** (see page 165).

Also here is the **Jim Thompson Center for the Arts** (ⓦ jimthompsonartcenter.org), a fascinating gallery that hosts both traditional and modern temporary exhibitions on textiles and the arts, such as royal maps of Siam in the nineteenth century or *mor lam*, the folk music of the northeast. Ignore any con-men at the entrance to the soi looking for gullible tourists to escort on rip-off shopping trips, who'll tell you that the house is closed when it isn't. To try to stop this scam, Jim Thompson's House now lays on a free shuttle service from the soi entrance.

The house

The grand, rambling **house** is in fact a combination of six teak houses, some from as far afield as Ayutthaya and most more than two hundred years old. Like all traditional houses, they were built in wall sections hung together without nails on a frame of wooden pillars, which made it easy to dismantle them, pile them onto a barge and float them to their new location. Although he had trained as an architect, Thompson had more difficulty in putting them back together again; in the end, he had to go back to Ayutthaya to hunt down a group of carpenters who still practised the old house-building methods. Thompson added a few unconventional touches of his own, incorporating the elaborately carved front wall of a Chinese pawnshop between the drawing room and the bedroom, and reversing the other walls in the drawing room so that their carvings faced into the room.

The impeccably tasteful **interior** has been left as it was during Jim Thompson's life, even down to the place settings on the dining table – Thompson entertained guests most nights and to that end designed the house like a stage set. Complementing the fine artefacts from throughout Southeast Asia is a stunning array of Thai arts and crafts, including one of the best collections of traditional Thai paintings in the world. Thompson picked up plenty of bargains from the Thieves' Quarter (Nakhon Kasem) in Chinatown, before collecting Thai art became fashionable and expensive. Other pieces were liberated from decay and destruction in upcountry temples, while many of the Buddha images were turned over by ploughs, especially around Ayutthaya. Some of the exhibits are very rare, such as a headless but elegant seventh-century Dvaravati Buddha and a seventeenth-century Ayutthayan teak Buddha.

After the guided tour, you're free to look again, at your leisure, at the former rice barn and gardener's and maid's houses in the small, jungly **garden**, which display some gorgeous traditional Thai paintings and drawings, as well as small-scale statues and Chinese ceramics.

THE LEGEND OF JIM THOMPSON

Thai silk-weavers, art dealers and conspiracy theorists all owe a debt to **Jim Thompson**, who even now, nearly fifty years after his disappearance, remains Thailand's most famous farang. An architect by trade, Thompson left his New York practice in 1940 to join the Office of Strategic Services (later to become the CIA), a tour of duty that was to see him involved in clandestine operations in North Africa, Europe and, in 1945, the Far East, where he was detailed to a unit preparing for the invasion of Thailand. When the mission was pre-empted by the Japanese surrender, he served for a year as OSS station chief in Bangkok, forming links that were later to provide grist for endless speculation.

After an unhappy and short-lived stint as part-owner of the *Oriental Hotel*, Thompson found his calling with the struggling **silk-weavers** of the area near the present Jim Thompson House, whose traditional product was unknown in the West and had been all but abandoned by Thais in favour of less costly imported textiles. Encouragement from society friends and an enthusiastic write-up in *Vogue* convinced him there was a foreign market for Thai silk, and by 1948 he had founded the Thai Silk Company Ltd. Success was assured when, two years later, the company was commissioned to make the costumes for the Broadway run of *The King and I*. Thompson's celebrated eye for colour combinations and his tireless promotion – in the early days, he could often be seen in the lobby of the *Oriental* with bolts of silk slung over his shoulder, waiting to pounce on any remotely curious tourist – quickly made his name synonymous with Thai silk.

Like a character in a Somerset Maugham novel, Thompson played the role of Western exile to the hilt. Though he spoke no Thai, he made it his personal mission to preserve traditional arts and architecture (at a time when most Thais were more keen to emulate the West), assembling his famous Thai house and stuffing it with all manner of Oriental objets d'art. At the same time he held firmly to his farang roots and society connections: no foreign gathering in Bangkok was complete without Jim Thompson, and virtually every Western luminary passing through Bangkok – from Truman Capote to Ethel Merman – dined at his table (even though the food was notoriously bad).

If Thompson's life was the stuff of legend, his disappearance and presumed death only added to the mystique. On Easter Sunday, 1967, Thompson, while staying with friends in a cottage in Malaysia's Cameron Highlands, went out for a stroll and never came back. A massive search of the area, employing local guides, tracker dogs and even shamans, turned up no clues, provoking a rash of fascinating but entirely unsubstantiated theories. The grandfather of them all, advanced by a Dutch psychic, held that Thompson had been lured into an ambush by the disgraced former prime minister of Thailand, Pridi Panomyong, and spirited off to Cambodia for indeterminate purposes; later versions, supposing that Thompson had remained a covert CIA operative all his life, proposed that he was abducted by Vietnamese Communists and brainwashed to be displayed as a high-profile defector to Communism. More recently, an amateur sleuth claims to have found evidence that Thompson met a more mundane fate, having been killed by a careless truck driver and hastily buried.

Bangkok Art and Cultural Centre

Junction of Rama I and Phrayathai roads • Free • ⓦ bacc.or.th • BTS National Stadium

A striking, white hunk of modernity, the prestigious **Bangkok Art and Cultural Centre** houses several galleries on its upper floors, connected by spiralling ramps like New York's Guggenheim, as well as performance spaces, cafés, boutiques and private art galleries on the lower floors. It hosts temporary shows by contemporary artists from Thailand and abroad across all media, from the visual arts to music and design, and there's usually something interesting on here – coming in from BTS National Stadium, there's a blackboard inside the entrance where the day's events and shows are chalked up in English. BACC is one of the main venues for the **Bangkok Art Biennale** (BAB;

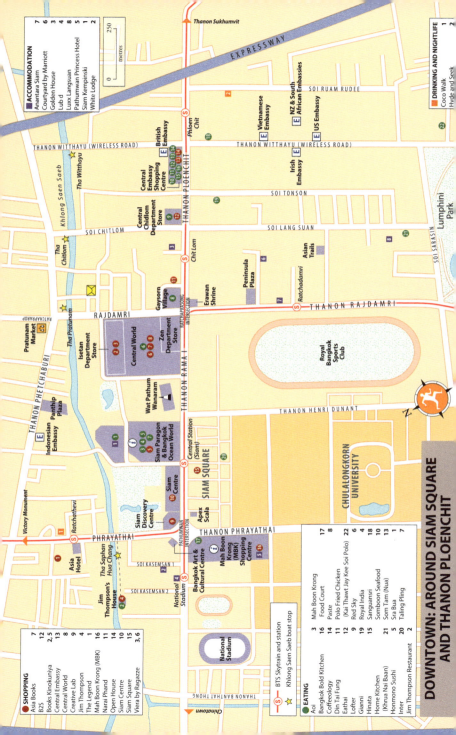

wbkkartbiennale.com), featuring dozens of Thai and international artists, cinema, music and performing arts; its next appearance will be in late 2026 and early 2027.

Sea Life Bangkok Ocean World

Basement of Siam Paragon shopping centre (east end), Thanon Rama I • daily jackass penguin feeds, as well as many other timed feedings (detailed on the website) • Charge (online and off-peak discounts available; extra charges for glass-bottomed boat ride, shark dive and 4D films) • w sealifebangkok.com • BTS Siam

Spread over two spacious floors, **Bangkok Ocean World** is an impressive, Australian-built aquarium. Despite the high admission price, it gets crowded at weekends and during holidays, and can be busy with school groups on weekday afternoons. Among outstanding features of this US$30-million development are an 8m-deep glass-walled tank, which displays the multicoloured variety of a coral reef drop-off to great effect, and a long, under-ocean tunnel where you can watch sharks and rays swimming over your head. In this global piscatorial display of around four hundred species, locals such as the Mekong giant catfish are not forgotten, while regularly spaced touch-screen terminals provide information in English about the creatures on view. It's even possible to dive with the sharks, whether you're a licensed diver or not. You can also see sharks and stingrays on a glass-bottomed boat ride and watch – through 3D glasses – underwater cartoons in the "4D Cinema".

The Erawan Shrine

Corner of Thanon Ploenchit and Thanon Rajdamri • Daily 24hr • Free • BTS Chit Lom

For a glimpse of the variety and ubiquity of Thai religion, drop in on the **Erawan Shrine** (*Saan Phra Prom* in Thai). Remarkable as much for its setting as anything else, this shrine to Brahma, the Hindu creation god, squeezes in on one of the busiest and noisiest intersections in modern Bangkok. And it's not the only one: half a dozen other Hindu shrines and spirit houses are dotted around Ratchaphrasong intersection, most notably **Trimurti**, who combines the three main gods, Brahma, Vishnu and Shiva, on Thanon Rajdamri outside Central World near the intersection's opposite corner. Modern Bangkokians see Trimurti as a sort of Cupid figure, and those looking for love bring red offerings.

The *Grand Hyatt Erawan Hotel*, towering over the Erawan Shrine, is the reason for its existence and its name. When a string of calamities held up the building of the original hotel in the 1950s, spirit doctors were called in, who instructed the owners to build a new home for the offended local spirits, in the form of a shrine to Brahma (who had created the many-headed elephant, Erawan, as a vehicle for the god Indra): the hotel was then finished without further mishap. Ill fortune, however, has struck the shrine itself twice in recent years. In 2006, a young, mentally ill Muslim man smashed the Brahma statue to pieces with a hammer – and was then brutally beaten to death by an angry mob. An exact replica of the statue was quickly installed, incorporating the remains of the old statue to preserve the spirit of the deity. Then in 2015, a bomb exploded on the grounds of the shrine (which was largely undamaged), killing twenty people, the most deadly act of terrorism in Thailand's history. There were speculations that the device was planted by Uighur separatists, in retaliation for Thailand's forced repatriation of a planeload of their kinsmen to China.

Be prepared for sensory overload here: the main structure shines with lurid glass of all colours and the overcrowded precinct around it is almost buried under scented garlands and incense candles. You might also catch a group of traditional dancers performing here to the strains of a small classical orchestra to entertain Brahma – worshippers hire them to give thanks for a stroke of good fortune. People set on less abstract rewards will invest in a lottery ticket from one of the physically disabled sellers: they're thought to be the luckiest you can buy.

Pratunam Market

Corner of Thanon Phetchaburi and Thanon Ratchaprarop

Ten minutes' walk north of the Erawan Shrine and extending northwest from the corner of Rajaprarop and Phetchaburi roads, **Pratunam Market** is famous for its low-cost, low-quality casual clothes. The vast, dark warren of stalls is becoming touristy near the hotels on its north side, but there are still bargains to be had elsewhere, especially along the market's western side.

Ban Kamthieng (Kamthieng House)

131 Thanon Asok Montri (Soi 21 off Thanon Sukhumvit) • Closed for renovations at the time of writing • ⓦ thesiamsociety.org • BTS Asok or Sukhumvit subway

A traditional northern Thai residence, **Ban Kamthieng** was moved in the 1960s from Chiang Mai to Thanon Sukhumvit and set up as an ethnological museum by the Siam Society, an august academic institution founded in 1904 to promote knowledge of Thailand. The delightful complex of polished teak buildings makes a pleasing oasis beneath the towering glass skyscrapers that dominate Sukhumvit. It differs from Suan Pakkad, Jim Thompson's House and M.R. Kukrit's Heritage Home in being the home of a rural family, and the objects on display give a fair insight into country life for the well-heeled in northern Thailand. In a traditional central Thai house at the front of the grounds, there's a nice little **café-restaurant** run by the Black Canyon chain.

The house was built on the banks of the Ping River in the mid-nineteenth century for local bigwigs, the Nimmanhaemins, and the ground-floor video will show you how to build your own northern Thai house. Also here are assorted looms and fish traps, which evoke the upcountry practice of fishing in flooded rice paddies to augment the supply from the rivers. Upstairs, the main display focuses on the ritual life of a typical Lanna household, explaining the role of the spirits, the practice of making offerings, and the belief in amulets, talismans, magic shirts and male tattoos. The rectangular lintel above the door is a *hum yon*, carved in floral patterns that represent testicles and are designed to ward off evil spirits. Walk along the open veranda to the authentically equipped kitchen, and to the granary to find an interesting exhibition on the ritual practices associated with rice farming.

The Queen Saovabha Memorial Institute (Snake Farm)

Corner of Thanon Rama IV and Thanon Henri Dunant • Live shows Mon–Fri 2pm, Sat, Sun & hols 11am; displays of venom extraction Mon–Fri 11am • Charge • ⓦ saovabha.org • 10min walk from BTS Sala Daeng, or from Sam Yan or Si Lom subway stations

The **Queen Saovabha Memorial Institute** (*Sathan Saovapha*) is a bit of a circus act, but an entertaining, informative and worthy one at that. Taking its formal name from one of Rama V's wives, it's often simply known as the **Snake Farm**, though it's not to be confused with other, more exploitative snake shows around Bangkok. Run by the Thai Red Cross, the institute has a double function: to produce snake-bite serums, and to educate the public on the dangers of Thai snakes. The latter mission involves putting on live shows of snake handling and feeding. Well presented and safe, these displays gain a perverse fascination from the knowledge that the strongest

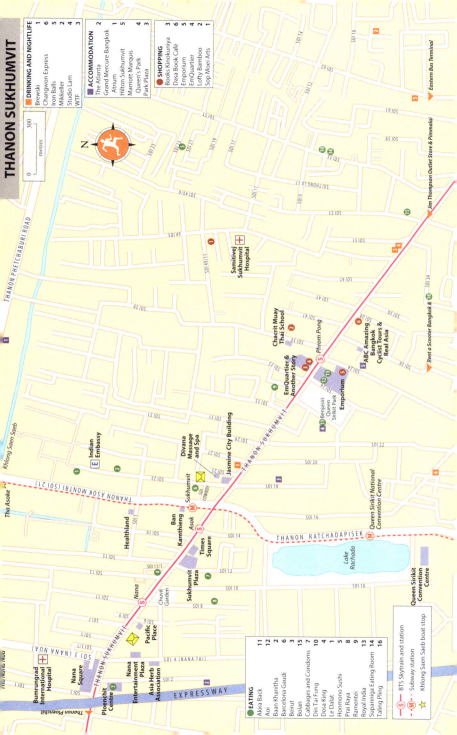

venoms of the snakes on show can kill in only three minutes. If you're still not herpetologically sated, you can look round the attached exhibition space, where dozens of Thai snakes live in cages.

Lumphini Park

Thanon Rama IV • Free • BTS Saladaeng or Si Lom or Lumphini subway stations

If you're sick of cars and concrete, head for **Lumphini Park** (*Suan Lum*), where the air is almost fresh and the traffic noise dies down to a low murmur. Named after the town in Nepal where the Buddha was born, it was the country's first public park, donated by Rama VI in the 1920s, whose statue by Silpa Bhirasri (see page 218) stands at the main, southwest entrance. The park is arrayed around two lakes, where you can join the locals in feeding the turtles and fish with bread or take out a pedalo or rowing boat, and is landscaped with a wide variety of local trees and numerous pagodas and pavilions, usually occupied by chess-players. In the early morning and at dusk, people hit the outdoor gym on the southwest side of the park, or en masse do aerobics, balletic t'ai chi or jogging along the yellow-marked circuit, stopping for the twice-daily broadcast of the national anthem. On late Sunday afternoons in the cool season (usually mid-Dec to mid-Feb), free classical concerts by the Bangkok Symphony Orchestra (wbangkoksymphony.org) draw in scores of urban picnickers.

Patpong

Concentrated into two lanes running between the eastern ends of Thanon Silom and Thanon Suriwong, the neon-lit go-go bars of the **Patpong** district loom like rides in a tawdry sexual Disneyland. In front of each bar, girls cajole passers-by with a lifeless sensuality while insistent touts proffer printed menus and photographs detailing the degradations on show. Inside, bikini-clad women gyrate to Western music and play hostess to the (almost exclusively male) spectators; upstairs, live shows feature women who, to use Spalding Gray's phrase in *Swimming to Cambodia*, "do everything with their vaginas except have babies".

Patpong was no more than a sea of mud when the capital was founded on the marshy river bank to the west, but by the 1960s it had grown into a flash district of dance halls for rich Thais, owned by a Chinese millionaire godfather, educated at the London School of Economics and by the OSS (forerunner of the CIA), who gave his name to the area. In 1969, an American entrepreneur turned an existing teahouse into a luxurious nightclub to satisfy the tastes of soldiers on R&R trips from Vietnam, and so Patpong's transformation into a Western sex reservation began. At first, the area was rough and violent, but over the years it has wised up to the desires of the affluent *farang*, and now markets itself as a packaged concept of Oriental decadence.

The centre of the skin trade lies along the interconnected sois of **Patpong 1 and 2**, where lines of go-go bars share their patch with respectable restaurants, a 24-hour supermarket and an overabundance of pharmacies. Even the most demure tourists – of both sexes – turn out to do some shopping at the night market down the middle of Patpong 1, where hawkers sell fake watches, bags and designer T-shirts. By day, a relaxed hangover descends on the place. Farang men slump at the open-air bars on Patpong 2, drinking and watching videos, unable to find anything else to do in the whole of Bangkok. Running parallel to the east, **Soi Thaniya** is Patpong's Japanese counterpart, lined with hostess bars and some good restaurants, while the focus of Bangkok's gay scene, **Silom 2** (ie Soi 2, Thanon Silom) and the more mixed **Silom 4**, flank Thaniya.

THAILAND'S SEX INDUSTRY

Bangkok owes its reputation as the carnal capital of the world to a **sex industry** adept at peddling fantasies of cheap thrills on tap. More than a thousand sex-related businesses operate in the city, but the gaudy neon fleshpots of Patpong and Sukhumvit's Soi Nana and Soi Cowboy give a misleading impression of an activity that is deeply rooted in Thai culture: the overwhelming majority of Thailand's prostitutes of both sexes (estimated at anywhere between 200,000 and 700,000) work with Thai men, not farangs.

Prostitution and polygamy have long been intrinsic to the Thai way of life. Apart from a few recent exceptions, Thai kings have always kept concubines, only a few of whom would be elevated to royal mothers. The practice was aped by the nobility and, from the early nineteenth century, by newly rich merchants keen to have lots of sons. Many men of all classes still keep **mistresses**, known as *mia noi* (minor wives), or have casual girlfriends (*gig*); the common view is that an official wife (*mia luang*) should be treated like the temple's main Buddha image – respected and elevated upon the altar – whereas the minor wife is like an amulet, to be taken along wherever you go. For less wealthy men, prostitution is a far cheaper option: at least two-fifths of sexually active Thai men are thought to visit brothels twice a month.

The **farang sex industry** is a relatively new development, having started during the Vietnam War, when the American military set up seven bases around Thailand. The GIs' appetite for "entertainment" attracted women from surrounding rural areas to cash in on the boom, and Bangkok joined the fray in the late 1960s. By the mid-1970s, the GIs had left, but tourists replaced them, lured by advertising that diverted most of the traffic to Bangkok and Pattaya. Sex tourism has since grown to become an established part of the Thai economy and has spread to Phuket, Hat Yai, Ko Samui and Chiang Mai.

The majority of the women who work in the country's go-go bars and "bar-beers" (outdoor hostess bars) come from the poorest areas of north and northeast Thailand. **Economic refugees**, they're easily drawn into an industry in which they can make in a single night what would take a month to earn in the rice fields. Many women opt for a couple of years in the sex bars to help pay off family debts and improve the living conditions of parents stuck in the poverty trap.

Many bar girls, and male prostitutes too, are looking for longer-term **relationships** with their farang customers, bringing a temporary respite from bar work and perhaps even a ticket out. A surprising number of one-night transactions do develop into some sort of holiday romance, with the young woman accompanying her farang "boyfriend" (often twice her age) around the country and maintaining contact after he's returned home. An entire sub-genre of novels and confessional memoirs (among them the classic *Hello, My Big Big Honey!: Letters to Bangkok Bar Girls and Their Revealing Interviews*) testifies to the role money plays in all this, and highlights the delusions common to both parties, not to mention the cross-cultural incomprehension.

Despite its ubiquity, prostitution has been **illegal** in Thailand since 1960, but sex-industry bosses easily circumvent the law by registering their establishments as clubs, karaoke bars or massage parlours, and making payoffs to the police and politicians. Sex workers, on the other hand, often endure exploitation and violence from pimps and customers rather than face fines and long rehabilitation sentences. Hardly surprising that many prefer to go freelance, working the clubs and bars in non-red-light zones such as Thanon Khao San. The **anti-prostitution law**, however, does attempt to treat sex workers as victims rather than criminals and penalizes parents who sell their children. A high-profile voice in the struggle to improve the **rights of sex workers** is the Empower Foundation (facebook.com/empowerfoundation.com)

Inevitably, **child prostitution** is a significant issue in Thailand, but NGOs such as ECPAT (ecpat.org) say numbers have declined over the last decade, due to zero-tolerance and awareness campaigns. The government has also strengthened legislation against hiring a prostitute under the age of 18, and anyone caught having sex with an under-15 can now be charged with rape. The disadvantaged are still targeted by traffickers however, who "buy" children from desperately poor hill tribe and other minority families and keep them as bonded slaves until the debt has been repaid.

M.R. Kukrit's Heritage Home

19 Soi Phra Pinit (Soi 7, Thanon Narathiwat Ratchanakharin) • Closed for renovations at the time of writing • 02 286 8185 • 10min walk south then east from Thanon Sathorn; 20min walk from BTS Chong Nonsi

M.R. Kukrit's Heritage Home (*Baan Mom Kukrit*) is the beautiful traditional house and gardens of one of Thailand's leading figures of the twentieth century. M.R. (*Mom Rajawongse*, a princely title) **Kukrit Pramoj** (1911–95) was a remarkable all-rounder, descended from Rama II on his father's side and, on his mother's side, from the influential ministerial family, the Bunnags. Kukrit graduated in Philosophy, Politics and Economics from Oxford University and went on to become a university lecturer back in Thailand, but his greatest claim to fame is probably as a writer: he founded, owned and penned a daily column for *Siam Rath*, the most influential Thai-language newspaper, and wrote short stories, novels, plays and poetry. He was also a respected performer in classical dance-drama (*khon*), and he starred as an Asian prime minister, opposite Marlon Brando, in the Hollywood film, *The Ugly American*. In 1974, during an especially turbulent period for Thailand, life imitated art, when Kukrit was called on to become Thailand's prime minister at the head of a coalition of seventeen parties. However, just four hundred days into his premiership, the Thai military leadership dismissed him for being too anti-American.

The **residence**, which has been left just as it was when Kukrit was alive, reflects his complex character. In the large, open-sided *sala* (pavilion) for public functions, near the entrance, is an attractive display of *khon* masks, including a gold one that Kukrit wore when he played the demon king, Totsagan (Ravana). In and around the adjoining Khmer-styled garden, keep your eyes peeled for the *mai dut*, sculpted miniature trees similar to bonsai, some of which Kukrit worked on for decades. The living quarters beyond are made up of five teak houses on stilts, assembled from various parts of central Thailand and joined by an open veranda. The bedroom, study and various sitting rooms are decked out with beautiful objets d'art; look out especially for the carved bed that belonged to Rama II and the very delicate, two-hundred-year-old nielloware (gold inlay) from Nakhon Si Thammarat in the formal reception room. In the small family prayer room, Kukrit Pramoj's ashes are enshrined in the base of a reproduction of the Emerald Buddha.

The west end of Thanon Silom

Further west along **Thanon Silom** from Patpong, in a still-thriving South Indian enclave, lies the colourful landmark of the **Maha Uma Devi Temple**. Also known as **Sri Mahamariamman** or **Wat Khaek**, this vibrant, gaudy Hindu shrine was built by Tamils in 1895 in honour of Shiva's consort, Uma. Carrying on to the river, the strip west of Charoen Krung (New Road) around Thanon Silom reveals some of the history of Bangkok's early dealings with foreigners in the fading grandeur of the old trading quarter. Here you'll find the only place in Bangkok where you might be able to eke out an architectural walk, though it's hardly compelling. Incongruous churches and "colonial" buildings – the best being the Authors' Wing of the *Oriental Hotel*, where nostalgic afternoon teas are served – are hemmed in by the spice shops and *halal* canteens of the Muslim area around Thanon Charoen Krung.

Thailand Creative and Design Center (TCDC)

Grand Postal Building, Thanon Charoen Krung • Free • tcdc.or.th • BTS Saphan Taksin, then a 20min walk, or Chao Phraya express boat or Urban Line Thai Smile boat to Tha Si Phraya

The **Thailand Creative and Design Centre** seeks to celebrate, promote and inspire innovative design through a resource centre, talks, a café and often fascinating temporary exhibitions. It's now housed in the former General Post Office, which was built in 1940 under the quasi-fascist government of Field Marshal Phibun (on the former site of the British Embassy), in a brutal modernist style that's hard to love. TCDC is the main venue for **Bangkok Design Week** every February (Wbangkokdesignweek.com), Southeast Asia's largest design festival with over two thousand participants and around half a million visitors.

TCDC is also the hub of the **Charoenkrung Creative District** project (Wfacebook.com/CharoenkrungCD), designed as a catalyst for art and design in the Thanon Charoen Krung area. Around the corner from TCDC off Soi 30 (aka Captain Bush Lane, named after an influential British sea captain who lived there at the turn of the twentieth century) is **Warehouse 30** (Wwarehouse30.com), a prestigious but hard-to-categorize redevelopment of seven 1940s warehouses. It encompasses boutiques and stalls selling clothes, furniture and flowers, a variety of food and drink outlets, galleries and spaces for temporary art exhibitions.

SANPHET PRASAT PALACE

Chatuchak Weekend Market and the outskirts

The amorphous clutter of Greater Bangkok doesn't harbour many attractions, but there are a handful of places on the outskirts of the city that make pleasant half-day outings. Nearly all the places described in this chapter can be reached fairly painlessly by some sort of city transport, either by ferry up the Chao Phraya River or by Skytrain, subway or city bus. If you're in Bangkok on a Saturday or Sunday, it's well worth making the effort to visit the enormous Chatuchak Weekend Market, where you could browse away an entire day among the thousands of stalls selling everything from handmade paper to bargain-priced sarongs.

The open-air Prasart Museum boasts many finely crafted replicas of traditional Thai buildings and is recommended for anyone who hasn't got the time to go upcountry and admire Thailand's temples and palaces *in situ*. Taking a boat ride up the Chao Phraya River makes a nice change to sitting in city-centre traffic, and the upstream town of Nonthaburi and the tranquil but less easily accessible island of Ko Kred provide the ideal excuse for doing just that.

Chatuchak Weekend Market (JJ)

Occupies a huge patch of ground extending northwest from the corner of Phaholyothin and Kamphaeng Phet roads • Sat & Sun roughly 9am–6/7pm, though many stalls open earlier and some close later • W chatuchak.org

With over ten thousand open-air stalls to peruse, 200,000 visitors each day and wares as diverse as Lao silk, Siamese kittens and designer lamps, the enormous **Chatuchak Weekend Market** (or **JJ** as it's usually abbreviated, from "Jatu Jak") is Bangkok's most enjoyable – not to mention hot and exhausting – shopping experience.

The market also contains a controversial **pets** section. In the past this has doubled as a clearing house for protected and endangered species such as gibbons, palm cockatoos and Indian pied hornbills, many of them smuggled in from Laos and Cambodia and sold to private animal collectors and foreign zoos. Crackdowns by the authorities, however, now seem to have driven this trade underground.

Where to shop

Chatuchak is divided into 27 numbered **sections**, plus half a dozen unnumbered ones, each of them more or less dedicated to a particular genre, for example household items, plants and secondhand books. The demarcation is nowhere near as clear-cut as the market's website would have you believe, but if you have several hours to spare, it's fun just to browse at whim. The market's primary customers are Bangkok residents in search of idiosyncratic fashions (try sections 2, 3 and 4), including used clothing (sections 5 and 6) and homeware (especially in sections A, B and C, behind the market's head office and information centre), but Chatuchak also has plenty of collector- and tourist-oriented **stalls**; best buys include antique lacquerware, unusual sarongs, traditional cotton clothing and crafts from the north, silver jewellery, and ceramics, particularly the five-coloured *bencharong*. For handicrafts (including musical instruments) and traditional textiles, you should start with sections 22, 24, 25 (which features textiles from northern Thailand) and 26, which are all in a cluster at the southwest (Kamphaeng Phet subway) end of the market. Section 7, meanwhile, at the north end of the market, is full of art galleries, often staffed by the artists themselves.

There are dozens of food stalls at Chatuchak, but foodies will want to check out **Talat Or Tor Khor** (the Agricultural Marketing Organization), a covered market that sells a fantastic array of fruit, veg and other produce from around the country, as well as prepared dishes to take away or to eat at the food court; it's on the south side of Thanon Kamphaeng Phet, next to Kamphaeng Phet subway station. The modern building next door to Talat Or Tor Khor, the **Siam Orchid Centre**, is a lovely market for orchids and other plants. The best place in Chatuchak Market to get a drink, and perhaps a plate of paella, is *Viva 8* (see page 173).

ARRIVAL AND GETTING AROUND — CHATUCHAK WEEKEND MARKET

Arrival Kamphaeng Phet subway station exits right into the most interesting, southwestern, corner of the market; on the northeast side of the market are Chatuchak Park subway and Mochit BTS stations.

Getting around A few very small electric trams circulate around the market's main inner ring road, transporting weary shoppers for free, though they always seem to be full.

INFORMATION

Maps Nancy Chandler's Map of Bangkok has a fabulously detailed and informatively annotated map of all the sections in the market. Maps are also posted at various points around the market, including in the subway stations, or go to ⓦchatuchak.org. For specific help you can ask at the market office, on the main inner ring road near Gate 1 off Thanon Kamphaeng Phet 2, which also has ATMs and currency exchange booths.

The Prasart Museum

9 Soi 4A, Soi Krungthep Kreetha, Thanon Krungthep Kreetha • Charge • Call ☎ 02 379 3601 or 02 379 3607 in advance to book the compulsory tour

Located on the far eastern edge of the city, the **Prasart Museum** is an unusual open-air exhibition of traditional Asian buildings, put together by wealthy entrepreneur and art-lover Khun Prasart. The museum is rarely visited – partly because of the intentionally limited opening hours and inflated admission price, and partly because it takes a long time to get there by public transport – but it makes a pleasant day out and is worth the effort.

Set in a gorgeously lush tropical garden, the museum comprises about a dozen beautifully crafted replicas of **traditional buildings**, including a golden teak palace inspired by the Tamnak Daeng at the National Museum, a Chinese temple and water garden, a Khmer shrine and a Sukhothai-era teak library set over a lotus pond. Some have been pieced together from ruined originals, while others were constructed from scratch. Many are filled with antique **artefacts**, including Burmese woodcarvings, prehistoric pottery from Ban Chiang and Lopburi-era statuettes. There's also an exquisite collection of *bencharong* ceramics.

ARRIVAL AND DEPARTURE   THE PRASART MUSEUM

By bus Bus #93 runs almost to the door: pick it up near its starting point on Thanon Si Phraya near River City and TCDC, or anywhere along its route on Phetchaburi and Phetchaburi Mai roads (both the Khlong Saen Saeb canal boats and the subway have potentially useful stops at the Thanon Asok Montri/Sukhumvit Soi 21 junction with Thanon Phetchaburi Mai). The #93 terminates on Thanon Krungthep Kreetha, but you should get off a couple of stops before the terminus, at the first stop on Thanon Krungthep Kreetha, as soon as you see the sign for the Prasart Museum (about 1hr 15min by bus from Si Phraya). Follow the sign down Soi Krungthep Kreetha, go past the golf course and, after about a 15min walk, turn off down Soi 4A.
By boat To speed things up, instead of a bus ride, you could take the Khlong Saen Saeb canal boat all the way to The Mall Bangkapi pier (about 40min from Phan Fah, seven stops after the confusingly similar The Mall Ram pier). It is then a very short taxi ride to the museum.
By train Another time saver is to take the Suvarnabhumi Airport Rail Link from Phaya Thai to Hua Mark station, which leaves you within a very short taxi ride of the museum.

Nonthaburi

Chao Phraya Express boat or Urban Line Thai Smile boat to Nonthaburi, the last stop upriver for most boats (N30), under 1hr from Central Pier (Sathorn)

A trip to **NONTHABURI**, the first town and province beyond the northern boundary of Bangkok, is the easiest excursion you can make from the centre of the city and affords a perfect opportunity to recharge your batteries. Nonthaburi is the last stop upriver for most express boats and the ride itself is most of the fun, weaving round huge, crawling sand barges and tiny canoes. The slow pace of the boat gives you plenty of time to take in the sights on the way. On the north side of Banglamphu, beyond the elegant, modern **Rama VIII Bridge**, which shelters the Mekong whisky distillery on the west bank, you'll pass in turn, on the east bank: the Bangkhunprom Palace and the adjacent Devaves Palace, two gleamingly restored former princely residences in the Bank of Thailand compound; the royal boathouse at Tha Wasukri in front of the National

CHATUCHAK WEEKEND MARKET AND THE OUTSKIRTS NONTHABURI

Library, where you can glimpse the minor ceremonial boats that escort the grand royal barges; the city's first Catholic church, Holy Conception, founded in the seventeenth century during King Narai of Ayutthaya's reign and rebuilt in the early nineteenth; and, beyond Krungthon Bridge, the Singha brewery and the new parliament complex. Along the route are dazzling Buddhist temples and drably painted mosques, catering for Bangkok's growing Muslim population, as well as a few remaining communities who still live in houses on stilts or houseboats.

Disembarking at suburban Nonthaburi, on the east bank of the river, you won't find a great deal to do, in truth. There's a market that's famous for the quality of its

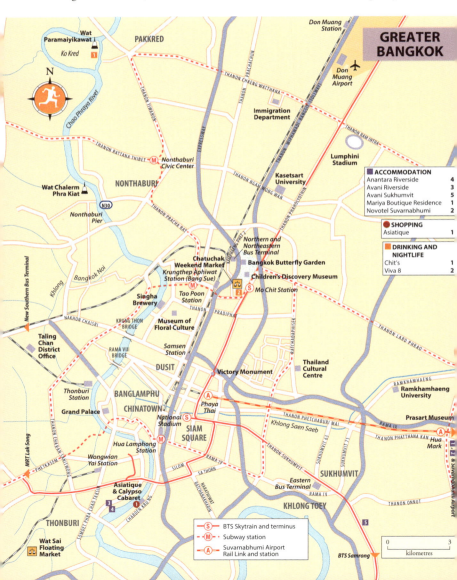

DURIANS

The naturalist Alfred Russel Wallace, eulogizing the taste of the **durian**, compared it to "rich butter-like custard highly flavoured with almonds, but intermingled with wafts of flavour that call to mind cream cheese, onion sauce, brown sherry and other incongruities". He neglected to discuss the smell of the fruit's skin, which is so bad – somewhere between detergent and dog excrement – that durians are barred from Thai hotels and aeroplanes. The different **varieties** bear strange names that do nothing to make them more appetizing: "frog", "golden pillow", "gibbon" and so on. However, the durian has fervent admirers, perhaps because it's such an acquired taste, and because it's considered a strong aphrodisiac. Aficionados discuss the varieties with as much subtlety as if they were vintage Champagnes, and treat the durian as a social fruit, to be shared around, despite a price tag of up to B3000 each. They also pour scorn on the Thai government scientists who have recently genetically developed an odourless variety, the Chanthaburi 1 durian.

The most famous durian orchards are around Nonthaburi, where the fruits are said to have an incomparably rich and nutty flavour due to the fine clay soil. To see these and other plantations such as mango, pomelo and jackfruit, your best bet is to hire a longtail from Nonthaburi pier to take you west along Khlong Om Non. If you don't smell them first, you can recognize durians by their sci-fi appearance: the shape and size of a rugby ball, but slightly deflated, they're covered in a thick, pale-green shell which is heavily armoured with short, sharp spikes (*duri* means "thorn" in Malay). By cutting along one of the faint seams with a good knife, you'll reveal a white pith in which are set a handful of yellow blobs with the texture of a wrinkled soufflé: this is what you eat. The taste is best when the smell is at its highest, about three days after the fruit has dropped. Be careful when out walking near the trees: because of its great weight and sharp spikes, a falling durian can lead to serious injury, or even an ignominious death.

fruit, while the attractive, old Provincial Office across the road is covered in wooden latticework. To break up your trip with a slow, scenic drink or lunch, you'll find a floating seafood restaurant, *Rim Fang*, to the right at the end of the prom.

Wat Chalerm Phra Kiat

1km north of Nonthaburi pier on the west bank of the river • From the express-boat pier take the ferry straight across the Chao Phraya and then catch a motorbike taxi or walk

Set in relaxing grounds on the west bank of the river, elegant **Wat Chalerm Phra Kiat** injects a splash of urban refinement among a grove of breadfruit trees. The beautifully proportioned temple, which has been lavishly restored, was built by Rama III in memory of his mother, whose family lived and presided over vast orchards in the area. Inside the walls of the temple compound, you feel as if you've come upon a stately folly in a secret garden, and a strong Chinese influence shows itself in the unusual ribbed roofs and elegantly curved gables, decorated with pastel ceramics. The restorers have done their best work inside: look out especially for the simple, delicate landscapes on the shutters.

Ko Kred

The tiny island of **KO KRED** lies in a particularly sharp bend in the Chao Phraya, about 7km north of Nonthaburi pier, cut off from the east bank by a waterway created in the eighteenth century to make the cargo route from Ayutthaya to the Gulf of Thailand just that little bit faster. Although it get busy with day-trippers from Bangkok at weekends, when there's a lively market near Wat Paramaiyikawat, this artificial island remains something of a time capsule, a little oasis of village life completely at odds with the metropolitan chaos downriver. Roughly 10 square kilometres in all, Ko Kred has no roads, just a concrete track that follows its circumference, with a few arterial walkways branching off towards the interior. Villagers, the majority of whom are Mon, descendants of refugees from Myanmar during the reigns of Taksin and Rama II, use a small fleet of motorbike taxis to cross their island, but as a sightseer you're much better off on a rental bicycle or just on foot: a round-island walk takes about an hour and a half.

There are few sights as such on Ko Kred, but its lushness and comparative emptiness make it a perfect place in which to wander, perhaps rounded off with a craft beer at *Chit's* (see page 173). You'll no doubt come across one of the island's potteries and kilns, which churn out the regionally famous earthenware flowerpots and small water-storage jars and employ a large percentage of the village workforce. The island's clay is very rich in nutrients and therefore excellent for fruit-growing, and banana trees, coconut palms, pomelo, papaya, mango and durian trees all grow in abundance on Ko Kred, fed by an intricate network of irrigation channels that crisscrosses the interior. In among the orchards, the Mons have built their wooden houses, mostly in traditional style and raised high above the marshy ground on stilts.

Wat Paramaiyikawat

Ko Kred boasts a handful of attractive riverside wats, most notably **Wat Paramaiyikawat** (also called **Wat Poramai**), at the main pier at the northeast tip of the island. This engagingly ramshackle eighteenth-century temple was restored by Rama V in honour of his grandmother, with a Buddha relic placed in its leaning, white, riverside chedi, which is a replica of the Mutao Pagoda in Hanthawadi (later Pegu, now Bago), capital of the Mon kingdom in Myanmar. Among an open-air scattering of Burmese-style alabaster Buddha images, the tall bot shelters some fascinating nineteenth-century murals, depicting scenes from temple life at ground level and the life of the Buddha above, all set in delicate imaginary landscapes.

ARRIVAL AND DEPARTURE

The Chao Phraya Express Boat company sometimes arrange good-value boat trips to Ko Kred from central Bangkok on weekends, which they advertise on Facebook (wfacebook.com/cpxcare).

From Pakkred From Pakkred, opposite Ko Kred on the river's east bank, the easiest way of getting across to the island is to hire a longtail boat, although shuttle boats cross at the river's narrowest point to Wat Poramai from Wat Sanam Neua, about 1km walk or motorbike-taxi ride south of the main Pakkred pier.

From Nonthaburi If you take a Chao Phraya Express boat to Nonthaburi, or a Thai Smile Urban Line boat to Nonthaburi or its terminus at Phra Nang Klao Bridge, you can then take a taxi (about B100) to Pakkred or a chartered longtail boat direct to Ko Kred (about B500).

From central Bangkok Either take the subway (MRT Blue Line) to Tao Poon, then change onto the MRT Purple Line to Nonthaburi Civic Center, then the MRT Pink Line to Yaek Pak Kred, or take the Skytrain to Wat Phra Sri Mahathat (N17), then the MRT Pink Line to Yaek Pak Kred; from Yaek Pak Kred station, it's a 20min walk to the shuttle boats at Wat Sanam Neua. On Mon–Fri, you could join the afternoon commuters on a Chao Phraya yellow-and-green-flag express boat to the main Pakkred pier on your outward journey; then use the MRT/Skytrain Lines to get back to central Bangkok later.

ANCIENT AYUTTHAYA

Excursions from Bangkok

Regular bus and train services from Bangkok give access to a number of enjoyable excursions, all of which are perfectly feasible as day-trips, though some also merit an overnight stay. The fertile plain to the north of the capital is bisected by the country's main artery, the Chao Phraya River, which carries boat tours to supplement the area's trains and buses. The monumental kitsch of the nineteenth-century palace at Bang Pa-In provides a sharp contrast with the atmospheric ruins further upriver at the former capital of Ayutthaya, where ancient temples, some crumbling and overgrown, others still very much in use, are arrayed in a leafy setting. You could visit the two sites on a long day-trip from Bangkok, but separate outings or an overnight stay in Ayutthaya will let you make the most of the former capital's many attractions.

To the west of the capital, the enormous nineteenth-century stupa at **Nakhon Pathom** is undeniably impressive and well worth the short journey from Bangkok; it's often visited in conjunction with an early-morning outing to the floating markets of **Damnoen Saduak**, though these are so popular with tourists that they seem staged and contrived. Better to venture a few kilometres further south to the more authentic floating markets around **Amphawa**, near **Samut Songkhram**, whose quaint canalside neighbourhoods are complemented by some appealing riverside accommodation that makes this a perfect overnight break from Bangkok. Getting there – on a rural, single-track train line – is half the fun. Tradition is also central to the untouristed town of **Phetchaburi**, with its many charming temples and hilltop royal palace.

Northwest of the capital, **Kanchanaburi** has long attracted visitors to the notorious **Bridge over the River Kwai**, and the extraordinary, POW-built Death Railway that crosses it. But the town harbours many even more affecting World War II memorials and occupies a gloriously scenic riverside location, best savoured by spending a night in a raft house moored to the river bank. Finally, for a taste of Thailand's finest monuments and temples in just one rewarding bite, just beyond Bangkok's southeastern suburbs there's the well-designed open-air museum at **Muang Boran Ancient City**, which contains beautifully crafted replicas of the country's top buildings.

Muang Boran Ancient City

33km southeast of central Bangkok in Samut Prakan • Charge • ⓦ ancientcitygroup.net • Skytrain to Keha station in Samut Prakan, then take minibus #36 or a taxi for the 5km trip to Muang Boran

A day-trip out to the **Muang Boran Ancient City** open-air museum is a great way to enjoy the best of Thailand's architectural heritage in relative peace and without much effort. Occupying a huge park shaped like Thailand itself, the museum comprises more than a hundred traditional Thai buildings scattered around pleasantly landscaped grounds and is best toured by rented **bicycle**, e-bike or golf cart (or the free tuk-tuk service), though doing it on foot is just about possible. Many of the buildings are copies of the country's most famous monuments, and are located in the appropriate "region" of the park, including Bangkok's Grand Palace (central region) and the spectacularly sited, hilltop Khmer Khao Phra Viharn sanctuary (northeast; make the most of it – the real temple is currently inaccessible from Thailand due to a border dispute with Cambodia). There are also some original structures, including a rare scripture library rescued from Samut Songkhram (south), and some painstaking reconstructions from contemporary documents of long-vanished gems, of which the Sanphet Prasat royal palace from Ayutthaya (central) is a particularly fine example, as well as recreated traditional villages and some purely imaginary designs. A sizeable team of restorers and skilled craftspeople maintains the buildings and helps keep some of the traditional techniques alive; if you come here during the week you can watch them at work.

Bang Pa-In

The village of **BANG PA-IN**, 60km north of Bangkok, has been put on the tourist map by its extravagant and rather surreal **Royal Palace**, even though most of the buildings can be seen only from the outside. King Prasat Thong of Ayutthaya first built a temple and palace on this site, 20km downstream from his capital, in the middle of the seventeenth century, and it remained a popular country residence for the kings of Ayutthaya. The palace was abandoned a century later when the capital was moved to Bangkok, only to be revived in the middle of the nineteenth century when the advent of steamboats shortened the journey time upriver. Rama IV (1851–68) built a modest residence here, which his son Chulalongkorn (Rama V), in his passion for westernization, knocked down in the 1870s to make room for the eccentric melange of European, Thai and Chinese architectural styles visible today.

The palace

Charge • Visitors are asked to dress respectfully, so no vests, shorts, short skirts, see-through shirts or open-back sandals

Set in manicured grounds on an island in the Chao Phraya River, and based around an ornamental lake, the **palace** complex is flat and compact, and easy to see on foot. The best approach is to explore slowly, following walkways that crisscross the lake.

The lakeside and covered bridge

On the north side of the lake stand a two-storey, colonial-style residence for the royal relatives and the Italianate **Varobhas Bimarn** (**Warophat Phiman**, "Excellent and Shining Heavenly Abode"), which housed Chulalongkorn's throne hall and still contains private apartments where the present royal family sometimes stays, though the lavishly furnished rooms by the entrance are usually open to the public. A covered bridge links this outer part of the palace to the **Pratu Thewarat Khanlai** ("The King of the Gods Goes Forth Gate"), the main entrance to the inner palace, which was reserved for the king and his immediate family. The high fence that encloses half of the bridge allowed the women of the harem to cross without being seen by male courtiers.

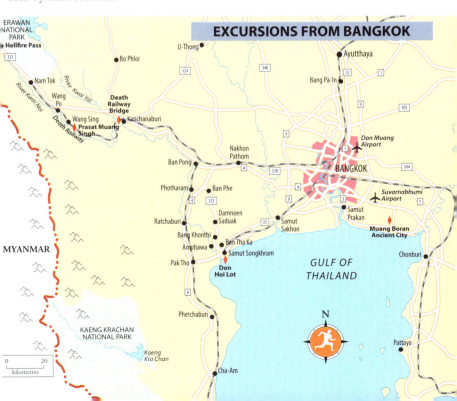

> **TRAVELLING OUT OF BANGKOK**
>
> **BY TRAIN**
> Managed by the State Railway of Thailand (SRT), the country's rail network consists of four main lines and a few branch lines, radiating out of Bangkok. The Northern Line connects Bangkok with Chiang Mai via **Bang Pa-in** and **Ayutthaya**. The Northeastern Line splits into two just beyond Ayutthaya, on its way to either Ubon Ratchathani or Nong Khai. The Southern Line extends via **Nakhon Pathom** and **Phetchaburi** to either Trang, Nakhon Si Thammarat or Hat Yai, where it forks on its way to the Malaysian border at either Padang Besar or Sungai Kolok. At Nakhon Pathom a branch of this line veers off to Nam Tok via **Kanchanaburi** – this is all that's left of the **Death Railway**, of Bridge on the River Kwai notoriety. (None of the places in this chapter are covered by the Eastern Line, which runs to either Aranyaprathet on the Cambodian border or Pattaya).
>
> Fares depend on the class of seat, whether or not you want air conditioning, and on the type of train, with supplements for the various "speed" types (see below). Hard, wooden or thinly padded third-class seats are much cheaper than buses; a few trains have air-conditioned third-class carriages. Second class has padded and often reclining seats in carriages that are either fan-cooled or a/c. Travelling first class generally means a two-person sleeping compartment (occasionally a one-person compartment), complete with washbasin and fierce air conditioning.
>
> There are several different **types of train**, most of which incur various "speed" supplements: slowest of all is the third-class-only "Ordinary" service, including Bangkok commuter trains, which has no speed supplement. Next come the misleadingly named "Rapid" trains and "Express" trains; only on "Special Express" trains will you notice much difference in speed. The fastest services are usually the daytime Special Expresses, which can usually be relied on to run roughly on time (most other services pay only lip service to their time-tables and are sometimes an hour or two late).
>
> Nearly all long-distance trains now depart from the new main terminal, **Krungthep Aphiwat Station**, to the north of the centre in Bang Sue, near the Northern Bus Terminal. Krungthep Aphiwat is served by the MRT subway and by the SRT Dark Red Line to Don Muang Airport. Many shorter-distance and slower trains still leave from **Hualamphong Station, which is** centrally located at the edge of Chinatown and on the subway line. (Trains from Hualamphong also stop at Bang Sue Junction station, which is just to the west

Aisawan Thiphya-art

You can't miss the glittering **Aisawan Thiphya-art** ("Divine Seat of Personal Freedom") in the middle of the lake: named after King Prasat Thong's original palace, it's the only example of pure Thai architecture at Bang Pa-In. The elegant tiers of the pavilion's roof shelter a bronze statue of Chulalongkorn.

The inner palace

In the inner palace, the **Uthayan Phumisathian** ("Garden of the Secured Land"), recently rebuilt in grand, neocolonial style, was Chulalongkorn's favourite house. After passing the candy-striped **Ho Withun Thasana** ("Sage's Lookout Tower"), built so that the king could survey the surrounding countryside, you'll come to the main attraction of Bang Pa-In, the **Phra Thinang Wehart Chamrun** ("Palace of Heavenly Light"), which was the favourite residence of Vajiravudh (Rama VI). A masterpiece of Chinese design, the mansion and its contents were shipped from China and presented as a gift to Chulalongkorn in 1889 by the Chinese Chamber of Commerce in Bangkok. The sumptuous interior gleams with fantastically intricate lacquered and gilded wooden screens, hand-painted porcelain floor tiles and ebony furniture inlaid with mother-of-pearl.

of Krungthep Aphiwat.) The other main route is the twice-daily service to Kanchanaburi and Nam Tok via Nakhon Pathom, which leaves from Thonburi Station (sometimes still referred to by its former name, Bangkok Noi Station), across the river from Banglamphu in Thonburi. The station is about a 750m walk east of Bang Khun Non subway station and an 850m walk west of the Thonburi Railway Station N11 express boat stop. The other departure from Bangkok is the service to Samut Sakhon (aka Mahachai), for connections to Samut Songkhram, which leaves from Wongwian Yai Station, also in Thonburi. Access is by Skytrain to Wongwian Yai (S8).

The State Railway of Thailand offers 24hr **train information in English** on its free hotline ☎ 1690. Its main website (W railway.co.th) carries English-language timetables, a train tracking function and now accepts **bookings** on the main long-distance trains in English. For more comprehensive information and advice, go to W seat61.com/thailand.htm.

BY BUS

Destinations in this chapter are served by air-conditioned buses (*rot air*) and air-conditioned minibuses (*rot tuu*) from two major terminals in Bangkok, both on the outskirts of the city. The huge, airport-like **Southern Bus Terminal**, or **Sathaanii Sai Tai**, is at the junction of Thanon Borom Ratchonani and Thanon Phutthamonthon Sai 1 in Taling Chan, an interminable 11km west of the Chao Phraya River and Banglamphu, so access to and from city accommodation can take an age, even in a taxi. It handles departures to destinations west of Bangkok, such as Nakhon Pathom, Damnoen Saduak, Samut Songkhram, Phetchaburi and Kanchanaburi, and to all points south of the capital. To reach the terminal from the east side of the Chao Phraya River, it's usually quickest to catch one of the urban railways to the Thonburi side then pick up a taxi: either the SRT Light Red Line from Bang Sue (Krungthep Aphiwat), which is on the MRT subway, to Taling Chan (4km from the **Southern Bus Terminal**); or even a Skytrain to Bang Wa (9km from the **Southern Bus Terminal**).

The **Northern Bus Terminal**, or **Sathaanii Mo Chit**, is the departure point for buses to Bang Pa-In, Ayutthaya and all northern and northeastern towns. It's on Thanon Kamphaeng Phet 2, near Chatuchak Weekend Market in the far north of the city; Mo Chit Skytrain station and Chatuchak Park and Kamphaeng Phet subway stations are within 15min walk or a short motorbike taxi or tuk-tuk ride.

The obelisk

The simple marble **obelisk** behind the Uthayan Phumisathian was erected by Chulalongkorn to hold the ashes of Queen Sunandakumariratana, his favourite wife. In 1881, Sunanda, who was then 21 and expecting a child, was taking a trip on the river here when her boat capsized. She could have been rescued quite easily, but the laws concerning the sanctity of the royal family left those around her no option: "If a boat founders, the boatmen must swim away; if they remain near the boat [or] if they lay hold of him [the royal person] to rescue him, they are to be executed." Following the tragedy, King Chulalongkorn set about reforming Thai customs and strove to make the monarchy more accessible.

Wat Niwet Thammaprawat

Perhaps the oddest building of all in Bang Pa-In's architectural melange is **Wat Niwet Thammaprawat**, reached by a cable car across the canal on the north side of the grounds. Chulalongkorn wanted a royal temple for his palace but, in his thirst for westernization, employed an Italian architect to build it in the style of a Gothic Revival church. Surmounted by a spire with a weather vane and lit by stained-glass windows, the main Buddha image sits beneath the pointed arches of a typically Gothic three-part altar.

ARRIVAL AND EATING

BANG PA-IN

Bang Pa-In can easily be visited on a day-trip from Bangkok, and tours to Ayutthaya from the capital usually feature a stop here (see page 117). From Ayutthaya, about 20km to the north, you could cycle or motorbike down the riverside Route 3477 beginning at Wat Phanan Choeng, or catch the train.

By train The best route from Bangkok is by train from Hualamphong station, which takes about ninety minutes to reach Bang Pa-in (on arrival, note the separate station hall built by Chulalongkorn for the royal family). All trains continue to Ayutthaya, with half going on to Lopburi. From Bang Pa-In's train station it's a 20min walk to the palace, or you can take a motorbike taxi. Returning to the station, you could catch a motorized samlor from the market, about 300m southwest of the palace entrance.

Destinations Ayutthaya (13–14 daily; 15min); Bangkok Hualamphong (13–14 daily; 1hr 30min).

By bus Buses leave Bangkok's Northern Mo Chit terminal (roughly every 30min; 1hr 30min–2hr) and stop at Bang Pa-In market, about 300m southwest of the palace entrance. This is also the easiest place to catch a bus back to Bangkok.

By songthaew From Ayutthaya, irregular and interminably slow songthaews leave Chao Phrom Market for the journey to Bang Pa-In market (very roughly hourly; about 1hr 30min), returning from the same spot.

Eating There are food stalls just outside the palace gates, and at Bang Pa-In market, plus a couple of well-appointed riverside restaurants between the railway station and the palace, opposite Wat Chumpol Nikayaram.

Ayutthaya

In its heyday as the booming capital of the Thai kingdom, **AYUTTHAYA**, 80km north of Bangkok, was so well-endowed with temples that sunlight reflecting off their gilt decoration was said to dazzle from 5km away. Wide, grassy spaces today occupy much of the atmospheric site, which now resembles a graveyard for temples: grand, brooding red-brick ruins rise out of the fields, satisfyingly evoking the city's bygone grandeur while providing a soothing contrast to more glitzy modern temple architecture. A few intact buildings help form an image of what the capital must have looked like, while several fine museums flesh out the picture.

The core of the ancient capital was a 4km-wide **island** at the confluence of the Lopburi, Pasak and Chao Phraya rivers, which was once encircled by a 12km-long wall, crumbling parts of which can be seen at the Phom Petch fortress in the southeast corner. A grid of broad roads now crosses the island, known as **Ko Muang**: the hub of the small modern town occupies its northeast corner, around the Thanon U Thong and Thanon Naresuan junction, but the rest is mostly uncongested and ideal for exploring by bicycle.

There is much pleasure to be had, also, from soaking up life on and along the encircling **rivers**, either by taking a boat tour or by dining at one of the waterside

> ### VISITING AYUTTHAYA – ORIENTATION AND TEMPLE PASS
>
> The majority of Ayutthaya's ancient remains are spread out across the western half of the island in a patchwork of parkland: **Wat Phra Mahathat** and **Wat Ratburana** stand near the modern centre, while a broad band runs down the middle of the parkland, containing the **Royal Palace** (Wang Luang) and temple, the most revered Buddha image, at **Viharn Phra Mongkol Bopit**, and the two main **museums**. To the north of the island you'll find the best-preserved temple, **Wat Na Phra Mane**, and **Wat Phu Khao Thong**, the "Golden Mount"; to the west stands the Khmer-style **Wat Chai Watthanaram**; while to the southeast lie the giant chedi of **Wat Yai Chai Mongkol**, **Wat Phanan Choeng**, still a vibrant place of worship, and **Baan Hollanda**, which tells the story of the Dutch settlement in Ayutthaya. The city's main temples can be visited for a slightly reduced rate when you buy the special six-in-one **pass** for Wat Phra Mahathat, Wat Ratburana, Wat Phra Ram, Wat Phra Si Sanphet, Wat Chai Watthanaram and easily missable Wat Maheyong (B220; valid for 30 days), which is available from the temples' ticket offices (all open daily 8am–6pm).

AYUTTHAYA TOURS AND CRUISES

Ayutthaya is relatively spread out, so if you're really pushed for time, you might consider joining one of the **day-trips** from Bangkok. With a little more time, you can tour by tuk-tuk, bicycle or boat. The widest choice of **tours** is offered by Ayutthaya Boat & Travel (wayutthaya-boat.com), whose itineraries include **cycling** around the ruins and to Bang Pa-In (see page 112), homestays, boat tours, lunch and dinner cruises on a teak rice-barge, cooking classes and packages by train and boat from Bangkok.

FROM BANGKOK

The most popular **day-trips** by bus to Ayutthaya from Bangkok feature only the briefest whizz around the old city's two or three main temples, making a stop at the Bang Pa-In summer palace en route (see page 112) and rounding the day off with a short river cruise down the Chao Phraya from just north of Bangkok; Grand Pearl Cruise is one of the main operators (wgrandpearlcruise.com). You can also cruise the river in more style, spending one or more nights on plushly converted teak rice-barges such as the *Namthip* (wasian-oasis.com) or the two owned by Loy Pela (wloypelavoyages.com).

BY TUK-TUK OR BOAT

If you're pushed for time you could hire a **tuk-tuk** for a whistle-stop tour of the old city. This will cost about B300 an hour from the station, where on busy days a queue forms, which is then divided into groups of four or five for the tours; or around B200 an hour if you walk away from the tourist hotspots and flag a tuk-tuk down on the street. Sunset tuk-tuk tours to see the ruins illuminated are sometimes organized by guesthouses.

Circumnavigating Ayutthaya by boat is a very enjoyable way to take in some of the outlying temples, and possibly a few lesser-visited ones too; many of the temples were designed to be approached and admired from the river, and you also get a leisurely look at twenty-first-century riverine residences. All guesthouses and agencies offer **boat tours**, usually in the early evening; tours can also be arranged – and boats chartered – from Chao Phrom pier.

---

restaurants. It's very much a working waterway, busy with barges carrying cement, rice and other heavy loads to and from Bangkok and the Gulf and with cross-river ferry services that compensate for the lack of bridges. In addition, kids – and children at heart – will enjoy the Million Toy Museum, which provides light relief from the sombre mood of Thailand's ancient heritage.

Ayutthaya comes alive each year for a week in mid-December, with a **festival** that commemorates the town's listing as a **World Heritage Site** by UNESCO on December 13, 1991. The highlight is the nightly *son et lumière* show, featuring fireworks and elephant-back fights, staged around the ruins.

Brief history

Ayutthaya takes its name from the Indian city of Ayodhya (Sanskrit for "invincible"), the legendary birthplace of Rama, hero of the *Ramayana* epic. It was founded in 1351 by U Thong – later **Ramathibodi I** – after Lopburi was ravaged by smallpox, and it rose rapidly through exploiting the expanding trade routes between India and China. Stepping into the political vacuum left by the decline of the Khmer empire at Angkor and the first Thai kingdom at Sukhothai, by the mid-fifteenth century Ayutthaya controlled an empire covering most of the area of modern-day Thailand. Built entirely on canals, few of which survive today, Ayutthaya grew into an enormous amphibious city, which by 1685 had one million people – roughly double the population of London at the same time – living largely on houseboats in a 140km network of waterways.

Ayutthaya's golden age

Ayutthaya's great wealth attracted a swarm of **foreign traders**, especially in the seventeenth century. At one stage around forty different nationalities were settled here, including Chinese, Persians, Portuguese (the first Europeans to arrive, in the early sixteenth century), Spanish, Dutch, English and French. Many of them lived in their own ghettos and had their own docks for the export of rice, spices, timber and hides. With deft political skill, the kings of Ayutthaya maintained their independence from outside powers, while embracing the benefits of their cosmopolitan influence: they employed foreign

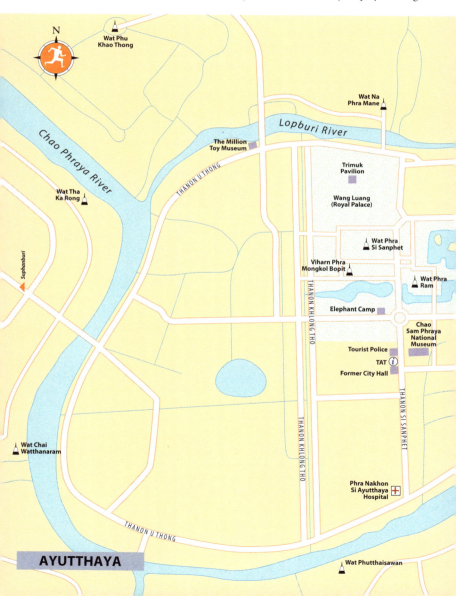

architects and navigators, used Japanese samurai – mostly Christians fleeing persecution at home – as royal bodyguards, and even took on outsiders as their prime ministers, who could look after their foreign trade without getting embroiled in the usual court intrigues.

The fall of Ayutthaya

In 1767, this four-hundred-year-long golden age of stability and prosperity came to an abrupt end. After more than two centuries of recurring tensions, the Burmese captured and ravaged Ayutthaya, taking tens of thousands of prisoners back to Myanmar.

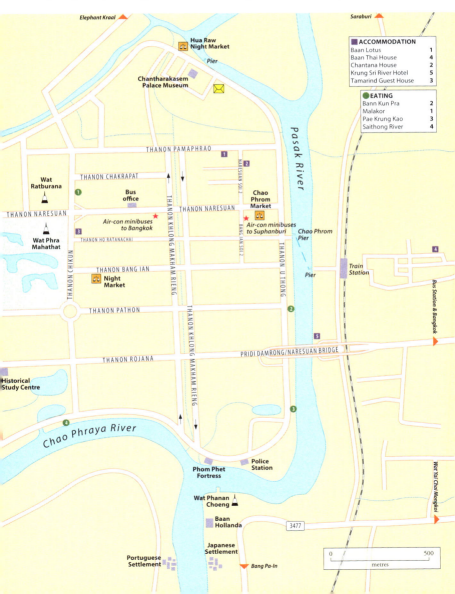

With even the wats in ruins, the city had to be abandoned to the jungle, but its memory endured: the architects of the new capital on Ratanakosin island in Bangkok perpetuated Ayutthaya's layout in every possible way.

On the island

Most of Ayutthaya's main sights, as well as most accommodation and restaurants, are located on the island, so it makes sense to begin your exploration here, then branch out to sights off the island if you have time.

Wat Phra Mahathat
1km west of the new town centre along Thanon Naresuan • Charge (included with the six-in-one pass)

Heading west out of the new town centre brings you to the first set of ruins – a pair of temples on opposite sides of the road. The overgrown **Wat Phra Mahathat**, on the left, is the epitome of Ayutthaya's nostalgic atmosphere of faded majesty. The name "Mahathat" (Great Relic Chedi) indicates that the temple was built to house remains of the Buddha himself: according to the royal chronicles – never renowned for historical accuracy – King Ramesuan (1388–95) was looking out of his palace one morning when ashes of the Buddha materialized out of thin air here. A gold casket containing the ashes was duly enshrined in a grand 38m-high prang, and the temple became home to Ayutthaya's supreme patriarch. The prang later collapsed, but the reliquary was unearthed in the 1950s, along with a hoard of other treasures, including a gorgeous marble fish, which opened to reveal gold, amber, crystal and porcelain ornaments – all now on show in the Chao Sam Phraya National Museum (see page 121).

You can climb what remains of the prang to get a good view of the broad, grassy complex, with dozens of brick spires tilting at impossible angles and headless Buddhas scattered around like spare parts in a scrapyard; look out for the serene (and much photographed) head of a stone Buddha that has become nestled in the embrace of a bodhi tree's roots.

Wat Ratburana
Across the road from Wat Phra Mahathat • Charge (included with the six-in-one pass)

The towering **Wat Ratburana** was built in 1424 by King Boromraja II to commemorate his elder brothers, Ay and Yi, who managed to kill each other in an elephant-back duel over the succession to the throne, thus leaving it vacant for Boromraja. Here, four elegant Sri Lankan-style chedis lean outwards as if in deference to the main prang, on which some of the original stuccowork can still be seen, some of which has been restored, including fine statues of garudas swooping down on nagas. It's possible to descend steep steps inside the prang to the crypt, where on two levels you can make out fragmentary murals of the early Ayutthaya period.

Wat Phra Ram
West of Wat Phra Mahathat • Charge (included with the six-in-one pass)

West of Wat Phra Mahathat you'll see a lake, now surrounded by a popular park, and the slender prang of **Wat Phra Ram**, built in the late fourteenth century on the site of Ramathibodi's cremation by his son and successor as king, Ramesuan. Sadly, not much of the prang's original stuccowork remains, but you can still get an idea of how spectacular it would have looked when the city was at its zenith.

Wat Phra Si Sanphet and the Wang Luang (Royal Palace)
To the west of Thanon Si Sanphet • Charge (included with the six-in-one pass)

Wat Phra Si Sanphet was built in 1448 by King Boromatrailokanat as a private royal chapel, and was formerly the grandest of Ayutthaya's temples. Even now, it's one of the best preserved.

The wat took its name from one of the largest standing metal images of the Buddha ever known, the **Phra Si Sanphet**, erected here in 1503. Towering 16m high and covered in 173kg of gold, it did not survive the ravages of the Burmese, though Rama I rescued the pieces and placed them inside a chedi at Wat Pho in Bangkok. The three remaining grey chedis in the characteristic style of the old capital were built to house the ashes of three kings, and have now become the most familiar image of Ayutthaya.

The site of this royal wat was originally occupied by Ramathibodi I's wooden palace, which Boromatrailokanat replaced with the bigger **Wang Luang** (Royal Palace; same hours and ticket as Wat Phra Si Sanphet), stretching to the Lopburi River on the north side. Successive kings turned the Wang Luang into a vast complex of pavilions and halls, with an elaborate system of walls designed to isolate the inner sanctum for the king and his consorts. The palace was destroyed by the Burmese in 1767 and plundered by Rama I for its bricks, which he needed to build the new capital at Bangkok. Now you can only trace the outlines of a few walls in the grass and inspect an unimpressive wooden replica of an open pavilion – better to consult the model of the whole complex in the Historical Study Centre.

Viharn Phra Mongkol Bopit
On the south side of Wat Phra Si Sanphet • Free

Viharn Phra Mongkol Bopit attracts tourists and Thai pilgrims in about equal measure. The pristine hall – a replica of a typical Ayutthayan viharn, with its characteristic chunky lotus-capped columns around the outside – was built in 1956, with help from the Burmese to atone for their flattening of the city two centuries earlier, in order to shelter the revered **Phra Mongkol Bopit**, which, at 12.45m high (excluding the base), is one of the largest bronze Buddhas in Thailand. The powerfully austere image, with its flashing mother-of-pearl eyes, was cast in the fifteenth century, then sat exposed to the elements from the time of the Burmese invasion until its new home was built. During restoration, the hollow image was found to contain hundreds of Buddha statuettes, some of which were later buried around the shrine to protect it.

The Million Toy Museum
In the northwest corner of the island, just west of the Royal Palace and the westernmost bridge over the Lopburi River • Charge • ⓦ facebook.com/p/million-toy-museum-by-krirk-yoonpun-100057456669529/

After a few hours gazing at the ruins of ancient temples, it comes as a welcome relief to enter the quirky, private **Million Toy Museum**, where cabinets on two floors are packed not only with toys, but also with odd items like Queen Elizabeth II coronation mugs from 1953. Kids love it, and even adults will recognize a few favourites from childhood, such as Superman, Minnie Mouse, Donald Duck and Goofy. There's a café out front that is also full of toy characters, and seats in a shady garden where you can rest your legs.

Chao Sam Phraya National Museum
10min walk south of Viharn Phra Mongkol Bopit • Charge • ⓦ facebook.com/chaosamphraya/

The largest of the town's three museums is the **Chao Sam Phraya National Museum**, where most of the moveable remains of Ayutthaya's glory – those that weren't plundered by treasure-hunters or taken to the National Museum in Bangkok – are exhibited. Apart from numerous Buddhas and some fine woodcarving, the museum is bursting with **gold treasures**, including the original relic casket from Wat Mahathat, betel-nut sets and model chedis, and a gem-encrusted fifteenth-century crouching elephant found in the crypt at Wat Ratburana.

Historical Study Centre
Thanon Rotchana, a 5min walk from Chao Sam Phraya National Museum • Closed for renovations at the time of writing • Charge • ⓦ facebook.com/Ayutthayahistoricalstudycenter

It's worth paying a visit to the **Historical Study Centre**, if only to check out its scale model of the Royal Palace before you set off to wander around the real thing. The visitors' exhibition upstairs puts Ayutthaya's ruins in context, dramatically presenting a broad social history of the city through videos, sound effects and reconstructions of temple murals. Other exhibits include model ships and a peasant's wooden house.

Chantharakasem Palace Museum
In the northeast corner of the island • Charge • ⓦ facebook.com/chantharakasemmuseum/

The **Chantharakasem Palace** was traditionally the home of the heir to the Ayutthayan throne. The Black Prince, Naresuan, built the first *wang na* (palace of the front) here in about 1577 so that he could guard the area of the city wall that was most vulnerable to enemy attack. Rama IV (1851–68) had the palace restored and it now houses a **museum** displaying many of his possessions, including a throne platform overhung by a white *chat*, a ceremonial nine-tiered parasol that is a vital part of a king's insignia. The rest of the museum features beautiful ceramics and Buddha images, and a small arsenal of cannon and musketry.

Off the island
It's easy enough to visit places off the island via various bridges across the river, especially if you're travelling around on a bike. If you're pushed for time, the two main sights are Wat Chai Watthanaram to the west, and Wat Yai Chai Mongkol to the southeast of the island.

Wat Na Phra Mane
On the north bank of the Lopburi River, opposite the Wang Luang • Charge

Wat Na Phra Mane (Wat Na Phra Meru) is in some respects Ayutthaya's most rewarding temple, being the only one from the town's golden age that survived the ravages of 1767 (because the Burmese used it as their main base during the siege), though frequent refurbishments make it appear quite new.

The main **bot**, built in 1503, shows the distinctive features of Ayutthayan architecture – outside columns topped with lotus cups, and slits in the walls instead of windows to let the air circulate. Inside, underneath a rich red-and-gold coffered ceiling that represents the stars around the moon, sits a powerful 6m-high Buddha in the disdainful, over-decorated royal style characteristic of the later Ayutthaya period.

In sharp contrast is the dark-green **Phra Khan Thavaraj** Buddha, which dominates the tiny viharn behind to the right. Seated in the "European position", with its robe delicately pleated and its feet up on a large lotus leaf, the gentle figure conveys a reassuring serenity. It's advertised as being from Sri Lanka, the source of Thai Buddhism, but more likely is a seventh- to ninth-century Mon image from Wat Phra Mane at Nakhon Pathom.

Wat Phu Khao Thong
2km northwest of Wat Na Phra Mane • Free

Head northwest of Wat Na Phra Mane and you're in open country, where the 50m-high chedi of **Wat Phu Khao Thong** rises steeply out of the fields. In 1569, after a temporary occupation of Ayutthaya, the Burmese erected a Mon-style chedi here to commemorate their victory. Forbidden by Buddhist law from pulling down a sacred monument, the Thais had to put up with this galling reminder of the enemy's success until it collapsed nearly two hundred years later, when King Borommakot promptly built a truly Ayutthayan chedi on the old Burmese base – just in time for the Burmese to return in 1767 and flatten the town. This "Golden Mount" has recently been restored, with a colossal equestrian statue of King Naresuan, conqueror of the Burmese, to keep it company. You can climb 25m of steps up the side of the chedi to look out over the countryside and the town, with glimpses of Wat Phra Si Sanphet and Viharn Phra Mongkok Bopit in the distance.

Wat Tha Ka Rong
Opposite the northwest corner of the island, near the confluence of the Chao Phraya and Lopburi rivers • Free

This modern temple is wild – think Buddha goes to Disneyland. Highlights include a room full of enormous statues of famous monks, motion-activated skeletons, robots and other mannequins that *wai* as you pass and ask for a donation, and the plushest bathrooms you'll see in town. There's also a floating market on the riverside selling souvenirs, and an interesting display of Buddha images from neighbouring countries.

Wat Chai Watthanaram
Across the river, west of the island • Daily 8am–6pm • Charge (included with the six-in-one pass)

It's worth the bike or boat ride to reach the elegant brick-and-stucco latticework of Khmer-style stupas at **Wat Chai Watthanaram**. Late afternoon is a popular time to visit, as the sun sinks photogenically behind the main tower.

King Prasat Thong commissioned the building of Wat Chai Watthanaram in 1630, possibly to commemorate a victory over Cambodia, designing it as a sort of Angkorian homage, around a 35m-high central Khmer corncob **prang** encircled by a constellation of four minor prangs and eight tiered and tapered chedis. Most of the stucco facing has weathered away to reveal the red-brick innards in pretty contrast, but a few tantalizing fragments of stucco relief remain on the outside of the chedis, depicting episodes from the Buddha's life. Around the gallery that connects them sits a solemn phalanx of 120 headless seated Buddhas, each on its own red-brick dais but showing no trace of their original skins, which may have been done in black lacquer and gold-leaf. To the east a couple of larger seated Buddhas look out across the river from the foundations of the old bot.

Wat Yai Chai Mongkol
Southeast of the island, about 2km from the station • If cycling here, avoid the multi-laned Pridi Damrong/Naresuan Bridge and Bangkok road by taking the river ferry across to the train station and then heading south 1.5km before turning east to the temple • Charge

Across the Pasak River southeast of the island, you pass through Ayutthaya's new business zone and some rustic suburbia before reaching the ancient but still functioning **Wat Yai Chai Mongkol**. Surrounded by formal lawns, flowerbeds and much-photographed saffron-draped Buddhas, the wat was established by Ramathibodi I in 1357 as a meditation site for monks returning from study in Sri Lanka. King Naresuan put up the beautifully curvaceous **chedi** to mark the decisive victory over the Burmese at Suphanburi in 1593, when he himself is said to have sent the enemy packing by slaying the Burmese crown prince in an elephant-back duel. Built on a colossal scale to outshine the Burmese Golden Mount on the opposite side of Ayutthaya, the chedi has come to symbolize the prowess and devotion of Naresuan and, by implication, his descendants right down to the present king. By the entrance, the **reclining Buddha** was also constructed by Naresuan. A huge modern glass-walled shrine to the revered king dominates the back of the temple compound.

Wat Phanan Choeng
Near the confluence of the Chao Phraya and Pasak rivers, to the west of Wat Yai Chai Mongkol • Charge

In Ayutthaya's most prosperous period, the docks and main trading area were located near the confluence of the Chao Phraya and Pasak rivers, and this is where you'll find the oldest and liveliest working temple in town, **Wat Phanan Choeng**. The main viharn is often filled with the sights, sounds and smells of an incredible variety of merit-making activities, as devotees burn huge pink Chinese incense candles, offer food and rattle fortune sticks. If you can get here during a festival, especially Chinese New Year, you're in for an overpowering experience.

The 19m-high Buddha, which almost fills the hall, has survived since 1324, shortly before the founding of the capital, and tears are said to have flowed from its eyes when Ayutthaya was sacked by the Burmese. However, the reason for the temple's popularity with the Chinese is to be found in the early eighteenth-century shrine by the pier, with its image of a beautiful Chinese princess who drowned herself here because of a king's infidelity: his remorse led him to build the shrine at the place where she had walked into the river.

Baan Hollanda
Just south of Wat Phanan Choeng • Charge • W baanhollanda.org

During Ayutthaya's heyday in the sixteenth and seventeenth centuries, foreign merchants were attracted here to trade with the Siamese, and were permitted to set up trading posts on either side of the Chao Phraya River to the southeast of the island. Three settlements have now been turned into museums recounting foreign relations with Siam, and of these, **Baan Hollanda** (the Dutch settlement) is the most interesting (the others are those of the Japanese and Portuguese). Established in 2013 to inform visitors about the history of the Dutch in Siam, the exhibition covers Siamese–Dutch relations from the first arrival of the Dutch East India Company in 1604. It's housed in a reconstruction of the original Dutch colonial-style lodge, following a description in the diary of a seventeenth-century Dutch merchant. The Dutch bought rice, tin, deerskins and wood from Siam and in return sold Japanese silver and Indian printed textiles to the Siamese. The centre also demonstrates how the Dutch have mastered the art of flood protection in their own country so that a large percentage of its population lives below sea level without fear, and there's a café and an opportunity for visitors to pick up a pair of ceramic clogs or a windmill at the museum shop.

The elephant kraal
Northeast of the island • W elephantstay.com

Now fully restored, the sixteenth-century kraal is where wild elephants were driven for capture, selection by the king and taming. These days it's the headquarters of Elephantstay (W elephantstay.com), an organization that runs one- to fourteen-day packages for visitors who want to ride, feed, water and bathe the seventy resident elephants.

ARRIVAL AND DEPARTURE — AYUTTHAYA

BY TRAIN
The best way of getting to Ayutthaya from Bangkok is by train (27 departures daily, mostly in the early morning and evening; 1hr 30min–2hr). Sixteen of these trains depart from the new main station, Krungthep Aphiwat, eleven from the old Hualamphong station ("Bangkok" on the State Railways of Thailand's timetable); those from Hualamphong tend to be shorter-distance and slower, but they also stop at Bang Sue Junction station, which is just to the west of Krungthep Aphiwat. Ayutthaya's station is on the east bank of the Pasak; to get to the centre of town, take a ferry from the jetty 100m west of the station (last ferry around 8pm) across and upriver to Chao Phrom pier; it's then a 5min walk to the junction of Thanon U Thong and Thanon Naresuan, near most guesthouses. The station has a useful left-luggage service.

BY BUS OR MINIBUS
From/to Bangkok Frequent a/c minibuses to Ayutthaya depart Bangkok's Northern (Mo Chit) and Southern bus terminals, pulling in at the stop on Thanon Naresuan, near the main accommodation area, after 1hr 30min–2hr.

From/to Kanchanaburi Travelling from Kanchanaburi, it's possible to bypass the Bangkok gridlock, either by hooking up with an a/c tourist minibus direct to Ayutthaya (daily; 3hr) arranged through guesthouses in Kanchanaburi or, under your own steam, by taking a public bus to Suphanburi (every 20min; 2hr 30min), then changing to an Ayutthaya a/c minibus, which will drop you off on Soi 2, Thanon Bang Ian, near Chao Phrom Market. To travel from Ayutthaya to Kanchanaburi, the easiest option is to book a seat on a minibus through one of the guesthouses.

GETTING AROUND
Busloads of tourists descend on Ayutthaya's sights during the day, but the area covered by the old capital is large enough not to feel swamped. Distances are deceptive, so it's not a good idea to walk everywhere. There are plenty of

ART AND HISTORY AT THE AYUTTHAYA TOURIST OFFICE

While visiting the Tourist Information Centre, it's well worth heading upstairs to the smartly presented multi-media **exhibition** on Ayutthaya (free), which provides an engaging introduction to the city's history, an overview of all the sights, including a scale-model reconstruction of Wat Phra Si Sanphet, and insights into local traditional ways of life. Also on this floor, there's the **Ayutthaya National Art Museum** (free), which houses depictions of animals, people and landscapes by Thai artists as well as temporary exhibitions.

---

bicycle and other tours around Ayutthaya (see page 117), and tuk-tuks can be hired by the hour.

By bicycle or motorbike Bicycles can be rented from most guesthouses, from around the train station and, more conveniently, from Chao Phrom pier across the river; if you do rent from the station, put the bike on the ferry to Chao Phrom pier rather than take on the busy, steep Pridi Damrong Bridge. Some guesthouses and a few outlets in front of the station and at Chao Phrom pier rent small motorbikes.

By tuk-tuk or motorbike taxi Tuk-tuks and motorbike taxis are easy enough to flag down on the street.

INFORMATION

Tourist information TAT's helpful Ayutthaya Tourist Information Centre (daily 8.30am–4.30pm; ☎ 035 246076–7, ✉ tatyutya@tat.or.th) is in a room on the ground floor of the former city hall (on the west side of Thanon Si Sanphet, opposite the Chao Sam Phraya National Museum).

Website If you want to delve further into the city's history, have a look at Ayutthaya Historical Research (⊛ ayutthaya-history.com), a labour of love by three expat enthusiasts.

ACCOMMODATION   SEE MAP PAGE 118

Ayutthaya offers a good choice of accommodation, including a small ghetto of **budget guesthouses** on and around the soi that runs north from Chao Phrom Market to Thanon Pamaphrao; it's sometimes known as Soi Farang (or "Khao San Road"), but is actually signed as Naresuan Soi 2 at the southern end and Pamaphrao Soi 5 at the northern. Competing singers at the clutch of bar-restaurants at its southern end can mean this stretch turns into a battle of the bands in the late evening.

Baan Lotus 20 Thanon Pamaphrao ☎ 035 251988. Two old wooden houses with polished wooden floors and large, plain, but clean rooms (with either shared or en-suite hot showers), at the end of a garden with a lotus pond and pavilion. It's a wonderfully restful location just a few steps from the restaurants and bars on Soi Farang. B̄

Baan Thai House 199/19 Moo 4, Sri Krung Villa, 600m east of the train station ⊛ baanthaihouse.com. Twelve immaculate a/c villas with traditional sloping roofs, set around manicured tropical gardens and a huge artificial pond with its own wooden water wheel. Rooms have flatscreen TVs, wooden floors and delicately carved furnishings, plus classy outdoor showers. Perks include free bicycles, a spa and an outdoor pool. BBB

Chantana House 12/22 Naresuan Soi 2 ☎ 035 323200; map page 119. Towards the quieter end of the travellers' soi, this low-key guesthouse has simple, boxy but spotlessly clean rooms with en-suite hot showers, though not all have outward-facing windows; it's set in a two-storey house with lots of common areas behind a well-kept garden. Kind, friendly staff, but not much English spoken. B̄

Krung Sri River Hotel 27/2 Moo 11, Thanon Rojana ⊛ krungsririver.com. Ayutthaya's most prominent central hotel occupies nine storeys in a prime if noisy position beside the Pridi Damrong Bridge, with some standard rooms and all suites enjoying river views. Furnishings aren't exactly chic, but there are minibars, safes and TVs in all two hundred large bedrooms, as well as an attractive third-floor pool and a fitness centre. BBB

★ **Tamarind Guest House** On a lane off Thanon Chikun, in front of the entrance to Wat Mahathat ⊛ facebook.com/p/Tamarind-Guest-House-100057450219803. Tucked away from the main road, this quirky guesthouse has bags of character and its stylish a/c rooms are all different in design, though all have bright colour schemes and en-suite hot showers. There's a great, multi-level family room and the owner can help with sightseeing plans. If this place is full, ask about nearby *Good Morning*, a slightly cheaper guesthouse under the same ownership. B̄

EATING   SEE MAP PAGE 118

Other than the restaurants listed below, the *roti* (Muslim pancake) stalls near the hospital at the southern end of Thanon Si Sanphet are good for daytime snacks and after dark there are a couple of **night markets**. There's an excellent one with a wide range of food beside the river at Hua Raw, about ten minutes' walk north of Naresuan Soi 2, and another at the west end of Thanon Bang Ian, 150m south of Wat Phra Mahathat.

Bann Kun Pra Thanon U Thong, just north of Pridi Damrong Bridge w facebook.com/ayutthayabankunpra. The atmospheric riverside dining terrace here enjoys fine views. It specializes in creative and reasonably priced fish, seafood and river prawns, in dishes such as an intensely flavoured seafood *tom yam*, with a thicker soup than usual. BB

★ **Malakor** Thanon Chikun, opposite Wat Ratburana w facebook.com/papayayoda. Handy for the sights, this all-round café-restaurant is set on appealing wooden decks among shady trees. As well as a wide choice of breakfasts, espresso coffees and icy-cold beers, it offers some tasty and unusual Thai dishes that can be spiced to order, such as *tom klong pla yang* (sour and spicy smoked fish soup), as well as one-plate meals and salads. B

★ **Pae Krung Kao** Thanon U Thong, just south of Pridi Damrong Bridge w facebook.com/Paekrungkao. official. Festooned with plants, *mai dut* (Thai bonsai trees), waterfalls and curios, this rustic restaurant with breezy wooden decks built over the river specializes in river prawns. They're pricy but huge, sweet and juicy and come with a delicious *nam jim*, spicy, sour dipping sauce. Other noteworthy dishes include green curry with fish balls. BB

Saithong River 45 Moo 1, Thanon U Thong w facebook. com/saithongriverofficial. On the south side of the island, this place has an attractive riverside terrace and a cosy a/c room, and its reasonably priced seafood is popular with locals, so it's often full on weekend evenings. Try the seabass with spicy lemon sauce or the *yum Saithong* – a spicy salad with shrimp, chicken, squid and ham. Live music in the evening. BB

DIRECTORY

Banks and ATMs There are plenty of banks with exchange services and ATMs around the junction of Thanon Naresuan and Naresuan Soi 2.

Hospital The government Phra Nakhon Si Ayutthaya hospital is at the southern end of Thanon Si Sanphet (☎ 035 211888).

Tourist police Based just to the north of the TAT office on Thanon Si Sanphet (☎ 035 243444 or ☎ 1155).

Nakhon Pathom

Even if you're just passing through, you can't miss the star attraction of **NAKHON PATHOM**: the enormous stupa **Phra Pathom Chedi** dominates the skyline of this otherwise unexceptional provincial capital, 56km west of Bangkok. Probably Thailand's oldest town, Nakhon Pathom (derived from the Pali for "First City") is thought to be the point at which **Buddhism** first entered the region now known as Thailand, more than two thousand years ago. Then the capital of a sizeable Mon kingdom, it was important enough to rate a visit from two missionaries dispatched by King Ashoka of India, one of Buddhism's great early evangelists.

The **Phra Pathom Chedi** is easily visited as a day-trip from Bangkok or while travelling from the capital west to Kanchanaburi or south to Phetchaburi, Surat Thani and Malaysia, with plenty of overnight trains on the latter route. As such, there's no earthly reason to overnight in Nakhon Pathom – which is reflected in the town's poor choice of hotels. Everything described below is within walking distance of the railway station.

Phra Pathom Chedi

400m south of the train station • Charge

Although the Buddha never actually came to Thailand, legend held that he rested in Nakhon Pathom after wandering the country, and the original **Phra Pathom Chedi** may have been erected to represent this. The first structure resembled Ashoka's great stupa at Sanchi in India, with its inverted bowl shape and spire that topped 39m. Local chronicles, however, tell how the chedi was built in the sixth century as an act of atonement by the foundling Phraya Pan who murdered the tyrant Mon king before realizing that he was his father. Statues of both father and son stand inside the viharns of the present chedi.

Whatever its true origins, the first chedi fell into disrepair and was later rebuilt with a prang during the Khmer period, between the eighth and twelfth centuries. Abandoned to the jungle once more, it was rediscovered by the future Rama IV in 1853 who, mindful that all Buddhist monuments are sacred however dilapidated, set about encasing the old prang in the enormous new 120m-high plunger-shaped chedi, making it one of the tallest stupas in the world. Its distinctive cladding of shimmering golden-brown tiles was completed several decades later.

The present-day chedi is much revered and holds its own week-long Phra Pathom Chedi **fair**, around the time of Loy Krathong in November, which attracts musicians, fortune-tellers and of course plenty of food stalls.

Around the chedi

Approaching the chedi from the main (northern) staircase, you're greeted by the 8m-high Sukhothai-style Buddha image known as **Phra Ruang Rojanarit**, which contains some of Rama VI's ashes and stands in front of the north viharn. There's a viharn at each of the cardinal points and they all have an inner and an outer chamber containing tableaux of the life of the Buddha.

Proceeding clockwise around the chedi, as is the custom at all Buddhist monuments, you can weave between the outer promenade and the inner cloister via ornate doors that punctuate the dividing wall. The outer promenade is ringed by Buddha images employing a wide variety of mudras, or hand gestures, each of which has a specific meaning for Buddhists, and most of them are explained on plaques beside them. Throughout the rest of the country, most Buddha images portray one of just five or six common mudras, making this collection rather unique. The promenade is also dotted with **trees**, many of which have religious significance, such as the bodhi tree (*ficus religiosa*), under one of which the Buddha was meditating when he achieved enlightenment.

In the **east viharn**, look out for a mural showing a diagrammatic cross-section of the chedi with the encased original at its core. Further round, the **south viharn** staircase, about halfway up, is flanked by a three-dimensional replica of the original chedi topped by a Khmer prang (east side) and a model of the venerated chedi at Nakhon Si Thammarat (west side). The **west viharn** houses two reclining Buddhas: a sturdy, 9m-long figure in the outer chamber and a more delicate portrayal in the inner one.

Phra Pathom Chedi National Museum
Just east from the bottom of the chedi's south staircase • Charge

Within the chedi compound are a couple of similarly named museums. The newer, more formal setup, the **Phra Pathom Chedi National Museum**, displays a good collection of Dvaravati-era (sixth to eleventh centuries) artefacts excavated nearby, including Wheels of Law (*dharmachakra*) – an emblem introduced by Theravada Buddhists before naturalistic images were permitted – and Buddha statuary with the U-shaped robe and thick facial features characteristic of Dvaravati sculpture. Together, the exhibits tell the story of how external influences, particularly those from India, shaped local beliefs.

Phra Pathom Chedi Museum
Halfway up the steps near the east viharn • Free

The **Phra Pathom Chedi Museum** is a magpie's nest of a collection, offering a broader, more domestic introduction to Nakhon Pathom's history than the National Museum. More a curiosity shop than a museum, the small room and entranceway are filled with Buddhist amulets, seashells, gold and silver needles, Chinese ceramics, Thai musical instruments and ancient statues – enough for a short but satisfying browse.

Sanam Chandra Palace
A 10min walk west of the chedi along Thanon Rajdamnoen • Closed for renovations at the time of writing

Before ascending to the throne in 1910, Rama VI made several pilgrimages to the Phra Pathom Chedi, eventually choosing this 335-acre plot west of the pagoda as the location for a convenient new country retreat. The resulting complex of elegant wooden buildings, known as **Sanam Chandra Palace**, was designed to blend Western and Eastern styles, and a handful of its main buildings are now open to the public. Its principal structure, the **Jalimangalasana Residence**, evokes a miniature Bavarian castle, complete with turrets and red-tiled roof; the **Marirajrattabalang Residence** is a more oriental-style pavilion, built of teak and painted a deep rose colour inside and out; and the **Thub Kwan Residence** is an unadorned traditional Thai-style house of polished, unpainted golden teak. They each contain royal artefacts and memorabilia and, as such, visitors should take care to dress appropriately.

Sanamchandra Art Gallery

Just outside Sanam Chandra Palace's southern perimeter, behind the Thub Kwan Residence on Thanon Rajamanka Nai • Free • ⓦ art-centre.su.ac.th • If coming from the chedi, expect to pay around B40 for a motorbike taxi

If you're interested in modern Thai art, it's well worth seeing what's on at the **Sanamchandra Art Gallery**. A purpose-built art centre set among outlying Sanam Chandra villas, it's one of the exhibition spaces for Bangkok's premier art school, Silpakorn University, whose satellite campus is just across the road. Their annual student show, held here every September and October, is usually very interesting.

ARRIVAL AND DEPARTURE   NAKHON PATHOM

By train To get to the chedi compound's northern gate from the train station, walk south for 200m down Thanon Rotfai, across the khlong and past the covered market.
Destinations Bangkok Hualamphong (2 daily; 1hr 25min; stopping at Sanam Chandra Palace Station 15min later); Bangkok Krungthep Aphiwat (10–12 daily; 1hr); Bangkok Thonburi (9 daily, with 3 stopping at Sanam Chandra Palace Station 15min later; 1hr 10min); Kanchanaburi (2 daily; 1hr 30min); Nam Tok (2 daily; 3hr 30min); Phetchaburi (12–14 daily; 1hr 20min–2hr 30min).
By bus There are buses and a/c minibuses to Nakhon Pathom from Bangkok's Southern Bus Terminal, and buses from Damnoen Saduak and Kanchanaburi. On arrival, buses drop passengers either in front of the police station across Thanon Kwaa Phra from the chedi's southern entrance, or beside the khlong, 100m from the northern gate towards the train station. Buses heading for Kanchanaburi and Damnoen Saduak collect passengers outside the police station across from the chedi's southern gate. Buses bound for Bangkok pick up from Thanon Phaya Pan on the north bank of the khlong near the train station.
Destinations Bangkok (every 30min; 40min–1hr 20min); Damnoen Saduak (roughly hourly; 1hr); Kanchanaburi (every 20min; 1hr 45min–2hr).

EATING

Fairy Tale West side of Thanon Rotfai at no. 307, just south of the train station ⓦ facebook.com/profile.php?id=100066834052602. Almost hidden behind the food stalls that line the street, this cosy a/c café-bakery serves yummy crêpes, waffles and even French fries. It's an ideal spot to while away time waiting for a train. B̲B̲
Hot-food stalls Just outside the chedi compound's southern wall, near the museum. The obvious place to eat during the day. There are lots of options here, from noodle soup to grilled chicken and rice dishes. B̲
Lung Loy Pa Lan North side of Highway 4: to get there from the southwest corner of the chedi compound, head west on Thanon Rajvithee, then immediately south on winding Thanon Bhudtharucksa for just over 1km ⓦ facebook.com/krualoonglypalan. Nakhon Pathom's best local restaurant is very popular with pilgrims visiting the chedi. Top choices are whole snakehead fish, salted and grilled on bamboo sticks, as well as very good grilled river prawns, but there are also more affordable regional specialities such as very spicy *kaeng pa* (jungle curry) with catfish. B̲B̲

Damnoen Saduak

To get an idea of what shopping in Bangkok used to be like before all the canals were tarmacked over, many people take an early-morning trip to the century-old **floating market** at **DAMNOEN SADUAK**. Sixty kilometres south of Nakhon Pathom and just over a hundred kilometres from Bangkok, it's just about accessible on a day-trip from the capital with a very early start – the market is open every day from about 6am to

11am. Vineyards and orchards here back onto a labyrinth of narrow canals, and every morning local market gardeners ply these waterways in paddleboats full of fresh fruit, vegetables and tourist-tempting soft drinks and souvenirs. Most dress in the blue denim jacket and high-topped straw hat traditionally favoured by Thai farmers, so it all looks very picturesque; however, the setup is clearly geared to tourists rather than locals, so the place lacks an authentic aura. For a more engaging experience, consider going instead to the floating markets at Amphawa, 10km south of Damnoen Saduak (see page 132), or at Tha Kha, 10km to the east of Damnoen Saduak (see page 133).

The market

The target for most tour groups is **Talat Khlong Ton Kem**, 2km west of Damnoen Saduak's tiny town centre at the intersection of Khlong Damnoen Saduak and Khlong Thong Lang. Many of the wooden houses here have been converted into warehouse-style souvenir shops and tourist restaurants, diverting trade away from the khlong vendors and into the hands of large commercial enterprises. Nonetheless, a semblance of traditional water trade continues, and the two bridges between Ton Kem and **Talat Khlong Hia Kui** (a little further south down Khlong Thong Lang) make decent vantage points.

Touts invariably congregate at the Ton Kem pier to hassle you into taking a **rowing boat trip** around the khlong network; this is worth considering and far preferable to being propelled between markets at top speed in one of the noisy longtail boats,

VISITING THE FLOATING MARKETS

For many visitors to Thailand, an essential item on their itinerary is a trip to a **floating market** (*talat nam*), to witness scenes of vendors selling fruit, flowers, vegetables and noodle dishes from **sampans** on the canals that were once the principal means of travelling around the country. Unfortunately, such bucolic scenes are from a bygone era, and while it's still possible to visit a floating market, many visitors regret the experience, feeling they've been led into a tourist trap, which is often exactly the case.

Most day tours from Bangkok head for **Damnoen Saduak**, where visitors are whisked around in noisy longtail boats, which pause for souvenir hawkers to make their pitch in between staged photos of smiling vendors dressed in traditional outfits with neatly arranged boatloads of produce. Such day-trips also include visits to dubious animal shows or handicraft workshops in an attempt to extract more tourist dollars.

In recent years, Thais have started heading for **Amphawa** (see page 132) at weekends, which has a more authentic atmosphere than Damnoen Saduak, though the least commercialized floating market is at **Tha Kha** (see page 133) on weekends. While most boat trips in these places focus on the markets, it's also possible to venture out onto the canals after dark to **watch the fireflies** twinkling romantically in their favourite lamphu trees like delicate strings of fairylights (best in the rainy season).

One problem of visits to this area is that most markets, with the exception of Amphawa, are at their best at the crack of dawn, but since they are around 100km from Bangkok, it takes at least a couple of hours for tour groups to get there. If you're keen to see them in the early hours, it's worth staying overnight in Damnoen Saduak, Amphawa or even Samut Songkhram (see page 130) and making arrangements for an early morning start; Tha Kha market is about 10km from each of these places.

While they cover less distance than the longtail boats, rowing boats make for a much more relaxing experience; they are available for hire from Ton Kem pier in Damnoen Saduak and at Tha Kha. Don't forget to take a hat or umbrella and plenty of sunscreen. There are no longer any rowing boats at Amphawa, only longtail boats offering roughly hour-long trips to see the fireflies.

which cost far more to charter. For a less hectic and more sensitive look at the markets, explore via the walkways beside the canals.

ARRIVAL AND ACCOMMODATION DAMNOEN SADUAK

BY BUS
From/to Bangkok Damnoen Saduak is 109km from Bangkok, so to reach the market in good time you have to catch one of the earliest buses or a/c minibuses from the capital's Southern Bus Terminal (roughly every 30min from 5.30am; 1hr 30min–2hr). Alternatively, you can join one of the day-trips from Bangkok, which generally give you two hours at the market, then stop at a handicraft village and/or animal show before dropping you back in the capital.
From Kanchanaburi Take a Ratchaburi-bound bus as far as Bang Phe (every 20min from 5.10am; 1hr 30min), then change for the 30min journey to Damnoen Saduak.
From Phetchaburi To get to Damnoen Saduak from Phetchaburi, catch any Bangkok-bound bus and change at Samut Songkhram.
Getting into town Damnoen Saduak's bus terminal is just north of Thanarat Bridge and Khlong Damnoen Saduak, on the main Nakhon Pathom–Samut Songkhram road, Highway 325. Frequent yellow songthaews cover the 2km to Ton Kem.

ACCOMMODATION
Maikaew Damnoen Resort 333 Moo 9 ⓦmaikaew.com. Just a few steps east of the floating market, this relaxing resort has a variety of smart, comfortable rooms, bungalows and traditional-style teak houses, a canalside restaurant that uses vegetables from their hydroponic farm, two saltwater swimming pools, a kids' pool and a Jacuzzi. They also have complimentary bicycles and offer a range of boat trips in the area (see website for details), so it makes a good springboard for exploration of the nearby canals. Prices rise a little at weekends. **BB**

Samut Songkhram

Rarely visited by foreign tourists and yet within easy reach of Bangkok, the tiny estuarine province of **Samut Songkhram** is nourished by the Mae Klong River as it meanders through on the last leg of its route to the Gulf. Fishing is an important industry round here, and big wooden boats are still built in riverside yards near the estuary; further inland, fruit is the main source of income, particularly pomelos, lychees, guavas and coconuts. But for visitors it is the network of three hundred **canals** woven around the river, and the traditional way of life the waterways still support, that makes a stay of a few days appealing. As well as some of the most interesting **floating markets** in Thailand – notably at **Amphawa** and **Tha Kha** – there are chances to witness traditional cottage industries such as palm-sugar production and *bencharong* ceramic-painting, plus more than a hundred historic temples to admire, a number of them dating back to the reign of Rama II, who was born in the province. The other famous sons of the region are Eng and Chang, the "original" Siamese twins, who grew up in the province (see page 86).

Samut Songkhram town

The provincial capital – officially called **SAMUT SONGKHRAM** but usually referred to by locals as **Mae Klong**, after the river that cuts through it – is a useful base for trips to the floating markets at Amphawa and Tha Kha. It's a pleasant enough market town, which, despite its proximity to Bangkok, remains relatively unaffected by Western influences. However, there's little reason to linger here during the day as all the local sights are out of town, mainly in **Amphawa** district a few kilometres upriver (see page 132).

To savour a real Thai seaside atmosphere, make the 10km trip to **Don Hoi Lot** at the mouth of the Mae Klong estuary (regular songthaews run there from the bus station), from where you can gaze out across the murky waters of the Gulf of Thailand from the shade of casuarina trees. Thais flock here in droves to gobble up *hoi lot*, or razor clams, which are harvested in their sackloads at low tide and typically served sun-dried and grilled on a stick or in a spicy stir-fry, *hoi lot pat cha*. You can order them – and lots of

> **THE SLOW TRAIN TO SAMUT SONGKHRAM**
>
> The most enjoyable way of travelling to Samut Songkhram is by **train** from Bangkok – a scenic, albeit convoluted, journey that involves changing lines and catching a boat across the river in Samut Sakhon and could take up to three hours. It's a very unusual route, being single track and for much of the way squeezed in between homes, palms and mangroves, and, most memorably, between market stalls, so that at both the Samut Sakhon and Samut Songkhram termini the train really does chug to a standstill amid the trays of seafood.
>
> Trains to Samut Sakhon (1hr) leave approximately hourly from Bangkok's **Wongwian Yai Station** in southern Thonburi (which is within walking distance of Wongwian Yai Skytrain station). The train pulls up right inside the wet market at **Samut Sakhon** (also known as **Mahachai** after the main local canal), a busy fishing port near the mouth of the Maenam Tha Chin. From the station, work your way through the market and take a ferry across the river to get the connecting train from **Ban Laem** on the opposite, west bank.
>
> There are only four trains a day in each direction between Ban Laem and Samut Songkhram at the end of the line (called "Mae Klong" on railway timetables; 1hr), a journey through marshes, lagoons, prawn farms, salt flats and mangrove and palm growth. Once again, at Samut Songkhram, the station is literally enveloped by the town-centre market, with traders gathering up their goods and awnings from the trackside for the arrival and departure of the train.

other cheap seafood – in any restaurant here, or buy them from street stalls, rent a mat and enjoy a picnic Thai-style.

ARRIVAL AND DEPARTURE

SAMUT SONGKHRAM TOWN

BY TRAIN
Samut Songkhram's train station is in the middle of town, on the eastern side of the Mae Klong River, with four trains a day making the 1hr trip from and to Ban Laem, where you can connect with trains from/to Bangkok (see page 131).

BY BUS FROM BANGKOK
The journey to Samut Songkhram by bus or a/c minibus from Bangkok's Southern Bus Terminal (every 20min in both directions; 1hr 30min) is fast, but the views are mostly dominated by urban sprawl. Samut Songkhram's bus station is south of the market, across from the Siam Commercial Bank off Thanon Ratchayadruksa.

CONNECTIONS TO AMPHAWA AND DAMNOEN SADUAK
By songthaew or a/c minibus Songthaews to Amphawa (approximately every 30min; 15min) and a/c minibuses to Amphawa and Damnoen Saduak, via Highway 325, leave from the bus station.

By taxi-boat Taxi-boats operate from the Mae Klong River pier, 50m west of the train station and market in the town centre. The journey upstream to Amphawa should take 20–30min.

ACCOMMODATION AND EATING

For accommodation, choose between staying in the town itself and a growing number of well-equipped resorts tucked away in the countryside. The **food stalls** near the pier, in the centre of town, make a pleasant spot for a cheap seafood lunch – for dessert, head to the **market**, near the train station, where you can buy fresh bananas, rambutans and watermelon slices. In the evening, food stalls just off Thanon Si Jumpa just north of the railway station offer a wide variety of options.

Asita Eco Resort Beside a small canal about 4km southwest of the train station and just north of Highway 35 (Thanon Rama II) w asitaresort.com. Choose between a Thai house and thatched villa at this small, luxurious resort, which is crafted from eco-friendly materials. There's a good-sized pool, a spa and bicycles for rent, plus a variety of tours on offer. Considerable discounts for weekday stays. __BBBB__

Baan Tai Had Resort On the west bank of the Mae Klong River, a couple of kilometres northwest of town w facebook.com/baantaihadresort. Good-value resort, 15min by taxi-boat from Samut Songkhram's pier (alternatively, take the ferry across the river, then a 10min ride on a motorbike taxi). With its stylish, comfortable rooms and bungalows set around an attractive garden, swimming pool and restaurant, Baan Tai Had makes a good base, not least because of its local tour programmes. __BB__

DIRECTORY

Banks and ATMs Currency exchange and ATMs are available at the branches of the main banks around the edge of Samut Songkhram market.

Amphawa

The district town of **AMPHAWA** is smaller and more atmospheric than Samut Songkhram, retaining original charm alongside modern development. Its old neighbourhoods hug the banks of the Mae Klong River and the Khlong Amphawa tributary, the wooden homes and shops facing the water and accessed either by boat or on foot along one of the waterfront walkways. The tradition of holding a **floating market** on the canal near Wat Amphawan has been revived for weekending Bangkokians and tourists, with traders setting up at around lunchtime and staying out until around 9pm every Friday, Saturday and Sunday. Amphawa's main street, Thanon Prachaset, runs west for about a kilometre from a T-junction with Highway 325 (the road from Damnoen Saduak to Samut Songkhram), before hitting the floating market at Khlong Amphawa (about 200m north of its confluence with the Mae Klong River), then Wat Amphawan and the Rama II Memorial Park.

Rama II Memorial Park

5min walk west of Amphawa market and khlong • Park and Museum Charge • **W** facebook.com/kingrama2samutsongkram/

Rama II was born in Amphawa (his mother's home town) in 1767 and is honoured with a memorial park and temple erected on the site of his probable birthplace, beside the Mae Klong River on the western edge of Amphawa town.

Rama II, or Phra Buddhalertla Naphalai as he is known in Thai, is remembered as a cultured king who wrote poems and plays, and the **museum** at the heart of the **Rama II Memorial Park** displays lots of rather esoteric kingly memorabilia in traditional Thai-style houses, including a big collection of nineteenth-century musical instruments and a gallery of *khon* masks used in traditional theatre.

On the eastern edge of the park, **Wat Amphawan** is graced with a statue of the king and decorated with murals that depict scenes from his life, including a behind-the-altar panorama of nineteenth-century Bangkok, with Ratanakosin Island's Grand Palace, Wat Pho and Sanam Luang still recognizable to modern eyes.

Amphawa Chaipattananurak

On the west bank of Khlong Amphawa, a 5min walk north of Amphawa market • **W** amphawanurak.com • Free

The **Amphawa Chaipattananurak** centre was established to conserve the cultural heritage of the town, and is divided into five areas, each of which provides interesting information about the traditional lifestyle of the region. The Community Exhibition Room reflects the way of life of local communities, the Agricultural Demonstration Farm features many of the local fruit trees, and the Nakhawarang Cultural Ground is used for performances of traditional music, puppet shows and cooking demonstrations. There are also community shops selling local products and souvenirs, and an atmospheric coffee shop and tea house beside the canal with a retro interior.

Pinsuwan bencharong showroom and workshop

About 1km (15min walk) east of Amphawa Chaipattananurak, just west of H325 (look for the P Ben sign in front of a compound of traditional houses) **W** facebook.com/p/Pinsuwan-Benjarong-100057756274084 • Free

The **Pinsuwan bencharong workshop** specializes in reproductions of famous antique *bencharong* ceramics, the exquisite five-coloured pottery that used to be the tableware of choice for the Thai aristocracy and is now a prized collectors' item. Here you can watch the manufacturing process in action (the shop is open but the workshop is closed on Sundays), and then buy items off the shelf or even order your own glittering, custom-made bowls, which can then be delivered to your hotel or shipped back home.

Wat Chulamani
A few hundred metres east of Pinsuwan, across H325, or a 5min boat ride from Amphawa market along Khlong Amphawa

The canalside **Wat Chulamani** was until the late 1980s the domain of the locally famous abbot Luang Pho Nuang, a man believed by many to possess special powers, and followers still come to the temple to pay respects to his body, which is preserved in a glass-sided coffin in the main viharn. The breathtakingly detailed decor inside the viharn is testament to the devotion he inspired: the intricate black-and-gold lacquered artwork that covers every surface took years and cost millions of baht to complete. Across the temple compound, the bot's modern, pastel-toned murals tell the story of the Buddha's life, beginning inside the door on the right with a scene showing the young Buddha emerging from a tent (his birth) and being able to walk on lilypads straight away. The death of the Buddha and his entry into Nirvana are depicted on the wall behind the altar.

ARRIVAL AND DEPARTURE   AMPHAWA

From/to Bangkok A/c minibuses (at least hourly; 2hr) run to Amphawa from Bangkok's Southern Bus Terminal (*Sathaanii Sai Tai Mai*). There's no bus station in tiny Amphawa, but you'll find the a/c minibus offices on the high street, Thanon Prachaset, just east of Khlong Amphawa in the town centre.

From/to Samut Songkhram Frequent songthaews from the market in Samut Songkhram (approximately every 30min; 15min) arrive at Amphawa's high street, Thanon Prachaset, just east of Khlong Amphawa.

GETTING AROUND AND INFORMATION

By boat The most appealing way to explore the area is by boat (see page 129).
By bicycle Some resorts, such as *Baan Amphawa Resort & Spa* (see below), rent out bicycles.

Tourist office TAT has an office on the east side of H325, just south of the T-junction with Thanon Prachaset (daily 8.30am–4.30pm; ☏ 034 752847–8, ✉ tatsmsk@tat.or.th).

ACCOMMODATION AND EATING

Amphawa Na Non 96 Thanon Prachaset ⓦ amphawa nanon.com. This stylish place sits on Amphawa's main street just a minute's walk east of the floating market. It caters mostly to Thais but staff speak English and the big, bright, balconied rooms offer every comfort. Higher rates on Fri & Sat nights. B̲B̲B̲

Baan Amphawa Resort & Spa 22 Thanon Bangkapom Kaewfah, off Highway 325 about 2km south of the T-junction with Thanon Prachaset ⓦ baanamphawa. com. A large, business-friendly resort hotel on the Mae Klong River, with attractive rooms in a series of traditional-style wooden buildings as well as more contemporary villas. There are two swimming pools, a spa, and a good riverfront restaurant. B̲B̲B̲B̲

Chaba Baan Cham Resort Just across Khlong Amphawa from Amphawa Chaipattananurak ⓦ facebook.com/chababaancham.resort. Twelve appealing contemporary rooms with French windows and lots of varnished wood, equipped with a/c, hot showers, TVs and fridges. Slightly higher rates on Fri & Sat nights. B̲B̲

Jao Sam Ran On the bank of the Mae Klong River, about 100m east of Khlong Amphawa, near the police station (the English sign says "Chal Sam Rhand") ☏ 034 751811. On a shady terrace overlooking the broad river, this evening-time restaurant specializes in fresh seafood, including lots of mackerel dishes and very good grey mullet in a three-flavoured sauce, and hosts live music. B̲B̲

Tha Ka floating market
Ban Tha Kha, 10km northeast of Amphawa and 10km north of Samut Songkhram • Sat, Sun & public holidays roughly 7am–noon • By boat, it can be reached in about half an hour from Amphawa; by car, it's signposted to the east of H325 between Damnoen Saduak and Amphawa

Unlike at the over-touristed market at nearby Damnoen Saduak, the **floating market** in the village of **Tha Kha** is still largely the province of local residents. It's possible to get here by boat from Amphawa, though most visitors come by road and begin their boat tour here. Market gardeners paddle up here in their small wooden sampans, or motor along in their noisy longtails, the boats piled high either with whatever's in season, be it pomelos or betel nuts, rambutans or okra, or with perennially popular snacks like hot noodle soup and freshly cooked satay. Their main customers are canalside residents and other traders, so the atmosphere is still pleasingly, but not artificially, traditional. As with the other markets in the area, boatmen also offer evening rides to watch the fireflies. The Tha Kha market attracts Thai tourist groups and occasional adventurous foreigners; it's best to pre-arrange a trip the day before through your accommodation in the area.

Phetchaburi

Straddling the Phet River about 120km south of Bangkok, the provincial capital of **PHETCHABURI** (sometimes "Phetburi"; meaning "Diamond City") has been settled since at least the eleventh century, when the Khmers ruled the region. It was an important producer of salt, gathered from the nearby coastal salt pans, and rose to greater prominence in the seventeenth century as a trading post between the Andaman Sea ports and Ayutthaya. Despite periodic incursions from the Burmese, the town gained a reputation as a cultural centre – as the ornamentation of its older temples testifies – and after the new capital was established in Bangkok it became a favourite country retreat of Rama IV, who had a hilltop palace, **Phra Nakhon Khiri**, built here in the 1850s. Modern Phetchaburi is known for its limes and rose apples, but its main claim to fame is as one of Thailand's finest sweet-making centres, the essential ingredient for its assortment of *khanom* being the sugar extracted from the sweet-sapped palms that cover the province. This being very much a cottage industry, today's downtown Phetchaburi has lost relatively little of the ambience that so attracted Rama IV: the central riverside area is hemmed in by historic wats in varying states of disrepair, along with plenty of traditional wooden shophouses. The town's top three temples, described below, can be seen on a leisurely two-hour circular walk beginning from Chomrut Bridge, while Phetchaburi's other significant sight, the palace-museum at Phra Nakhon Khiri, is on a hill about 1km west of the bridge.

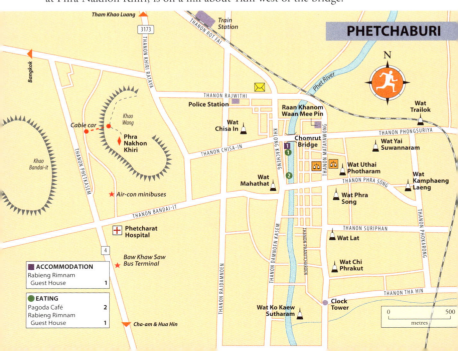

Despite the attractions of its old quarter, Phetchaburi gets few overnight visitors as most people see it on a day-trip from Bangkok, Hua Hin or Cha-am. The town sees more overnighters during the **Phra Nakhon Khiri Fair**, spread over at least a week in February or March, which features traditional cultural performances, handicraft demonstrations and fireworks displays.

Wat Yai Suwannaram
Thanon Phongsuriya, about 700m east of Chomrut Bridge

Of all Phetchaburi's temples, the most attractive is the still-functioning seventeenth-century **Wat Yai Suwannaram**. The temple's fine old teak **sala** has elaborately carved doors, bearing a gash reputedly inflicted by the Burmese in 1760 as they plundered their way towards Ayutthaya. Across from the *sala* and hidden behind high, whitewashed walls stands the windowless Ayutthaya-style bot. The bot compound overlooks a pond, in the middle of which stands a small but well-preserved scripture library, or **ho trai**: such structures were built on stilts over water to prevent ants and other insects destroying the precious documents. Enter the walled compound from the south and make a clockwise tour of the cloisters filled with Buddha statues before entering the bot itself via the eastern doorway (if the door is locked, one of the monks will get the key for you). The **bot** is supported by intricately patterned red and gold pillars and contains a remarkable, if rather faded, set of murals, depicting Indra, Brahma and other lower-ranking divinities ranged in five rows of ascending importance. Once you've admired the interior, walk to the back of the bot, passing behind the central cluster of Buddha images, to find another Buddha image seated against the back wall: climb the steps in front of this statue to get a close-up of the left foot, which for some reason was cast with six toes.

Wat Kamphaeng Laeng
Thanon Phra Song, a 15min walk east and then south of Wat Yai

The five tumbledown prangs of **Wat Kamphaeng Laeng** mark out Phetchaburi as the likely southernmost outpost of the Khmer empire. Built probably in the thirteenth century to honour the Hindu deity Shiva and set out in a cruciform arrangement facing east, the laterite corncob-style prangs were later adapted for Buddhist use, as can be seen from the two that now house Buddha images. There has been some attempt to restore a few of the carvings and false balustraded windows, but these days worshippers congregate in the modern whitewashed wat behind these shrines, leaving the atmospheric and appealingly quaint collection of decaying prangs and casuarina topiary to chickens, stray dogs and the occasional tourist.

Wat Mahathat
Thanon Damnoen Kasem

Heading west along Thanon Phra Song from Wat Kamphaeng Laeng, across the river you can see the prangs of Phetchaburi's most fully restored and important temple, **Wat Mahathat**, long before you reach them. Boasting the "Mahathat" title only since 1954 – when the requisite Buddha relics were donated by the king – it was probably founded in the fourteenth century, but suffered badly at the hands of the Burmese. The five landmark prangs at its heart are adorned with stucco figures of mythical creatures, though these are nothing compared with those on the roofs of the main viharn and the bot. Instead of tapering off into the usual serpentine *chofa*, the gables are studded with miniature *thep* and *deva* figures (angels and gods), which add an almost mischievous vitality to the place. In a similar vein, a couple of gold-embossed crocodiles snarl above the entrance to the bot, and a caricature carving of a bespectacled man rubs shoulders with mythical giants in a relief around the base of the gold Buddha, housed in a separate mondop nearby.

Khao Wang

Dominating Phetchaburi's western outskirts stands Rama IV's palace, a stew of mid-nineteenth-century Thai and European styles scattered over the crest of the hill known as **Khao Wang** ("Palace Hill"). During his day, the royal entourage would struggle its way up the steep brick path to the summit, but now there's a **cable car** (charge, including admission to the palace; visitors are asked to dress modestly, covering knees and shoulders) which starts from the western flank of the hill off Highway 4; there's also a path up the eastern flank, starting near Thanon Rajwithi. If you do walk up the hill, be warned that hundreds of quite aggressive monkeys hang out at its base and on the path to the top.

Up top, the wooded hill is littered with wats, prangs, chedis, whitewashed gazebos and lots more, in an ill-assorted combination of architectural idioms – the prang-topped viharn, washed all over in burnt sienna, is particularly ungainly. Whenever the king came on an excursion here, he stayed in the airy summer house, **Phra Nakhon Khiri**, with its Mediterranean-style shutters and verandas. Now a museum, it houses a moderately interesting collection of ceramics, furniture and other artefacts given to the royal family by foreign friends. Besides being cool and breezy, Khao Wang also proved to be a good stargazing spot, so Rama IV, a keen astronomer, had an open-sided, glass-domed observatory built close to his sleeping quarters.

ARRIVAL AND DEPARTURE　　　　　　　　　　　　　　　　　　　　　PHETCHABURI

BY TRAIN
Phetchaburi station is on the north side of the town centre. Destinations Bangkok (Hualamphong Station 1 daily, Krungthep Aphiwat 10–12 daily, Thonburi Station 2 daily; 2hr 45min–3hr 45min); Nakhon Pathom (13–15 daily; 1hr 30min–2hr).

BY BUS
There's no longer a dedicated service between Bangkok and Phetchaburi, which is now served by through-buses on their way to or from Bangkok – all services between the capital and southern Thailand have to pass through the town on Highway 4.
Through-buses There's a small Baw Khaw Saw terminal on the east side of Highway 4 (Thanon Phetkasem), which is where southbound through-buses will set you down or pick you up. Northbound through-buses on their way to Bangkok stop on the opposite side of the highway at "Sii Yaek Phetcharat", the crossroads of Highway 4 and Thanon Bandai-It by Phetcharat Hospital. Songthaews and motorbike taxis run between Highway 4 and the town centre.

BY MINIBUS
Several companies, which all now congregate to the south of Khao Wang near Wat Tham Kaeo, offer licensed a/c minibuses to the Southern Bus Terminal in Bangkok, Ratchaburi, Nakhon Pathom and Kanchanaburi.

GETTING AROUND

By samlor or songthaew Shared songthaews circulate round the town, but to see the major temples in a day and have sufficient energy left for climbing Khao Wang, you might want to hire a samlor or a songthaew for a couple of hours.

INFORMATION AND TOURS

Tourist information There's no TAT office in town, but *Rabieng Rimnam Guest House* is a good source of local information. It can also book day-trips and multi-day visits to Kaeng Krachan National Park for hiking (two or three nights are ideal for trekking into the jungle), roughly from November to June or July.

ACCOMMODATION　　　　　　　　　　　　　　　　　　　　　　　　SEE MAP PAGE 134

Rabieng Rimnam Guest House 1 Thanon Chisa-in, on the southwest corner of Chomrut Bridge ⓦ facebook.com/rabiengrimnampetchbur. Occupying a century-old house next to the Phet River and, less appealingly, a noisy main road, this popular, central guesthouse offers very simple rooms with shared, cold-water bathrooms, lots of local information and the best restaurant in town. Good rates for singles. B̄

EATING　　　　　　　　　　　　　　　　　　　　　　　　　　　　　SEE MAP PAGE 134

As well as for *khanom*, Phetchaburi is famous for savoury **khao chae**: originally a Mon dish designed to cool you down in the hot season, it consists of rice in chilled, flower-scented water served with delicate, fried side dishes, such

> **SWEET PHETBURI**
>
> Almost half the shops in Phetchaburi stock the town's famous **khanom** (sweet snacks), as do many of the souvenir stalls crowding the base of Khao Wang and vendors at the day market on Thanon Matayawong. The most well-known local speciality is *maw kaeng* (best sampled from Raan Khanom Waan Mae Pin on the west side of Thanon Matayawong, just north of Phongsuriya), a baked sweet egg custard made with mung beans and coconut and sometimes flavoured with lotus seeds, durian or taro. Other Phetchaburi classics to look out for include *khanom taan*, small, steamed, saffron-coloured cakes made with local palm sugar, coconut and rice flour, and wrapped in banana-leaf cases; and *thong yot*, orange balls of palm sugar and baked egg yolk.

as shredded Chinese radish and balls of shrimp paste, dried fish and palm sugar. It's available at the day market until sold out, usually around 3pm. There's a nice little **night market** on the small road parallel to and immediately west of Thanon Matayawong.

Pagoda Café Thanon Khlong Kacheng, opposite Wat Mahathat ⓦ facebook.com/PagodaCafePhetburi. The cool industrial look of polished concrete and red bricks may be looking all-too-familiar by now on your travels, but the espresso coffees are very good, and it serves cakes and teas, too. B̄

Rabieng Rimnam Guest House 1 Thanon Chisa-in, on the southwest corner of Chomrut Bridge ⓦ facebook.com/rabiengrimnampetchburi. The town's best restaurant, an airy, wooden house with riverside tables, attached to the guesthouse of the same name. It offers a long and interesting menu of inexpensive Thai dishes, from banana-blossom salad to the tasty Phetchaburi speciality, sugar-palm fruit curry with prawns and is deservedly popular with local diners. B̄B̄

Kanchanaburi

Set at the confluence of two rivers, the Kwai Noi and the Kwai Yai, the provincial capital of **KANCHANABURI** makes the perfect getaway from Bangkok, 140km away. With its rich wartime history, plentiful supply of traveller-oriented accommodation and countless possibilities for easy forays into the surrounding countryside, there are plenty of reasons to linger here, and many visitors end up staying longer than planned. The big appeal is the river: that it's the famous River Kwai (pronounced "*khwae*" as in "quell" rather than "*kwai*" as in "quite") is a bonus, but the more immediate attractions are the guesthouses and restaurants that overlook the waterway, many of them offering fine views of the jagged limestone peaks beyond. The other main attraction is the drama of a ride on the **Death Railway** (see page 140).

The heart of Kanchanaburi's ever-expanding travellers' scene dominates the southern end of **Thanon Maenam Kwai** (also spelt Kwae) and is within easy reach of the train station, but the real town centre is some distance away, running north from the bus station up the town's main drag, **Thanon Saeng Chuto**. Between this road and the river you'll find most of the town's **war sights**, with the infamous **Bridge over the River Kwai** marking the northern limit. Every day, tour groups and day-trippers descend on the Bridge, a symbol of Japanese atrocities in the region that's now insensitively commercialized – the town's main **war museums** and **cemeteries** are actually much more moving. Overlooking the huge **Don Rak Kanchanaburi war cemetery**, the **Thailand–Burma Railway Centre** provides shockingly instructive accounts of a period not publicly documented outside this region. The **JEATH War Museum** at the southeast end of town is also worth a visit, though you're strongly advised to avoid the insensitive World War II Museum by the Bridge (which also misleadingly labels itself as the "JEATH War Museum").

The **Chungkai war cemetery** and a handful of moderately interesting temples – including **Wat Tham Khao Poon** and **Wat Ban Tham** – provide the focus for pleasurable trips west of the town centre.

Kanchanaburi gets packed during its annual *son et lumière* **River Kwai Bridge Festival**, held over ten nights from the end of November to commemorate the first Allied bombing of the Bridge on November 28, 1944, so book accommodation well ahead at this time.

Thailand–Burma Railway Centre

Across from the train station, next to the Don Rak Kanchanaburi War Cemetery on Thanon Jaokannun • Charge • tbrconline.com

The modern **Thailand–Burma Railway Centre** is by far the best place to start any tour of Kanchanaburi's World War II memorials. It was founded to provide an informed context and research centre for the thousands who visit the POW graves every week. The result is a comprehensive and sophisticated history of the entire Thailand–Burma Railway line, with plenty of original artefacts, illustrations and scale models, and particularly strong sections on the planning and construction of the railway, and on the subsequent operation, destruction and decommissioning of the line. There is more of a focus on the line itself here than at the more emotive Hellfire Pass Memorial Museum (see page 148), but the human stories are well documented too, notably via some extraordinary original photographs and video footage shot by Japanese engineers, as well as through unique interviews with surviving Asian labourers on the railway.

There's a friendly café upstairs, and the shop inside the entrance stocks some interesting books on the railway. If you want to learn more about the area's World War II history, guides can be hired for half-, full- and multi-day tours.

Kanchanaburi War Cemetery (Don Rak)

Across Thanon Saeng Chuto from the train station • Free

One Allied POW died for each railway sleeper laid on the Thailand–Burma Railway (see page 140), or so the story goes, and many of them are buried in Kanchanaburi's two war cemeteries, **Don Rak Kanchanaburi War Cemetery** and Chungkai Cemetery (see page 141). Of all the region's war sights, the cemeteries are the only places to have remained untouched by commercial enterprise. Don Rak is the bigger of the two, with 6982 POW graves laid out in straight lines amid immaculate lawns and flowering shrubs, maintained by the Commonwealth War Graves Commission. It was established after the war, on a plot adjacent to the town's Chinese cemetery, as the final resting place for the remains that had been hurriedly interred at dozens of makeshift POW-camp gravesites all the way up the line. Many of the identical stone memorial slabs in Don Rak state simply, "A man who died for his country"; others, inscribed with names, dates and regiments, indicate that the overwhelming majority of the dead were under 25 years old. A commemorative service is held here, and at Hellfire Pass (see page 147), every year on April 25, Anzac Day.

The Bridge over the River Kwai

Just west of the River Kwai Bridge Train Station • The public songthaews along Thanon Saeng Chuto pass close by or it's a 15–20min walk north of the main Thanon Maenam Kwai guesthouse area

For most people, the plain steel arches of the **Bridge over the River Kwai** come as a disappointment: as a war memorial it lacks both the emotive punch of the museums and the perceptible drama of spots further up the line, and as a bridge it looks nothing out of the ordinary – certainly not as awesomely hard to construct as it appears in David Lean's famous 1957 film, *Bridge on the River Kwai* (which was in fact shot in Sri Lanka). But it is the link with the multi-Oscar-winning film, of course, that draws tour buses by the dozen, and makes the Bridge approach seethe with trinket-sellers and touts. For all the commercialization of the place, however, you can't really come to the Kwai and not see it.

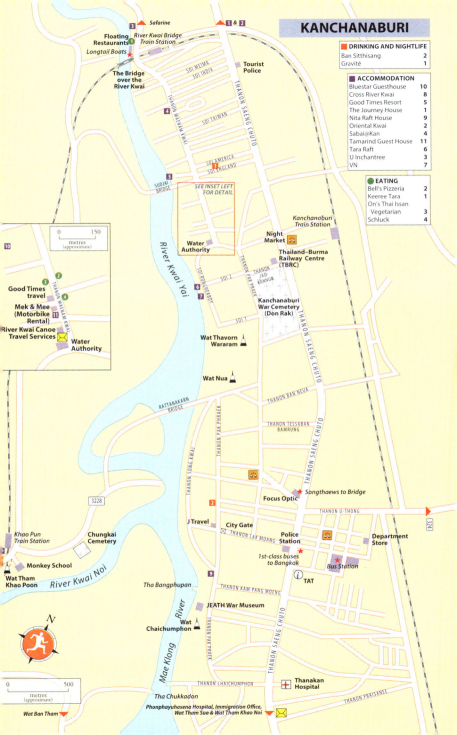

THE DEATH RAILWAY

Shortly after entering World War II in December 1941, with the Straits of Malacca still mined and patrolled by the Allies, Japan began looking for an alternative supply route to connect its newly acquired territories that stretched from Singapore to the Myanmar–India border, with the eventual aim of being able to invade India from the northeast. In spite of the almost impenetrable terrain, the River Kwai basin was chosen as the route for a new **Thailand–Burma Railway**, the aim being to join the existing terminals of Nong Pladuk in Thailand (51km southeast of Kanchanaburi near Ban Pong, on Thailand's Southern Railway Line) and Thanbyuzayat in Myanmar – a total distance of 415km. British engineers had investigated the possibility of constructing such a railway before the war and had estimated it would take six years to build.

Over 60,000 British, Australian, Dutch and American POWs were shipped up from captured Southeast Asian territories to work on the link, their numbers augmented by as many as 250,000 conscripted Asian labourers. Work began at both ends in October 1942. Three million cubic metres of rock were shifted and 14km of bridges built with little else but picks and shovels, dynamite and pulleys. By the time the line was completed, just a year later, it had more than earned its nickname, the **Death Railway**: 12,400 POWs and an estimated 90,000 Asian labourers died while working on it.

The appalling conditions and Japanese brutality were the consequences of the **samurai code**: Japanese soldiers abhorred the disgrace of imprisonment – to them, ritual suicide was the only honourable option open to a prisoner – and therefore considered that Allied POWs had forfeited any rights as human beings. Food rations were meagre for men forced into backbreaking eighteen-hour shifts, often followed by night-long marches to the next camp. Many suffered from beriberi, many more died of dysentery-induced starvation, but the biggest killers were cholera and malaria, particularly during the monsoon. It is said that one man died for every sleeper laid on the track.

The two lines finally met at Konkoita, just south of present-day Sangkhlaburi, in October 1943. But as if to underscore its tragic futility, the Thailand–Myanmar link saw less than two years of active service: after the Japanese surrender on August 15, 1945, the railway came under the jurisdiction of the British who, thinking it would be used to supply Karen separatists in Myanmar, tore up 4km of track at Three Pagodas Pass, thereby cutting the Thailand–Myanmar link forever. When the Thais finally gained control of the rest of the railway, they destroyed the track all the way down to Nam Tok, apparently because it was uneconomic. Recently, however, an Australian–Thai group of volunteers and former POWs has salvaged sections of track near the fearsome stretch of line known as **Hellfire Pass**, creating a memorial walk at the pass and founding an excellent museum at the site (see page 138). There have been a number of **books** written about the Death Railway, including *The Bridge over the River Kwai* by Pierre Boulle and *The Railway Man* by Eric Lomax, both of which were made into successful films, and 2014 Booker Prize-winner *The Narrow Road to the Deep North* by Richard Flanagan. The Thailand–Burma Railway Centre stocks a selection of such books, as do the town's bookshops.

The fording of the Kwai Yai at the point just north of Kanchanaburi known as Tha Makkham was one of the first major obstacles in the construction of the Thailand–Burma Railway. Sections of a steel bridge were brought up from Java and reassembled by POWs using only pulleys and derricks. A temporary **wooden bridge** was built alongside it, taking its first train in February 1943; three months later the steel bridge was finished. Both bridges were severely damaged by Allied bombers (rather than commando-saboteurs as in the film) in 1944 and 1945, but the steel bridge was repaired after the war and is still in use today. The best way to see the bridge is by walking gingerly across it, or taking the **train** right over it: the Kanchanaburi–Nam Tok service crosses it three times a day in each direction, stopping briefly at the River Kwai Bridge station on the east bank of the river.

Thanon Pak Phraek

Between Rattanakarn Bridge and the City Gate

The historical significance of the stretch of **Thanon Pak Phraek** that runs north from Kanchanaburi's only remaining city gate has led the TAT to place information boards outside many of the old buildings, explaining their origin and use over the years. Most of these houses were built just outside the city walls in the late nineteenth or early twentieth century by Chinese and Vietnamese immigrants and reflect a variety of architectural styles. While some of the properties along the street are nothing more than run-down shophouses, others have been carefully restored and boast elaborate balconies with balustrades. Sadly, the tangle of electric cables along the street makes them less photogenic than they would otherwise be.

The more interesting buildings include the former Sumitrakarn Hotel, the first hotel in Kanchanaburi, which was built in 1937 and finally closed its doors to the public in 1979; it now functions as a shop selling household goods. Others worth a close look are Sitthisang house, built in 1920, renovated in 2009 and now opened as a charming coffee shop (see page 145); and Boonyiam Jiaranai house, which has some elaborate stucco arches on the upstairs balcony.

Kanchanaburi Skywalk

Beside the Mae Klong River on Thanon Song Kwai, towards the southern end of town • facebook.com/Skywalkkanchanaburi • Charge

Visitors now have the dubious privilege of paying to climb the stairs up to this twelve-metre-high, glass-bottomed platform that runs along the river bank. Skywalks are a recent fad in Thailand, but this one seems particularly value-free, considering that it closes well before sunset and given that the town already has a rather famous bridge with fine views over the river.

JEATH War Museum

Beside the Mae Klong River on Thanon Pak Phraek, at the southern end of town • Charge

Founded by the abbot of adjacent Wat Chaichumphon in 1977 and housed partly in reconstructed Allied POW huts of *attap* (thatched palm), the unashamedly low-tech **JEATH War Museum** was the town's first public repository for the photographs and memories of the POWs who worked on the Death Railway. The name JEATH is an acronym of six of the countries involved in the railway: Japan, England, Australia, America, Thailand and Holland. The museum has since been surpassed by the slicker and more informative exhibitions at the Thailand–Burma Railway Centre and the Hellfire Pass Memorial Museum, and is now of most interest for its small collection of wartime photographs and for its archive of newspaper articles about, and letters from, former POWs who have revisited the River Kwai.

Chungkai Cemetery

On the west bank of the Kwai Noi, 2km from Rattanakarn Bridge, along Route 3228 • Usually included in boat trips from the bridge (see page 138)

Scrupulously well-trimmed **Chungkai Cemetery** occupies a fairly tranquil roadside spot on the west bank of the Kwai Noi, at the site of a former POW camp. Some 1750 POWs are buried here; most of the gravestone inscriptions include a name and regimental insignia, and some with epitaphs such as "One corner of the world which is forever England". However, a number of the graves remain unnamed – at the upcountry camps, bodies were thrown onto mass funeral pyres, making identification impossible. The cemetery makes a pleasant cycle ride from Rattanakarn Bridge – much of the land in this area is sugar-cane country, for which Kanchanaburi has earned the title "sugar capital of Thailand".

Wat Tham Khao Poon

On the west bank of the Kwai Noi, 2km west along Route 3228 from Chungkai Cemetery and then Route 3305 (turn left at the railway line) • Charge • Usually included in boat trips from the bridge (see page 138)

At the top of Route 3305's only hill, the cave temple **Wat Tham Khao Poon** stands on the former site of a POW camp. The attraction here is a nine-chambered cave connected by a labyrinth of dank stalactite-filled passages, where almost every ledge and knob of rock is filled with religious icons, the most important being the Reclining Buddha in the main chamber. Once out of the cave system, you can walk through a bamboo "museum" with some blurry pictures from World War II. If you arrived by road, follow the sealed road through the temple compound for 150m to reach a good vantage point over the Kwai Noi, just above the train tracks, presided over by an outsized, pot-bellied golden Buddha statue; if arriving by boat, you enter the wat compound via the cliff-side steps here.

Wat Ban Tham

12km south of town on the south bank of the Mae Klong River • Head south down Thanon Saeng Chuto for about 5km, turn right onto Thanon Mae Klong (Route 3429) to cross the Mae Klong River, then turn left along the south bank; alternatively, it can be reached by boat in around 30min from the centre

Because of the limestone landscape, caves are found right around Kanchanaburi and many of them have been sanctified as shrines. **Wat Ban Tham** is one such place, and is intriguing enough to make the 12km trip from the town centre worthwhile. Travelling south down the Mae Klong to get to the temple is especially pleasant by longtail or kayak, but can also be done by road.

Wat Ban Tham was founded around six hundred years ago but its fame rests on the seventeenth-century love story that was supposedly played out in a cave on this site. A young woman called Nang Bua Klee was forced to choose between duty to her criminal father and love for the local hero by whom she had fallen pregnant; her father eventually persuaded Bua Klee to poison her sweetheart's food, but the soldier learned of the plot and killed both Bua Klee and their unborn son, whose souls are now said to be trapped in the cave at Wat Ban Tham. The cave is approached via an ostentatious Chinese-style dragon's mouth staircase, whose upper levels relate the legend in a gallery of brightly painted modern murals on the right-hand walls. Inside the cave, a woman-shaped stone has been painted in the image of the dead mother and is a popular object of worship for women trying to conceive: hopeful devotees bring pretty dresses and shoes for the image, which are hung in wardrobes to the side of the shrine, as well as toys for her son.

Wat Tham Sua and Wat Tham Khao Noi

17km south of the town centre • From Wat Ban Tham, follow the river road east for 5km and you'll see the hilltop complex on the south side of the road. If coming direct from town, the quickest route is to head south along Thanon Saeng Chuto, which becomes Highway 323, and cross the river via the signed Mae Klong Dam, then follow signs to the right. Otherwise, take any local bus as far as Tha Muang, 12km south along Highway 323, then change to a motorbike taxi to the temples

If you're in the mood for more temples, the modern hilltop wats of Tham Sua and Tham Khao Noi both afford expansive views over the Mae Klong River valley and out to the mountains beyond. Designed by a Thai architect at the end of the twentieth century, **Wat Tham Sua** was conceived in typical grandiose style and boasts a very short funicular railway. It centres on a massive seated Buddha, sheltering under a strange half-chedi, his huge palm facing forward to show the Wheel of Law inscribed across it like one of Christ's stigmata. The neighbouring Chinese-designed **Wat Tham Khao Noi** was built at the same time and is a fabulously gaudy, seven-tiered Chinese pagoda, within which a laughing Buddha competes for attention with a host of gesturing and grimacing statues and painted characters. Neighbourly relations are now obviously a little frosty: Wat Tham Seua has built an eight-storey tower that partly obstructs the pagoda's view; and, though they share the same hilltop, a wall and barbed wire now separates the two temples, so that you're obliged to descend the slope and ascend again to get from one to the other.

ARRIVAL AND DEPARTURE KANCHANABURI

BY TRAIN
The main Kanchanaburi train station (not to be confused with the River Kwai Bridge station) is just off Thanon Saeng Chuto, about 2km north of the town centre. It's within walking distance of some of the Thanon Maenam Kwai accommodation.

Services to Kanchanaburi Trains are the most scenic way to get to Kanchanaburi, but there are only two daily from Bangkok's Thonburi station (7.45am and 1.55pm), both of which are slow, all-third class (no a/c), non-reservable, ordinary trains via Nakhon Pathom and continue along the "Death Railway" to Nam Tok (see page 146). If coming from Phetchaburi, take the train to Nong Pla Duk Junction, just east of Ban Pong (or to Nakhon Pathom), and then change to a Kanchanaburi-bound train.

Destinations Bangkok Thonburi (2 daily; 2hr 35min); Nakhon Pathom (2 daily; 1hr 25min); Nam Tok (3 daily; 2hr); Nong Pla Duk Junction (3 daily; 1hr).

BY BUS
Kanchanaburi's bus station is at the southern edge of the town centre, a good 2km from most accommodation. Tuk-tuks wait here and will run you into the main Thanon Maenam Kwai accommodation area, or you could catch a public songthaew up Thanon Saeng Chuto and walk.

Services to Kanchanaburi The buses and a/c minibuses from Bangkok's Southern Bus Terminal and Northern Mo Chit terminal are generally faster than the train. From Ayutthaya, you'll have to return to Bangkok, use a tourist a/c minibus service direct to Kanchanaburi or change buses at Suphanburi, about 90km north of Kanchanaburi. Coming from Phetchaburi, there's now a government-licensed a/c minibus service.

Moving on Government buses and a/c minibuses run from the bus station to Bangkok's Northern Mo Chit bus terminal, the Southern Bus Terminal, and to all destinations listed below. The first-class ticket office and departure point is beside the main road on the edge of the bus station, while the office for all other services is in the middle of the depot.

Destinations Bangkok (Northern Mo Chit terminal; roughly hourly; 3hr); Bangkok (Southern Bus Terminal; every 20min; 2hr 30min); Nam Tok (every 30min; 1hr 30min); Phetchaburi (every 60–90min; 2hr 30min).

BY TOURIST A/C MINIBUS
Guesthouses and travel agents can book you on a/c minibuses for Ayutthaya, Suvarnabhumi Airport and Thanon Khao San in Bangkok, which will usually pick you up at your guesthouse at a designated time.

GETTING AROUND

With songthaews plying the main route between the bus station and the Bridge, boatmen waiting to ferry you along the waterways, and plenty of tuk-tuks, it's easy to get to and from Kanchanaburi's main sights.

By songthaew Orange public songthaews run along Thanon Saeng Chuto, originating from outside the Focus Optic optician's, three blocks north of the bus station, and travelling north via the Kanchanaburi War Cemetery (Don Rak), Thai–Burma Railway Centre, train station and access road to the Bridge (#2; roughly every 20min until 7pm; 15min to the Bridge turn-off).

By motorbike Many outlets, such as Mek and Mee (📞 081 757 1194) on Thanon Maenam Kwai, rent out motorbikes.

By longtail boat Boats wait beside the Bridge for trips to riverside sights. A typical tour of the JEATH War Museum, Chungkai Cemetery and Wat Tham Khao Poon will cost around B1000 and last 1hr 30min–2hr, though shorter jaunts on the water are also possible.

By bicycle Guesthouses and tour agencies rent out bicycles – ideal for exploring the main town sights and the quiet rural backroads.

By kayak A green and sedate way of exploring the area is on a kayak tour. Try River Kwai Canoe Travel Services, 11 Thanon Maenam Kwai (📞 086 168 5995, 🌐 facebook.com/riverkwaicanoe), or Safarine, 117 Soi Tha Makham, Moo 2 (to the northwest of town; 📞 086 049 1662, 🌐 safarine.com).

INFORMATION

Tourist information The TAT office (daily 8.30am–4.30pm; 📞 034 511200 or 034 512500, ✉ tatkan@tat.or.th) is just south of the bus station on Thanon Saeng Chuto and keeps up-to-date bus and train timetables. They also have decent maps of the town and province, and a booklet on Pak Phraek Cultural Road.

ACCOMMODATION SEE MAP PAGE 139

Many people choose to make the most of the inspiring scenery by staying on or near the river, in a **raft house**, a guesthouse or a hotel, and the options are constantly increasing as the town's building boom continues. The most popular area is the southern end of **Thanon Maenam Kwai**, which is *the* backpackers' hub, crammed with sometimes-noisy bars, restaurants and tour agents; most guesthouses are at the riverside end of the small sois running off this thoroughfare, though few rooms actually have river views. For those that have views (which naturally have higher rates), the idyll can be disturbed by roaring longtail engines and jet skis during the day, so you might want to book in for just one night until you've experienced the decibel levels for yourself. Bring mosquito repellent too, as many huts float among lotus swamps.

KANCHANABURI

Bluestar Guesthouse 241 Thanon Maenam Kwai w bluestar-guesthouse.com; map page 139. Popular, clued-up guesthouse in a quiet, leafy garden that runs down to the riverside, with a wide range of good-value accommodation including very cheap, basic fan bungalows with en-suite cold showers, smarter fan rooms with hot water and a choice of a/c bungalows and rooms, some with good views of the river. B̄

Good Times Resort 265/5–7 Thanon Maenam Kwai w good-times-resort.com; map page 139. This is one of the most attractive resorts in town, with a prime location by the river just north of the Sudjai Bridge. Just about all of the 36 spacious rooms have a balcony, some with a view of the small swimming pool, but only one with river view. It's a good base for families as some rooms are connecting. B̄B̄

The Journey House Just off Thanon Maenam Kwai, about 3km northwest of the Bridge w facebook.com/thejourneyhousekanchanaburi; map page 139. Set in a large white villa with a pretty lily pond and swimming pool in the tranquil garden, this welcoming boutique hotel provides spacious rooms that are stylishly decorated with dark teak furniture. B̄B̄B̄

Nita Raft House Thanon Pak Phraek w facebook.com/nitarafthouse95; map page 139. Away from the Thanon Maenam Kwai fray, a friendly, laidback, old-school guesthouse, whose simple floating rooms, some en-suite with river views, are among the cheapest in town; the very cheapest share bathrooms and face inland. Also does great food. B̄

★ **Sabai@Kan** 317/4 Thanon Maenam Kwai w sabaiatkan.com; map page 139. This relaxing boutique hotel is located towards the northern end of Thanon Maenam Kwai, handy for the River Kwai Bridge railway station, and while there are no river views, all rooms have wall-to-wall windows that overlook a pleasant prospect of a swimming pool and shady garden. Rooms are spacious and well-equipped, with thick king-size mattresses on the beds. Staff are very efficient and helpful. B̄B̄

Tamarind Guest House 29/1 Thanon Maenam Kwai w facebook.com/tamarindkan; map page 139. Smaller rooms than in some of the other riverside guesthouses, but the place is very clean throughout and managed by considerate, friendly staff. Sleep in the two-storey house, or down by the waterfront in one of the raft-house rooms (all en suite with hot showers), which have river views and share a breezy, orchid-strewn terrace. B̄

★ **Tara Raft** 15/1 Soi Rongheaboy w facebook.com/tararaft1; map page 139. In a picturesque location on a quiet stretch of the river just south of the Maenam Kwai hub, this place has probably the nicest raft-house rooms in town: colourfully decorated, they come with king-size beds, a/c, hot showers, safes, fridges, big TVs and lovely outlooks from tiny terraces. The cheapest rooms are back on land with no view, but have the same facilities. They also run the even cheaper *Tara Bed and Breakfast* at 99–101 Thanon Maenam Kwai (w facebook.com/tarabed). B̄

U Inchantree 443 Thanon Maenam Kwai w ukanchanaburi.com; map page 139. Spectacularly located on a bend in the Kwai Yai River, a 5min walk north of the Bridge (get off at the River Kwai Bridge station if arriving by train), this luxurious, 50-room retreat has charming staff and what must be Kanchanaburi's most style-conscious rooms. Standard rooms aren't huge, but the powerful rain showers and snuggly white duvets more than compensate. Outside, facilities include a waterfront pool, a peaceful glass-fronted library and an attractive restaurant by the river. All-day breakfast and bicycles included; 24hr use of pool. Discounts available for early booking and for midweek stays. B̄B̄B̄B̄

VN 44 Soi Rongheaboy w facebook.com/VnGuesthouse Restaurant; map page 139. A quiet, pretty place just south of the Maenam Kwai hub, with good food and decent raft-house rooms: they're large and come with terraces, en-suite hot showers and either fan or a/c. The cheapest rooms are in a concrete building, but all have hot-water bathrooms. B̄

OUT OF TOWN

Cross River Kwai Southwest of town, off Route 3228, about 10km beyond Chungkai Cemetery w crosshotelsandresorts.com; map page 139. The idea – a resort built mostly of shipping containers on the banks of the River Kwai Noi – may not sound promising, but the execution is stunningly and ingeniously modern, with bold architectural features and elements of industrial-chic and Japanese style. Most of the rooms float on the placid waters, with riverside balconies and chill-out rooftops, while some give directly onto the infinity-edged pool. There are kayaks to explore the river. B̄B̄B̄B̄

★ **Oriental Kwai** 194/5 Moo 1, Ladya (off Route 3199) w orientalkwai.com; map page 139. In a lovely, quiet spot beside the Kwai Yai, 15km north of town, this small Dutch–Thai hotel offers thoughtfully designed cottages in a lush tropical garden with a pool and gym, and gracious service. Cottages are a/c and tastefully decorated in modern Asian accents; some are wheelchair accessible. The owners will give you plenty of ideas for exploring the area, including boat rides to the Bridge and route maps for tours by bicycle or motorbike (both available for rent). BBB

EATING
SEE MAP PAGE 139

Most of Kanchanaburi's guesthouses and raft houses have **restaurants**, and there's a cluster of floating restaurants beside the Bridge, serving good if rather pricey seafood to accompany the river views. A cheaper place to enjoy genuine local food is at the ever-reliable **night market**, which sets up alongside Thanon Saeng Chuto on the edge of the bus station. There are also a few food stalls at the **night bazaar**, which operates in front of the train station in the evening, and at Thanon Lak Muang's "walking street" market on Saturday evenings from about 6pm.

Bell's Pizzeria 24/5 Thanon Maenam Kwai ⓦrestaurant-pizzeria-bells.com; map page 139. Lively, Swiss-run, evening-time place with pavement tables that's justly popular for its great pizzas. Also offers pastas, salads and a handful of Thai dishes. BB

★ **Keeree Tara** 431/1 Thanon Maenam Kwai, about 100m north of the Bridge ⓦfacebook.com/keereetara; map page 139. Beyond the grandiose fountain at the entrance, scenic terraces slope down to a floating platform, all with fine views of the Bridge. Fortunately, the style is matched by the substance, on a diverse, creative menu: the *laap muu thawt* (deep-fried spicy pork salad) and the *kaeng khua muu yang khamin khao* (roast pork and white turmeric curry) are both very good, and there's plenty of river fish and prawns. BBB

On's Thai Issan Vegetarian 77/9 Thanon Maenam Kwai ⓦfacebook.com/OnsThaiIssan; map page 139. There's a lively buzz around this simple streetside place, which only serves vegan and vegetarian dishes such as seaweed soup and *phat thai*. The buzz comes from On's students who learn how to make their favourite dishes during the day (see page 145). B

Schluck 222 Thanon Mahathai ⓦfacebook.com/SchluckRestaurant; map page 139. Cosy a/c restaurant with outdoor seating, serving salads, pizzas and steaks as well as Thai food, but what really makes it stand out are its mouthwatering, home-made cakes such as vanilla choux buns and lemon meringue tart. BB

DRINKING
SEE MAP PAGE 139

Nightlife in Kanchanaburi is relatively low-key, though there's a string of hostess bars at the southern end of Thanon Maenam Kwai, offering loud music and cheapish beer, with sports on TV as an added attraction. Further north up the strip are several simple bars without hostesses, and some classy venues that attract a mostly Thai crowd.

Ban Sitthisang Thanon Pak Phraek ⓦfacebook.com/baansittisang; map page 139. This attractively renovated, hundred-year-old mansion, with ornate wooden lintels and sepia-toned décor, serves good espresso coffees, speciality teas, cakes and ice cream during the day.

Gravité 5/1 Soi England ⓦfacebook.com/gravitedrip; map page 139. Cool, friendly little café-bar serving drip coffee – their own blend is very good, but you can also try Ethiopian and Guatemalan beans – as well as home-made cakes and Thai craft beers.

DIRECTORY

Banks and ATMs There are several banks with money-changing facilities and ATMs on Thanon Saeng Chuto, immediately to the north of the Thanon U Thong junction, and around the Bridge.

Cookery classes Vegetarians and vegans should sign up for two-hour classes with Khun On at On's Thai Issan Vegetarian (see page 145).

Hospitals The private Thanakan Hospital (☎034 622358) is at 20/20 Thanon Saeng Chuto, at the southern end of town, near the junction with Thanon Chukkadon; the government-run Phahon Phonphayulasena Hospital (☎034 511233 or ☎034 622999) is further south at 572/1 Thanon Saeng Chuto, near the junction with Thanon Mae Khlong.

Tourist police For all emergencies, call the tourist police on the free, 24hr phone line (☎1155), or contact them at their office at 123 Thanon Maenam Kwai (☎034 512795).

Around Kanchanaburi

The railway that originates at Bangkok's Thonburi Station continues northwest of Kanchanaburi up the valley of the River Kwai Noi to **Nam Tok**, running dramatically along the line of the **Death Railway**. Halfway along, the railway gives access to some much older remnants of the valley's history, the twelfth-century Khmer temple ruins of **Prasat Muang Singh**. The most informative museum about the Death Railway, the excellent **Hellfire Pass Memorial Museum and Walk**, is not served by trains, but fully justifies the extra bus journey, 18km northwest of Nam Tok.

Prasat Muang Singh

Take the train towards Nam Tok and get off at Tha Kilen (1hr 15min from Kanchanaburi), then walk straight out of the station for 500m, turn right at the crossroads and continue for another 1km to reach the ruins • Charge • ⓦ facebook.com/muangsinghp

Eight hundred years ago, the Khmer empire extended west as far as Muang Singh (City of Lions), an outpost strategically sited on the banks of the River Kwai Noi, 43km west of present-day Kanchanaburi. Thought to have been built at the end of the twelfth century, the temple complex of **Prasat Muang Singh** follows Khmer religious and architectural precepts, but its origins are obscure – the City of Lions gets no mention in any of the recognized chronicles until the nineteenth century.

Prasat Muang Singh covers one-third of a square kilometre, bordered by moats and ramparts that had cosmological as well as defensive significance, and with an enclosed **shrine complex** at its heart. Restorations now give an idea of the crude grandeur of the original structure, which was constructed entirely from blocks of rough, russet laterite.

As with all Khmer prasats, the pivotal feature of Muang Singh is the main prang, surrounded by a series of walls and a covered gallery, with gateways marking the cardinal points. The prang faces east, towards Angkor, and is guarded by a fine sandstone statue of **Avalokitesvara**, one of the five great *bodhisattvas* of Mahayana Buddhism, would-be Buddhas who have postponed their entrance into Nirvana to help others attain enlightenment. He's depicted here in characteristic style, his eight arms and torso covered with tiny Buddha reliefs and his hair tied in a topknot. In Mahayanist mythology, Avalokitesvara represents mercy, while the other statue found in the prasat, the female figure of **Prajnaparamita**, symbolizes wisdom – when wisdom and mercy join forces, enlightenment ensues. Just visible on the inside of the north wall surrounding the prang is the only intact example of the stucco carving that once ornamented every facade. Other fragments and sculptures found at this and nearby sites are displayed in a small museum; especially tantalizing is the single segment of what must have been a gigantic face hewn from several massive blocks of stone.

Nam Tok

There's not much more to the tiny town of **NAM TOK** than the terminus of the Death Railway line. Tour groups of Thais and foreigners flock to the pretty, roadside **Sai Yok Noi Falls**, 2km north, and if you're filling time between trains, you could walk along the continuation of the railway tracks to join them. It's also straightforward to get a bus on to Hellfire Pass.

ARRIVAL AND DEPARTURE NAM TOK

By train The train station is at the top of the town, 900m north of Highway 323, and a further 2km from the Kwai Noi River. To reach the highway from the station, walk up the station approach road, cross the tracks, turn left at the spirit-house roundabout, then first right through the small town, passing a water tower and market on your left.

By bus All Kanchanaburi–Hellfire Pass–Thong Pha Phum/Sangkhlaburi buses pass through Nam Tok, generally making a stop near the T-junction of the highway and the station road (every 30min; last bus back to Kanchanaburi at about 5pm); it's about 1hr 30min from Kanchanaburi to Nam Tok and 30min from Nam Tok to Hellfire Pass.

ACCOMMODATION

Boutique Raft Resort Just west of Pak Saeng pier on the river bank ⓦ boutiqueraft-riverkwai.com. In a tranquil spot, accommodation either on land or in large, thatched bamboo and wood floating rafthouses with a/c, hot showers, fridges and their own waterside balconies, from which you could dive into the river. There's also a large raft enclosing a river-water swimming pool and plenty of simple bamboo rafts for pootling about on. **BBB**

RIDING THE DEATH RAILWAY

The two-hour journey along the notorious Thailand–Burma **Death Railway** from Kanchanaburi to Nam Tok is one of Thailand's most scenic and popular train rides. Though the views are lovely, it's the history that makes the ride so special, so it's worth visiting the Thailand–Burma Railway Centre in Kanchanaburi before making the trip, as this provides a context for the enormous loss of human life and the extraordinary feat of engineering behind the line's construction (see page 140). Alternatively, take a bus from Kanchanaburi to the **Hellfire Pass Memorial Museum and Walk** (see page 138), 18km from the line's current Nam Tok terminus, which offers an equally illuminating introduction to the railway's history, as well as a chance to walk along part of the original track, then take a bus back to Nam Tok and return to Kanchanaburi by train. A good tip, to get the best views, is to make sure you sit (or stand) on the right-hand side of the train on the journey back to Kanchanaburi, and on the left-hand side when travelling towards Nam Tok.

Leaving Kanchanaburi via the Bridge over the River Kwai, the train chugs through the fertile, red-soiled Kwai Noi valley, passing plantations of teak, tapioca, sugar cane, papaya and watermelon, and stopping frequently at country stations decked with frangipani and jasmine. The first stop of note is Tha Kilen (1hr 15min), where you can alight for Prasat Muang Singh (see page 146). About twenty minutes later, the most hair-raising section of track begins: at **Wang Sing**, also known as Arrow Hill, the train squeezes through 30m-deep solid rock cuttings, dug at the cost of numerous POW lives; 6km further, it slows to a crawl at the approach to the **Wang Po viaduct**, where a 300m-long trestle bridge clings to the cliff face as it curves with the Kwai Noi – almost every man who worked on this part of the railway died. The station at the northern end of the trestle bridge is called **Tham Krasae**, after the cave that's hollowed out of the rock face beside the bridge; you can see the cave's resident Buddha image from the train. North of Tham Krasae, the train pulls in at **Wang Po Station** before continuing alongside a particularly lovely stretch of the Kwai Noi, its banks thick with jungle and not a raft house in sight, the whole vista framed by distant tree-clad peaks. Thirty minutes later, the train reaches **Nam Tok**, a small town that thrives chiefly on its position at the end of the line.

Three trains operate daily along the Death Railway in both directions, but they don't always run on time. Currently they're scheduled to leave Kanchanaburi at 6.08am (originating at Nong Pladuk Junction), 10.35am and 4.26pm (the latter two originating at Bangkok's Thonburi Station) and to return from Nam Tok at 5.20am, 12.55pm (both continuing to Thonburi Station) and 3.30pm (terminating at Nong Pla Duk Junction). If you're up at the Bridge, you can join the train five minutes later, though you're more likely to get a seat if you board at the main station. The Death Railway is classified as a historic line, so foreigners are charged an over-the-odds B100 to go to Nam Tok, even though the carriages are third class without a/c. All Kanchanaburi–Hellfire Pass–Thong Pha Phum/Sangkhlaburi **buses** pass through Nam Tok (every 30min; last bus back to Kanchanaburi at about 5pm); it's about 1hr 30min from Kanchanaburi to Nam Tok.

EATING

There are several tourist-oriented **restaurants** at the station (open all day), and cheap **hot-food stalls** in the market (evening only), halfway along the station road, but your best bet for something to eat is *Raenu Restaurant* on Highway 323, about 2km north of town.

Raenu (Renu) Restaurant Opposite Sai Yok Noi Falls on the main road ⓦ facebook.com/Renurestaurant. Big, open-sided wooden restaurant overlooking the valley, that's hugely popular with Thai tourists, and for good reason: dished up in generous portions, the *pla khao thawt man pla*, a locally caught river fish deep-fried with fish sauce, is delicious, and goes well with stir-fried local vegetables served with spicy shrimp-paste relish. $\overline{\text{BB}}$

Hellfire Pass

Although the rail line north of Nam Tok was ripped up soon after the end of World War II, it casts its dreadful shadow all the way up the Kwai Noi valley into Myanmar.

> **BOAT TRIPS FROM NAM TOK**
>
> You can rent a longtail **boat** (plus driver) from Nam Tok's **Pak Saeng pier** ("Tha Pak Saeng") for the ride upstream to **Tham Lawa**, the largest stalactite cave in the area, which is home to three species of bat, or **Sai Yok Yai Falls**, which flow into the river. To reach the pier from the Highway 323 T-junction, cross the road, turn southeast towards Kanchanaburi, then take the first road on your right; it's 2km from here to the river. The return journey to the cave takes roughly two hours, including 30–45min there. You could continue to Sai Yok Yai Falls, a five- or six-hour return trip, though this trip is not possible when water levels are low (Feb–May). You can also rent a boat for an hour's sightseeing along this pretty stretch of river.

The remnants of track are most visible at **Hellfire Pass**, and many of the villages in the area are former POW sites – locals frequently stumble across burial sites, now reclaimed by the encroaching jungle. To keep the Death Railway level through the uneven course of the Kwai valley, the POWs had to build a series of embankments and trestle bridges and, at dishearteningly frequent intervals, gouge deep cuttings through solid rock. The most concentrated digging was at **Konyu**, 18km beyond Nam Tok, where seven separate cuttings were made over a 3.5km stretch. The longest and most brutal of these was Hellfire Pass, which got its name from the hellish-looking lights and shadows of the fires the POWs used when working at night. The job took three months of round-the-clock labour with the most primitive tools.

Hellfire Pass Memorial Museum
Donation requested • W dva.gov.au

The story of the POWs who died on the Hellfire Pass is documented at the beautifully designed **Hellfire Pass Memorial Museum**, the best and most informative of all the World War II museums in the Kanchanaburi region. Inside, wartime relics, POW memorabilia, photos and informative display boards tell the sobering history of the construction of this stretch of the Thailand–Burma Railway, along with slide shows and videos. Founded by an Australian–Thai volunteer group, the museum now serves as a sort of pilgrimage site for the families and friends of Australian POWs.

Hellfire Pass Memorial Walk
No set hours for the walk, but the audio tour must be returned to the museum by 4pm

The same Australian–Thai group responsible for the Hellfire Pass Memorial Museum has also cleared a one-hour circular **memorial walk**, which begins at the museum and descends to follow the old rail route through the 20m-deep, 70m-long cutting and back. Only adding to the poignancy, it's a beautiful trail through woods and bamboo stands, with bucolic views of the mountain ridges across the valley. It's also possible to extend the walk by continuing northwards along the line of the railway to the Hin Tok Road, just beyond Hin Tok Cutting, along a course relaid with some of the original narrow-gauge track (about 2hr 30min out and back; if you have a car with driver, you could arrange to be picked up at the Hin Tok Road). It's well worth getting the excellent, free **audio tour** available at the museum, which gives a detailed commentary, including vivid first-person testimonies by Australian former POWs, all along both sections of walk. Bring water and sturdy shoes as the walk along the old railway line goes over large chippings.

ARRIVAL AND DEPARTURE — HELLFIRE PASS

Hellfire Pass is 18km north of Nam Tok, on the west side of Highway 323 after kilometre-stone 139. It's easy to get here by a combination of train and bus, taking the Death Railway (see page 140) to Nam Tok, then a bus to Hellfire Pass.

By bus From Kanchanaburi or Nam Tok, take any bus bound for Thong Pha Phum or Sangkhlaburi and ask to be dropped off at Hellfire Pass; it's about a 2hr journey from Kanchanaburi or 30min from Nam Tok.

THE ANANTARA SIAM HOTEL

Accommodation

Bangkok has appalling traffic jams, so think carefully about what you want to see and do before deciding which part of town to stay in: easy access to relevant train networks and river transport can be crucial. Advance reservations are recommended where possible during high season (Nov–Feb); many guesthouses and cheaper hotels no longer maintain their own websites (only Facebook pages), but are available to book on sites such as booking.com and agoda.com. In the reviews that follow, accommodation is air-conditioned, unless specified.

ACCOMMODATION PRICES

Throughout the Guide, the price codes given for accommodation represent the **minimum** you can expect to pay in each establishment in the **high season** (roughly July, Aug and Nov–Feb in most parts of the country) for a typical **double room**, booked via the hotel website where available; there may however be an extra "peak" supplement for the Christmas–New Year period. If travelling on your own, expect to pay between sixty and one hundred percent of the rates quoted for a double room. Top-end hotels will add **seven percent tax** (though this may increase to ten percent) and **ten percent service charge** to your bill; the prices given in the Guide are net rates after these taxes (usually referred to as "plus plus") have been added.

B̲ = under B1000
B̲B̲ = B1000–2000
B̲B̲B̲ = B2000–3000
B̲B̲B̲B̲ = over B3000

For cheap double rooms at around B500, your widest choice lies with the guesthouses on and around **Banglamphu**'s Thanon Khao San. The most inexpensive rooms here are no-frills crash-pads – small and often windowless, with fans, thin walls and shared bathrooms – but Banglamphu also offers plenty of modern-style hostels and well-appointed, mid-priced small hotels with swimming pools. Other, far smaller and less interesting travellers' ghettoes that might be worth considering are the generally dingy **Soi Ngam Duphli**, off the south side of Thanon Rama IV, which nevertheless harbours a couple of decent shoestring options; and **Soi Kasemsan I**, which is very handily placed next to Siam Square and firmly occupies the moderate range, though with a few rooms for around B700. Otherwise, the majority of the city's moderate and expensive rooms are scattered widely across the **downtown areas**, around Siam Square and Thanon Ploenchit, to the south of Thanon Rama IV and along **Thanon Sukhumvit**, and to a lesser extent in **Chinatown**. As well as easy access to transport links and shops, the downtown views from accommodation in these areas are a real plus.

Bangkok boasts an increasing number of exceptionally stylish **super-deluxe** hotels, with chic decor and excellent facilities that often include a **spa**. The cream of this accommodation, with rates starting from around B5000, is scenically sited along the banks of the Chao Phraya River, though there are a few top-notch hotels in the downtown area, which is also where you'll find the best business hotels.

ESSENTIALS

Family accommodation Many of the expensive hotels listed offer special deals for families, usually allowing one or two under-12s to share their parents' room for free, so long as no extra bedding is required. It's also sometimes possible to cram two adults and two children into the twin rooms in inexpensive and mid-priced hotels (as opposed to guesthouses), as beds in these places are often big enough for two. A number of guesthouses offer three-person rooms.

Long-stay accommodation If you plan on staying in Bangkok longer, the most economical option is usually a room with a bathroom in an apartment building, which is likely to cost at least B7000 a month. Many foreigners end up living in apartments off Thanon Sukhumvit, around Victory Monument and Pratunam, or on Soi Boonprarop, off Thanon Rajaprarop just north of Pratunam. Visit the website for teachers of English in Thailand, w ajarn.com, for tips on living in Bangkok and finding an apartment.

RATANAKOSIN AND AROUND   SEE MAP PAGE 51

Several small, upmarket hotels and hostels have recently opened on the west side of Ratanakosin, which put you in a peerless location, in a quiet, traditional, heavily Chinese neighbourhood of low-rise shophouses, overlooking the river and on the doorsteps of Wat Pho and the Grand Palace. The restaurants and nightlife of Banglamphu are within walking distance if you fancy a bit more of a buzz, while the sights of Thonburi and Chinatown, and Sanam Chai subway station are also nearby.

Aurum The River Place 394/27–29 Soi Pansook,

Thanon Maharat ⓦaurum-bangkok.com. Modelled on a French townhouse, with wooden shutters and wrought-iron balconies, this spruce, four-storey hotel is set back very slightly from the river and four of the rooms are "City View" only, but the other eight offer at least partial views of the water. Splashed with colourful Thai fabrics and sporting heavily varnished wooden floors, the well-equipped rooms are a little on the small side, apart from those on the top floor. There's a daytime riverside café, *Vivi: The Coffee Place*, where complimentary breakfast is served. **B̲B̲B̲B̲**

★ **Bangkok Bed and Bike** 19/6 Th Charoen Krung ⓦbangkokbedandbike.com. Excellent hostel with a smart urban look, close to Wat Pho and the Grand Palace. Private rooms, women's and mixed dorms are a/c with hot showers, and there are bicycle tours, bikes for rent (with great hand-drawn maps of the area) and an impressive array of amenities, including a washing machine and drier. **B̲**

Chakrabongse Villas 396 Thanon Maharat ⓦchakrabongsevillas.com. Upmarket riverside accommodation with a difference: seven tranquil suites, villas and compact rooms beautifully furnished in a choice of Thai, Chinese and Moroccan styles, set in the luxuriant

TOP FIVE RIVERSIDE STAYS

Anantara Riverside See page 155
Chakrabongse Villas See below
Four Seasons See page 156
Peninsula Bangkok See page 156
Praya Palazzo See page 152

gardens of hundred-year-old Chakrabongse House overlooking Wat Arun. All have cable TV, and there's a small, attractive swimming pool and a riverfront terrace restaurant for dinner (set menu, reservations required). **B̲B̲B̲B̲**

Sala Arun 47 Soi Tha Thien, Thanon Maharat ⓦsalaarun.com. At this riverside inn, the nine teak-floored rooms feature objets d'art from the owners' worldwide travels and balconies (in most), while complimentary breakfast is served in the boldly coloured ground-floor café, which has a small terrace with armchairs facing Wat Arun (bedrooms with views of the river and temple are more expensive than city-side rooms). The Eagle Nest rooftop bar offers peerless views of the floodlit temple and the river in the evening. **B̲B̲B̲B̲**

BANGLAMPHU AND DEMOCRACY MONUMENT AREA   SEE MAP PAGE 68

Nearly all backpackers head straight for Banglamphu, Bangkok's long-established travellers' ghetto just north of the Grand Palace, location of the cheapest accommodation, the best traveller-oriented facilities and some of the most enjoyable bars and restaurants in the city. A growing number of Banglamphu guesthouses are reinventing themselves as good-value mini-hotels boasting chic decor, swimming pools, and even views from the windows, and have now been joined by twenty-first-century hostels, which throw in a measure of style and sociability with your wi-fi-enabled bunk. The cheap guesthouses are still there, particularly immediately west of Khao San, around the neighbourhood temple Wat Chana Songkhram, and along riverside Thanon Phra Arthit – where you'll also find some upscale places offering prime views over the Chao Phraya.

About a 10min walk north from Thanon Khao San, the handful of guesthouses and small hotels scattered among the shophouses of the Thanon Samsen sois enjoy a more authentically Thai environment, while the Thewet area, a further 15min walk in the same direction or a 7min walk from the Thewet express-boat stop, is more local still. Heading south from Khao San, across multi-laned Rajdamnoen Klang, to the upscale places in the area immediately south of Democracy also puts you plumb in the middle of an interesting old neighbourhood, famous for its traditional shophouse restaurants. Theft is a problem in Banglamphu, particularly at the cheaper guesthouses, so don't leave anything valuable in your room and heed the guesthouses' notices about padlocks and safety lockers.

THANON KHAO SAN AND AROUND

Buddy Lodge 265 Thanon Khao San ⓦbuddylodge.com. Stylish hotel right in the thick of the action, whose charming, colonial-style rooms are done out in cream, with louvred shutters, balconies, marble bathrooms and polished dark-wood floors. There's a beautiful rooftop pool, a gym, a sauna and several bars downstairs in the *Buddy Village* complex. Specify an upper-floor location away from Khao San to ensure a quieter night's sleep. **B̲B̲B̲**

Nap Park 5 Thanon Tani ⓦnappark.com;. On a surprisingly untouristed street just north of Thanon Khao San, this lively hostel shelters smart dorm beds with lockers and hot showers (some with personal TVs), as well as plenty of space for lounging, either inside in front of the TV or outside in the tamarind-shaded front yard. Lockers and laundry available. **B̲**

Suneta Hostel 209–11 Trok Kraisi ⓦsunetahostel.com. Welcoming, well-equipped place, 5min walk from Thanon Khao San, done out with acres of wood to give a retro look, offering wide, souped-up bunk beds and private rooms. Women-only dorm available. **B̲**

AROUND WAT CHANA SONGKHRAM AND PHRA ARTHIT

Bella Bella House Soi Ram Bhuttri ⓦfacebook.com/bella.bella.house.phraathit. Above a plant-strewn café, the pastel-coloured rooms here are no frills but well priced, and a few boast lovely views over Wat Chana Songkhram. The cheapest share cold-water bathrooms, a notch up gets you an en-suite hot shower, while the most expensive have

TOP FIVE CHEAP SLEEPS
Chern See page 153
Lamphu House See below
Lub d See page 154
New Siam 2 See below
Tavee See page 153

a/c. Good prices for single rooms, especially the en-suite ones. B̄

KC Guest House 64 Trok Kai Chae, corner of Thanon Phra Sumen w facebook.com/kcguesthouse. Friendly, family-run guesthouse offering exceptionally clean bedrooms, with either en-suite or shared, hot-water bathrooms; try to get a room away from the noisy street. There's also a rooftop terrace and a decked eating area on the soi next to 7-Eleven. B̄

★ **Lamphu House** 75 Soi Ram Bhuttri w lamphuhouse.com. With smart bamboo beds, coconut-wood furniture and elegant rattan lamps in nearly all the rooms, this travellers' hotel set round a quiet courtyard has a calm, modern feel. Cheaper options share facilities (including good-value singles) and the cheapest fan rooms have no outside view; the more expensive options have balconies overlooking the courtyard and the triples and four-person rooms are popular with families. B̄

Merry V Soi Ram Bhuttri ☏ 02 282 9267. Large, utterly plain but efficiently run guesthouse offering some of the cheapest accommodation in Banglamphu. Bottom-end rooms are basic and small, many share bathrooms and it's pot luck whether you get a window or not. Better en-suites with hot showers and a/c versions are also available. Good rates for singles. B̄

New Siam 1 21 Soi Chana Songkhram w newsiam.net. Above a pleasant terrace restaurant, the cheaper options here are well-kept tiled-floor rooms (doubles, twins and singles), all with windows and shared cold showers, while the a/c rooms boast en-suite hot showers. B̄

★ **New Siam 2** 50 Trok Rong Mai w newsiam.net. Very pleasant and well-run small hotel whose en-suite rooms with a/c and hot shower stand out for their thoughtfully designed extras such as in-room safes, cable TV and drying rails on the balconies. Occupies a fairly quiet but convenient location and has a small pool. Popular with families, and triple rooms are also available. B̄B̄

New Siam Riverside 21 Thanon Phra Arthit w newsiam.net. Occupying a prime spot on the Chao Phraya, the riverside branch of the *New Siam* empire offers well-designed, good-value rooms. Even the cheapest have a/c and full amenities, while the best of them boast fabulous river views from windows or private balconies. Also has a large riverside swimming pool and terrace restaurant. B̄B̄B̄

★ **Praya Palazzo** 757/1 Soi 2, Thanon Somdet Phra Pinklao w prayapalazzo.com. A peaceful riverside sanctuary right opposite Banglamphu, this large, graceful, Italianate palace has been lovingly restored by an architecture professor, with great attention to detail – right down to the wallpaper and lampshades – to give the feel of its 1920s origins. Twenty-first-century luxuries have been overlaid, of course, such as rain showers in the bathrooms to go alongside the brass taps and swathes of coloured marble. There's a lovely pool in the lush waterfront garden, too, and an excellent Thai royal-cuisine restaurant. Access is by the free hotel boat, which shuttles across to Phra Arthit express-boat pier. B̄B̄B̄B̄

SAMSEN SOIS AND THEWET

Lamphu Treehouse 155 Saphan Wanchat, Thanon Phracha Thipatai w lamphutreehotel.com. Named after the *lamphu* trees that line the adjacent canal, after which Banglamphu ("the riverside village with mangrove apple trees") is named, this attractively turned-out guesthouse offers a pool and smart rooms, with plenty of polished wood fittings made of recycled golden teak, among other traditional Thai decorative elements; most have balconies, though the cheapest in the nearby annexe are windowless. It's in a quiet neighbourhood but just a few minutes' walk from Democracy. B̄B̄

Nakorn Ping 9/1 Soi 6, Thanon Samsen w nakornpinghotel.com. In a low-rise, orange building dotted with plants on a fairly quiet soi, this place sports some classic elements of a Thai-Chinese hotel: spittoons for waste baskets, gnarly wooden furniture and little natural light. However, it's very clean, efficiently run and good value, offering fridges, cable TV and bathrooms in all rooms. B̄

★ **Phra Nakorn Norn Len** 46 Thewet Soi 1, Thanon Krung Kasem, Thewet w phranakorn-nornlen.com. What was once a seedy short-time motel has been transformed into a leafy bohemian haven with genuine eco-conscious and socially engaged sensibilities and a tangible fair-trade philosophy. Every one of the comfortable, though not luxurious, rooms has been cheerily hand-painted to a different retro Thai design, and each has a cute bathroom and balcony. Mostly organic vegetarian breakfast included. B̄B̄B̄

Rajata Soi 6, Thanon Samsen w rajatahotel.com. This traditional motel of large bedrooms and bathrooms around a quiet courtyard café has been subtly transformed with retro furniture, hundreds of plants and a friendly welcome. All of the shining white, spotlessly clean accommodation has satellite TV, hot showers and mini-bars. B̄B̄

Shanti Lodge 37 Thanon Sri Ayutthaya (at Soi 16), Thewet w shantilodge.com. Colourful, old-school-hippy guesthouse with a mostly vegetarian restaurant festooned with pot plants. The cheapest "traditional" rooms (fan or a/c) are in a wooden building at the back with shared hot-water bathrooms, but it's worth paying a bit extra for a bright en-suite room in the main building – or splash out for the penthouse with its leafy roof terrace. Dorm beds, free bicycles and free weekly Thai cooking classes available. B̲

Sri Ayutthaya 23/11 Thanon Sri Ayutthaya (at Soi 14), Thewet ⓦ facebook.com/sriayuttaya. The most attractive guesthouse in Thewet, where most of the good-sized rooms (choose between fan rooms without private bathroom and en suites with a/c) are elegantly done out with wood-panelled walls and beautiful polished wood floors; these have been augmented by a few modern, "Superior" rooms done out in bright, fetching colours. Hot showers throughout. B̲

Ssip 42 Thanon Phitsanulok, Thewet ⓦ ssiphotel thailand.com. Genteel and helpful upmarket B&B. It's in a new building on busy Thanon Phitsanulok, but fitted with antique furniture and fixtures and polished-wood floors, as well as hot showers, TVs and fridges. It's worth opting for the delicious and beautifully presented Thai breakfasts. B̲B̲B̲B̲

★ **Tavee** 83 Soi 14, Thanon Sri Ayutthaya, Thewet ⓦ facebook.com/taveeguesthouse. *Tavee* is located down a pedestrian alley behind *Sri Ayutthaya* and is owned by the same family, but is the quieter and friendlier of the two options. Behind the stylish little café, the fan rooms sport attractive wood floors and share chic hot-water bathrooms, while the en-suite a/c options are larger and enjoy a few more decorative touches. B̲

SOUTH AND EAST OF DEMOCRACY

Baan Dinso 113 Trok Sin, Thanon Dinso ⓦ baandinso. com. This tasteful, upmarket little guesthouse occupies an elegant, carefully restored 1920s Thai house all done out in cool buttermilk paintwork and polished teak floors. Prices are a little steep considering that all but the deluxe rooms have to use shared ground-floor, hot-water bathrooms, but they all have a/c, mini-bars and kettles. Very good single rates. B̲B̲

Bangkok Publishing Residence 31/1 Thanon Lan Luang ⓦ bpresidence.com. Luxurious, friendly B&B in a beautifully converted printing house, which is also something of a museum to its most famous publication, the *Bangkok Weekly* magazine, scattered with old typewriters and printing blocks. The very comfortable rooms evoke a gentleman's club, with leather armchairs and acres of polished wood, plus modern touches like espresso machines and Bluetooth speakers, and there's a rooftop garden and Jacuzzi. No children under 15. B̲B̲B̲B̲

★ **The Bhuthorn** 96 Thanon Phraeng Phuthon, just off Thanon Kanlayana Maitri ⓦ thebhuthorn.com. The architect-owners have beautifully converted this hundred-year-old shophouse into a B&B. Behind the small lobby lie just three elegant rooms (including a junior suite with a mezzanine), fitted with Chinese, Thai and Western dark-wood antique furniture, chandeliers, *khon* masks and other objets d'art, as well as modern comforts. B̲B̲B̲B̲

★ **Chern** 17 Soi Ratchasak, Thanon Bamrung Muang ⓦ chernbangkok.com. This friendly boutique hostel "invites" (*chern*) you to stay in its sleek, minimalist accommodation, done out in gleaming whites, light wood and quirky murals illustrating Thai proverbs. Choose between four- or eight-bed dorms and good-value, large private rooms with desks, fridges, safes and TVs. B̲

★ **Old Capital Bike Inn** 607 Thanon Phra Sumen ⓦ oldcapitalbkk.com. Formerly the *Old Bangkok Inn*, this chic little boutique guesthouse with an eco-friendly philosophy and a vintage bike theme has just ten rooms, each of them individually styled in dark wood, with nostalgic murals, ironwork lamps and elegant contemporary-accented bathrooms. Most of the suites are split-level and some also have a tiny private garden. The guesthouse is located a 10min walk from Khao San. Sit-up-and-beg bicycles and thrice-weekly evening bike tours are free to guests. B̲B̲B̲

Siri Oriental 120 Thanon Bunsri ⓦ sirihotelsgroup. com/SiriOrientalBangkok. This low-rise hotel is an appealing conversion of a former warehouse. The good-sized en-suite rooms sport balconies, plenty of wooden furniture and crisp white linens, and there's a decked, leafy roof garden. B̲B̲

CHINATOWN AND PAHURAT

SEE MAP PAGE 77

Set between the Ratanakosin sights and downtown, Chinatown is among the most frantic and fume-choked parts of Bangkok – and there's quite some competition. If you're in the mood, however, it's got plenty of interest, sees barely any Western overnighters, and is handy for the river, Hualamphong Station and the subway system.

Grand China 215 Thanon Yaowarat ⓦ grandchina. com. The poshest hotel in Chinatown boasts fairly luxurious accommodation in a richly coloured, contemporary style, in its 25-storey tower close to the heart of the bustle, with stunning views over all the city landmarks (the best take in the river). Facilities include a gym, a pool, the revolving *Sky Restaurant* and two panoramic rooftop bars. B̲B̲B̲B̲

Lub d 777 Thanon Mahachai, ⓦ lubd.com. Branch of the popular, well-run *Siam Square* hostel (see page 156), though here there are no dorms, only private rooms. Located at the west end of Chinatown towards Ratanakosin, it's especially handy for Sam Yot subway station and Khlong Ong Ang. B̲B̲

★ **Shanghai Mansion** 479 Thanon Yaowarat, next to Scala shark's fin restaurant ⓦ shanghaimansion.com. The most design-conscious accommodation in Chinatown has embraced the modern Chinoiserie look with gusto. It's not actually an historic mansion, but has been purpose-built on the site of a former Beijing opera house, with most bedrooms (and their windows and private terraces) facing onto an appealing, four-storey atrium, and thus cosily isolated from the Chinatown frenzy. Rooms are prettily done out in silks, lacquer-look furniture and lanterns, featuring a lot of sumptuous reds and purples, as well as hot showers and complimentary mini-bars. **BBB**

DOWNTOWN: AROUND SIAM SQUARE AND THANON PLOENCHIT   SEE MAPS PAGES 92 AND 96

Siam Square and nearby Thanon Ploenchit are as central as Bangkok gets: all the accommodation listed here is within walking distance of a Skytrain or subway station. On hand are the city's best shopping possibilities – notably the phalanx of malls along Thanon Rama I – and a wide choice of Thai and international restaurants and food courts. There's no ultra-cheap accommodation around here, but a few scaled-up guesthouses complement the hotels. Concentrated in their own small "ghetto" on Soi Kasemsan 1, which runs north off Thanon Rama I, between the Bangkok Art and Cultural Centre and Jim Thompson's House, these offer typical travellers' facilities and basic hotel comforts – a/c and en-suite hot-water bathrooms – at moderate prices; the Khlong Saen Saeb canal-boat pier, Tha Saphan Hua Chang (easily accessed via Thanon Phrayathai), is especially handy for heading west to the Golden Mount and beyond.

★ **Anantara Siam** 155 Thanon Rajdamri w anantara.com. The stately home of Bangkok's top hotels, formerly the *Regent*. Afternoon tea is still served in the monumental lobby, which is adorned with magnificent, vibrant eighteenth-century-style murals depicting the Thai cosmology, and flanked by acclaimed Thai, Italian, Japanese and South American restaurants, a steakhouse, an opulent spa and lovely gardens. The large and luxurious rooms are decorated in warm Thai colours and dark wood. **BBBB**

Courtyard by Marriott 155/1 Soi Mahadlekluang 1, Thanon Rajdamri w marriott.com. On a quiet but very handy soi, this hotel offers most of the facilities of a five-star, but at more manageable prices. The modern design is seductive, gleaming white outside, muted colours and plenty of natural light inside, and there's a long, narrow, infinity pool, a fitness centre and a spa. **BBBB**

Golden House 1025/5–9 Thanon Ploenchit w goldenhousebangkok.com. A clean and welcoming small hotel in a peerless location, situated down a short soi by Chit Lom BTS. The colourful, parquet-floored bedrooms are equipped with hot water, cable TV and mini-bar – ask for one of the larger front rooms with bay windows, which leave just enough space for an armchair or two. **BB**

Lub d 925/9 Thanon Rama I w lubd.com. Meaning "sleep well" (*lap dii*), this buzzing, upmarket hostel has a/c and hot water throughout and an industrial feel to its stylishly lit decor. This crisp modernity extends to the bedrooms, among which the mixed dorms and the standard private rooms share large bathroom areas, while the top-of-the-range en-suite deluxe doubles boast TVs. The hostel has a popular bar and café, a co-working space and plenty of social spaces, and laundry facilities, but no kitchen. It's right on Thanon Rama I, under BTS National Stadium, so handy for just about everything but rather noisy. **B**

Luxx Langsuan 82/8 Soi Lang Suan w staywithluxx.com. Quietly set back just off Soi Lang Suan, this boutique hotel is the younger, but bigger, sister of the original *Luxx Silom* (see page 156). It shelters large, balconied "Studio" rooms and suites in a seductive contemporary style, all red wood and grey stone, as well as a 13m, infinity-edge pool in the leafy garden. **BBB**

Pathumwan Princess Hotel 444 Thanon Phrayathai w pprincess.com. Central luxury hotel in a crisp, modern style, at the southern end of MBK Shopping Centre. Service is of a high standard, and the facilities include a large, saltwater swimming pool on the eighth floor, a spa and a huge, popular fitness club, The Olympic, that encompasses squash and tennis courts and a 400m jogging track. **BBBB**

Siam Kempinski 991/9 Thanon Rama I w kempinski.com/bangkok. Though it's in downtown's throbbing heart, this top-of-the-range offering from Europe's oldest luxury hotel group styles itself as a resort: all rooms turn in on a landscaped triangular garden with three pools (some ground-floor rooms even have direct access to one of the pools). As the site used to be part of the "lotus-pond palace", Wang Sra Pathum, the interior designers have made use of lotus motifs, complemented by over two hundred specially commissioned paintings and sculptures by Thai artists, amid the Art Deco-inspired architecture. There's also a beautiful spa and an excellent contemporary Thai restaurant, *Sra Bua* (see page 166). **BBBB**

The Sukosol 477 Thanon Si Ayutthaya, just east of Thanon Phrayathai w thesukosol.com. Cherished, long-standing hotel offering fine service and a good measure of luxury at great prices. As well as an attractive rooftop swimming pool, there's an appealing clubby bar on the ground floor, a small museum of Asian antiques and a good dim sum restaurant (see page 165). Handy for Suan Pakkad Palace Museum, Phaya Thai Skytrain station and the Suvarnabhumi Airport Rail Link. **BBB**

White Lodge 36/8 Soi Kasemsan 1, Thanon Rama I w whitelodgebangkok.com. The cheapest guesthouse on the soi, with plain white cubicles and a lively, welcoming atmosphere – the best rooms, bright and quiet, are on the upper floors. **B**

THANON SUKHUMVIT
SEE MAP PAGE 99

Thanon Sukhumvit is Bangkok's longest road – it keeps going east all the way to Cambodia – but for such an important artery it's far too narrow for the volume of traffic that needs to use it, and is further hemmed in by the Skytrain line that runs above it. Packed with high-rise office blocks and business hotels (though very little budget accommodation), an impressive array of specialist restaurants (from Lebanese to Lao), and stall after stall selling cheap souvenirs and T-shirts, it's a lively place that attracts a high proportion of single male tourists to its enclaves of girlie bars on Soi Nana Tai and Soi Cowboy. But for the most part it's not a seedy area, and is home to many expats and middle-class Thais. Even at the west end of Sukhumvit, many of the sois are refreshingly quiet, even leafy; transport down the longer sois is provided by motorbike-taxi (*mohtoesai*) drivers who wait at the soi's mouth, clad in numbered waistcoats. Odd-numbered sois run off the north side of Thanon Sukhumvit, even-numbered off the south side; some of the sois have become important enough to earn their own names, which are often used in preference to their numbers; many sois are long enough to have sub-sois running off them, which usually have their own numbers (or names).

The Atlanta At the far southern end of Soi 2 ⓦtheatlantahotelbangkok.com. A Bangkok institution, this classic, five-storey budget hotel was built in 1952 around a famously photogenic Art Deco-style lobby and continues to emphasize an old-fashioned, conservative style of hospitality. It offers some of the cheapest accommodation on Sukhumvit: rooms are plain and simple, though they are all en suite and some have a/c and hot water; many have small balconies. There's a swimming pool and kids' pool in the garden, a good restaurant and a free left-luggage facility. **BB**

Grand Mercure Bangkok Atrium 1880 Thanon Phetchaburi Mai ⓦall.accor.com. Good-value, 600-room luxury hotel that's a little to the north of the Sukhumvit strip, but handy for the subway (Phetchaburi), the airport rail link (Makkasan) and Khlong Saen Saeb boats. Well-equipped, tasteful rooms enjoy great views of downtown, and there's a delicious and theatrical Japanese teppanyaki restaurant, *Benihana*. **BBB**

Hilton Sukhumvit 11 Soi 24 ⓦhilton.com. This high-end luxury hotel cleverly links the skyscraper cities of New York and Bangkok, with an Art Deco-influenced contemporary design that's intended to suggest 1920s Manhattan. The design continues in the excellent Italian restaurant, *Scalini*, and in the capacious bedrooms and their opulent bathrooms; on the rooftop are an infinity pool and a gym. **BBBB**

Marriott Marquis Queens Park 199 Soi 22 ⓦmarriott.com. This 1400-room hotel overlooks and has direct access to Benjasiri Park (and its jogging track). Luxurious rooms offer subtly appealing hints of Thai style in their contemporary decor, and there's a lovely spa. A wide choice of eating outlets includes a Thai-Western tea room, a Chinese restaurant and, on the rooftop, a clubby cocktail bar and a spectacular contemporary Asian restaurant, *Akira Back*, that fuses Japanese, Korean and Western influences (see page 166). **BBBB**

Park Plaza 9 Soi 18 ⓦparkplaza.com. The quieter and newer of two nearby Park Plazas, this small hotel is topped by an appealing, open-air 20m pool, gym and bar-restaurant on the eighth floor. The rooms sport a perky contemporary look, with bright colours set against businessman's black. **BBB**

DOWNTOWN: SOUTH OF THANON RAMA IV
SEE MAPS PAGES 102 AND 108

South of Thanon Rama IV, the area sometimes known as Bangrak contains a wide cross-section of accommodation. As well as a fair scattering of medium-range places, the arc between Thanon Rama IV and the river also lays claim to the capital's biggest selection of top hotels, which are among the most opulent in the world. Traversed by the Skytrain, this area is especially good for eating and for gay and straight nightlife, mostly near the east end of Thanon Silom (around which several gay-friendly hotels are scattered). Staying by the river itself in the atmospheric area around Thanon Charoen Krung, also known as New Road, has the added advantage of easy access to express boats.

★ Anantara Riverside 257 Thanon Charoennakorn ⓦanantara.com. A luxury retreat from the frenetic city centre, well to the south on the Thonburi bank, but connected to Taksin Bridge (for the Skytrain and express river boats), 15min away, by regular hotel ferries. Arrayed around a highly appealing, landscaped swimming pool, the tranquil, riverside gardens are filled with birdsong, while the stylish and spacious bedrooms come with varnished hardwood floors and balconies. There's a fitness centre, tennis courts, kids' club, a spa, and among a wide choice of places to eat, an excellent Japanese teppanyaki house. **BBBB**

Avani Riverside 257 Thanon Charoennakorn ⓦavanihotels.com. Thoroughly modern luxury hotel with creative touches such as stylish work stations in the *Long Bar* and a deli-coffee bar. Though the hotel is set back a little from the Chao Phraya, towering views of the city and its riverscape are enjoyed by all of the rooms, the rooftop, infinity-edge pool and the excellent bar-restaurant on the same floor, *Seen*, which is staffed by fine chefs, mixologists and late-night DJs. Guests can use most of the facilities of the adjacent *Anantara Riverside* (see left), including its shuttle boats. **BBBB**

Como Metropolitan 27 Thanon Sathorn Tai

comohotels.com. The height of chic, minimalist urban living, where the spacious, Zen-like rooms are decorated in dark wood and creamy Portuguese limestone. There's a very seductive pool, a fine spa, a well-equipped fitness centre with bubbling hydro-pools, a yoga studio with free daily classes, and an excellent restaurant, *Nahm* (see page 168). BBBB

Dusit Thani Corner of Thanon Rama IV and Thanon Silom dusit.com. Thailand's tallest building when it opened in 1970, the *Dusit Thani* has recently reopened after a thorough makeover, as part of the Dusit Central Park mixed-use development, which will feature a three-acre roof park and jogging track. The hotel's reincarnation makes even more of its landmark location (it's also at the intersection of the subway and Skytrain lines), with all the luxurious bedrooms now enjoying views over Lumphini Park from their floor-to-ceiling windows. In addition to a tempting range of dining venues, the hotel now makes the most of its rooftop with a convivial bar beneath its trademark golden spire. BBBB

★ **Four Seasons** 300/1 Thanon Charoen Krung, 1km south of Saphan Taksin fourseasons.com. The newest addition to Bangkok's luxury hotel scene features beautiful landscaped gardens with riverside infinity-edge and lap swimming pools, alongside other striking water features. The interior decor of earth tones with hints of contemporary primitivism extends to the bedrooms, lofty spaces with floor-to-ceiling windows and acres of marble in the bathrooms. An art gallery, a spa and wellness centre, Cantonese and Italian restaurants and a French brasserie and patisserie round out the picture. BBBB

Le Siam 3 Thanon Convent lesiamhotel.com. Friendly – and genuinely eco-friendly – boutique hotel, with high standards of service, just off Thanon Silom and ideally placed for business and nightlife. Staying true to the origins of the hotel, which was founded as Bangkok's first guesthouse, *The Swiss Guesthouse*, in 1953, the swish, well-designed rooms offer very good value, and there's a tiny terrace swimming pool. BBB

Luxx Silom 6/11 Thanon Decho staywithluxx. com. Welcoming boutique hotel offering a good dose of contemporary style at reasonable prices. Decorated in white, grey and natural teak, the rooms feature cute wooden Japanese-style baths surmounted by rain showers. BBB

Peninsula Bangkok 333 Thanon Charoennakorn peninsula.com. Located on the Thonburi bank, with shuttle boats down to Taksin Bridge and its BTS station, this is an excellent top-class hotel, where the ultra-luxurious decor stylishly blends traditional Western and Asian design, and every room has a panoramic view of the Chao Phraya. The lovely riverside gardens shelter a three-tiered pool, a beautiful spa, a fitness centre and a tennis court, while restaurants include the classy *Mei Jiang* Cantonese restaurant (see page 168). BBBB

Rose 118 Thanon Suriwong facebook.com/people/Rose-Hotel/100066967370477. Set back from the main road but very handy for the city's nightlife, the compact rooms here (all with bathtubs) boast a simple but stylish, modernist look, enhanced by paintings and silk cushions. The ground-floor public rooms are more elegant again, and there's a beautiful swimming pool, a small gym, saunas and a good Thai restaurant, *Ruen Urai* (see page 168), at the back. BB

★ **Sukhothai** 13/3 Thanon Sathorn Tai sukhothai. com. The most elegant of Bangkok's top hotels, its decor inspired by the walled city of Sukhothai, offers low-rise accommodation, as well as a beautiful garden spa, all coolly furnished in silks, teak and granite. Service is of the highest standard and the architecture makes the most of the views of the surrounding six acres of gardens, lotus ponds and pools dotted with statuary. There's also a health club, a 25m infinity pool and excellent restaurants including *Celadon* (see page 167). BBBB

Tarntawan Hotel 119/5–10 Thanon Suriwong tarntawansurawong.com. Set back from the main road, a pretty, plant-strewn lobby announces this welcoming and well-run, gay-friendly hotel. The decent-sized, well-equipped rooms are gracefully furnished in natural colours with traditional Thai design elements, and all have bathtubs. BB

SUVARNABHUMI AIRPORT SEE MAP PAGE 108

Avani Sukhumvit 2089 Thanon Sukhumvit avanihotels.com. Well placed between Suvarnabhumi and the city centre, this sleek, contemporary hotel is a great four-star choice, with a spa, a gym and a seductive rooftop pool. Less than thirty minutes' drive from the airport, it has direct access to Exit 3 of On Nut Skytrain station and also offers four-hour and day packages. BBB

Mariya Boutique Residence 1627/2 Thanon Latkrabang mariyahotel.com. A 5min drive from the airport to the northeast (with pick-ups available 24hr), this well-organized hotel offers hot showers, double-glazed windows, minibars, cable TV, microwaves and kettles in all of the bedrooms, which feature some traditional Thai touches in the appealing decor. BB

Novotel Suvarnabhumi novotel.com. The official airport hotel, set within the complex and a 10min walk from arrivals via a walkway in the basement (or catch the shuttle bus from outside arrivals Gate 4). Offering smart, contemporary rooms with marble bathrooms, Thai, Japanese, Cantonese and international restaurants, a spa, swimming pool and fitness centre, the eco-friendly *Novotel* operates on a 24hr basis – you can check in at any time, and check out 24hr later. BBBB

STREET FOOD VENDOR

Eating

Bangkok boasts an astonishing fifty thousand places to eat, ranging from makeshift streetside noodle shops to the most elegant of restaurants. Despite this glut, an awful lot of visitors venture no further than the front doorstep of their guesthouse, preferring the dining room's ersatz Thai or Western dishes to the more adventurous food to be found in even the most touristy accommodation areas.

Thai restaurants of all types are found all over the city. The best **gourmet Thai** restaurants operate from the downtown districts, proffering wonderful royal, traditional and regional cuisines that definitely merit a visit – though even here, you're unlikely to spend more than B600 per person. Over in Banglamphu, Thanon Phra Arthit is known for its idiosyncratic little restaurant-bars angled at young Thai diners. At the other end of the scale, as well as the **food courts** of shopping centres and department stores listed below, there are the **night markets** and **street stalls**, where you can generally get a lip-smacking feast for around B150 or less. However in 2017 – just after CNN declared Bangkok the best city in the world for street food – the city authorities announced that they were going to rid the pavements of all vendors. They later backtracked, saying the street stalls in Chinatown and Banglamphu could stay, and, at the time of writing, it didn't seem that the ban was being rigorously enforced in the rest of the city.

Most restaurants in Bangkok are open every day for lunch and dinner. Inexpensive Thai restaurants and cafés specialize in one general food type or preparation method, charging around B50 a dish – a "noodle shop", for example, will do fried noodles and/or noodle soups, plus maybe a basic fried rice, but they won't have curries or meat or fish dishes. Similarly, a restaurant displaying whole roast chickens and ducks in its window will offer these sliced, usually with chillies and sauces and served over rice, but their menu probably won't extend to noodles or fish, while in "curry shops" your options are limited to the vats of curries stewing away in the hot cabinet. Some large markets have separate food court areas where you buy coupons first and select food and

REGIONAL THAI FOOD

In Bangkok, you'll be served mostly central Thai cuisine, but all of the country's regional cuisines are also on offer. Northeastern food is the most prevalent, partly due to the large numbers of migrants from the northeast (or Isaan) who work in the capital.

Many of the specialities of **northern Thailand** originated in Burma, including *khao soi*, featuring both boiled and crispy egg noodles plus beef, chicken or pork in a curried coconut soup; and *kaeng hang lay*, a pork curry with ginger, turmeric and tamarind. Also look out for spicy dipping sauces such as *nam phrik ong*, made with minced pork, roast tomatoes and lemon grass, and served with crisp cucumber slices. The crop most suited to the infertile lands of **Isaan** is sticky rice (*khao niaw*), which replaces the standard grain as the staple for northeasterners. Served in a rattan basket, it's usually eaten with the fingers, rolled up into small balls and dipped into chilli sauces. It's perfect with such local delicacies as basted barbecued chicken (*kai yaang*) and *som tam*, a spicy green-papaya salad with raw chillies, green beans, tomatoes, peanuts and dried shrimps (or fresh crab). Raw minced pork, beef or chicken is the basis of another popular Isaan and northern dish, *laap*, a salad that's subtly flavoured with mint and lime. A similar northeastern salad is *nam tok*, featuring grilled beef or pork and roasted rice powder, which takes its name, "waterfall", from its refreshing blend of complex tastes.

Aside from putting a greater emphasis on seafood, **southern Thai cuisine** displays a marked Malaysian and Muslim aspect, notably in *khao mok kai*, the local version of a biryani: chicken and rice cooked with turmeric and other Indian spices, and served with chicken soup. Southerners often eat *khao yam* for breakfast or lunch, a delicious salad of dried cooked rice, dried shrimp and grated coconut served with a sweet sauce. You'll also find many types of roti in Bangkok, a pancake sold from pushcart griddles and, in its plain form, rolled with condensed milk. Other versions include savoury *mataba*, with minced chicken or beef, and *roti kaeng*, served with curry sauce for breakfast. A huge variety of especially spicy curries also come from the south, many substituting shrimp paste for fish sauce. Two of the most distinctive are *kaeng luang*, "yellow curry", featuring fish, turmeric, pineapple, squash, beans and green papaya; and *kaeng tai plaa*, a powerful combination of fish stomach with potatoes, beans, pickled bamboo shoots and turmeric.

drink to their value at the stalls of your choice. This is also usually the modus operandi in the food courts found in department stores and shopping centres, though some of the more modern ones issue each diner with a plastic card, on which is recorded their expenditure, for payment at the end.

For those interested in **learning to cook Thai food**, short courses designed for visitors are on offer (see page 161).

ESSENTIALS

HOW TO EAT

Thai food is eaten with a fork (left hand) and a spoon (right hand); there is no need for a knife as food is served in bite-sized chunks, which are forked onto the spoon and fed into the mouth. Cutlery is often delivered to the table wrapped in a perplexingly tiny pink napkin: Thais use this, not for their lap, but to give their fork, spoon and plate an extra wipe-down before they eat. Steamed rice (*khao*) is taken with most meals, and indeed the most commonly heard phrase for "to eat" is *kin khao* (literally, "eat rice"). Chopsticks are provided only for noodle dishes, and northeastern and northern sticky-rice dishes are usually eaten with the fingers of your right hand. Never eat with the fingers of your left hand, which is used for washing after going to the toilet.

So that complementary taste combinations can be enjoyed, the dishes in a Thai meal are served all at once, even the soup, and shared communally. The more people, the more taste and texture sensations; if there are only two of you, it's normal to order three dishes, plus your own individual plates of steamed rice, while three diners would order four dishes, and so on. Only put a serving of one dish on the side of your rice plate each time, and then only one or two spoonfuls.

Bland food is anathema to Thais, and restaurant tables everywhere come decked out with condiment sets featuring the four most basic flavours (salty, sour, sweet and spicy): usually fish sauce with chopped chillies; vinegar with chopped chillies; sugar; and dried chillies – and often extra bowls of ground peanuts and a bottle of chilli ketchup as well. Similarly, many individual Thai dishes are served with their own specific, usually spicy, condiment dip (*nam jim*). If you do bite into a chilli, the way to combat the searing heat is to take a mouthful of plain rice and/or beer: swigging water just exacerbates the sensation.

THAI CUISINE

Thai food is now hugely popular in the West, but nothing, of course, beats coming to Thailand to experience the full range of subtle and fiery flavours, constructed from the freshest ingredients. Five fundamental tastes are identified in Thai cuisine – spiciness, sourness, bitterness, saltiness and sweetness. Lemon grass, basil, coriander, galangal, chilli, garlic, lime juice, coconut milk and fermented fish sauce (used instead of salt) are just some of the distinctive components that bring these tastes to life.

Curries (kaeng) Thai curries have as their foundation a variety of curry pastes, elaborate blends of herbs, spices, garlic, shallots and chilli peppers traditionally ground together with a pestle and mortar. The use of some of these spices, as well as of coconut cream, was imported from India long ago; curries without coconut cream are naturally less sweet and thinner, with the consistency of soups. While some curries, such as *kaeng karii* (mild and yellow) and *kaeng matsaman* (literally "Muslim curry", with potatoes, peanuts and usually beef), still show their roots, others have been adapted into quintessentially Thai dishes, notably *kaeng khiaw wan* (sweet and green), *kaeng phet* (red and hot) and *kaeng phanaeng* (thick and savoury, with peanuts). *Kaeng som* generally contains vegetables and fish and takes its distinctive sourness from the addition of tamarind or, in the northeast, okra leaves. Traditionally eaten during the cool season, *kaeng liang* uses up gourds or other bland vegetables, but is made aromatic by the heat of peppercorns and shallots and the fragrance of basil leaves.

Soups (tom) An essential component of most shared meals, thai soups are eaten simultaneously with other dishes, not as a starter. They are often flavoured with the distinctive tang of lemon grass, kaffir lime leaves and galangal, and garnished with fresh coriander – and can be extremely hot, if the cook adds liberal handfuls of chillies to the pot. Two favourites are *tom kha kai*, a creamy coconut chicken soup; and *tom yam kung*, a hot and sour prawn soup without coconut milk. *Khao tom* and *jok*, starchy rice soups often eaten for breakfast, meet the approval of few Westerners, except as a traditional hangover cure.

Salads (yam) One of the lesser-known delights of Thai cuisine is salad, which can often impart all five of the fundamental flavours in an unusual and refreshing harmony. *Yam* can be made in many permutations – with noodles, meat, seafood or vegetables – but at the heart of most varieties is fresh lime juice and a fiery sprinkling of chopped chillies. As well as *som tam, laap* and northeastern Thailand's *nam tok* (see box below), salads to look out for include *yam som oh* (pomelo), *yam hua plee* (banana flowers) and *yam plaa duk foo* (deep-fried catfish).

Noodle dishes Thais eat noodles when Westerners would dig into a sandwich – for lunch or as a late-night snack. Sold on street stalls everywhere, they come in assorted varieties – including *kway tiaw* (made with rice flour) and *ba mii* (egg noodles), *sen yai* (wide) and *sen lek* (thin) – and get boiled up as soups (*nam*), doused in gravy (*rat na*) or stir-fried (*haeng*, "dry", or *phat*, "fried"). Most famous of noodle dishes is *kway tiaw phat thai* – usually abbreviated to *phat thai*, meaning "Thai fry-up" – a delicious mix of fried noodles, bean sprouts, egg, tofu and spring onions, sprinkled with ground peanuts and lime juice, and often spiked with tiny dried shrimps.

Rice dishes Fried rice (*khao phat*) is the other faithful standby that features on menus right across the country. Also popular are cheap, one-dish meals served on a bed of steamed rice, notably *khao kaeng* (with curry), *khao na pet* (with roast duck) and *khao muu daeng* (with red-roasted pork).

Desserts (khanom waan) Desserts are usually sold at specialist shops and don't really figure on most restaurant menus, though a few places offer bowls of *luk taan cheum*, a jellied concoction of lotus or palm seeds floating in a syrup scented with jasmine or other aromatic flowers. Coconut milk is a feature of most other desserts, notably delicious coconut ice cream; *khao niaw mamuang/thurian* (sticky rice with mango or durian); *khao niaw daeng* (sticky red rice mixed with coconut cream); *takoh*, which consists of squares of transparent jelly (jello) topped with coconut cream; and a royal Thai cuisine special of coconut custard (*sangkhayaa*) cooked inside a small pumpkin, whose flesh you can also eat.

INTERNATIONAL CUISINES

For the non-Thai cuisines, Chinatown naturally rates as the most authentic district for pure Chinese food; likewise neighbouring Pahurat, the capital's Indian enclave, is best for unadulterated Indian dishes, while there's a sprinkling of Indian and (mostly southern Thai) Muslim restaurants around Silom's Maha Uma Devi Temple and nearby Thanon Charoen Krung. Sukhumvit's Soi 3 is a hub for Middle Eastern cafés, complete with hookah pipes at the outdoor tables; good, comparatively cheap Japanese restaurants can be found, for example, on and around Soi Thaniya, at the east end of Thanon Silom; and there's a Korean enclave in Sukhumvit Plaza, at the corner of Soi 12. The place to head for inexpensive, Western, travellers' food – from herbal teas and hamburgers to muesli – as well as a hearty range of veggie options, is Thanon Khao San; standards vary, but there are some definite gems among the blander establishments.

VEGETARIANS AND VEGANS

Very few Thais are **vegetarian** (*mangsawirat*) but, if you can make yourself understood, you can often get a non-meat or fish alternative to what's on the menu; simply ask the cook to exclude meat and fish: *mai sai neua, mai sai plaa*. You may end up eating a lot of unexciting vegetable fried rice and *phat thai* minus the shrimps, but in better restaurants you should be able to get veggie versions of most curries; the mushroom version of chicken and coconut soup is also a good standby: ask for *tom kha hed*. Browsing food stalls also expands your options, with barbecued sweetcorn, nuts, fruit and other non-meaty goodies all common. The two ingredients that you will have to consider compromising on are the fermented **fish sauce** and **shrimp paste** that are fundamental to most Thai dishes; only in the vegan Thai restaurants described below, and in tourist spots serving specially concocted Thai and Western veggie dishes, can you be sure of avoiding them.

If you're **vegan** (*jay*, sometimes spelt "*jeh*") you'll need to stress when you order that you don't want egg, as they get used a lot; cheese and other dairy produce, however, don't feature at all in Thai cuisine. Dotted around Bangkok are **vegan restaurants** (*raan ahaan jay*), which are usually run by members of a temple or Buddhist sect and operate from unadorned premises off the main streets; because strict Buddhists prefer not to eat late in the day, most of the restaurants open early, at around 6 or 7am, and close by 2pm. Most of these places have a yellow and red sign, though few display an English-language name. Nor is there ever a menu: customers simply choose from the trays of veggie stir-fries and curries, nearly all of them made with soya products, that are laid out canteen-style. Most places charge around B50 for a couple of helpings served over a plate of brown rice.

PRACTICALITIES

Tipping In the more expensive restaurants listed below you may have to pay a ten percent service charge and seven percent VAT (which may be increased to ten percent).

Health Hygiene is a consideration when eating anywhere in Bangkok, but being too cautious means you'll end up spending a lot of money and missing out on some real treats – you can be pretty sure any noodle stall or curry shop that's permanently packed with customers is a safe bet. Foods that are generally considered high risk include salads, shellfish, raw or undercooked meat, fish or eggs, ice and ice cream. Thais don't drink water straight from the tap and neither should you: plastic bottles of drinking water (*nam plao*) are sold everywhere for around B10, as well as the usual multinational panoply of soft drinks.

EATING PRICE CODES

Each restaurant and café reviewed in this Guide is accompanied by a price category, based on the cost of a one-dish meal for one, including a non-alcoholic drink.

B̲ = under B100
B̲B̲ = B100–200
B̲B̲B̲ = B200–300
B̲B̲B̲B̲ = over B300

YELLOW-FLAG HEAVEN FOR VEGGIES

Every year, for nine days during the ninth lunar month (between late Sept and Nov), Thailand's Chinese community goes on a **meat-free** diet to mark the onset of the **Vegetarian Festival** (Ngan Kin Jeh), a sort of Taoist version of Lent. Though the Chinese citizens of Bangkok don't go in for skewering themselves like their compatriots in Phuket, they do celebrate the Vegetarian Festival with gusto: some people choose to wear only white for the duration, all the temples throng with activity, and nearly every restaurant and food stall in Chinatown turns vegetarian for the period, flying small yellow flags to show that they are upholding the tradition and participating in what's essentially a nightly veggie food jamboree. For vegetarian tourists this is a great time to be in town – just look for the yellow flag and you can be sure all dishes will be one hundred percent vegetarian. Soya substitutes are a popular feature on the vegetarian Chinese menu, so don't be surprised to find pink prawn-shaped objects floating in your noodle soup or unappetizingly realistic slices of fake duck. Many hotel restaurants also get in on the act during the Vegetarian Festival, running special veggie promotions for a week or two.

RATANAKOSIN   SEE MAP PAGE 51

The places reviewed below are especially handy for sightseers, but there are also plenty of street stalls around Tha Chang and a load of simple, student restaurants off the north end of Thanon Maharat near Thammasat University, as well as a riverside café at *Aurum The River Place* (see page 150).

Navy Club (Krua Khun Kung) Tha Chang ☎ 02 222 0081. This place is immediately on the south side of the express-boat pier, but a little tricky to get to: from the corner of Na Phra Lan road, walk down Thanon Maharat a short way and go in through the car park of the navy compound. The decor's deeply institutionalized but the real draw is the shaded terrace built over the river, where you can enjoy excellent dried prawn and lemon-grass salad, *haw mok thalay* (seafood curry soufflé) and other marine delights. BB

★ **Supanniga Eating Room** Riva Arun Hotel, 392/25–26 Thanon Maharat ⓦ supannigaeatingroom. com. The upstairs terrace at this riverside restaurant-coffee bar, with head-on views of freshly renovated Wat Arun, is a great place to try the distinctive cuisine of Chanthaburi, famous for its herbs and spices – the delicious mixed appetiser platter is a great place to start, followed by *moo cha muang*, a mild red curry of stewed pork. The restaurant's other speciality is food from Isaan, where the family have a boutique hotel in Khon Kaen. BBB

BANGLAMPHU AND THE DEMOCRACY MONUMENT AREA   SEE MAP PAGE 68

Copycat entrepreneurship means that Khao San is stacked full of backpacker restaurants serving near-identical Western and (mostly) watered-down Thai food; there's even a lane, one block east, parallel to Thanon Tanao (behind *Burger King*), that's dominated by vegetarian cafés, following a trend started by *May Kaidee*. Hot-food stalls selling very cheap night-market snacks operate until the early hours. Things are more varied over on Thanon Phra Arthit, with its arty little café-restaurants favoured by Thammasat University students, while the riverside places, on Phra Arthit and further north off Thanon Samsen and in Thewet, tend to be best for seafood with a view. For the real old-fashioned Thai taste though, browse southern Thanon Tanao, where traditional shophouses have been selling specialist sweets and savouries for generations.

AROUND THANON KHAO SAN

Madame Musur Soi Ram Bhuttri ⓦ facebook.com/madamemusur. Mellow bar-restaurant festooned with vines and paper lanterns with good people-watching tables on the alley, serving a wide range of drinks, including good espressos, and authentic northern Thai food – try the *khantoke*, two kinds of chilli dip with pork scratchings and organic vegetables. BB

★ **May Kaidee** East off Thanon Tanao ⓦ maykaidee. com. Simple, neighbourhood Thai vegan restaurant that still serves some of the best veggie and vegan food in Banglamphu despite having spawned several competitors on the same alley. Come for the tasty green curry, the Vietnamese-style veggie spring rolls or the sticky black-rice pudding with mango or banana. Also runs a variety of cookery courses (see page 164). BB

Nittaya 136 Thanon Chakrabongse; map page 68. This shop is nationally famous for its *nam phrik* (chilli dips) and curry pastes (which are available vacuum-packed), but it serves all kinds of food to take away – perhaps to eat in nearby Santichaiprakarn Park (see page 67) – including snacks and desserts. B

PHRA ARTHIT AREA

★ **Hemlock** 56 Thanon Phra Arthit ⓦ facebook.com/HemlockBangkok. Small, stylish, a/c restaurant that's

DINNER AND BREAKFAST CRUISES

The **Chao Phraya River** looks fabulous at night, when most of the noisy longtails have stopped terrorizing the ferries, and the riverside temples, other fine monuments such as the Grand Palace and an increasing number of historic houses are elegantly illuminated. Joining one of the nightly **dinner cruises** along the river is a great way to appreciate it all, especially on one of the teak barges listed below, which are preferable to the big, modern boats with live music. The latter – also with options for sunset cruises, Indian food and cabaret – are offered by the Chao Phraya River Cruises agency (W thairivercruise.com). Contact ahead of time to reserve a table and check departure details – some cruises may not run during the rainy season (May–Oct).

Baan Khanitha W baan-khanitha.com. Two-hour cruises from Icon Siam shopping centre on a teak barge, offering a choice of Thai set dinners catered by the famous Bangkok restaurant (see page 166).

Manohra W manohracruises.com. Beautiful converted teak rice-barges operated by the *Anantara Riverside Resort*, south of Taksin Bridge in Thonburi, serving a choice of Thai set dinners on thrice-nightly two-hour cruises; take the first cruise if you want to make the most of the sunset. They also offer weekend breakfast cruises, including a guided tour of Wat Arun.

---

very popular with students and young Thai couples. Offers a long, mid-priced menu, including delicious *tom yam* and green and *phanaeng* curries, as well as more unusual dishes such as several kinds of *laap* (spicy ground meat salad). The traditional *miang* starters (shiny green wild tea leaves filled with chopped vegetables, fish, prawn or meat) are also very tasty, and there's a good vegetarian selection. Worth reserving a table on Friday and Saturday nights. **BB**

Kway Jap Yuan Khun Daeng Thanon Phra Arthit T 085 246 0111. This basic, bustling canteen does a roaring trade with Thammasat University students, who come for the delicious *kway jap yuan*, noodle soup similar to Vietnamese *pho* but a little starchier – go for the "extra" version with egg and you're set up for the day. Find it in an historic shophouse, unmistakably painted white and green – colours which the flamboyant owner often sports himself. **B**

★ **Praya Palazzo** 757/1 Soi 2, Thanon Somdet Phra Pinklao W prayapalazzo.com. Superb royal Thai cuisine, using hard-to-find recipes that came out of Rama V's palace. Complex flavours come together in perfect harmony, in roast shrimp dip with crispy catfish, spicy beef soup with shrimp paste, and pork with yellow chili paste. Or make the most of the boat ride and the historic architecture of this small garden hotel by coming for afternoon tea, which features delicious Thai sweets and cakes. Call to make a booking and arrange a free pick-up from Tha Phra Arthit express-boat pier. **BBBB**

Roti Mataba Karim 136 Thanon Phra Arthit W roti-mataba.net. Famous 70-year-old halal outlet for the ever-popular fried Indian breads, or *rotis*, served here in lots of sweet and savoury varieties, including stuffed with meat and veg (*mataba*), served with vegetable and meat curries, or with bananas and condensed milk; biryanis (*khao mok*) are also on offer. Choose between pavement tables and a basic upstairs a/c room. **B**

THANON SAMSEN AND THEWET

Jok Phochana On a side soi running between Soi 2 and Soi 4, Thanon Samsen. This bare-basics, forty-year-old night-time restaurant, which has featured on national TV, is about as real as you're going to get near Thanon Khao San, and serves a mean green curry. The day's ingredients are colourfully displayed at the front of the shop, and the quiet pavement tables get more crowded as the night wears on. **B**

Kaloang Home Kitchen Beside the river (follow the bend round) at the far western end of Thanon Sri Ayutthaya W facebook.com/kaloanghomekitchen. Flamboyant service and excellent seafood attracts a largely Thai clientele to this open-air, no-frills, bare-wood restaurant that perches on a stilted deck over the river. Dishes well worth sampling include the fried rolled shrimps served with a sweet dip and any of the host of Thai salads. **BB**

Kinlom Chom Saphan Riverside end of Soi 3, Thanon Samsen W facebook.com/Khinlomchomsaphan. This sprawling, waterside restaurant merits its poetic name, "eat the wind and savour the bridge", enjoying river breezes and close-up views of the lyre-like Rama VIII Bridge. It's always busy with a youngish Thai crowd who are entertained by live music. The predominantly seafood menu features everything from crab to grouper cooked in multiple ways, but never with MSG. **BBB**

★ **Krua Apsorn** Thanon Samsen, opposite Thanon Uthong Nok on the southwestern edge of Dusit W facebook.com/kruaapsorn; Thanon Dinso T 02 685 4531. Very good, spicy and authentic food and a genteel welcome make this unpretentious, a/c restaurant popular with the area's civil servants – as well as the royalty whom they serve. Try the green fish-ball curry or the yellow curry with river prawns and lotus shoots, both recommended by the leading Thai restaurant guide, MacDang, and then put out the fire in your mouth with home-made coconut sorbet. **BBB**

★ **May Kaidee** Soi 5, Thanon Samsen ⓦ maykaidee. com. Branch of the famous vegan restaurant off Thanon Khao San (see page 161), where cookery courses are held (see page 164). __BB__

Somsong Pochana Soi Lamphu (Soi Wat Sangwet), Thanon Samsen (though closer to Thanon Phra Sumen)

ⓦ facebook.com/CoconutPalmThaiFood. Excellent lunch place serving unusual dishes such as Sukhothai-style noodles and *khanom jiin sao nam*, rice noodles with pineapple, dried shrimp and coconut cream. __B__

Steve Café and Cuisine Wat Thawarad ⓦ stevecafeandcuisine.com. In a lovely riverside setting with views

FRUITS OF THAILAND

You'll find **fruit** (*phonlamai*) offered everywhere in Bangkok – neatly sliced in glass boxes on hawker carts, blended into delicious shakes and served as a dessert in restaurants. The fruits described here come from all parts of Thailand; with enhanced agricultural techniques – and imports – many of them can now be found year-round, but we've given the traditional seasons where applicable below, which is when they should be at their best and cheapest. The country's more familiar fruits include forty varieties of **banana** (*kluay*), dozens of different **mangoes** (*mamuang*), several types of **pineapple** (*sapparot*), **coconuts** (*maprao*), **oranges** (*som*), **limes** (*manao*) and **watermelons** (*taeng moh*). Thailand's most prized and expensive fruit is the **durian** (*thurian*).

To avoid stomach trouble, **peel all fruit** before eating it, and use common sense if you're tempted to buy it pre-peeled on the street, avoiding anything that looks fly-blown or seems to have been sitting in the sun for hours.

Custard apple (*noina*; July–Sept). Inside the knobbly, muddy green skin is a creamy, almond-coloured blancmange-like flesh, with a strong flavour of strawberries and pears, and a hint of cinnamon, and many seeds.

Guava (*farang*; year-round). The apple of the tropics has green textured skin and sweet, crisp pink or white flesh, studded with tiny edible seeds. Has five times the vitamin C content of an orange and is sometimes eaten cut into strips and sprinkled with sugar and chilli.

Jackfruit (*khanun*; year-round). This large, pear-shaped fruit can weigh up to 20kg and has a thick, bobbly, greeny-yellow shell protecting sweet yellow flesh. Green, unripe jackfruit is sometimes cooked in curries or pounded in salads, especially in the north.

Longan (*lamyai*; July–Oct). A close relative of the lychee, with succulent white flesh covered in thin, brittle skin.

Lychee (*linjii*; April–May). Under rough, reddish-brown skin, the lychee has sweet, richly flavoured white flesh, rose scented and with plenty of vitamin C.

Mangosteen (*mangkut*; April–Sept). The size of a small apple, with smooth, purple skin and a fleshy inside that divides into succulent white segments that are sweet though slightly acidic.

Papaya (paw-paw; *malakaw*; year-round). Looks like an elongated watermelon, with smooth green skin and yellowy-orange flesh that's a rich source of vitamins A and C. It's a favourite in fruit salads and shakes, and sometimes appears in its green, unripe form in salads, notably *som tam*.

Pomelo (*som oh*; Oct–Dec). The largest of all the citrus fruits, it looks rather like a grapefruit, though it is sweeter; sometimes used in delicious salads.

Rambutan (*ngaw*; May–Sept). The bright red rambutan's soft, spiny exterior has given it its name – *rambut* means "hair" in Malay. Usually about the size of a golf ball, it has a white, opaque flesh of delicate flavour, similar to a lychee.

Rose apple (*chomphuu*; year-round). Linked in myth with the golden fruit of immortality; small and pear-shaped, with white, rose-scented flesh.

Sapodilla (sapota; *lamut*; Sept–Dec). These small, brown, rough-skinned ovals look a bit like kiwi fruit and conceal a grainy, yellowish pulp that tastes almost honey-sweet.

Tamarind (*makhaam*; Dec–Jan). A Thai favourite and a pricey delicacy – carrying the seeds is said to make you safe from wounding by knives or bullets. Comes in rough, brown pods containing up to ten seeds, each surrounded by a sticky, dry pulp which has a lemony taste; generally sour, but some parts of the country, notably Phetchabun, produce sweet tamarinds.

> ### THAI COOKERY CLASSES IN BANGKOK
>
> **Baipai** 8/91 Soi 54, Thanon Ngam Wongwan w baipai.com. Thorough, four-hour classes in an attractive garden house in northern Bangkok. Transfers from central hotels included.
>
> **Cooking with Poo and Friends** Klong Toey w cookingwithpoo.com. Set up by the ebullient Khun Poo with the help of a Christian charity, a chance to experience the slums of Klong Toey and spend a morning learning to cook. Also included are a market tour and free transfers from next to Phrom Pong BTS station.
>
> **May Kaidee** Soi 5, Thanon Samsen w maykaidee. com. Banglamphu's famous vegetarian and vegan restaurant (see page 161) offers courses in Thai vegan cooking, tofu making and fruit carving, and hopes to add a wider variety of classes again in the future.
>
> **Thai House** 22km from central Bangkok in Bangmuang w thaihouse.co.th. Set in a rural part of Nonthaburi province, here you can do one- to three-day cooking courses, all including transfers from downtown. The three-day course includes a market visit, all meals and homestay accommodation in a lovely traditional teak house with a kitchen garden.

of Rama VIII Bridge, come here for great service and a huge menu that encompasses southern, northern and northeastern Thai specialities and fusion dishes, including a very tasty and spicy salmon *laap*. It's easy to see, right across the mouth of Khlong Krung Kasem from Tha Thewet express-boat pier, though harder to get there, walking round and right through the grounds of the temple. BBB

SOUTH OF DEMOCRACY

Kai Yang Boran 474–476 Thanon Tanao, immediately to the south of the Chao Poh Seua Chinese shrine t 02 622 2349. Locally famous grilled chicken and *som tam* (green papaya salad) restaurant (with a/c), wallpapered with photos of celebrities who have eaten here. *Nam tok* salad with roast pork and several kinds of *laap* round out the northeastern menu. BB

Kor Panit (K. Panich) 431–433 Thanon Tanao, on the east side, directly opposite Thanon Phraeng Phuton. Outstanding coconut-laced sticky rice has been sold at this daytime spot since 1932; no English sign, but look for the mango vendors outside. You can choose your own variety to accompany the delicious *khao niaw* (sticky rice with coconut milk) to take away, or the shop will do you a plate of *khao niaw mamuang* to eat in, sitting on their one large wooden bench. BB

★ **Krua Apsorn** Thanon Dinso w facebook.com/kruaapsorn. Branch of the excellent Samsen restaurant (see page 162). BBB

Nattaporn 94 Thanon Phraeng Phuton, just off Thanon Kanlayana Maitri w facebook.com/nuttapornicecream94. This family has been specializing in its famous ice cream homemade from the milk of fresh coconuts for over sixty years, topping it with classic Thai condiments like sweetcorn, red beans and taro balls. They also do coconut-milk ice cream in mango, chocolate, coffee and tea flavours, as well as durian when in season. No English sign, but it's a basic daytime shophouse, right next door to *The Bhuthorn* guesthouse. B

Padthai Thipsamai 313 Thanon Mahachai, near Wat Rajnadda w thipsamai.com. The most famous *phat thai* in Bangkok, flash-fried by the same family since 1966. The "special" option is huge, comes with especially juicy prawns, and is wrapped in a translucent, paper-thin omelette. Best washed down with fresh coconut juice. B

CHINATOWN AND PAHURAT   SEE MAP PAGE 77

Much of the fun of Chinatown dining is in the browsing of the night-time hot-food stalls that open up all along Thanon Yaowarat, around the mouth of Soi Issaranuphap (Yaowarat Soi 11) and along Soi Phadungdao (Soi Texas); wherever there's a crowd you'll be sure of good food. Pan Siam's *Good Eats: Chinatown* map, available from major bookshops, is a great resource for the weirder local specialities.

Hua Seng Hong 371 Thanon Yaowarat w huasenghong.com. Vibrant, ever-popular, few-frills restaurant with an open kitchen out front, the original branch of what's now a citywide chain. Dishes range from noodle soup, dim sum and roast duck on rice, to delicacies such as braised geese's feet. B

Raan Khun Yah Wat Traimit. Just to the right inside the temple's Thanon Mittaphap entrance, this basic, very cheap central Thai restaurant, now in its third generation of operation, is especially famous for its delicious *kaeng khiaw wan neua* (green beef curry), on a menu that otherwise changes daily – look out for *lon*, a chilli dip with coconut milk, and *khanom jiin nam yaa*, rice noodles topped with spicy fish sauce. Open weekdays for breakfast and lunch, but some dishes will sell out early. B

Royal India Just off Thanon Chakraphet at 392/1 w royalindiathailand.com. Great dhal, perfect parathas and famously good North Indian curries, with plenty of vegetarian options, served in a dark, basic little a/c restaurant in the heart of Bangkok's most Punjabi of neighbourhoods to an almost exclusively South Asian clientele. BB

T&K (Toi & Kid's Seafood) 49 Soi Phadungdao, corner of Thanon Yaowarat w facebook.com/tkseafood. Hectic,

DOWNTOWN: AROUND SIAM SQUARE AND THANON PLOENCHIT   SEE MAPS PAGES 92 AND 96

Notable street food in this area includes delicious *khao man kai*, boiled chicken breast with broth, dipping sauces and rice that's been cooked in chicken stock, which is served at a strip of late-night canteens on the south side of Thanon Phetchaburi, running east from the corner of Thanon Rajdamri.

★ **Aoi** Ground floor, Siam Paragon ⓦ aoi-bkk.com. Shopping centre branch of the excellent Japanese restaurant on Silom (see page 167). **BBBB**

Bangkok Bold Kitchen Lower Ground Floor, Central Embassy ⓦ facebook.com/bangkokboldkitchen. This restaurant's retro look is in keeping with its menu of traditional, home-style recipes with bold flavours, mostly from central Thailand, which have earned it a "Bib Gourmand" from the Thailand Michelin guide. Don't miss the excellent signature dish, stir-fried mackerel with acacia and pork crackling, which goes well with the crabmeat "relish" (*lon*). **BBB**

Coffeeology Open House, Floor 6, Central Embassy ⓦ facebook.com/coffeeologybangkok. Possibly the best espresso in Bangkok, made with beans from Chiang Dao in northern Thailand. Also offers drip, cold-brew and nitro-cold-brew coffees. **BB**

Din Tai Fung Floor 5, Central Embassy ⓦ dintaifung.com.sg. At this attractive and efficient all-day dim sum place, the superb speciality is steamed pork dumplings with clear broth inside each one, but other dishes such as spring rolls with duck and spring onion are also very tasty. **BB**

Eathai Basement, Central Embassy ⓦ centralembassy.com/eathai. This upmarket food court is a great place to learn about the huge variety of Thai food, with kitchens from the various regions rustling up their local dishes, plus seafood and vegetarian specialities, traditional drinks, ice cream and dessert stalls. **BB**

Gianni Ground Floor, Athenee Tower, Thanon Witthayu ⓦ giannibkk.com. Probably Bangkok's best independent Italian restaurant, offering a sophisticated blend of traditional and modern in both its decor and food. Twice-weekly shipments of artisan ingredients from the old country are used in dishes such as risotto with porcini mushrooms and parmesan and squid-ink spaghetti with clams, prawns and asparagus. Best to come for lunch Mon–Fri when there's a good-value set menu. **BBBB**

★ **Hinata** Central Embassy, Thanon Ploenchit ⓦ shin-hinata.com. This branch of a famous Nagoya restaurant offers exquisite sushi and good wines by the glass. Very good-value lunchtime sets are available before 2pm, or you could blow the bank on a multi-course *kaiseki* meal, featuring appetizers, sushi, sashimi, seasonal dishes, soup and dessert. **BBBB**

Home Kitchen (Khrua Nai Baan) 90/2 Soi Lang Suan ⓦ khruanaibaan.com. This congenial, unpretentious spot in an attractive a/c villa is like an upcountry restaurant in the heart of the city. On the reasonably priced Thai and Chinese picture menu, you're bound to find something delicious, including dozens of soups – try the *kaeng som*, with shrimp and acacia shoot omelette – six kinds of *laap* and a huge array of seafood. **BBB**

Honmono Sushi Ground Floor, Siam Paragon, Thanon Rama I ⓦ honmono.xyz. Owned by the Japanese expert on Thailand's version of Iron Chef, this place – and its half-dozen branches around the city – imports its seafood from Tokyo's seafood market five times a week and offers delights such as lobster sushi and scallop sashimi. **BBBB**

Inter 432/1–2 Soi 9, Siam Square ⓦ facebook.com/InterRestaurants1981. Honest, efficient Thai restaurant that's popular with students and shoppers, serving good one-dish meals, as well as curries, soups, salads and fish, in a no-frills, fluorescent-lit canteen atmosphere. **B**

Jim Thompson Restaurant Jim Thompson's House, 6 Soi Kasemsan 2, Thanon Rama I ⓦ jimthompsonrestaurant.com. A civilized haven for lunch or dinner in the must-see house museum (see page 94), serving delicious dishes such as pomelo salad with prawns and *matsaman* curry with chicken, as well as Thai desserts. Also in the complex are two cafés, a bar and a venue for afternoon tea. **BBB**

Lin Fa The Sukosol Hotel, 477 Thanon Si Ayutthaya, just east of Thanon Phrayathai ⓦ thesukosol.com. Congenial Cantonese restaurant overlooking the garden at this old hotel favourite (see page 154), serving excellent dim sum for lunch and dinner. The businessman's set lunch served from Monday to Friday is particularly good value. **BBB**

Lofter Floor 7, Central Chidlom, Thanon Ploenchit ⓦ facebook.com/HappyLofter. Bangkok's top department store lays on a suitably upscale food court that brings together in one place more than twenty of Bangkok's most famous street-food and global food names, offering everything from lobster spaghetti, through noodles and roast duck, to Thai desserts. **B**

Mah Boon Krong Food Court Corner of Rama I and Phrayathai rds ⓦ mbk-center.co.th. This long-running food-court at the north end of MBK on Floor 6 is a good introduction to Thai food, with English names and pictures of a huge variety of tasty, cheap one-dish meals from all over the country displayed at the various stalls (including

> **TOP FIVE RESTAURANTS WITH A VIEW**
> **Akira Back** See below
> **Kaloang Home Kitchen** See page 162
> **Navy Club** See page 161
> **Red Sky** See below
> **Supanniga Eating Room** See page 161

vegetarian options), as well as fresh juices and a wide range of desserts. B

Paste Gaysorn Village shopping centre, Thanon Ploenchit w pastebangkok.com. Arrayed around a striking woven spiral sculpture that evokes a silk cocoon, this Michelin-starred restaurant offers innovative updates of centuries-old Thai techniques, in dishes such as yellow curry with spanner crab, hummingbird flowers and Thai samphire. There are plenty of vegetarian options and great desserts on the a la carte and tasting menus. BBBB

★ **Polo Fried Chicken (Kai Thawt Jay Kee Soi Polo)** 137/13 Soi Polo, Thanon Witthayu ☎ 02 251 2772. On the access road to the snobby polo club, this simple restaurant is Bangkok's most famous purveyor of the ultimate Thai peasant dish, fried chicken. All manner of northeastern dishes, including fish, sausages and loads of salads, fill out the menu, but it would be a bit perverse to come here and not have the classic combo of finger-licking chicken, *som tam* and sticky rice. BB

Red Sky Centara Grand at Central World Hotel, 999/99 Thanon Rama I w centarahotelsresorts.com. Opulent, blow-out restaurant, named for the great sunset views from its indoor-outdoor, rooftop perch on the fifty-fifth floor. It purveys "the best of the land, sky and water" – be that Maine lobster, Hokkaido scallops or *wagyu* beef – beautifully presented in complex, meticulous preparations. BBBB

Royal India Basement Floor, Siam Paragon w royalindiathailand.com. Branch of a famous North Indian restaurant in Phahurat (see page 164). BB

★ **Sanguansri** 59/1 Thanon Witthayu ☎ 02 251 9378. The rest of the street may be a multi-storey building site but this low-rise, canteen-like old-timer, run by a friendly bunch of middle-aged women, clings on. And where else around here can you lunch on a sweet, thick and toothsome *kaeng matsaman* for less than B100? It goes well with *kung pla*, a tasty, fresh prawn and lemon-grass salad that can be spiced to order. The menu changes daily, and in the hot season they serve delicious *khao chae*, rice in chilled, flower-scented water served with delicate, fried side dishes. Lunchtime only – if possible, avoid the rush between noon and 1pm. B

Som Tam (Nua) Floor 5, Central Embassy w central embassy.com. This lively modern restaurant, with several branches around town, is a great place to get to know the full range of Thai spicy salads. The *som tam* with pork crackling and sausage goes well with the very tasty deep-fried chicken, or there's northeastern *laap* and *nam tok*, and central Thai salads (*yam*) by the dozen. BBB

Somboon Seafood Floor 5, Central Embassy w somboonseafood.com. Shopping centre branch of the justly famous seafood restaurant (see page 168). BBB

Sra Bua Siam Kempinski Hotel (see page 154). Molecular gastronomy comes to Bangkok, with great success. Operated by Copenhagen's Michelin one-star, Kiin Kiin, this place applies some serious creativity and theatricality to Thai cuisine. Dishes such as frozen red curry with lobster salad, which perfectly distils the taste of the *kaeng daeng*, match the dramatic decor, which encompasses two lotus ponds (*sra bua*). BBBB

★ **Taling Pling** Ground Floor, Siam Paragon w facebook.com/TalingplingRes. Branch of the excellent Silom restaurant (see page 168). BBB

THANON SUKHUMVIT

SEE MAP PAGE 99

Akira Back Marriott Marquis Queens Park Hotel, 129 Soi 2, Thanon Sukhumvit. In a spectacular setting on the 37th floor, this restaurant and sushi bar by a renowned Korean-American chef offers luxurious reimaginings of Japanese cuisine, with Korean touches, in dishes full of vibrant flavours such as scallops with strawberry salsa and sushi rolls with spicy crab, asparagus, cucumber and pop rocks. A la carte and tasting set menus available. BBBB

★ **Aoi** 3rd Floor, Emporium shopping centre w aoi-bkk.com. Shopping centre branch of the excellent Japanese restaurant on Silom (see page 167). BBBB

Baan Khanitha 36/1 Soi 23 w baan-khanitha.com. The big attraction at this long-running favourite haunt of Sukhumvit expats is the setting in a traditional Thai house and leafy garden. The food is upmarket Thai and fairly pricey, and includes lots of fiery salads (*yam*) and a good range of *tom yam* soups, as well as green, *matsaman* and seafood curries. BBB

Barcelona Gaudí Ground floor, Le Premier 1 Condo, Soi 23 w facebook.com/barcelonagaudithailand. This appealing café offers lovely outdoor tables under a broad, shady tree and plenty of very good Spanish and Catalan dishes, including salads, paellas, cold cuts and tapas, as well as tasty *crema catalana* (a bit like a crème brûlée) and on-the-money espressos. It's especially good value at lunchtime (Mon–Fri), and is also popular at weekends for watching Barcelona's football games, when the good-value house wine by the glass goes down a storm. BBB

★ **Beirut** Basement, Ploenchit Centre, at the mouth of Soi 2 w beirut-restaurant.com. It's worth crossing the road from Bangkok's main Middle Eastern ghetto (Soi 3 and Soi 3/1) for the top-notch Lebanese food in this comfortable, a/c restaurant. Among dozens of salads and stuffed breads, the superb *motabel* (baba ganoush) is fluffy and smoky, while the falafels are suitably moist inside and crunchy out. Good baklava, too. **BBB**

★ **Bolan** 24 Soi 53 (5min walk from BTS Thong Lo) ⓦbolan.co.th. Meticulous and hugely successful attempt to produce authentic traditional food in all its complexity, while upholding the "Slow Food" philosophy. It's only open from Thursday to Sunday evenings, serving a chef's tasting menu, but it'll give you a lipsmacking education in Thai cuisine. **BBBB**

Cabbages and Condoms 10 Soi 12 ⓦcabbagesandcondomsbkk.com. The Population and Community Development Association of Thailand (PDA) runs this relaxing restaurant, decorated with condoms from around the world and the slogan "our food is guaranteed not to cause pregnancy". Try the chicken in pandanus leaves or the seafood green curry; there's also a varied vegetarian menu. **BBBB**

Din Tai Fung Eight Thonglor shopping centre, 88/1 Soi 55 (Soi Thonglor) ⓦdintaifung.com.sg. Branch of the excellent all-day dim sum restaurant in Central Embassy (see page 165). **BB**

Dosa King Soi 11/1, with a back entrance on Soi 11 ⓦdosaking.net. Usually busy with expat Indian diners, this vegetarian Indian restaurant serves good food from both north and south, including over a dozen different dosas (southern pancake dishes), tandooris and the like. It's an alcohol-free zone so you'll have to make do with sweet lassi instead. **BB**

Honmono Sushi 17–19 Soi 23 off Soi Thonglor (Sukhumvit Soi 55) ⓦhonmono.xyz. Branch of the famous sushi restaurant in Siam Paragon (see page 165). **BBBB**

Le Dalat 57 Soi 23 (Soi Prasanmit) ⓦfacebook.com/ledalatrestaurant. There's Indochinese romance aplenty at this delightful, re-created Vietnamese brick mansion decked out with pot plants, plenty of photos and eclectic curiosities. The extensive, high-class Vietnamese menu features favourites such as a *goi ca* salad of aromatic herbs and raw fish and *chao tom* shrimp sticks on sugar cane. **BBBB**

Prai Raya 59 Soi 8 ☎02 253 5556. Set in a grand, modern villa done out in Sino-Portuguese style, this branch of a famous Phuket Town restaurant brings that city's distinctive cuisine to the capital – with a welcome offer to spice things down if requested. Dishes include *muu hong* (stewed pork belly with cinnamon), but it's worth forking out a bit extra for the yellow curry with coconut milk and big chunks of fresh crabmeat. Also offers a good selection of vegetarian southern Thai dishes. **BBB**

★ **Ramentei** Soi 33/1 ⓦfacebook.com/ramentei. Branch of the excellent Japanese noodle café on Soi Thaniya (see page 168). **BBB**

Royal India Floor 5, Emporium shopping centre ⓦroyalindiathailand.com. Branch of a famous North Indian restaurant in Pahurat (see page 164). **BB**

★ **Supanniga Eating Room** Soi 55 (Soi Thonglor) ⓦsupannigaeatingroom.com. Branch of the famous Chanthaburi-style restaurant in Ratanakosin (see page 161). **BBB**

★ **Taling Pling** 25 Soi 34 ⓦfacebook.com/TalingplingRes. Branch of the excellent Silom restaurant (see page 168). **BBB**

> **TOP FIVE TRADITIONAL THAI RESTAURANTS**
>
> **Bolan** See left
> **Celadon** See below
> **Krua Apsorn** See page 162
> **Sanguansri** See page 166
> **Taling Pling** See page 168

DOWNTOWN: SOUTH OF THANON RAMA IV   SEE MAPS PAGES 92 AND 102

★ **Aoi** 132/10–11 Soi 6, Thanon Silom ⓦaoi-bkk.com. One of the best places in town for a Japanese blowout, justifiably popular with the expat community, with excellent authentic food, including great sushi, and elegant décor. Prices are higher in the evening, but at lunchtime you can get bento boxes. **BBBB**

Baan Khanitha 69 Thanon Sathorn Tai, at the corner of Soi Suan Phlu ⓦbaan-khanitha.com. Branch of a much-loved Sukhumvit restaurant (see page 166). **BBB**

Bangkok Bold Kitchen Floor 2, Riverside Plaza, Thanon Charoennakorn ⓦfacebook.com/bangkokboldkitchen. Original branch of the Central Embassy shopping centre restaurant (see page 165). A bit out of the centre, but you can use the *Anantara Riverside* hotel's shuttle boats (see page 155) from Saphan Taksin to get here (Riverside Plaza is right behind the hotel). **BBB**

★ **Beirut** 64 Silom Building, set back off Thanon Silom between Soi 4 and Soi Thaniya ⓦbeirut-restaurant.com. Branch of a great Lebanese restaurant on Thanon Sukhumvit (see page 167). **BBB**

★ **Celadon** Sukhothai Hotel, 13/3 Thanon Sathorn Tai ⓦbangkok.sukhothai.com. Consistently rated as one of the best hotel restaurants in Bangkok and a favourite with locals, serving outstanding traditional and contemporary Thai food from all over the country – try the delicious pomelo salad with chicken and prawns and the northern-style egg noodles in curry soup (*khao soi*) – in an elegant setting surrounded by lotus ponds. A la carte and tasting set menus. **BBBB**

★ **Eat Me** 1/6 Soi Phiphat 2, Thanon Convent ⓦeatmerestaurant.com. Justly fashionable art gallery and late-night restaurant in a striking, white modernist building, with changing exhibitions on the walls and a temptingly relaxing balcony. The eclectic, far-reaching menu features such mains as grilled squid with fennel, pomegranate and white bean purée, there's an extensive wine list with many available by the glass, and the lemongrass crème brûlée is not to be missed. **BBBB**

Harmonique 22 Soi 34, Thanon Charoen Krung, on the lane leading to Wat Muang Kae pier ⓦfacebook.com/harmoniqueth. A relaxing, welcoming, moderately priced restaurant that's well worth a trip: tables are scattered throughout several converted wooden shophouses, decorated with antiques and bric-a-brac, and a quiet, leafy courtyard, and the Thai food is varied and excellent, notably the house speciality crab curry. **BB**

★ **Krua Aroy Aroy** 3/1 Thanon Pan (opposite the Maha Uma Devi Temple) ⓦfacebook.com/kruaaroyaroy. Aptly named "Delicious, Delicious Kitchen", this simple daytime shophouse restaurant stands out for its choice of cheap, tasty, well-prepared dishes from all around the kingdom, notably chicken *matsaman* curry, *khao soi* (a curried soup with egg noodles from northern Thailand) and *khanom jiin* (rice noodles topped with curry). **BB**

Le Bouchon 50 Soi 1 (Soi Atthakarn Prasit), Thanon Sathorn Tai ⓦfacebook.com/lebouchonbangkok. Lyonnais bistro, much frequented by the city's French expats, that's recently moved from Patpong to a more spacious and salubrious location, with plenty of garden tables. It offers home cooking such as duck confit and a good-value lunch set menu (Mon–Fri). **BBBB**

★ **Le Du** 399/3 Soi 7, Thanon Silom ⓦledubkk.com. Excellent evening-time restaurant that takes authentic Thai flavours and ingredients and develops them creatively and very successfully with modern cooking techniques. The kitchen is strong on fish and seafood, in dishes such as superb soft-shell crab with bitter gourd and pineapple in a southern-style curry, accompanied by excellent wines, many available by the glass. No a la carte – four- or six-course tasting menus only (with wine pairings available). **BBBB**

Mei Jiang Peninsula Hotel, 333 Thanon Charoennakorn ⓦpeninsula.com. Probably Bangkok's best Chinese restaurant, with beautiful views of the riverside gardens of this luxury hotel (see page 156), and very attentive and graceful staff. Cantonese specialities include excellent lunchtime dim sum, lobster rolls, lobster dumplings and brassica in clear broth and delicious teas. Free shuttle boats from Taksin Bridge. **BBBB**

★ **Nahm** Como Metropolitan Hotel, 27 Thanon Sathorn Tai ⓦcomohotels.com/metropolitanbangkok. This seductive Japanese-designed restaurant offers esoteric but authentic Thai dishes such as oyster and Thai samphire salad, which are complex, intensely flavoured but well balanced, using the best of local ingredients. Set menu, with wine pairings available; book early. **BBBB**

★ **Ramentei** 23/8–9 Soi Thaniya ⓦfacebook.com/ramentei. Excellent Japanese noodle café, bright, clean and welcoming, under the same ownership as *Aoi* (see page 167). The open kitchen turns out especially good, huge bowls of miso ramen, which goes very well with the gyoza dumplings. **BBB**

Ruen Urai Rose Hotel, 118 Thanon Suriwong ⓦruen-urai.com. Set back behind the hotel, this peaceful, hundred-year-old, traditional house, with fine balcony tables overlooking the beautiful hotel pool, comes as a welcome surprise in this full-on downtown area. The varied Thai food, which includes a good *matsaman* curry, is of a high quality. **BBBB**

Sara Jane's 55/21 Thanon Narathiwat Ratchanakharin, between sois 4 & 6 ⓦsara-janes.com. Long-standing, basic, a/c restaurant, popular with Bangkok's Isaan population, serving good, simple northeastern dishes, including a huge array of *nam tok*, *laap* and *som tam*, as well as Italian food – and a very tasty fusion of the two, spaghetti with *sai krok*, spicy Isaan sausage. **BB**

Somboon Seafood Thanon Suriwong, corner of Thanon Narathiwat Ratchanakharin ⓦsomboonseafood.com. Highly favoured, bustling seafood restaurant, one of several branches around town, with functional, modern decor and an array of marine life lined up in tanks awaiting its gastronomic fate. Known especially for its crab curry, hence the slogan "Sawatdii Crab". **BBB**

★ **Supanniga Eating Room** 28 Soi 10, Thanon Sathorn ⓦsupannigaeatingroom.com. Branch of the famous Chanthaburi-style restaurant in Ratanakosin (see page 161). **BBB**

★ **Taling Pling** 653 Building 7, Ban Silom Arcade, Thanon Silom ⓦfacebook.com/TalingplingRes. One of the best traditional Thai restaurants in the city outside of the big hotels, specializing in classic dishes from the four corners of the kingdom. The toothsome green beef curry with roti, which is recommended by the leading Thai restaurant guides, goes well with the delicious and refreshing house deep-fried fish salad. The atmosphere's convivial and relaxing, too. **BBB**

SPIRITS LINING A BANGKOK BAR

Drinking and nightlife

For many of Bangkok's male visitors, nightfall is the signal to hit the city's sex bars, most notoriously in the area off the east end of Thanon Silom known as Patpong (see page 100). Fortunately, Bangkok's *nightlife* has thoroughly grown up in the past couple of decades to leave these neon sumps behind, and now offers everything from craft-beer pubs and vertiginous, rooftop cocktail bars to fiercely chic clubs and dance bars, hosting top-class DJs. The high-concept bars of Sukhumvit and the lively, teeming venues of Banglamphu, in particular, pull in the style-conscious cream of Thai youth and are tempting an increasing number of travellers to stuff their party gear into their rucksacks.

NIGHTLIFE HOURS, ID CHECKS AND ADMISSION CHARGES

Most bars and clubs in Bangkok are meant to **close** at 1am, while those in designated nightlife zones, such as the east end of Silom and Royal City Avenue, can stay open until 2am. In previous years, there have been regular "social order" clampdowns by the police, strictly enforcing these closing times, conducting occasional urine tests for drugs on bar customers, and setting up widespread ID checks to curb under-age drinking (you have to be 20 or over to drink in bars and clubs). However, at the time of writing, things were more chilled, with some bars and clubs staying open into the wee hours on busy nights and ID checks in only a few places. It's hard to predict how the situation might develop, but you'll soon get an idea of how the wind is blowing when you arrive in Bangkok – and there's little harm in taking a copy of your passport out with you, just in case. Nearly all bars and clubs in Bangkok are free, but the most popular of them will sometimes levy an admission charge of a couple of hundred baht on their busiest nights (which will usually include a drink or two), though this can vary from week to week.

Among the city's **club nights**, look out for the interesting regular events organized by Zudrangma Record Store (wzudrangmarecords.com), especially at their own bar *Studio Lam*, which mix up dance music from all around Thailand and from all over the world; and Dudesweet's parties all over town, featuring Thai and international DJs and indie bands (wfacebook.com/dudesweetworld).

During the cool season, an evening out at one of the pop-up beer gardens (usually Dec) is a pleasant way of soaking up the urban atmosphere (and the traffic fumes); you'll find them in hotel forecourts or sprawled in front of shopping centres all over the city.

Getting back to your lodgings should be no problem in the small hours: many bus routes run a (reduced) service throughout the night, and tuk-tuks and taxis are always at hand – though it's probably best for unaccompanied women to avoid using tuk-tuks late at night.

BANGLAMPHU AND THE DEMOCRACY MONUMENT AREA   SEE MAP PAGE 68

The travellers' enclave of Banglamphu takes on a new personality after dark, when its hub, Thanon Khao San, becomes a "walking street", closed to all traffic but open to almost any kind of makeshift stall, selling everything from fried bananas and buckets of "very strong" cocktails to share, to bargain fashions and one-off artworks. Young Thais come to the area to browse and snack before piling in to Banglamphu's more stylish bars and live-music clubs, most of which are free to enter (though some ask you to show ID first).

Adhere the 13th (Blues Bar) 13 Thanon Samsen, opposite Soi 2, right by the start of the bridge over Khlong Banglamphu wfacebook.com/adhere13thbluesbar. Relaxed little neighbourhood live-music joint with sociable seats out on the pavement, where musos congregate nightly to listen to Thai and expat blues and jazz bands (from about 9.30pm onwards). Well-priced beer and plenty of cocktails.

Brick Bar Buddy Village complex, 265 Thanon Khao San wfacebook.com/BrickBarKhaoSanRoad. Massive red-brick vault of a live-music bar whose regular roster of reggae, ska, rock'n'roll and Thai pop bands, and occasional one-off appearances, is hugely popular with Thai twenty-somethings and teens. Big, sociable tables are set right under the stage and there's food too. The biggest nights are Fri and Sat when there's sometimes an entry charge, depending on who's on.

The Club 123 Thanon Khao San wtheclubkhaosan.com. Thumping electronic dance music from an elevated, central DJ station with state-of-the-art lighting draw a young Thai and international crowd; check the website for upcoming events with imported DJs.

Culture Café 249 Thanon Samsen wfacebook.com/profile.php?id=100063617379926. Long-running Bangkok institution that has been through many incarnations, but may now have settled down on the northern edge of Banglamphu. This is about as underground as Bangkok's clubs get, a bare-bones place where no expense has been spent on the décor, apart from glitter balls and a few comfy sofas. Nothing is allowed to distract from the music, which is pumped out from a great sound system. Techno, minimal house, italo-disco, everything's on offer – "Fuck Genres, Just Dance" is the motto – check out their Facebook page for line-ups.

★ **Hippie de Bar** 46 Thanon Khao San wfacebook.com/Hippiedebar46. Inviting courtyard bar set away from the main fray, with an indie-pop soundtrack and its own-brand fashion boutique. Attracts a mixed studenty/arty/high-society, mostly Thai, crowd, to drink cheapish beer at its wrought-iron tables and park benches. Indoors is totally given over to retro kitsch, with plastic armchairs, Donny Osmond posters and floral prints.

Phra Nakorn 58/2 Soi Damnoen Klang Tai facebook.com/phranakornbarandgallery. Styles itself as "a hangout place for art lovers", and it successfully pulls in the capital's artists and art students, who can admire the floodlit view of the Golden Mount from the candlelit rooftop terrace, tuck into good food and reasonably priced drinks and browse one of the regular exhibitions on the first floor.

Sheepshank Tha Phra Arthit express-boat pier sheepshankpublichouse.com. Set in a former boat-repair yard overlooking the Chao Phraya and the riverside walkway, this cool bar-restaurant sports an industrial look that features black leather, silver studs, pulleys and girders. There's a wide selection of craft beers from Thailand, the US and Japan, as well as imaginative bar snacks and a long menu of more substantial gastropub dishes.

CHINATOWN SEE MAP PAGE 77

Chinatown has never had a reputation for its bars, but a handful of chic places, all affecting a rough-edged air of oriental mystique, have now made Soi Nana a small hub of nightlife, just 5min walk from Hualamphong subway station.

★ **Ba Hao** 8 Soi Nana, Thanon Maitri Chit facebook.com/8bahao. Announced by paper lanterns, friendly *Ba Hao* conjures up the spirit of old Chinatown with low red lighting and traditional, marble-topped tables. As well as teas, ginseng shots and a short menu of Chinese food, it serves creative, Chinese-inspired cocktails – which Jamie Oliver likes, apparently – such as Opium, a Negroni using a ginseng and herbs liquor.

Brown Sugar 18 Soi Nana, Thanon Maitri Chit facebook.com/brownsugarbangkok. Bangkok's best and longest-running jazz club has recently moved into an atmospheric old shophouse in Chinatown, hung with colourful modernist gig posters. Music usually starts around 8.30pm, sometimes with an acoustic session. Entry is usually free (there's an occasional admission fee for special acts) and the prices of drinks are pumped up to pay for the talent, though they include imported beers on draught and in bottles.

Teens of Thailand (TOT) 76 Soi Nana, Thanon Maitri Chit facebook.com/teensofthailand. The creaking of an ancient wooden door announces your arrival at this misleadingly named bar. Inside, old movie posters and a piano provide the setting for a cocktail menu that uses dozens of gins from around the world.

Tep Bar 69–71 Soi Nana, Thanon Maitri Chit facebook.com/tepbarbkk. Down a side alley off the main Soi Nana, *Tep* evokes the atmosphere of Bangkok of yore, with a bar that looks like the base of a chedi, candles and distressed walls. There's a long menu of Thai snacks, grilled meats and rice dishes, to be washed down with Thai rice whisky and herb liquor cocktails.

DOWNTOWN: AROUND SIAM SQUARE AND THANON PLOENCHIT SEE MAPS PAGES 92 AND 96

Downtown, Siam Square has much less to offer after dark than Thanon Sukhumvit, further east. Out to the northeast, running south off Thanon Rama IX, lies RCA (Royal City Avenue). An officially sanctioned "nightlife zone" that's allowed to stay open until 2am, it's lined mostly with warehouse-like clubs that have a reputation as meat markets.

Coco Walk Thanon Phrayathai. It would be hard not to enjoy yourself at this covered parade of loosely interchangeable but buzzing good-time bars, right beside Ratchathevi BTS. Popular with local students, they variously offer pool tables, live musicians, DJs and a small skateboarding ramp, but all have reasonably priced beer and food.

Hyde and Seek Floor 9, Silom Edge shopping centre, corner of Thanon Silom and Thanon Rama IV hydeandseek.com. Classy but buzzy gastrobar, with nightly DJs and an outdoor rooftop area with great views of Lumphini Park. Amid a huge range of drinks, there's a good selection of wines by the glass and imported beers on draught; the food menu features bar bites, pastas, salads and creative takes on familiar gastropub dishes.

Raintree 116/63–4 Soi Ruamjit, Thanon Rangnam 081 926 1604. Near Victory Monument, two ordinary shophouses have been converted into this friendly, typical "good ol' boys" bar, with good food, lots of rough timber furniture and the biggest water-buffalo skulls you've ever seen. Live, nightly music (from about 9pm) is mostly Songs for Life, mixed in with some *luk thung*, starting out low-key and soothing, and getting more raucous and danceworthy as the night hots up.

Saxophone 3/8 Victory Monument (southeast corner), just off Thanon Phrayathai saxophonepub.com. Lively, easy-going, spacious venue with decent Thai and Western food and a diverse roster of bands – including acoustic, jazz and blues, funk, rock and reggae (details on their website) – which attracts a good mix of locals and foreigners.

THANON SUKHUMVIT SEE MAP PAGE 99

A night out on Thanon Sukhumvit could be subsumed by the girlie bars and hostess-run bar-beers on sois Nana and Cowboy, but there's plenty of style on Sukhumvit too, especially in the rooftop bars and craft-beer pubs. The scene has been gravitating eastwards over the last few years: the fashionable bars and clubs on and around Soi Thonglor (Soi 55) attract a "hi-so" (high-society) crowd, while those over on Soi Ekamai (Soi 63) are perhaps a little more studenty.

Brewski Radisson Blu Plaza Hotel, Thanon Sukhumvit between sois 25 and 27 Ⓦ facebook.com/brewskirooftop. Winning (though pricy) combination of views and brews: a thirtieth-floor rooftop bar with a 270-degree vista of all the other downtown skyscrapers; plus sports on TV and a dozen craft beers on tap (a hundred more in bottles), with regular takeovers by the likes of Scotland's Brewdog.

★ **Changwon Express** 37 Thanon Asok–Din Daeng Ⓦ facebook.com/changwonexpress. Off-strip but right next to Phetchaburi subway station, this small, friendly, Korean-owned bar brews its own ales. Staff know what they're talking about and there are plenty of other Thai craft beers on tap, as well as British and US imports – plus all manner of Korean chicken dishes.

Iron Balls Park Lane shopping mall, 5min walk up Soi Ekamai (Soi 63) from the Skytrain Ⓦ facebook.com/ironballsdistillery. An unlikely spot for a gin distillery, but the product – using German juniper, ginger and lemongrass – is great; try their excellent Negroni, with Campari and charred sandalwood bitters. The small, attached DJ bar mixes clubbiness – leather armchairs, library lamps – with a low-tech, early industrial feel – bell jars, coils and lots of wrought iron.

Mikkeller 26 Yaek 2, Soi 10, Soi Ekamai (Soi 63) Ⓦ mikkeller.com. This branch of the famous Danish microbrewery offers thirty craft beers on tap in a handsome 1950s villa furnished in blonde wood, with bean bags out on the lawn. Located (and signposted) down a sub-soi of a sub-soi of Ekamai and with the beer working out at about B500/pint, it's one for the beer geeks.

★ **Studio Lam** About 100m up Soi 51 on the left, on the corner of the first sub-soi, about 5min walk west of BTS Thong Lo Ⓦ facebook.com/studiolambangkok. This friendly, cosy neighbourhood bar is run by Zudrangma Records, whose record shop is just up the sub-soi to the left. The soundproofing and massive, purpose-built sound system give the game away: the music's the thing here, with DJs and live musicians playing driving *mor lam* and an eclectic choice of world sounds nightly.

★ **WTF** 7 Soi 51 Ⓦ wtfbangkok.com. Small, ground-floor bar-café with an influential art gallery on the floors above, that hosts half-a-dozen exhibitions on social and political issues each year. Popular with Bangkok creatives, it offers tapas and a tempting variety of cocktails and wines. It's 5min walk west of BTS Thong Lo, 100m up Soi 51, near the mouth of a small sub-soi on the left.

DOWNTOWN: SOUTH OF THANON RAMA IV

SEE MAP PAGE 102

There are one or two mixed bars on the mostly gay Soi 4 at the east end of Thanon Silom – and, of course, a slew of go-go bars on Patpong – but otherwise the action in this area is widely scattered. If, among all the choice of nightlife in Bangkok, you do end up at one of Patpong's sex shows, watch out for hyper-inflated bar bills and other cons – plenty of customers get ripped off in some way, and stories of menacing bouncers are legion.

ALCOHOLIC DRINKS

The two most famous **local beers** (*bia*) are Singha (ask for *"bia sing"*) and Chang, though many travellers find Singha's weaker brew, Leo, more palatable than either. In shops you can expect to pay around B35–40 for a 330ml bottle of these beers, B70 for a 660ml bottle. All manner of slightly pricier foreign beers are now brewed in Thailand, including Heineken and Asahi, and in Bangkok you'll find imported bottles from all over the world.

Wine is now found on plenty of upmarket and tourist-oriented restaurant menus, but expect to be disappointed both by the quality and by the price, which is jacked up by heavy taxation. Thai wine is now produced at several vineyards, including by the family behind Red Bull at the Monsoon Valley Vineyard near Hua Hin, which produces an especially tasty rosé.

At about B150 for a hip-flask-sized 375ml bottle, local **spirits are** a lot better value, and Thais think nothing of consuming a bottle a night, heavily diluted with ice and soda or Coke. One of the most popular and widely available of these is Sang Som, a **rum** made from sugar cane, at forty percent proof. Mekong, a whisky distilled from rice at 35 percent proof, is hard to come by these days as it's kept for the export market. Check the menu carefully when ordering a bottle of Sang Som from a bar in a tourist area, as they sometimes ask up to five times more than you'd pay in a guesthouse or shop. You can **buy** beer and spirits in food stores, guesthouses, bars and most restaurants (by a law that's spottily enforced, it's not meant to be for sale between 2pm and 5pm, when schools are finishing for the day).

KO KRED DRINKING AND NIGHTLIFE

★ **Changwon Chicken and Beer** 15/245 Soi 11, Thanon Sathorn Tai w facebook.com/changwonexpress. Branch of a great Korean craft-beer place (see page 172), next to St Louis Skytrain station.

Chithole Montien Mall, 54 Thanon Suriwong w facebook.com/chitbeer or chitbrewery.com. Branch of the famous Ko Kred craft-beer bar, *Chit's* (see page 173).

★ **The Sky Bar & Distil** Floors 63 & 64, State Tower, 1055 Thanon Silom, corner of Thanon Charoen Krung w lebua.com. Thrill-seekers and view addicts shouldn't miss forking out for an alfresco drink here, 275m above the city's pavements – come around 6pm to enjoy the stunning panoramas in both the light and the dark. It's standing-only at *The Sky Bar*, a circular restaurant-bar built over the edge of the building with almost 360-degree views, but for the sunset itself, you're better off on the outside terrace of *Distil* one floor up on the other side of the building, which has a wider choice of drinks, charming service and huge couches to recline on. The bars have become very popular since featuring in *The Hangover II* movie and have introduced a strict, smart-casual dress code.

★ **Tawandang German Brewery** 462/61 Thanon Rama III w tawandang.com. A taxi-ride south of Chong Nonsi BTS down Thanon Narathiwat Ratchanakharin – and best to book a table in advance – this vast all-rounder is well worth the effort. Under a huge dome, up to 1600 revellers enjoy good Thai and German food, great micro-brewed German beer and a mercurial, hugely entertaining cabaret, featuring live pop and *luk thung*, magic shows and dance numbers.

Viva Aviv: The River Ground floor, River City shopping centre w vivaaviv.com. With a lovely open deck right on the river and a gnarly interior decor of hide-bound chairs and ships' winches, this bar offers cool sounds, some serious cocktails, good coffees and smoothies, as well as comfort food such as pasta, pizzas and salads.

CHATUCHAK WEEKEND MARKET   SEE MAP PAGE 108

Viva 8 Section 8 w facebook.com/viva8jj. Classy, relaxing bar that serves great cocktails, juices and coffees, where you can rest your feet while listening to DJs or tuck into paella that's theatrically prepared in a huge pan.

KO KRED   SEE MAP PAGE 108

Chit's 5min walk south of the pier on the river w facebook.com/chitbeer or w chitbrewery.com. Huge selection of craft beers on tap and in bottle by Thailand's most famous home brewer, Chit (motto: "It's Good Chit"), plus Thai guest beers, pub grub and lovely riverside tables. Weekends only.

BANGKOK PRIDE PARADE

LGBTQ+ Bangkok

Buddhist tolerance and a national abhorrence of confrontation and victimization combine to make Thai society relatively relaxed about homosexuality. Although most Thais are private and discreet about being gay, generally pursuing a "don't ask, don't tell" understanding with their family, the majority are accepting of and welcoming to the LGBTQ+ community. Indeed, same-sex marriage became legal in Thailand in January 2025. Meanwhile, nightlife concentrated around Silom caters to (mainly male) LGBTQ+ partygoers from around the world. The age of consent for gay sex is fifteen, the same as for heterosexuals. Hardly any public figures are out, yet the predilections of several respected social, political and entertainment figures are widely known and accepted.

THE SCENE

Bangkok's **gay scene** is mainly focused on mainstream venues like karaoke bars, restaurants, massage parlours, gyms, saunas and escort agencies. Much of the action happens on Silom 4 (Thanon Silom, Soi 4; near Patpong) and on the more exclusive Silom 2 (towards Thanon Rama IV). After a break of more than ten years, **Bangkok Pride** returned to the city in June 2022, with a parade and all manner of other events for Pride Month. Now supported by the Bangkok Metropolitan Administration and the Ministry of Tourism and Sports, it has taken place every June since.

The farang-oriented gay **sex industry** is a tiny but highly visible part of Bangkok's gay scene and, with its tawdry floor shows and host services, it bears a dispiriting resemblance to the straight sex trade. Like their female counterparts in the heterosexual fleshpots, many of the boys working in the gay sex bars that dominate these districts are underage (anyone caught having sex with a prostitute below the age of 18 faces imprisonment). A significant number of gay prostitutes are gay by economic necessity rather than by inclination. As with the straight sex scene, we do not list the commercial gay sex bars.

The gay scene is heavily male, and there are hardly any **lesbian**-only venues, though quite a few gay bars are mixed. Thai lesbians generally eschew the word lesbian, which in Thailand is associated with male fantasies, instead referring to themselves as either *tom* (for tomboy) or *dee* (for lady).

Although excessively physical displays of affection are frowned upon for both heterosexuals and homosexuals, Western gay couples should get no hassle about being seen together in public. **Katoey** (which can refer both to transgender women and to effeminate gay men, so often translated as "ladyboys") are also a lot more visible in Thailand than in the West. You'll find transgender women doing ordinary jobs and there are a number of *katoey* in the public eye too – including national volleyball stars and champion *muay thai* boxers. The government tourist office promotes transgender cabarets in Bangkok (see page 178), which are seen as family entertainment.

LISTINGS AND RESOURCES

The Gay Passport ⓦ thegaypassport.com. Regularly updated listings for the main tourist centres.
Gay People in Thailand ⓦ aseannow.com/forum/27-gay-people-in-thailand. Forum for gay expats.
Travel Gay Asia ⓦ travelgayasia.com/destination/gay-thailand. Active, frequently updated site that covers listings and events all over the country.
Utopia ⓦ utopia-asia.com. Lists clubs, bars, restaurants, accommodation, tour operators, organizations and resources for gay men and lesbians.

BARS AND CLUBS   SEE MAP PAGE 102

The bars, clubs and café-restaurants listed here, located around the east end of Thanon Silom and especially in the narrow alleys of Soi 2 and Soi 4, are the most notable of Bangkok's **gay nightlife** venues. Advice on opening hours, admission charges and ID is given in Drinking and Nightlife (see page 170) – Soi 2, for example, operates a strict ID policy.

The Balcony Soi 4, Thanon Silom ⓦ balconypub.com. Unpretentious, fun place with plenty of outdoor seats for people-watching, welcoming staff, reasonably priced drinks and decent Thai and Western food. All kinds of drink and food special offers are detailed on their website. There's live music every night, with an open-mike session early in the evening, and upstairs is free karaoke.

DJ Station Soi 2, Thanon Silom ⓦ facebook.com/djstationbangkok. Bangkok's most famous club, a highly fashionable, good-time venue on three floors, packed at weekends, attracting a mix of Thais and farangs, with a cabaret show nightly.

G Bangkok 60/18–21 Soi 2/1, Thanon Silom, in a small pedestrianized alley between Soi Thaniya and Soi 2 ⓦ x.com/GBangkokGOD. Large, full-on, three-level club, somewhat more Thai-oriented than *DJ Station*, that's still often referred to by its former name, *GOD* (for *Guys on Display*). It tends not to fill up until *DJ Station* has closed. Hosts a big festival of parties over Songkran.

The Stranger Bar Soi 4, Thanon Silom ⓦ facebook.com/thestrangerbar. Stylish "pub theatre" with drag shows most nights and good cocktails. Free entry most nights, with a minimum two-drink spend.

THAI BOXING AT RAJADAMNERN STADIUM

Entertainment

The most accessible of the capital's performing arts is Thai dancing, particularly when served up in bite-size portions in tourist shows. Thai boxing is also well worth watching: the raucous live experience at either of Bangkok's two main national stadia far outshines the TV coverage. Two main companies put on spectacular ladyboy cabaret shows, while central Bangkok has more than forty cinemas, many of them on the top floors of shopping centres.

THAI DANCING

Thai dancing is performed for its original ritual purpose, usually several times a day, at the Lak Muang Shrine (see page 60) behind the Grand Palace and the Erawan Shrine (see page 97) on the corner of Thanon Ploenchit. Both shrines have resident troupes of dancers who are hired by worshippers to perform *lakhon chatri*, a sort of *khon* **dance-drama**, to thank benevolent spirits for answered prayers. The dancers are always dressed up in full gear and accompanied by musicians, but the length and complexity of the dance and the number of dancers depend on the amount of money paid by the supplicant: a price list is posted near the dance area. The musicians at the Erawan Shrine are particularly highly rated, though the almost comic apathy of the dancers there doesn't do them justice.

CULTURE SHOWS AND PERFORMING ARTS

Non-Thai-speaking audiences are likely to struggle with much of the **drama** performed in the city, so the best way to experience the traditional performing arts is usually at a show designed for tourists, where background knowledge and stoic concentration are not essential; the *khon* shows at the Chalermkrung Theatre are good introductions. Several tourist restaurants offer nightly **culture shows** that usually feature a medley of Thai dancing and classical music, perhaps with a martial-arts demonstration thrown in. In some cases there's a set fee for dinner and show, in others the performance is free but the à la carte prices are slightly inflated; it's always worth calling ahead to reserve, especially if you want a vegetarian version of the set menu.

Chalermkrung Theatre (Sala Chalermkrung) 66 Thanon Charoen Krung, on the intersection with Thanon Triphet in Pahurat, next to Old Siam Plaza ⓦ salachalermkrung.com or ⓦ palaces.thai.net. This Art Deco former cinema, dating from 1933, hosts 25-minute *khon* performances with English subtitles Mon–Fri at 1pm, 2.30pm and 4pm. Admission is included with tickets to the Grand Palace and Wat Phra Kaeo, with a free shuttle bus laid on 30min before each performance; at the end of the show you're very close to Sam Yot subway station.

National Theatre Sanam Luang, Ratanakosin ☎ 02 224 1342. Hosts traditional performing arts such as *khon*, *lakhon* and medley shows of music and dancing roughly twice a month (not in the hot season), usually on Sun. However, it's difficult to get information about what's on in English – the nearby Bangkok Tourism Division (see page 34) often has a schedule.

Thailand Cultural Centre Thanon Ratchadapisek ⓦ thaiticketmajor.com; Thailand Cultural Centre subway. All-purpose venue, under the control of the Ministry of Culture, that hosts mainstream classical concerts, traditional and contemporary theatre, and visiting international dance and theatre shows. The acoustics of the Main Hall are superb and the Royal Bangkok Symphony Orchestra performs here. There have also been ballet performances, such as Swan Lake. Note that drinks can't be taken into the auditoriums.

RITUALS OF THE RING

Thai boxing (*muay thai*) enjoys a following similar to football or baseball in the West: every province has a stadium, and whenever a big fight is shown on TV you can be sure that large, noisy crowds will gather round the sets in streetside restaurants. The best place to see Thai boxing is at one of Bangkok's two main stadia, which between them hold bouts every night of the week (see page 178).

There's a strong spiritual and **ritualistic** dimension to *muay thai*, adding grace to an otherwise brutal sport. Each boxer enters the ring to the wailing music of a three-piece *phipat* orchestra, wearing the statutory red or blue shorts ands, on his head, a sacred rope headband or *mongkhon*. Tied around his biceps are *phra jiat*, pieces of cloth that are often decorated with cabalistic symbols and may contain Buddhist tablets. The fighter then bows, first in the direction of his birthplace and then to the north, south, east and west, honouring both his teachers and the spirit of the ring. Next he performs a slow dance, claiming the audience's attention and demonstrating his prowess as a performer.

Any part of the body except the head may be used as an **offensive weapon** in *muay thai*, and all parts except the groin are fair targets. Kicks to the head are the blows that cause most knockouts. As the action hots up, so the orchestra speeds up its tempo and the betting in the audience becomes more frenetic. It can be a gruesome business, but it was far bloodier before modern boxing gloves were introduced in the 1930s, when the Queensbury Rules were adapted for *muay* – combatants used to wrap their fists with hemp impregnated with a face-lacerating dosage of ground glass.

TRADITIONAL DANCE-DRAMA

Drama pretty much equals dance in classical Thai theatre, and many of **the traditional dance-dramas** are based on the Hindu epic the *Ramayana* (in Thai, *Ramakien*), a classic adventure tale of good versus evil, which is taught in all the schools (see page 55). Not understanding the plots can be a major disadvantage, so try reading an abridged version beforehand such as *Thai Ramayana* (see page 222) and check out the wonderfully imaginative murals at Wat Phra Kaeo (see page 52), after which you'll certainly be able to sort the goodies from the baddies, if little else.

KHON

The most spectacular form of traditional Thai theatre is **khon**, a stylized drama performed in masks and elaborate costumes by a troupe of highly trained classical dancers. There's little room for individual interpretation in these dances, as all the movements follow a strict choreography that's been passed down through generations: each graceful, angular gesture depicts a precise event, action or emotion which will be familiar to educated *khon* audiences. The dancers don't speak, and the story is chanted and sung by a chorus who stand at the side of the stage, accompanied by a classical *phipat* orchestra.

A typical *khon* performance features several of the best-known **Ramakien** episodes, in which the main characters are recognized by their masks, headdresses and heavily brocaded costumes. Gods and humans don't wear masks, but the hero Rama and heroine Sita always wear tall gilded headdresses and often appear as a trio with Rama's brother Lakshaman. Monkey **masks** are wide-mouthed: monkey army chief Hanuman always wears white, and his two right-hand men – Nilanol, the god of fire, and Nilapat, the god of death – wear red and black respectively. In contrast, the demons have grim mouths, clamped shut or snarling; Totsagan, the ten-headed king of the demons, wears a green face in battle and a gold one during peace, but always sports a two-tier headdress carved with two rows of faces.

Even if you don't see a show, you're bound to come across finely crafted real and replica *khon* masks both in museums and in souvenir shops all over the country.

CABARET

Glitzy and occasionally ribald entertainment is the order of the day at the capital's **ladyboy cabaret shows**, where it's all glamorous outfits and over-the-top song and dance routines.

Calypso Cabaret Asiatique shopping centre (see page 184), Thanon Charoen Krung, 2km south of Saphan Taksin w calypsocabaret.com. Shows twice nightly. Combination tickets with a pre-show set dinner or a dinner cruise available.

Golden Dome 252/5 Soi 18, Thanon Ratchadapisek, 10–15min walk from Sutthisarn subway station w goldendomecabaret.com. Shows three times nightly. Combination tickets with a pre-show set dinner or a dinner cruise available.

THAI BOXING

The violence of the average **Thai boxing** (*muay thai*) match may be offputting to some, but spending a couple of hours at one of Bangkok's two main stadia, Rajdamnoen and Lumphini (which has now moved out of the centre from Lumphini Park), can be immensely entertaining, not least for the enthusiasm of the spectators and the ritualistic aspects of the fights. Seats for foreigners start at around B1000–2000 (cheaper, standing tickets are reserved for Thais) – try w muaythaistadium.com for fight schedules and advance ticket booking. Sessions usually feature at least ten bouts, each consisting of five 3min rounds with 2min rests in between each round, so if you're not a big fan it may be worth turning up late, as the better fights tend to happen later in the billing. To engage in a little *muay thai* yourself, visit one of several gyms around Bangkok that offer classes to foreigners.

Chacrit Muay Thai School 15/2 Soi 39, Thanon Sukhumvit w chakritmuaythai.com. Drop-in one-on-one sessions and longer courses are available.

Lumphini Stadium Thanon Ram Intra, 15min walk from Wat Phra Mahathat Skytrain station w facebook.com/p/Lumpinee-MuayThai-100064710500629. This sixty-year-old stadium has moved way out into the northern suburbs near Don Muang Airport.

Rajdamnoen Stadium Thanon Rajdamnoen Nok w rajadamnern.com. Thailand's oldest stadium (established

LAKHON

Serious and refined, lakhon is derived from khon but is used to dramatize a greater range of stories, including Buddhist Jataka tales, local folk dramas and of course the Ramakien.

The form you're most likely to come across is lakhon chatri, which is performed at shrines like Bangkok's Erawan as entertainment for the spirits and a token of gratitude from worshippers. Usually female, the lakhon chatri dancers perform as an ensemble, executing sequences that, like khon movements, all have minute and particular symbolism. They also wear ornate costumes, but no masks, and dance to the music of a phipat orchestra. Unfortunately, as resident shrine troupes tend to repeat the same dances a dozen times a day, it's rarely the sublime display it's cracked up to be. Bangkok's National Theatre stages the more elegantly executed lakhon nai, a dance form that used to be performed at the Thai court and often re-tells the Ramakien.

LIKAY

Likay is a much more popular and dynamic derivative of khon – more light-hearted, with lots of comic interludes, bawdy jokes and panto-style over-the-top acting and singing. Some likay troupes perform Ramakien excerpts, but a lot of them adapt pot-boiler romances or write their own, and most will ham things up with improvisations and up-to-the-minute topical satire. Costumes might be traditional as in khon and lakhon, modern and Western as on TV, or a mixture of both.

Likay troupes travel around the country doing shows on makeshift outdoor stages wherever they think they'll get an audience, most commonly at temple fairs. Performances are often free and generally last for about five hours, with the audience strolling in and out of the show, cheering and joking with the cast throughout. Televised likay dramas get huge audiences and always follow romantic soap-opera-style plot-lines. Short likay dramas are also a staple of Bangkok's National Theatre, but for more radical and internationally minded likay, look out for performances by Makhampom (Wmakhampom.org), a famous, long-established troupe with bases in Bangkok and Chiang Dao that pushes likay in new directions to promote social causes and involve minority communities.

---

in 1945) is handily located near Banglamphu (and handily surrounded by restaurants selling northeastern food).
Sor Vorapin's Gym Soi 1, Thanon Suan Pak, Taling Chan Wthaiboxings.com. Holds training courses at a gym and homestay in Thonburi.

CINEMAS

Most Bangkok cinemas show recent American and European releases with their original dialogue and Thai subtitles, screening shows around four times a day. In recent years Thailand's own film industry has been enjoying a boom, and in Bangkok you may be lucky enough to come across one of the bigger Thai hits showing with English subtitles. Several websites give showtimes of movies in Bangkok, including Wcinematic.asia, which also carries details of screenings at the Thai Film Archive, and has links to the Goethe Institut, the Japan Foundation and other film clubs in the city. Some cinema-goers in Bangkok still stand for the king's anthem, which is played before every performance.

Alliance Française Off Thanon Witthayu, opposite the east side of Lumpini Park behind the Japanese Embassy Wafthailande.org. The movie screenings at the French cultural centre are usually subtitled in English.

House Samyan Floor 5, Samyan Mitrtown shopping centre, corner of Thanon Rama IV and Thanon Phraya Thai Whousesamyan.com. Bangkok's main art-house cinema, handy for Sam Yan subway station and walkable from Sala Daeng Skytrain station.

THAI MASSAGE

Mind and body

The last few years have seen an explosion in the number of spas opening in Bangkok – mainly inside the poshest hotels, but also as small, affordable walk-in centres around the city. With their focus on indulgent self-pampering, spas are usually associated with high-spending tourists, but the treatments on offer at Bangkok's five-star hotels are often little different from those used by traditional medical practitioners, who have long held that massage and herbs are the best way to restore physical and mental well-being. Even in the heart of the city, it's also possible to undergo a bit of highly traditional mental self-help by practising meditation.

SPAS AND MASSAGE CENTRES

Thais visit a masseur for many conditions, including fevers, colds and muscle strain, but bodies that are not sick are also considered to benefit from the restorative powers of a **massage**, and nearly every hotel and guesthouse will be able to put you in touch with a masseur. A session should ideally last at least one and a half hours and will cost B300–1500, or a lot more in the most exclusive spas. All **spas** in Bangkok feature traditional Thai massage and herbal therapies in their programmes, but most also offer dozens of other international treatments, including facials, aromatherapy, Swedish massage and various body wraps. Spa centres in upmarket hotels are usually open to non-guests but generally need to be booked in advance; day spas that are not attached to hotels may not require reservations.

Asia Herb Association 20 Soi 4 (Soi Nana Tai), Thanon Sukhumvit ⓦasiaherbassociation.com. The speciality here is massage with hot herbal balls (*phrakop*), which are freshly made each day with ingredients from their organic farm in Khao Yai. Also on offer are regular Thai massages, aromatherapy oil massages, foot massages and body scrubs, with several other locations, mostly around Sukhumvit.

Divana Massage and Spa 10 Thanon Srivieng ⓦdivanaspa.com. Delightful spa serving up Thai massages, foot, aromatherapy and herbal massages, as well as facials, body scrubs and other treatments, with several other locations around Bangkok.

Health Land 55/5 Soi 1, Thanon Asok Montri (Sukhumvit Soi 21) ⓦhealthlandspa.com. Excellent, inexpensive Thai and other massages, Ayurvedic treatments, facials and body polishes, in swish surroundings, with several other locations around Bangkok.

Pimmalai Thanon Sukhumvit, 50m east of BTS On Nut,

THAI MASSAGE

Thai massage (*nuad boran*, "traditional massage") is based on the principle that many physical and emotional problems are caused by the blocking of vital energy channels within the body. The masseur uses his or her feet, heels, knees and elbows, as well as hands, to exert a gentle pressure on these channels, supplementing this acupressure-style technique by pulling and pushing the limbs into yogic stretches. This distinguishes Thai massage from most other massage styles, which are more concerned with tissue manipulation. One is supposed to emerge from a Thai massage feeling both relaxed and energized, and it is said that regular massages produce long-term benefits in muscles as well as stimulating the circulation and aiding natural detoxification.

The **science** behind Thai massage has its roots in Indian Ayurvedic medicine, which classifies each component of the body according to one of the four elements (earth, water, fire and air), and holds that balancing these elements within the body is crucial to good health. Many of the stretches and manipulations fundamental to Thai massage are thought to have derived from yogic practices introduced to Thailand from India by Buddhist missionaries in about the second century BC; Chinese acupuncture and reflexology have also had a strong influence. In the nineteenth century, King Rama III ordered a series of murals illustrating the principles of Thai massage to be painted around the courtyard of Bangkok's Wat Pho (see page 57), and they are still in place today, along with statues of ascetics depicted in typical massage poses. **Wat Pho** has been the leading school of Thai massage for hundreds of years, and it's possible to take courses there as well as to receive a massage. Masseurs who trained at Wat Pho are considered to be the best in the country and masseurs all across the city advertise this as a credential, whether it's true or not. Many Thais consider blind masseurs to be especially sensitive practitioners.

The same Indian missionaries who introduced yogic practices to Thailand are also credited with spreading the word about the therapeutic effects of herbal saunas and **herbal massages**, in which the masseur will knead you with a ball of herbs (*phrakop*) wrapped in a cloth and steam-heated; they're said to be particularly good for stiffness of the neck, shoulders and back. The **herbs** themselves, however, are resolutely Thai and feature in Thai cuisine as well as herbal treatments. Among these the most popular are tamarind, whose acidic content makes it a useful skin exfoliant, and turmeric, which is known for its disinfectant and healing properties; both are a common component of the scrubs and body wraps offered at many spas. The same places will also use lemon grass, probably Thailand's most distinctive herb, and the ubiquitous jasmine as soothing agents in aromatherapy treatments.

MASSAGE PRACTICALITIES

Traditional Thai masseurs do not use oils or lotions and the client is treated on a mat or mattress; you'll often be given loose-fitting trousers and a loose top to change into. English-speaking masseurs will often ask if there are any areas that you would like them to concentrate on, or if you have any problem areas that you want them to avoid; if your masseur doesn't speak English, the simplest way to signal the latter is to point at the area while saying *mai sabai* ("not well"). If you're in pain during a massage, wincing usually does the trick, perhaps adding *jep* ("it hurts"); if your masseur is pressing too hard, say *bao bao na khrap/kha* ("gently please"). If you're wary of submitting to the full works, try a **foot massage** first, which will apply the same techniques to just your feet and lower legs.

exit 1, between sois 81 and 83 ⓦpimmalai.com. In a nice old wooden house, inexpensive Thai massages, plus foot, herbal and oil massages, herbal steam treatments, body scrubs, masks and facials.

Wat Pho (see page 57). Excellent body and foot massages are available in two a/c buildings on the east side of Wat Pho's main compound; allow 2hr for the full works. There are often long queues here, however, so you might be better off heading over to one of the massage centre's other branches just outside the temple, as detailed on the website (ⓦwatpomassage.com). Here you can also enrol on a 30hr massage training course in English, over five days, and foot-massage courses.

MEDITATION SESSIONS AND RETREATS

Most of Thailand's retreats are out in the provinces, but a few temples and centres in Bangkok cater for foreigners by holding **meditation sessions** in English; novices and practised meditators alike are generally welcome. The meditation taught is mostly Vipassana, or "insight", which emphasizes the minute observation of internal sensations; the other main technique is Samatha, which aims to calm the mind and develop concentration (these two techniques are not entirely separate, since you cannot have insight without some degree of concentration). Little Bangkok Sangha (ⓦlittlebang.org) is a handy blog maintained by a British-born monk, Phra Pandit, which gives details of group meditation sessions and talks in Bangkok and retreats. Also in Bangkok, there are sessions at Wat Mahathat (see page 61) and keep an eye out for events for English-speakers at the Buddhadasa Indapanno Archives in Chatuchak Park in the north of the city (ⓦbia.or.th).

House of Dhamma Insight Meditation Centre 26/9 Soi Lardprao 15, Chatuchak, Bangkok ⓦhouseofdhamma.com. Regular courses in Vipassana by a respected British-born teacher, lasting one (for beginners) or two (for those with some experience of meditation) days; courses in reiki (lasting two to four days) and other subjects also available.

Thailand Vipassana Centres ⓦdhamma.org. Frequent retreats in a Burmese Vipassana tradition (ten days), in ten centres around Thailand, including Bangkok and nearby Chanthaburi, Kanchanaburi, Phetchaburi and Prachinburi.

World Fellowship of Buddhists (WFB) 616 Benjasiri Park, Soi Medhinivet off Soi 24, Thanon Sukhumvit, Bangkok ⓦwfbhq.org. Headquarters of an influential worldwide organization of (mostly Theravada) Buddhists, founded in Sri Lanka in 1950, which holds occasional dhamma talks.

MEDITATION RETREATS

Longer retreats are for the serious-minded only. Strict segregation of the sexes is enforced and many places observe a vow of silence. Reading and writing are also discouraged, and you'll not be allowed to leave the retreat complex unless absolutely necessary, so try to bring whatever you'll need in with you. All retreats expect you to wear modest clothing, and some require you to wear white – check ahead whether there is a shop at the retreat complex or whether you are expected to bring this with you. An average day at any one of these monasteries starts with a **wake-up** call at around 4am and includes several hours of **group meditation** and chanting, as well as time put aside for chores and personal reflection. However long their stay, visitors are expected to keep the eight main Buddhist precepts, the most restrictive of these being the abstention from food after midday and from alcohol, tobacco, drugs and sex at all times. Most wats ask for a minimal daily **donation** (around B200) to cover the costs of the simple accommodation and food.

SIAM PARAGON MALL

Shopping

Bangkok has a good reputation for shopping, particularly for antiques, gems, contemporary interior design and fashion, where the range and quality are streets ahead of other Thai cities. Fabrics and handicrafts are good buys too. Watch out for fakes: cut glass masquerading as precious stones, damaged goods being passed off as antiques, counterfeit designer clothes and accessories, even mocked-up international driver's licences (Thai travel agents and other organizations aren't easily fooled). Bangkok also has Thailand's best English-language bookshops.

Downtown is full of smart, multi-storey **shopping plazas** like Siam Centre, Siam Paragon and Central World on Thanon Rama I, Central Embassy on Thanon Ploenchit and Emporium and EmQuartier on Thanon Sukhumvit, which is where you'll find the majority of the city's fashion stores, as well as designer lifestyle goods and bookshops. The plazas tend to be pleasantly air-conditioned and thronging with trendy young Thais, but don't hold much interest for tourists unless you happen to be looking for a new outfit.

Shopping centres, department stores and tourist-oriented shops in the city keep late **hours**, opening daily at 10 or 11am and closing at about 9pm; many small, upmarket boutiques, for example along Thanon Charoen Krung and Thanon Silom, close on Sundays, one or two even on Saturdays. Monday is meant to be no-street-vendor day throughout Bangkok, a chance for the pavements to get cleaned and for pedestrians to finally see where they're going, but plenty of stalls manage to flout the rule.

MARKETS

For travellers, spectating, not shopping, is apt to be the main draw of Bangkok's neighbourhood markets and the bazaars of Chinatown. The massive Chatuchak Weekend Market is an exception, being both a tourist attraction and a marvellous shopping experience (see page 106). With the notable exception of Chatuchak, most markets operate daily from dawn till early afternoon; early morning is often the best time to go to beat the heat and crowds.

Asiatique About 2km south of Taksin Bridge, between the river and Thanon Charoen Krung ⓦasiatique thailand.com; see map page 108. Market for tourists in ten rebuilt 1930s warehouses and sawmills that belonged to the Danish East Asiatic Company, which are now dotted with information points and exhibits as a kind of "living museum"; the market opens late morning but is liveliest in the evening. Several of the warehouses are given over to souvenir stalls and clothes stalls, which tend to morph into bigger, more chic and expensive fashion outlets the closer to the river you get. A few more interesting shops are devoted to furniture and home décor, featuring some creative contemporary designs. There's plenty to eat, of course, with the poshest restaurants occupying the pleasant riverside boardwalk, while attractions include a sixty-metre ferris wheel, Calypso Cabaret (see page 178) and the *Sirimahannop* on the river, a replica of a nineteenth-century three-masted sailing ship that now accommodates a restaurant and bar run by the *Marriott Marquis Queens Park* hotel (see page 155). Free ferries shuttle back and forth from Tha Sathorn pier, though the queues are sometimes long. Otherwise, the Chao Phraya Express tourist boats leaving Phra Arthit between 3.30pm and 6pm extend their route from Tha Sathorn to Asiatique. You could also catch an orange-flag express boat to Wat Rajsingkorn, leaving a 10min walk through the wat and down Thanon Charoen Krung to the shopping complex.

Jodd Fairs Corner of Thanon Ratchadaphisek and Thanon Rama IX ⓦfacebook.com/JoddFairs; see map page 92. Fun outdoor market that's the most accessible

> ### AXE PILLOWS
>
> Traditional triangular pillows (*mawn khwaan*) – so named because their shape supposedly resembles an axe head (*khwaan*) – are a lot more comfortable than they look and come in a range of sizes, fabrics and colours, both traditional and contemporary. **Axe pillows** have been used in Thai homes for centuries, where it's normal to sit on the floor and lean against a densely stuffed *mawn khwaan*; in wealthier homes one reclines on a polished teak chaise longue and props oneself against a *mawn khwaan*.
>
> Pillows are made up of seven or more triangular pods, each of which is packed with kapok, although the cheaper (but longer-lasting) versions are bulked out with cardboard. The **design** has been slightly adapted over the years, so it's now also possible to get *mawn khwaan* with up to four flat cushions attached, making lying out more comfortable. The trademark *khit* fabric used in traditional-style pillows is characterized by stripes of (usually yellow) supplementary weft and is mostly woven in north and northeast Thailand. Pillows made from the multi-coloured red, blue and green nylon *khit* are the most durable, but those covered in muted shades of cotton *khit* are softer and more fashionable.
>
> Axe pillows make fantastic souvenirs but are heavy to post home; some places sell unstuffed versions which are simple to mail home, but a pain to fill when you return.

SHOPPING FOR EVERYDAY STUFF

You're most likely to find useful everyday items in one of the city's numerous **department stores**: seven-storey Central Chidlom on Thanon Ploenchit (w central.co.th), which boasts handy services like watch-repair booths as well as a huge product selection (including large sizes), is probably the city's best. For **children's stuff**, Central Chidlom also has a branch of Mothercare (w mothercarethailand.com), as do the Emporium, Central World and Siam Paragon shopping centres. Meanwhile, the British chain of **pharmacies**, Boots (w th.boots.com), has scores of branches across the city, including on Thanon Khao San in Banglamphu, in Siam Paragon, in EmQuartier and at the Thanon Suriwong end of Patpong 1.

The best place to buy anything to do with **mobile phones** (see page 47) is the scores of small booths on Floor 4 of Mah Boon Krong (MBK) Shopping Centre at the Rama I/Phrayathai intersection. For **computer** hardware and software, and cameras and other photographic equipment, as well as repairs and secondhand, Fortune Town IT Lifestyle Centre, on Thanon Ratchadaphisek at the corner of Thanon Rama IX, is the best place; it's right next to Rama 9 subway station.

of several similar night-time operations in Bangkok, as it's 2min walk from Rama 9 subway station. Among the nail bars and tattoo parlours, hundreds of stalls purvey all the cool stuff a twenty-something urbanite might want, including new and pre-loved clothes, caps, bags and general kitsch. Dozens of food stalls and outdoor bars, some with live music and DJs, round out the picture. A second branch next to Thailand Cultural Centre subway station on Thanon Ratchadaphisek is planned (though it's also possible that the whole market will move to the new site).

HANDICRAFTS, TEXTILES AND CONTEMPORARY DESIGN

Samples of nearly all regionally produced **handicrafts** end up in Bangkok, so the selection is phenomenal. Many of the shopping plazas have at least one classy handicraft outlet, and competition keeps prices in the city at upcountry levels, with the main exception of household objects – particularly wickerware and tin bowls and basins – which get palmed off relatively expensively in Bangkok. Several places on and around Thanon Khao San sell reasonably priced triangular "axe" **pillows** (mawn khwaan) in traditional fabrics (see box below). The cheapest outlet for traditional northern and northeastern **textiles** is Chatuchak Weekend Market (see page 106), where you'll also be able to nose out some interesting handicrafts. Most Thai **silk**, which is noted for its thickness and sheen, comes from the northeast and the north. However, there is a decent range of outlets in the capital, including many branches of Jim Thompson. Bangkok also has a good reputation for its **contemporary interior design**, fusing minimalist Western ideals with traditional Thai and other Asian craft elements.

RATANAKOSIN, SEE MAP PAGE 51

Doi Tung Lifestyle Thanon Na Phra Lan (plus several other branches around town and at the airports) w doitung.com. Part of the late Princess Mother's development project based at Doi Tung near Chiang Rai, selling very striking and attractive cotton and linen in warm colours, made up into clothes, cushion covers, rugs and so on, as well as coffee and macadamia nuts from the Chiang Rai mountains.

Queen Sirikit Museum of Textiles Shop Grand Palace (near the exit from the palace complex) w qsmtthailand.org/shop. Not-for-profit shop under the auspices of the Queen Mother's Support Foundation, which is especially good for batik and hill-tribe jewellery.

DOWNTOWN: AROUND SIAM SQUARE AND THANON PLOENCHIT, SEE MAP PAGE 96

Creative Lab Siam Discovery, Thanon Rama I w siamdiscovery.co.th. The renovated Floor 3 of this mall is now an open-plan bazaar for all manner of contemporary Thai design, including lamps, vases, rugs, accessories, spa products and stationery.

Jim Thompson Jim Thompson House Museum (see page 94). Large branch of the iconic Thai silk shop (see page 186).

The Legend Just off Thanon Phraya Thai near the corner of Thanon Phetchaburi and Ratchathevi Skytrain station. Stocks a small selection of well-made Thai handicrafts, notably celadon, as well as other ceramics and basketware, at reasonable prices.

Narai Phand Ground floor, President Tower Arcade, just east of Gaysorn Village, Thanon Ploenchit w naraiphand.com. This souvenir centre was set up to ensure the preservation of traditional crafts and to maintain standards of quality, as a joint venture with the Ministry of Industry in the 1930s, and has a duly institutional feel, though it makes a reasonable one-stop shop for last-minute presents. It offers a huge assortment of reasonably priced, good-quality goods from all over the country, including silk and cotton, *khon* masks, *bencharong*, celadon, woodcarving, lacquerware, silver, brass, bronze, *yan lipao* basketware and axe cushions.

THANON SUKHUMVIT, SEE MAPS PAGES 96 AND 99

Another Story Floor 4, EmQuartier w facebook.com/anotherstoryofficial. Another Story shelters a bewildering anthology of cool stuff: lamps and interior décor, leather bags and accessories, gadgets, stationery and art books, sunglasses, and wine accessories.

Jim Thompson 153 Soi 93 w jimthompson.com. Outlet store of the iconic Thai silk shop (see page 186).

Lofty Bamboo 20/7 Soi 39 w facebook.com/LoftyBamboo. Japanese-run fair-trade outlet for crafts, accessories, clothes, bags and jewellery, including textiles and accessories made by Lisu people from northern Thailand.

Narai Phand Floor 1, Eight Thonglor shopping centre, 88/36 Soi 55 w naraiphand.com. Sukhumvit branch of the long-running Thai crafts souvenir centre (see page 185).

Sop Moei Arts 8 Soi 49 w sopmoeiarts.com. Gorgeous fabrics – scarves, wall-hangings, bags and cushion covers – and stylish basketware, with part of the profits going back to the eponymous Karen village and nearby refugee camp near Mae Sariang in northern Thailand, where they're made.

DOWNTOWN: SOUTH OF THANON RAMA IV, SEE MAP PAGE 102

Alexander Lamont Warehouse 30, 60/1 Soi 30, Thanon Charoen Krung w alexanderlamont.com. Beautiful lacquerware bowls, vases and boxes, as well as objects using bronze, glass, crystal, ceramic, parchment, gold leaf and petrified wood, all in imaginative contemporary, Asian-inspired styles.

Chabatik Floor 2, River City w chabatik.com. Gorgeous scarves, wraps, bags, accessories and hangings in a rainbow of colours, made from soft Khon Kaen silk, combining traditional weaving methods with contemporary designs.

Jim Thompson 9 Thanon Suriwong, corner of Thanon Rama IV; branches at the airports and many department stores, malls and hotels around the city w jimthompson.com. A good place to start looking for traditional Thai fabric, or at least to get an idea of what's out there. Stocks silk, linen and cotton by the metre and ready-made items from shirts to cushion covers, which are well designed and of good quality, but pricey. They also have a home-furnishings section.

Khomapastr 56–58 Thanon Naret, between Suriwong and Si Phraya roads w facebook.com/khomapastrfabrics. Famous outlet for *pha kiaw* (or *pha khomapastr*), brightly coloured, hand-printed cotton with lovely, swirling *kannok* patterns, usually with strong elements of gold – Khomapastr's founder, himself a prince, was inspired to start the business when rummaging through trunks of nineteenth-century royal clothing at Bangkok's National Museum in the 1940s. You can buy the cloth by the piece or metre, or made up into skirts, shirts, cushion covers and bags.

TAILORED CLOTHES   SEE MAP PAGE 102

Inexpensive tailoring shops crowd Silom, Sukhumvit and Khao San roads, but the best single area to head for is the short stretch of Thanon Charoen Krung between Thanon Suriwong and Thanon Silom (near the Chao Phraya express-boat stop at Tha Oriental, or a 10min walk from Saphan Taksin Skytrain station). It's generally advisable to avoid tailors in tourist areas such as Thanon Khao San, shopping malls and Thanon Sukhumvit, although if you're lucky it's still possible to come up trumps here. For cheap and reasonable shirt and dress material other than silk go for a browse around Pahurat market (see page 80), though the suit materials are mostly poor and best avoided.

A Song Tailor 8 Trok Chartered Bank (Soi 38), just round the corner from OP Place shopping centre off Thanon Charoen Krung, near the Oriental Hotel e asongtailor@gmail.com. Friendly, helpful small shop that's a good first port of call if you're on a budget. Men's and women's suits and shirts; preferably at least three to five days with two fittings, but can turn work around in a day or two. No walk-ins: email to make an appointment.

Ah Song Tailor 1203 Thanon Charoen Krung, opposite Soi 36 t 02 233 0992. Younger brother of the above (neither of them should be confused with the nearby Ah Sun Tailor), a meticulous tailor who takes pride in his work. Men's and women's suits and shirts in around four days, with two fittings.

World Group Tailor 38 Soi 40 (Oriental Avenue), Thanon Charoen Krung, near the Oriental Hotel w worldgrouptailor.com. Large shop that can turn around decent work in three or four days, though prices are slightly on the high side.

FASHION

Thanon Khao San is lined with stalls selling low-priced fashion clothing: the baggy cotton fisherman's trousers, elephant pants and embroidered blouses are all aimed at backpackers, but they're supplemented by cheap contemporary fashions that appeal to urban Thais as well. Downtown, the most famous area for low-cost, low-quality casual clothes is the warren-like Pratunam Market and surrounding malls such as Platinum Fashion Mall around

HAVING CLOTHES TAILOR-MADE

Bangkok can be an excellent place to get tailor-made suits, dresses, shirts and trousers at a fraction of the price you'd pay in the West. Tailors here can copy a sample brought from home and will also work from any photographs you can provide; most also carry a good selection of catalogues. The bad news is that many tourist-oriented tailors aren't terribly good, often attempting to get away with poor work and shoddy materials (and sometimes trying to delay delivery until just before you leave the city, so that you don't have time to complain). However, with a little effort and thought, both men and women can get some fantastic clothes made to measure.

Choosing a tailor can be tricky, and unless you're particularly knowledgeable about material, shopping around won't necessarily tell you much. However, don't make a decision wholly on prices quoted – picking a tailor simply because they're the cheapest usually leads to poor work, and cheap suits don't last. Special deals offering two suits, two shirts, two ties and a kimono for US$99 should be left well alone. Above all, ignore recommendations by anyone with a vested interest in bringing your custom to a particular shop.

Prices vary widely depending on material and the tailor's skill. As a very rough guide, for labour alone expect to pay B6000 for a two-piece suit, though some tailors will charge rather more (check whether or not the price you're quoted includes the lining). For middling **material**, expect to pay about B3000–5000, or anything up to B20,000 for top-class cloth. With the exception of silk, local materials are frequently of poor quality and for suits in particular you're far better off using English or Italian cloth. Most tailors stock both imported and local fabrics, but bringing your own from home can work out significantly cheaper.

Give yourself as much **time** as possible. For suits, insist on two fittings. Most good tailors require around three days for a suit (some require ten days or more), although a few have enough staff to produce good work in a day or two. The more **detail** you can give the tailor the better. As well as deciding on the obvious features such as single- or double-breasted and number of buttons, think about the width of lapels, style of trousers, whether you want the jacket with vents or not, and so forth. Specifying factors like this will make all the difference as to whether you're happy with your suit, so it's worth discussing them with the tailor; a good tailor should be able to give good advice. Finally, don't be afraid to be an awkward customer until you're completely happy with the finished product – after all, the whole point of getting clothes tailor-made is to get exactly what you want.

---

the junction of Phetchaburi and Ratchaprarop roads (see page 96), but for the best and latest trends from Thai designers, you should check out the shops in Siam Square and across the road in the more upmarket Siam Centre. Prices vary considerably: street gear in Siam Square is undoubtedly inexpensive, while genuine Western brand names are generally competitive but not breathtakingly cheaper than at home; larger sizes can be hard to find. Shoes and leather goods are good buys in Bangkok, being generally handmade from high-quality leather and quite a bargain.

Central Embassy Thanon Ploenchit w centralembassy.com; see map page 96. Constructed on land sold off by the British Embassy, this mall is bidding to become the most chic of the city's shopping plazas: here you'll find Gucci and McQ – and gentlemen can get a very civilized haircut or shave at a branch of the London barber, Truefitt and Hill – while a few upmarket Thai names have made it to the party, notably Sretsis and Scotch & Soda.

Central World Ratchaprasong Intersection, corner of Rama I and Rajdamri roads w central.co.th; see map page 96. This shopping centre is so huge that it defies easy classification, but you'll find plenty of Thai and international fashions on its lower floors and in the attached Central department store at its southern end or the Japanese Takashimaya department store at its northern end.

Emporium Thanon Sukhumvit, between sois 22 and 24 w emporium.co.th; see map page 99. Large and rather glamorous shopping plaza, with its own department store and a good range of fashion outlets, from exclusive designer wear to trendy high-street gear. Genuine brand-name shops include Prada, Chanel and Burberry, as well as established local labels such as Soda.

EmQuartier Thanon Sukhumvit, opposite Emporium w emquartier.co.th; see map page 99. Sprawled across three buildings, this mall runs the gamut from Chanel and Jimmy Choo to Boots the chemist. Less exclusive brands such as Tommy Hilfiger also find space alongside

Soda, Jaspal and other local names (and lots of good eating options).

Mah Boon Krong (MBK) At the Rama I/Phrayathai intersection ⓦmbk-center.co.th; see map page 96. Vivacious, labyrinthine shopping centre which most closely resembles a traditional Thai market that's been rammed into a huge mall. It houses hundreds of small, mostly fairly inexpensive outlets, including plenty of high-street fashion shops.

Siam Centre Thanon Rama I ⓦsiamcenter.co.th; see map page 96. Particularly good for local labels – look out for Greyhound, Jaspal and Kloset, which mounts dramatic displays of women's party and formal gear – many of which have made the step up from the booths of Siam Square across the road, as well as international names like Nike.

Siam Square Corner of Phayathai Road and Rama I Road; see map page 96. It's worth poking around the alleys here and the "mini-malls" inside the blocks. All manner of inexpensive boutiques, some little more than booths, sell colourful street-gear to the capital's fashionable students and teenagers.

Viera by Ragazze Floor 2, Central World and in the attached Central and Takashamiya department stores ⓦvierabyragazze.com; see map page 96. Stylish, Italian-influenced leather goods.

BOOKS

English-language **bookshops** in Bangkok are always well stocked with everything to do with Thailand, and most carry fiction classics and popular paperbacks as well. The capital's secondhand bookshops are not cheap, but you can usually part-exchange your unwanted titles.

Asia Books Flagship store in Central World on Thanon Rama I, plus dozens of other branches around town ⓦasiabooks.com; see map page 96. English-language bookshop (and publishing house) that's especially recommended for its books on Asia – everything from guidebooks to cookery books, novels to art. Also stocks bestselling novels and coffee-table books.

B2S Floor 7, Central Chidlom, Thanon Ploenchit ⓦb2s.co.th; see map page 96. This shop sells a decent selection of English-language books, but is most notable for its huge selection of magazines and stationery. There are dozens of branches around town.

Books Kinokuniya Floor 3, EmQuartier Shopping Centre, Thanon Sukhumvit; Floor 6, Central World, Thanon Rama I; Floor 3, Siam Paragon, Thanon Rama I ⓦthailand.kinokuniya.com; see maps pages 96 and 99. Huge, efficient, Japanese-owned, English-language bookshop with a wide selection of books ranging from bestsellers to travel literature and from classics to sci-fi; not so hot on books about Asia, though.

Dasa Book Café Between sois 26 and 28, Thanon Sukhumvit ⓦdasabooks.com; see map page 99. Bangkok's best secondhand bookshop, Dasa is appealingly calm and intelligently, and alphabetically, categorized, with sections on everything from Asia to biography, and a large children's area. Browse its regularly updated list of stock online, or enjoy coffee and cakes *in situ*.

Open House Floor 6, Central Embassy, Thanon Ploenchit ⓦcentralembassy.com; see map page 96.

GEM SCAMS

Gem scams are so common in Bangkok that TAT publishes regular warnings about it and there are lots of web pages on the subject, including ⓦen.wikipedia.org/wiki/Gem_scam. Never buy anything through a tout or from any shop recommended by a "government official"/"student"/"businessperson"/tuk-tuk driver who just happens to engage you in conversation on the street, and note that there are no government jewellery shops, despite any information you may be given to the contrary, and no special government promotions or sales on gems.

The basic **scam** is to charge a lot more than what the gem is worth based on its carat weight – at the very least, get it **tested** on the spot, ask for a written guarantee and receipt. Don't even consider **buying gems in bulk** to sell at a supposedly vast profit elsewhere: many a gullible traveller has invested thousands of dollars on a handful of worthless multicoloured stones, believing the vendor's reassurance that the goods will fetch at least a hundred percent more when resold at home.

If you're determined to buy precious stones, check that the shop is a member of the **Thai Gem and Jewelry Traders Association** by visiting their website, which has a directory of members (ⓦthaigemjewelry.or.th). To be doubly sure, you may want to seek out shops that also belong to the TGJTA's **Jewel Fest Club** (look for the window stickers, or look at the directory of members on ⓦjewelfestclub.com), which guarantees quality.

As well as posh restaurants and a great coffee bar (see page 165), this novel take on a food court shelters lots of sofas and books to browse and to buy in a bright and welcoming space, as well as a playground for kids.

JEWELLERY AND GEMS

Bangkok boasts Thailand's best **gem and jewellery** shops, and some of the finest lapidaries in the world, making this *the* place to buy cut and uncut stones such as rubies, blue sapphires and diamonds. However, countless gem-buying tourists get badly ripped off, so remember to be extremely wary.

Asian Institute of Gemological Sciences Floor 48, Jewelry Trade Center, 919 Thanon Silom ⓦaigsthailand.com; see map page 102. Independent professional advice and precious stones certification from its laboratory. Also runs reputable courses, such as a five-day introduction to gems and gemology.

Jewelry Trade Center West end of Thanon Silom ⓦjewelrytradecenter.com; see map page 102. Dozens of members of the Thai Gem and Jewelry Traders Association have outlets in this shopping mall (and on the surrounding streets).

Lambert Floor 4, Shanghai Building, Soi 17, 807–9 Thanon Silom ⓦlambertgems.com; see map page 102. Thoroughly reputable, forty-year-old, American-owned outlet, offering a full service: loose stones and pearls, including collectors' stones, ready-made pieces, cutting, design, redesign and repairs.

ANTIQUES

Bangkok is the entrepôt for the finest Thai, Burmese and Cambodian antiques, but the market has long been sewn up, so don't expect to happen upon any undiscovered treasure. Even experts admit that they sometimes find it hard to tell real antiques from fakes, so the best policy is just to buy on the grounds of attractiveness. The River City shopping complex (ⓦrivercitybangkok.com) off Thanon Charoen Krung, which is near Si Phraya pier (Chao Phraya Express and Thai Smile Urban Line boats), devotes its third, fourth and some of its second floors to a bewildering array of pricey treasures, ranging from Buddha images to tribal masks, as well as holding monthly auctions (ⓦrcbauctions.com). The other main area for antiques is the nearby section of Charoen Krung that runs down to the bottom of Thanon Silom, and the stretch of Silom running east from here up to and including the multistorey Jewelry Trade Center. Here you'll find a good selection of largely reputable individual businesses specializing in woodcarvings, ceramics, bronze statues and stone sculptures culled from all parts of Thailand and neighbouring countries as well. Remember that most antiques require an export permit (see page 45).

ROLLER-COASTER AT DREAM WORLD

Kids' Bangkok

Thais are very tolerant of children, so you can take them almost anywhere without restriction. The only drawback might be the constant attention lavished on your kids by complete strangers, which some adults and children might find tiring. Should you be in Thailand in January, your kids will be able to join in the free entertainment and activities staged all over the city on National Children's Day (Wan Dek), which is held on the second Saturday of January. They also get free entry to zoos that day and free rides on public buses.

ESSENTIALS

For babies, a **changing mat** may be worth bringing with you as, although there are public toilets in every shopping plaza and department store, few have baby facilities (toilets at posh hotels being a useful exception). International brands of powdered milk and baby food are available in Bangkok, though some parents find restaurant-cooked rice and bananas go down just as well. Thai women do not **breastfeed** in public.

Getting around Child-carrier backpacks are ideal for getting around (though make sure that the child's head extends no higher than yours, as there are countless low-hanging obstacles on Thai streets). Opinions are divided on whether or not it's worth bringing a buggy or three-wheeled stroller. Bangkok's pavements are bumpy at best and there's an almost total absence of ramps. Buggies and strollers do, however, come in handy for feeding small children (and even for daytime naps), as highchairs are provided only in some restaurants (and then often without restraints for smaller toddlers). Taxis almost never provide baby car seats, and even if you bring your own you'll often find there are no seat belts to strap them in with; branches of international car-rental companies should be able to provide car seats.

Accommodation and discounts Many of Bangkok's expensive hotels offer special deals for families (see page 150), and an increasing number of guesthouses offer three-person rooms. Decent cots are available free in the bigger hotels as well as at some smaller ones (though cots in these places can be a bit grotty) and top- and mid-range rooms usually come with a fridge. Many hotels can also provide a babysitting service. Kids get discounts at most of the theme parks and amusement centres listed below, though not at the majority of the city's museums, and there are no reductions on Bangkok buses and boats. One of the more bizarre provisos is the State Railway's regulation that a child aged 3 to 12 qualifies for half-fare only if under 150cm tall; some stations have a measuring scale painted onto the ticket-hall wall.

Shopping Although many Thai babies don't wear them, disposable nappies (diapers) are sold at supermarkets, department stores, pharmacies and convenience stores across the city – Mamy Poko is a reliable Japanese brand, available in supermarkets. Should you need to buy a crucial piece of children's gear while you're in Bangkok, you should be able to find it in one of the department stores (see page 185), which all have children's sections selling bottles, slings and clothes. There are even several branches of Mothercare in the main shopping plazas, including in the Emporium (between Sukhumvit sois 22 and 24; BTS Phrom Pong; see page 99); in Central World on Thanon Rama I; BTS Chit Lom or Central; see page 96); in Central Chidlom on Thanon Ploenchit (BTS Chit Lom; see map, page 96); and in Siam Paragon at Siam Square (BTS Central; see map, page 96). Children's clothes are very cheap in Thailand.

INFORMATION AND ADVICE

Bangkok Mothers and Babies International ⓦ bambiweb.org. For expat mothers and kids, but some of the information and advice on the website should be useful.

Bkk Kids ⓦ bkkkids.com. Especially good on activities for kids in Bangkok, but also covers health matters and other services thoroughly.

ACTIVITIES

The following places are all designed for kids, the main drawbacks being that many are located a long way from the city centre. Other attractions kids might enjoy include the Museum of Siam (see page 59), feeding the turtles at Wat Prayoon (see page 87), Sea Life Bangkok Ocean World aquarium (see page 95), the Snake Farm (see page 98), cycling around Muang Boran Ancient City (see page 112), taking a canal boat through Thonburi (see page 81), Open House in Central Embassy shopping centre (see page 187) and pedal-boating in Lumphini Park (see page 100).

HAZARDS

Even more than their parents, children need protecting from the sun, unsafe drinking water, heat and unfamiliar **food**. Consider packing a jar of a favourite spread so that you can always rely on toast if all else fails to please. As with adults, you should be careful about unwashed fruit and salads and about dishes that have been left uncovered for a long time. As diarrhoea can be dangerous for a child, rehydration solutions (see page 35) are vital if your child goes down with it; sachets formulated specially for children are available in local pharmacies. Avoiding **mosquitoes** is difficult, but low-strength DEET lotions should do the trick. You should also make sure, if possible, that your child is aware of the dangers of rabies; keep children away from **animals**, especially dogs and monkeys, and ask your medical adviser about rabies jabs.

Bangkok Butterfly Garden and Insectarium Suan Rotfai (Railway Park), just north of Queen Sirikit Park and Chatuchak Weekend Market; free; w facebook.com/butterfiyMBA2548. Over five hundred butterflies flutter within an enormous landscaped dome. There's also a study centre, plus family-oriented cycle routes and bikes (with infant seats) for rent in the adjacent park. The park is walkable from BTS Mo Chit or Ha Yaek Lat Phrao, or from Phahon Yothin or Chatuchak Park subway stations.

Children's Discovery Museum Queen Sirikit Park, just north of Chatuchak Weekend Market; free; w facebook.com/bkkchildrensmuseum. With different zones for different ages, ranging from babies to 12-year-olds, this recently renovated museum lets kids excavate in the sand for dinosaur bones, do hands-on experiments and frolic in the outdoor water-play park. The museum is handy for BTS Mo Chit station or Chatuchak Park subway station.

Dream World Twenty minutes' drive north of Don Muang Airport at kilometre-stone 7 Thanon Rangsit–Ongkarak; Charge; w dreamworld.co.th. Theme park with different areas such as Snow Town and Fantasy Land, including water rides, a hanging roller coaster and other amusements.

Siam Amazing Park On the far eastern edge of town at 101 Thanon Sukhapiban 2; Charge; w siamamazingpark.com. Waterslides, wave pool and artificial beach, plus roller coasters and other rides.

ANCIENT MURAL, WAT PHRA KAEO

Contexts

194 History
206 Religion: Thai Buddhism
212 Art and architecture
221 Books
224 Language
229 Glossary

History

Bangkok is a comparatively new capital, founded in 1782 after the previous capital of Ayutthaya, a short way upriver, had been razed by the Burmese, but it has established an overwhelming dominance in Thailand. Its history over the last two centuries directly mirrors that of the country as a whole, and the city has gathered to itself, in the National Museum and elsewhere, the major relics of Thailand's previous civilizations, principally from the eras of Ayutthaya and its precursor, Sukhothai.

Early history

The region's first distinctive civilization, **Dvaravati**, was established around two thousand years ago by an Austroasiatic-speaking people known as the Mon. One of its mainstays was Theravada Buddhism, which had been introduced to Thailand during the second or third century BC by Indian missionaries. From the discovery of monastery boundary stones (*sema*), clay votive tablets and Indian-influenced Buddhist sculpture, it's clear that the Dvaravati city-states (including **Nakhon Pathom**) had their greatest flourishing between the sixth and ninth centuries AD. Meanwhile, in the eighth century, peninsular Thailand to the south of Dvaravati came under the control of the **Srivijaya** empire, a Mahayana Buddhist state centred on Sumatra which had strong ties with India.

From the ninth century onwards, however, both Dvaravati and Srivijaya Thailand succumbed to invading **Khmers** from Cambodia, who consolidated their position during the watershed reign of **Jayavarman II** (802–50). To establish his authority, Jayavarman II had himself initiated as a *chakravartin* or universal ruler, the living embodiment of the **devaraja**, the divine essence of kingship – a concept which was adopted by later Thai rulers. From their capital at **Angkor**, Jayavarman's successors took control over northeastern, central and peninsular Thailand, thus mastering the most important trade routes between India and China. By the thirteenth century, however, the Khmers had overreached themselves and were in no position to resist the onslaught of a vibrant new force in Southeast Asia, the Thais.

The earliest Thais

The earliest traceable history of the **Thai people** picks them up in southern China around the fifth century AD, when they were squeezed by Chinese and Vietnamese expansionism into sparsely inhabited northeastern Laos. Their first significant entry into what is now Thailand seems to have happened in the north, where some time after the seventh century the Thais formed a state known as Yonok. Theravada Buddhism spread to **Yonok** via Dvaravati around the end of the tenth century, which served not only to unify the Thais themselves but also to link them to the wider community of Buddhists.

3rd century BC	6–9th centuries AD	Late 9th century
Theravada Buddhism probably first enters Thailand	Dvaravati civilization flourishes	Khmers, from Cambodia, begin to push into Thailand

By the end of the twelfth century they formed the majority of the population in Thailand, then under the control of the Khmer empire. The Khmers' main outpost, at Lopburi, was by this time regarded as the administrative capital of a land called **Syam** (possibly from the Sanskrit *syam*, meaning swarthy) – a mid-twelfth-century bas-relief at Angkor portraying the troops of Lopburi, preceded by a large group of self-confident Syam Kuk mercenaries, shows that the Thais were becoming a force to be reckoned with.

Sukhothai

At some time around 1238, Thais in the upper Chao Phraya valley captured the main Khmer outpost in the region at **Sukhothai** and established a kingdom there. For the first forty years it was merely a local power, but an attack by the ruler of the neighbouring principality of Mae Sot brought a dynamic new leader to the fore: the king's nineteen-year-old son, Rama, defeated the opposing commander, earning himself the name **Ramkhamhaeng**, "Rama the Bold". When Ramkhamhaeng himself came to the throne around 1278, he seized control of much of the Chao Phraya valley, and over the next twenty years, more by diplomacy than military action, gained the submission of most of Thailand under a complex tribute system.

Although the empire of Sukhothai extended Thai control over a vast area, its greatest contribution to the Thais' development was at home, in cultural and political matters. A famous **inscription** by Ramkhamhaeng, now housed in the Bangkok National Museum, describes a prosperous era of benevolent rule: "In the time of King Ramkhamhaeng this land of Sukhothai is thriving. There is fish in the water and rice in the fields… [The King] has hung a bell in the opening of the gate over there: if any commoner has a grievance which sickens his belly and gripes his heart… he goes and strikes the bell… [and King Ramkhamhaeng] questions the man, examines the case, and decides it justly for him."

Although this plainly smacks of self-promotion, it seems to contain at least a kernel of truth: in deliberate contrast to the Khmer god-kings (*devaraja*), Ramkhamhaeng styled himself as a **dhammaraja**, a king who ruled justly according to Theravada Buddhist doctrine and made himself accessible to his people. A further sign of the Thais' growing self-confidence was the invention of a new script to make their tonal language understood by the non-Thai inhabitants of the land.

The growth of Ayutthaya

After the death of Ramkhamhaeng around 1299, however, his empire quickly fell apart. By 1320 Sukhothai had regressed to being a kingdom of only local significance, though its mantle as the capital of a Thai empire was taken up shortly after at **Ayutthaya** to the south. Soon after founding the city in 1351, the ambitious king **Ramathibodi** united the principalities of the lower Chao Phraya valley, which had formed the western provinces of the Khmer empire. When he recruited his bureaucracy from the urban elite of Lopburi, Ramathibodi set the style of government at Ayutthaya, elements of which persisted into the Bangkok empire and up to the present day. The elaborate etiquette, language and rituals of Angkor were adopted,

Mid-12th century	**1238**	**1278**	**1299**
Bas-relief at Angkor Wat depicting Thai mercenaries, a new force to be reckoned with in the region	The Thais seize the Khmer outpost of Sukhothai	Ramkhamhaeng "the Bold" comes to the throne of Sukhothai	With the death of Ramkhamhaeng, Sukhothai begins its decline

and, most importantly, the conception of the ruler as *devaraja*: when the king processed through the town, ordinary people were forbidden to look at him and had to be silent while he passed.

The site chosen by Ramathibodi was the best in the region for an international port, and so began Ayutthaya's rise to prosperity, based on exploiting the upswing in trade in the middle of the fourteenth century along the routes between India and China. By 1540, the Kingdom of Ayutthaya had grown to cover most of the area of modern-day Thailand. Despite a 1568 invasion by the Burmese, which led to twenty years of foreign rule, Ayutthaya made a spectacular comeback, and in the seventeenth century its **foreign trade** boomed. In 1511 the Portuguese had become the first Western power to trade with Ayutthaya, and a treaty with Spain was concluded in 1598; relations with Holland and England were initiated in 1608 and 1612 respectively. European merchants flocked to Thailand, not only to buy Thai products, but also to gain access to Chinese and Japanese goods on sale there.

The Burmese invasion

In the mid-eighteenth century, however, the rumbling in the Burmese jungle to the north began to make itself heard again. After an unsuccessful siege in 1760, in February 1766 the Burmese descended upon the city for the last time. The Thais held out for over a year, during which they were afflicted by famine, epidemics and a terrible fire which destroyed ten thousand houses. Finally, in April 1767, the walls were breached and the city taken. The Burmese savagely razed everything to the ground and led off tens of thousands of prisoners to Myanmar, including most of the royal family. The city was abandoned to the jungle, and Thailand descended into banditry.

Taksin and Thonburi

Out of this lawless mess, however, emerged **Phraya Taksin**, a charismatic and brave general, who had been unfairly blamed for a failed counterattack against the Burmese at Ayutthaya and had quietly slipped away from the besieged city. Taksin was crowned king in December 1768 at his new capital of **Thonburi**, on the opposite bank of the river from modern-day Bangkok. Within two years he had restored all of Ayutthaya's territories; more remarkably, by the end of the next decade Taksin had outdone his Ayutthayan predecessors by bringing Cambodia and much of Laos into a huge new empire.

However, by 1779 all was not well with the king. Taksin was becoming increasingly paranoid about plots against him, a delusion that drove him to imprison and torture even his wife and sons. At the same time he sank into religious excesses, demanding that the monkhood worship him as a god. By March 1782, public outrage at his sadism and dangerously irrational behaviour had reached such fervour that he was ousted in a coup.

Chao Phraya Chakri, Taksin's military commander, was invited to take power and had Taksin executed. In accordance with ancient etiquette, this had to be done without royal blood touching the earth: the mad king was duly wrapped in a black velvet sack and struck on the back of the neck with a sandalwood club. (Popular belief has it that even this form of execution was too much: an unfortunate substitute got the velvet

1351	**1511**	**1767**
Ramathibodi founds the capital of Ayutthaya	The first Western power, Portugal, begins trading with Ayutthaya	Ayutthaya is razed to the ground by the Burmese

sack treatment, while Taksin was whisked away to a palace in the hills near Nakhon Si Thammarat, where he is said to have lived until 1825.)

The early Bangkok empire: Rama I

With the support of the Ayutthayan aristocracy, Chakri – reigning as **Rama I** (1782–1809) – set about consolidating the Thai kingdom. His first act was to move the capital across the river to what we know as **Bangkok**, on the more defensible east bank where the French had built a grand but short-lived fort in the 1660s. Borrowing from the layout of Ayutthaya, he built a new royal palace and impressive monasteries in the area of **Ratanakosin** – which remains the city's spiritual heart – within a defensive ring of two (later expanded to three) canals. In the palace temple, Wat Phra Kaeo, he enshrined the talismanic Emerald Buddha, which he had snatched during his campaigns in Laos. Initially, as at Ayutthaya, the city was largely amphibious: only the temples and royal palaces were built on dry land, while ordinary residences floated on thick bamboo rafts on the river and canals, and even shops and warehouses were moored to the river bank.

During Rama I's reign, trade with China revived, and the style of government was put on a more modern footing: while retaining many of the features of a *devaraja*, he shared more responsibility with his courtiers, as a first among equals.

Rama II and Rama III

The peaceful accession of his son as **Rama II** (1809–24) signalled the establishment of the **Chakri dynasty**, which is still in place today. This Second Reign was a quiet interlude, best remembered as a fertile period for Thai literature. The king, himself one of the great Thai poets, gathered round him a group of writers including the famous Sunthorn Phu, who produced scores of masterly love poems, travel accounts and narrative songs.

In contrast, **Rama III** (1824–51) actively discouraged literary development and was a vigorous defender of conservative values. To this end, he embarked on an extraordinary redevelopment of **Wat Pho**, the oldest temple in Bangkok. Hundreds of educational inscriptions and mural paintings, on all manner of secular and religious subjects, were put on show, apparently to preserve traditional culture against the rapid change which the king saw as corroding the country.

The danger posed by Western influence became more apparent in the Third Reign. As early as 1825, the Thais were sufficiently alarmed by British colonialism to strengthen Bangkok's defences by stretching a great iron chain across the mouth of the Chao Phraya River, to which every blacksmith in the area had to donate a certain number of links. In 1826 Rama III was obliged to sign the **Burney Treaty**, a limited trade agreement with the British by which the Thais won some political security in return for reducing their taxes on goods passing through Bangkok.

Mongkut

Rama IV, commonly known to foreigners as **Mongkut** (in Thai, Phra Chom Klao; 1851–68), had been a Buddhist monk for 27 years when he succeeded his brother.

1768	1782–1809	1782	1826
Taksin crowned king at the new capital, Thonburi	Reign of Rama I, founder of the current Chakri dynasty	A grandiose new capital, Bangkok, is established, modelled on Ayutthaya	The signing of the Burney Treaty, a trade agreement between Thailand and Britain

But far from leading a cloistered life, Mongkut had travelled widely throughout Thailand, had maintained scholarly contacts with French and American missionaries, and had taken an interest in Western learning, studying English, Latin and the sciences.

When his kingship faced its first major test, in the form of a threatening British mission in 1855 led by **Sir John Bowring**, Mongkut dealt with it confidently. Realizing that Thailand would be unable to resist the military might of the British, the king reduced import and export taxes, allowed British subjects to live and own land in Thailand and granted them freedom of trade. Furthermore, Mongkut quickly made it known that he would welcome diplomatic contacts from other Western countries: within a decade, agreements similar to the Bowring Treaty had been signed with France, the United States and a score of other nations.

Thus by skilful diplomacy the king avoided a close relationship with just one power, which could easily have led to Thailand's annexation. And as a result of the open-door policy, foreign trade boomed, financing the redevelopment of Bangkok's waterfront and, for the first time, the building of paved roads. However, Mongkut ran out of time for instituting the far-reaching domestic reforms which he saw were needed to drag Thailand into the modern world.

Chulalongkorn

Mongkut's son, **Chulalongkorn**, took the throne as Rama V (1868–1910) at the age of only fifteen, but he was well prepared by an excellent education which mixed traditional Thai and modern Western elements – provided by Mrs Anna Leonowens, subject of *The King and I*. When Chulalongkorn reached his majority after a five-year regency, he set to work on the reforms envisioned by his father.

One of his first acts was to scrap the custom by which subjects were required to prostrate themselves in the presence of the king. He constructed a new residential palace for the royal family in **Dusit**, north of Ratanakosin, and laid out that area's grand European-style boulevards. In the 1880s Chulalongkorn began to **restructure the government** to meet the country's needs, setting up a host of departments, for education, public health, the army and the like, and bringing in scores of foreign advisers to help with everything from foreign affairs to rail lines.

Throughout this period, however, the Western powers maintained their pressure on the region. The most serious threat to Thai sovereignty was the **Franco-Siamese Crisis** of 1893, which culminated in the French sending gunboats up the Chao Phraya River to Bangkok. Flouting numerous international laws, France claimed control over Laos and made other outrageous demands, to which Chulalongkorn had no option but to concede. During the course of his reign the country was obliged to cede almost half of its territory, and forewent huge sums of tax revenue, in order to preserve its independence; but by Chulalongkorn's death in 1910, the frontiers were fixed as they are today.

The end of absolute monarchy

Chulalongkorn was succeeded by a flamboyant, British-educated prince, **Vajiravudh** (Rama VI, 1910–25). However, in 1912 a group of young army lieutenants,

1855	1874	1893
The Bowring Treaty exacts further trade concessions for the British	Beginning of the abolition of slavery in Thailand	Gunboats up the Chao Phraya: the Franco–Siamese Crisis obliges Thailand to give up its claims to Laos and Cambodia

disillusioned by the absolute monarchy, plotted a coup. The conspirators were easily broken up, but this was something new in Thai history: the country was used to infighting among the royal family, but not to military intrigue by men from comparatively ordinary backgrounds.

By the time the young and inexperienced **Prajadhipok** – seventy-sixth child of Chulalongkorn – was catapulted to the throne as Rama VII (1925–35), Vajiravudh's extravagance had created severe financial problems. The vigorous community of Western-educated intellectuals who had emerged in the lower echelons of the bureaucracy were becoming increasingly dissatisfied with monarchical government. The Great Depression, which ravaged the economy in the 1930s, came as the final shock to an already moribund system.

On June 24, 1932, a small group of middle-ranking officials, led by a lawyer, **Pridi Phanomyong**, and an army major, Luang Phibunsongkhram (**Phibun**), staged a **coup** with only a handful of troops. Prajadhipok weakly submitted to the conspirators, and 150 years of absolute monarchy in Bangkok came to a sudden end. The king was sidelined to a position of symbolic significance, and in 1935 he abdicated in favour of his ten-year-old nephew, **Ananda**, then a schoolboy living in Switzerland.

Up to World War II

The success of the 1932 coup was in large measure attributable to the army officers who gave the conspirators credibility, and it was they who were to dominate the constitutional governments that followed. Phibun emerged as prime minister after the decisive elections of 1938, and encouraged a wave of nationalistic feeling with such measures as the official institution of the name Thailand in 1939 – Siam, it was argued, was a name bestowed by external forces, and the new title made it clear that the country belonged to the Thais rather than the economically dominant Chinese.

The Thais were dragged into **World War II** on December 8, 1941, when, almost at the same time as the assault on Pearl Harbor, the Japanese invaded the east coast of peninsular Thailand, with their sights set on Singapore to the south. The Thais resisted for a few hours, but realizing that the position was hopeless, Phibun quickly ordered a cease-fire.

The Thai government concluded a military alliance with Japan and declared war against the United States and Great Britain in January 1942, probably in the belief that the Japanese would win. However, the Thai minister in Washington, Seni Pramoj, refused to deliver the declaration of war against the US and, in cooperation with the Americans, began organizing a resistance movement called **Seri Thai**. Pridi Phanomyong, now acting as regent to the young king, furtively coordinated the movement under the noses of the occupying Japanese, smuggling in American agents and housing them in a European prison camp in Bangkok.

By 1944 Japan's defeat looked likely, and in July Phibun, who had been most closely associated with them, was forced to resign by the National Assembly. Once the war was over, American support prevented the British from imposing heavy punishments on the country for its alliance with Japan.

1912	1932	1939
The first of many coup attempts in modern Thailand takes place	A coup brings the end of the absolute monarchy and introduces Thailand's first constitution	The country's name is changed from Siam to the more nationalistic Thailand

Postwar upheavals

With the fading of the military, the election of January 1946 was for the first time contested by organized political parties, resulting in Pridi becoming prime minister. A new constitution was drafted and the outlook for democratic, civilian government seemed bright. Hopes were shattered, however, on June 9, 1946, when King Ananda was found dead in his bed, with a bullet wound in his forehead. Three palace servants were hurriedly tried and executed, but the murder has never been satisfactorily explained. Pridi resigned as prime minister, and in April 1948 Phibun, playing on the threat of communism, took over the premiership.

As **communism** developed its hold in the region with the takeover of China in 1949 and the French defeat in Indochina in 1954, the US increasingly viewed Thailand as a bulwark against the red menace. Between 1951 and 1957, when its annual state budget was only about $200 million a year, Thailand received a total $149 million in American economic aid and $222 million in military aid. This strengthened Phibun's dictatorship, while enabling leading military figures to divert American money and other funds into their own pockets.

Phibun narrowly won a general election in 1957, but only by blatant vote rigging and coercion. Although there's a strong tradition of foul play in Thai elections, this is remembered as the dirtiest ever: after vehement public outcry, **General Sarit**, the commander-in-chief of the army, overthrew the new government in September 1957. Believing that Thailand would prosper best under a unifying authority, Sarit set about re-establishing the monarchy as the head of the social hierarchy and the source of legitimacy for the government. Ananda's successor, **Bhumibol** (**Rama IX**), was pushed into an active role, while Sarit ruthlessly silenced critics and pressed ahead with a plan for economic development, achieving a large measure of stability and prosperity.

The Vietnam War

Sarit died in 1963, whereupon the military succession passed to **General Thanom**, closely aided by his deputy prime minister, General Praphas. Their most pressing problem was the **Vietnam War**. The Thais, with the backing of the US, quietly began to conduct military operations in Laos, to which North Vietnam and China responded by supporting anti-government insurgency in Thailand. The more the Thais felt threatened by the spread of communism, the more they looked to the Americans for help – by 1968 around 45,000 US military personnel were on Thai soil, which became the base for US bombing raids against North Vietnam and Laos.

The effects of the **American presence** were profound. The economy swelled with dollars, and hundreds of thousands of Thais became reliant on the Americans for a living, with a consequent proliferation of prostitution – centred on Bangkok's infamous Patpong district – and corruption. The sudden exposure to Western culture also led many to question traditional Thai values and the political status quo.

The democracy movement and civil unrest

Poor farmers in particular were becoming increasingly disillusioned with their lot, and many turned against the Bangkok government. At the end of 1964, the

1941	1946	1957–63
The Japanese invade, and Thailand forms an alliance with them	Rama VIII is mysteriously shot dead, to be succeeded by Rama IX (Bhumibol)	Successful coup-maker and military strongman, General Sarit, brings Thailand ever closer to the US

Communist Party of Thailand and other groups formed a broad left coalition which soon had the support of several thousand insurgents in remote areas of the northeast and the north. By 1967, a separate threat had arisen in southern Thailand, involving Muslim dissidents and the Chinese-dominated Communist Party of Malaya, as well as local Thais.

Thanom was now facing a major security crisis, especially as the war in Vietnam was going badly. In November 1971 he reimposed repressive military rule, under a triumvirate of himself, his son Colonel Narong and Praphas, who became known as the "Three Tyrants". However, the 1969 experiment with democracy had heightened expectations of power-sharing among the middle classes, especially in the universities. **Student demonstrations** began in June 1973, and in October as many as 500,000 people turned out at Thammasat University in Bangkok to demand a new constitution.

King Bhumibol intervened with apparent success, and indeed the demonstrators were starting to disperse on the morning of October 14, when the police tried to control the flow of people away. Tensions quickly mounted and soon a full-scale riot was under way, during which over 350 people were reported killed. The army, however, refused
to provide enough troops to suppress this massive uprising, and later the same day, Thanom, Narong and Praphas were forced to resign and leave the country.

In a new climate of openness, **Kukrit Pramoj** (see page 103) formed a coalition of seventeen elected parties and secured a promise of US withdrawal from Thailand, but his government was riven with feuding. In October 1976, the students demonstrated again, protesting against the return of Thanom to Bangkok to become a monk at Wat Bowonniwet. This time there was no restraint: supported by elements of the military and the government, the police and reactionary students launched a massive assault on **Thammasat University**. On October 6, hundreds of students were brutally beaten, scores were lynched and some even burned alive; the military took control and suspended the constitution.

"Premocracy"

Soon after the events of October 6, the military-appointed prime minister, **Thanin Kraivichien**, forced dissidents to undergo anti-communist indoctrination, but his measures seem to have been too repressive even for the military, who forced him to resign in October 1977. **General Kriangsak Chomanand** took over, and began to break up the insurgency with shrewd offers of amnesty. He in turn was displaced in February 1980 by **General Prem Tinsulanonda**, backed by a broad parliamentary coalition.

Untainted by corruption, Prem achieved widespread support, including that of the monarchy. Overseeing a period of rapid economic growth, Prem maintained the premiership until 1988, with a unique mixture of dictatorship and democracy sometimes called **Premocracy**: although never standing for parliament himself, Prem was asked by the legislature after every election to become prime minister. He eventually stepped down because, he said, it was time for the country's leader to be chosen from among its elected representatives.

1973	1976	1980–88
Bloody student demonstrations bring the downfall of Sarit's successor, General Thanom	The brutal suppression of further student demos ushers the military back in	Period of Premocracy, General Prem's hybrid of military rule and democracy

The 1992 demonstrations and the 1997 constitution

The new prime minister was indeed an elected MP, **Chatichai Choonhavan**, a retired general with a long civilian career in public office. He pursued a vigorous policy of economic development, but this fostered widespread corruption, in which members of the government were often implicated. Following an economic downturn and Chatichai's attempts to downgrade the political role of the military, the armed forces staged a bloodless coup on February 23, 1991, led by Supreme Commander Sunthorn and General Suchinda, the army commander-in-chief, who became premier.

When Suchinda reneged on promises to make democratic amendments to the constitution, hundreds of thousands of ordinary Thais poured onto the streets around Bangkok's Democracy Monument in **mass demonstrations** between May 17 and 20, 1992. Hopelessly misjudging the mood of the country, Suchinda brutally crushed the protests, leaving hundreds dead or injured. Having justified the massacre on the grounds that he was protecting the king from communist agitators, Suchinda was forced to resign when King Bhumibol expressed his disapproval in a ticking-off that was broadcast on world television.

Elections were held in September, with the **Democrat Party**, led by Chuan Leekpai, a noted upholder of democracy and the rule of law, emerging victorious. Chuan was succeeded in turn by Banharn Silpa-archa – nicknamed by the local press "the walking ATM", a reference to his reputation for buying votes – and General Chavalit Yongchaiyudh. The most significant positive event of the latter's tenure was the approval of a **new constitution** in 1997. Drawn up by an independent drafting assembly, its main points included: direct elections to the senate, rather than appointment of senators by the prime minister; acceptance of the right of assembly as the basis of a democratic society and guarantees of individual rights and freedoms; greater public accountability; and increased popular participation in local administration. The eventual aim of the new charter was to end the traditional system of patronage, vested interests and vote-buying.

Tom yam kung: the 1997 economic crisis

In February 1997 foreign-exchange dealers began to mount speculative attacks on the **baht**, alarmed at the size of Thailand's private foreign debt – 250 billion baht in the unproductive property sector alone, much of it accrued through the proliferation of prestigious skyscrapers in Bangkok. Chavalit's government defended the pegged exchange rate, spending $23 billion of the country's formerly healthy foreign-exchange reserves, but at the beginning of July was forced to give up the ghost – the baht was floated and soon went into free-fall. Thailand was obliged to seek help from the **IMF**, who in August put together a $17-billion **rescue package**, coupled with severe austerity measures.

In November, the inept Chavalit was replaced by Chuan Leekpai, who immediately took a hard line in following the IMF's advice, which involved maintaining cripplingly high interest rates to protect the baht and slashing government budgets. Although this played well abroad, at home the government encountered increasing hostility from its newly impoverished citizens – the downturn struck with such speed and severity that it was dubbed the **tom yam kung crisis**, after the searingly hot Thai soup.

1997	1997	2001
A landmark new constitution aims to end corruption and guarantee individual rights and freedoms	Tom yam kung: Thailand is ravaged by economic crisis	Thaksin Shinawatra, loved and hated in roughly equal measure, wins the general election

Chuan's tough stance paid off, however, with the baht stabilizing and inflation falling back, and in October 1999 he announced that he was forgoing almost $4 billion of the IMF's package.

Thaksin

The 2001 general election was won by a new party, **Thai Rak Thai** (Thai Loves Thai), led by one of Thailand's wealthiest men, **Thaksin Shinawatra**, an ex-policeman who had made a personal fortune from government telecommunications concessions. Instead of a move towards greater democracy, as envisioned by the new constitution, however, Thaksin began to apply commercial and legal pressure to try to silence critics in the media and parliament. As his standing became more firmly entrenched, he rejected constitutional reforms designed to rein in his power – famously declaring that "democracy is only a tool" for achieving other goals. Thaksin did, however, live up to his billing as a reformer. In his first year of government, he issued a three-year loan moratorium for perennially indebted farmers and set up a one-million-baht development fund for each of the country's seventy thousand villages. To improve public health access, a standard charge of B30 per hospital visit was introduced nationwide.

In early 2004, politically and criminally motivated violence in the **Islamic southern provinces** escalated sharply, and since then, there has been on average nearly a death a day on both sides in the troubles. The insurgents have targeted any representative of central authority, including monks and teachers, as well as setting off bombs in marketplaces and near tourist hotels. The authorities have inflamed opinion in the south by reacting violently, notably in crushing protests at Tak Bai and the much-revered Krue Se Mosque in Pattani in 2004, in which a total of over two hundred alleged insurgents died. In 2005, the government imposed **martial law** in Pattani, Yala and Narathiwat provinces and in parts of Songkhla province – this, however, has exacerbated economic and unemployment problems in what is Thailand's poorest region. Facing a variety of shadowy groups, whose precise aims are unclear, the authorities' natural instinct has been to get tough – which so far has brought the problem no nearer to a solution.

Despite these problems, Thaksin breezed through the **February 2005 election**, becoming the first prime minister in Thai history to win an outright majority at the polls, but causing alarm among a wide spectrum of Thailand's elites. When Thaksin's relatives sold their shares in the family's Shin Corporation in January 2006 for £1.1 billion, apparently without paying tax, tens of thousands of mostly middle-class Thais flocked to Bangkok to take part in protracted but peaceful demonstrations, under the umbrella of the **People's Alliance for Democracy (PAD)**. After further allegations of corruption and cronyism, in September Thaksin, while on official business in the United States, was ousted by a military government in a **coup**.

… and the spectre of Thaksin

Thaksin set up home in London, but his supporters, now the **People's Power Party (PPP)**, won the December 2007 general election. In response, the PAD – its

2004	2006	2010
The violence in the Islamic southern provinces sharply escalates	While in the US, Thaksin is ousted in a military coup and goes into exile	Red-shirted supporters of Thaksin set up a month-long protest camp in Bangkok, before being dispersed by force

nationalist and royalist credentials and its trademark yellow shirts (the colour of King Bhumibol) now firmly established – restarted its mass protests. Meanwhile, there was a merry-go-round of tribunals and court cases, including Thaksin's conviction *in absentia* for corruption.

Matters came to a head in November and December 2008: the PAD seized and closed down Bangkok's Suvarnabhumi airport; the ruling People's Power Party was declared illegal by the courts; and **Pheu Thai** (sometimes "Peua Thai"; meaning "For Thais"), the PPP's swift reincarnation, found itself unable to form a new coalition government. Instead, led by the Eton- and Oxford-educated **Abhisit Vejjajiva**, the Democrat Party jumped into bed with the Bhumjaithai Party, formerly staunch supporters of Thaksin, to take the helm.

This in turn prompted Thaksin's supporters – now **red-shirted** and organized into the **UDD** (United Front for Democracy against Dictatorship) – to hold mass protest meetings. In March 2009, Thaksin claimed by video broadcast that Privy Council President, Prem Tinsulanonda, had masterminded the 2006 coup and Abhisit's appointment as prime minister, and called for the overthrow of the *amat* (elite). Amid a clampdown by the Democrat government on free speech, including heavy-handed use of Article 112, the *lèse majesté* law, much more violent protests took place early the following year. Calling on Abhisit to hold new elections, thousands of red shirts set up a heavily defended camp around the **Ratchaprasong** intersection in central Bangkok in early April. On May 19, Abhisit sent in the army to break up the camp by force; altogether 91 people died on both sides in the two months of protests.

Mass popular support for Thaksin, however, did not wane, and in the general election of May 2011, Pheu Thai – now led by his younger sister, **Yingluck Shinawatra** – romped home with an absolute majority. Thailand's first woman prime minister, Yingluck proposed an amnesty bill for all those involved in the political turmoils of the last ten years, which would have included wiping out Thaksin's corruption convictions, thus allowing him to return to Thailand. However, in late 2013 this prompted further mass protests on the streets of Bangkok: led by Suthep Thaugsuban, who resigned his seat as a Democrat Party MP, thousands of nationalists – no longer wearing yellow shirts, but now blowing whistles as their trademark – occupied large areas of the city centre for several months, in an attempt to provoke the military into staging a coup.

In May 2014, this duly happened, Thailand's twelfth successful **coup d'état** in the period of constitutional monarchy since 1932 (not to mention seven failed attempts). The army chief, **General Prayut Chan-ocha**, installed himself as prime minister, at the head of a military junta known as the National Council for Peace and Order (NCPO).

All political gatherings and activities were banned, politicians, journalists, academics and activists were imprisoned or fled abroad and censorship of the media and social media was greatly tightened (which in turn fostered broad self-censorship). General elections were initially promised for 2015, but were postponed repeatedly.

In October 2016, the much-revered King Bhumibol passed away, to be succeeded by his 64-year-old son **Vajiralongkorn**, who initially continued to spend much of his time in Germany. A year-long nationwide period of mourning followed, until the funeral was held in October 2017; in May 2019, King Vajiralongkorn's coronation took place. The new king seems to favour a return to old ways and intervened in the drafting of the new constitution (Thailand's twentieth charter since 1932) to take direct

2011	2014	2016
Thaksin's sister, Yingluck, wins the general election with an outright majority	Thailand's twelfth military coup since 1932	The much-loved Rama IX dies, succeeded by Vajiralongkorn (Rama X)

control of the immense holdings of the Crown Property Bureau (the equivalent of the Royal Household). This 2017 constitution also reduced the power of elected politicians while bolstering the power of the military, with provisions for a prime minister who is not an elected representative and for a strong Senate of 250 members appointed by the junta. Also in 2017, Yingluck Shinawatra fled abroad just before she was sentenced to five years in prison for negligence.

When the general election eventually took place, in 2019, it was marked by interventions by the king, including to prevent his sister Princess Ubolratana being nominated by one of the opposition parties as their prime minister candidate; by the Constitutional Court, in banning two opposition parties; and by the junta-appointed Election Commission, in revising the allocation of votes after election day. The Palang Pracharat party was accordingly announced as the winner, with the unelected Prayut as prime minister.

Thailand weathered the COVID-19 pandemic comparatively well, though its economy, so dependent on tourism, was hit hard. A new general election was held on time in 2023. The winners were the progressive party, **Move Forward**, though with 151 MPs they failed to achieve an absolute majority in the House of Representatives. Second-placed Pheu Thai initially made to form a coalition with Move Forward but did an abrupt U-turn. With elaborate choreography, Pheu Thai instead did a deal with conservative, royalist, pro-military parties and on 22 August, its prime-ministerial candidate, Srettha Thavisin, was duly elected by parliament; on the very same day, Pheu Thai's *de facto* leader, Thaksin, returned to Thailand after fifteen years of self-imposed exile. He was taken to prison to begin serving an eight-year sentence for his outstanding corruption convictions, but within hours was transferred to a private suite at the Police General Hospital on grounds of ill health. The following day, the king endorsed Srettha as Thailand's 30th prime minister and, on 1 September, commuted Thaksin's sentence to one year. After six months, Thaksin was released on probation without having spent a night in jail. In August 2024, Thaksin's 37-year-old daughter, **Paetongtarn Shinawatra**, took over from Srettha as prime minister.

Just as happened to its previous incarnation, Future Forward, after surprise success in the 2019 election, Move Forward was banned from politics, along with all its leaders, after the 2023 election. Though by now deprived of much of its leading talent, the party was reborn as the **People's Party**, with 143 MPs and the little-known Natthaphong Ruengpanyawut as leader of the opposition in the House of Representatives.

2023	2024	2025
Pheu Thai comes to power again and Thaksin returns from exile	Thailand's Move Forward political party is dissolved by the Constitutional Court in Bangkok	Bangkok celebrates Thailand's new law to recognize gay marriage. Scores of people are killed when the Myanmar earthquake brings down a Bangkok high-rise

Religion: Thai Buddhism

Over 85 percent of Thais consider themselves Theravada Buddhists, followers of the teachings of a holy man usually referred to as the Buddha (Enlightened One), though more precisely known as Gautama Buddha to distinguish him from lesser-known Buddhas who preceded him. Theravada Buddhism is one of the two main schools of Buddhism practised in Asia, and in Thailand it has absorbed an eclectic assortment of animist and Hindu elements. Islam is the biggest of the minority religions in Thailand, practised by between five and ten percent of the population. Most Muslims live in the south, along the Malaysian border. The separatist violence in this region (see page 97) has caused great tension between local Buddhist and Muslim communities, which have traditionally co-existed peacefully; it has not, however, obviously affected inter-faith relationships elsewhere in Thailand. The rest of the Thai population comprises Mahayana Buddhists, Hindus, Sikhs, Christians and animists.

The Buddha: his life and beliefs

Gautama Buddha was born in Nepal as **Prince Gautama Siddhartha** in the seventh century BC according to the calculations for the Thai calendar, though scholars now think it may have been a century or two later. At his birth, astrologers predicted that he would become either a famous king or a celebrated holy man, depending on which path he chose. Much preferring the former, the prince's father forbade the boy from leaving the palace grounds, and set about educating Gautama in all aspects of the high life. Most statues of the Buddha depict him with elongated earlobes, which is a reference to this early pampered existence, when he would have worn heavy precious stones in his ears.

The prince married and became a father, but at the age of 29 he flouted his father's authority and sneaked out into the world beyond the palace. On this fateful trip he encountered successively an old man, a sick man, a corpse and a hermit, and thus for the first time was made aware that pain and suffering were intrinsic to human life. Contemplation seemed the only means of discovering why this was so – and therefore Gautama decided to leave the palace and become a **Hindu ascetic**.

For several years he wandered the countryside leading a life of self-denial and self-mortification, but failed to come any closer to the answer. Eventually concluding that the best course of action must be to follow a "Middle Way" – neither indulgent nor overly ascetic – Gautama sat down beneath the famous riverside bodhi tree at **Bodh Gaya** in India, facing the rising sun, to **meditate** until he achieved enlightenment. For 49 days he sat cross-legged in the "lotus position", contemplating the causes of suffering and wrestling with temptations that materialized to distract him. Most of these were sent by **Mara**, the Evil One, who was finally subdued when Gautama summoned the earth goddess **Mae Toranee** by pointing the fingers of his right hand at the ground – the gesture known as **Calling the Earth to Witness**, or *Bhumisparsa Mudra*, which has been immortalized by thousands of Thai sculptors. Mae Toranee wrung torrents of water from her hair and engulfed Mara's demonic emissaries in a flood, an episode that's also commonly reproduced, most famously in the statue in Bangkok's Sanam Luang.

Temptations dealt with, Gautama soon came to attain **enlightenment** and so become a Buddha. As the place of his enlightenment, the **bodhi tree** (or bo tree) has assumed special significance for Buddhists: not only does it appear in many Buddhist paintings, but there's often a real bodhi tree (*Ficus religiosa*) planted in temple compounds as well. In addition, the bot is nearly always built facing either a body of water or facing east (preferably both).

The Buddha preached his **first sermon** in a deer park in India, where he characterized his doctrine, or **Dharma**, as a wheel. From this episode comes the early Buddhist symbol the **Dharmachakra**, known as the Wheel of Law, which is often accompanied by a statue of a deer. Thais celebrate this first sermon with a public holiday in July known as **Asanha Puja**. On another occasion 1250 people spontaneously gathered to hear the Buddha speak, an event remembered in Thailand as **Maha Puja** and marked by a public holiday in February.

For the next forty-odd years the Buddha travelled the region converting non-believers and performing miracles. One rainy season he even ascended into the **Tavatimsa heaven** (Heaven of the 33 Gods) to visit his mother and to preach the doctrine to her. His descent from this heaven is quite a common theme of paintings and sculptures, and the **Standing Buddha** pose of numerous Buddha statues comes from this story.

The Buddha "died" at the age of 80 on the banks of a river at Kusinari in India – an event often dated to 543 BC, which is why the **Thai calendar** is 543 years out of synch with the Western one, so that the year 2019 AD becomes 2562 BE (Buddhist Era). Lying on his side, propping up his head on his hand, the Buddha passed into **Nirvana** (giving rise to another classic pose, the **Reclining Buddha**), the unimaginable state of nothingness which knows no suffering and from which there is no reincarnation. Buddhists believe that the day the Buddha entered Nirvana was the same date on which he was born and on which he achieved enlightenment, a triply significant day that Thais honour with the **Visakha Puja** festival in May.

Buddhists believe that Gautama Buddha was the five-hundredth incarnation of a single being: the stories of these five hundred lives, collectively known as the **Jataka**, provide the inspiration for a lot of Thai art. Hindus also accept Gautama Buddha into their pantheon, perceiving him as the ninth manifestation of their god Vishnu.

The spread of Buddhism

After the Buddha entered Nirvana, his **doctrine** spread relatively quickly across India, and probably was first promulgated in Thailand in about the third century BC, when the Indian emperor Ashoka (in Thai, Asoke) sent out missionaries. His teachings, the *Tripitaka*, were written down in the Pali language – a then-vernacular derivative of Sanskrit – in a form that became known as **Theravada**, or "The Doctrine of the Elders".

By the beginning of the first millennium, a new movement called **Mahayana** (Great Vehicle) had emerged within the Theravada school, attempting to make Buddhism more accessible by introducing a pantheon of **bodhisattva**, or Buddhist saints, who, although they had achieved enlightenment, postponed entering Nirvana in order to inspire the populace. Mahayana Buddhism spread north into China, Korea, Vietnam and Japan, also entering southern Thailand via the Srivijayan empire around the eighth century and parts of Khmer Cambodia in about the eleventh century. Meanwhile, Theravada Buddhism (which the Mahayanists disparagingly renamed "Hinayana" or "Lesser Vehicle") established itself most significantly in Sri Lanka, northern and central Thailand and Myanmar.

Buddhist doctrine and practice

Central to Theravada Buddhism is a belief in **karma** – every action has a consequence – and **reincarnation**, along with an understanding that craving is at the root of human suffering. The ultimate aim for a Buddhist is to get off the cycle of perpetual reincarnation and suffering and instead to enter the blissful state of non-being that is **Nirvana**. This enlightened state can take many lifetimes to achieve so the more realistic goal for most is to be reborn slightly higher up the karmic ladder each time. As Thai Buddhists see it, animals are at the bottom of the karmic scale and monks at the top, with women on a lower rung than men.

Living a good life, specifically a life of "pure intention", creates good karma and Buddhist doctrine focuses a great deal on how to achieve this. Psychology and an understanding of human weaknesses play a big part. Key is the concept of **dukka**, which holds that craving is the cause of all suffering or, to put it simplistically, human unhappiness is caused by the unquenchable dissatisfaction experienced when one's sensual, spiritual or material desires are not met. Accepting the truth of this is known as the **Four Noble Truths** of Buddhism. The route to enlightenment depends on a person being sufficiently detached from earthly desires so that *dukka* can't take hold. One acknowledges that the physical world is impermanent and ever-changing, and that all things – including the self – are therefore not worth craving. A Buddhist works towards this realization by following the **Eightfold Path**, or **Middle Way**, that is by developing a set of highly moral personal qualities such as "right speech", "right action" and "right mindfulness". Meditation is particularly helpful in this.

A devout Thai Buddhist commits to the **five basic precepts**, namely not to kill or steal, to refrain from sexual misconduct and incorrect speech (lies, gossip and abuse) and to eschew intoxicating liquor and drugs. There are **three extra precepts** for special *wan phra* holy days and for those laypeople including foreign students who study meditation at Thai temples: no eating after noon, no entertainment (including TV and music) and no sleeping on a soft bed; in addition, the no sexual misconduct precept turns into no sex at all.

Making merit

Merit-making in popular Thai Buddhism has become slightly skewed, so that some people act on the assumption that they'll climb the karmic ladder faster if they make bigger and better offerings to the temple and its monks. However, it is of course the purity of the intention behind one's merit-making (*tham buun*) that's fundamental.

Merit can be made in many ways, from giving a monk his breakfast to attending a Buddhist service or donating money and gifts to the neighbourhood temple, and most **festivals** are essentially communal merit-making opportunities. Between the big festivals, the most common days for making merit and visiting the temple are **wan phra** (holy days), which are determined by the phase of the moon and occur four times a month. The simplest **offering** inside a temple consists of lotus buds, candles and three incense sticks (representing the three gems of Buddhism – the Buddha himself, the Dharma or doctrine, and the monkhood). One of the more bizarre but common merit-making activities involves **releasing caged birds**: worshippers buy tiny finches from vendors at wat compounds and, by liberating them from their cage, prove their Buddhist compassion towards all living things. The fact that the birds were free until netted earlier that morning doesn't seem to detract from the ritual. In riverside and seaside wats, fish or even baby turtles are released instead.

For an accessible and insightful introduction to the Buddha and his thought, get hold of a copy of Michael Carrithers' The Buddha: A Very Short Introduction (see page 221). A number of Thai temples welcome foreign students of Buddhism and meditation (see page 182).

The monkhood

It's the duty of Thailand's 200,000-strong **Sangha** (monkhood) to set an example to the Theravada Buddhist community by living a life as close to the Middle Way as possible and by preaching the Dharma to the people. The life of a monk (*bhikkhu*) is governed by 227 precepts that include celibacy and the rejection of all personal possessions except gifts.

Each day begins with an alms round in the neighbourhood so that the laity can donate food and thereby gain themselves merit, and then is chiefly spent in meditation, chanting, teaching and study. As the most respected members of any community, monks act as teachers, counsellors and arbiters in local disputes. They also perform rituals at cremations, weddings and other events, such as the launching of a new business or even the purchase of a new car. Many young boys from poor families find themselves almost obliged to become either a *dek wat* (temple boy) or a **novice monk** because that's the only way they can get accommodation, food and, crucially, an education. This is provided free in exchange for duties around the wat, and novices are required to adhere to ten rather than 227 Buddhist precepts.

Monkhood doesn't have to be for life: a man may leave the Sangha three times without stigma, and in fact every Thai male (including royalty) is expected to **enter the monkhood** for a short period, ideally between leaving school and marrying, as a rite of passage into adulthood. Thai government departments and some private companies grant their employees paid leave for their time as a monk, but the custom is in decline as young men increasingly have to consider the effect their absence may have on their career prospects. Instead, many men now enter the monkhood for a brief period after the death of a parent, to make merit both for the deceased and for the rest of the family. The most popular time for temporary ordination is the three-month Buddhist retreat period – **Pansa**, sometimes referred to as "Buddhist Lent" – which begins in July and lasts for the duration of the rainy season. (The monks' confinement is said to originate from the earliest years of Buddhist history, when farmers complained that perambulating monks were squashing their sprouting rice crops.)

Monks in contemporary society

Some monks extend their role as village spokesmen to become influential activists: Wat Tham Krabok near Lopburi and Wat Nong Sam Pran in Kanchanaburi are among a growing number of temples that have established themselves as successful drug rehabilitation centres; monks at Wat Phra Bat Nam Pu in Lopburi run a hospice for people with HIV/AIDS as well as a famously hard-hitting AIDS-awareness museum; monks at Wat Phai Lom near Bangkok have developed the country's largest breeding colony of Asian open-billed storks; while the monks at Wat Pa Luang Ta Bua Yannasampanno in Kanchanaburi hit the headlines for the wrong reasons with their controversial, now closed tiger sanctuary. Other monks, such as the famous Luang Pho Khoon of Wat Ban Rai in Nakhon Ratchasima province, who died in 2015 aged 91, have acquired such a reputation for giving wise counsel and bringing good fortune to their followers that they have become national gurus and their temples now generate great wealth through the production of specially blessed amulets and photographs.

Though the increasing involvement of many monks in the secular world has not met with unanimous approval, far more disappointing to the laity are those monks who **flout the precepts** of the Sangha by succumbing to the temptations of a consumer society, flaunting Raybans, Rolexes and Mercedes (in some cases actually bought with temple funds), chain-smoking and flirting, even making pocket money from predicting lottery results and practising faith-healing. With so much national pride and integrity riding on the sanctity of the Sangha, any whiff of a deeper scandal is bound to strike deep into the national psyche. Cases of monks involved in drug-dealing, gun-running, even rape and murder have prompted a stream of editorials on the state of the Sangha and the collapse of spiritual values at the heart of Thai society. The inclusivity of the monkhood – which is open to just about any male who wants to join – has been highlighted as a particularly vulnerable aspect, not least because donning saffron robes has always been an accepted way for criminals, reformed or otherwise, to repent of their past deeds.

Interestingly, back in the late 1980s, the influential monk Phra Bodhirak (Photirak) was defrocked after criticizing what he saw as a tide of decadence infecting Thai Buddhism. He now preaches his ascetic code of anti-materialism through his breakaway **Santi Asoke** sect, famous across the country for its cheap vegetarian restaurants, its philosophy of self-sufficiency and for the simple blue farmers' shirts worn by many of its followers.

Women and the monkhood

Although the Theravada Buddhist hierarchy in some countries permits the ordination of **female monks**, or *bhikkhuni*, the Thai Sangha does not. Instead, Thai women are officially only allowed to become **nuns**, or *mae chii*, shaving their heads, donning white robes and keeping eight rather than 227 precepts. Their status is lower than that of the monks and they are chiefly occupied with temple upkeep rather than conducting religious ceremonies.

However, the progressives are becoming more vocal, and in 2002 a Thai woman became the first of several to break with the Buddhist authorities and get **ordained** as a novice *bhikkhuni* on Thai soil. Thailand's Sangha Council, however, still recognizes neither her ordination nor the temple, Watra Songdhammakalyani in Nakhon Pathom, where the ordination took place. The Watra (rather than Wat) is run by another Thai *bhikkhuni*, Dhammananda Bhikkhuni, the author of several books in English about **women and Buddhism** and of an informative website, Ⓦthaibhikkhunis.com.

Hindu deities and animist spirits

The complicated history of the area now known as Thailand has made Thai Buddhism a confusingly syncretic faith, as you'll realize when you enter a Buddhist temple compound to be confronted by a statue of a Hindu deity. While regular Buddhist merit-making insures a Thai for the next life, there are certain **Hindu gods and animist spirits** that many Thais – sophisticated city dwellers and illiterate farmers alike – also cultivate for help with more immediate problems; and as often as not it's a Buddhist monk who is called in to exorcise a malevolent spirit. Even the Buddhist King Vajiralongkorn employs Brahmin priests and astrologers to determine auspicious days and officiate at certain royal ceremonies and, like his royal predecessors of the Chakri dynasty, he also associates himself with the Hindu god Vishnu by assuming the title Rama X – Rama, hero of the Hindu epic the *Ramayana*, having been Vishnu's seventh manifestation on Earth.

If a Thai wants help in achieving a short-term goal, like passing an exam, becoming pregnant or winning the lottery, he or she will quite likely turn to the **Hindu pantheon**, visiting an enshrined statue of Brahma, Vishnu, Shiva or Ganesh, and making offerings of flowers, incense and maybe food. If the outcome is favourable, the devotee will probably come back to show thanks, bringing more offerings and maybe even hiring a dance troupe to perform a celebratory *lakhon chatri*. Built in honour of Brahma, Bangkok's Erawan Shrine is the most famous place of Hindu-inspired worship in the country.

Spirits and spirit houses

Whereas Hindu deities tend to be benevolent, **spirits** (or *phi*) are not nearly as reliable and need to be mollified more frequently. They come in hundreds of varieties, some more malign than others, and inhabit everything from trees, rivers and caves to public buildings and private homes – even taking over people if they feel like it.

So that these *phi* don't pester human inhabitants, each building has a special **spirit house** (*saan phra phum*) in its vicinity, as a dwelling for spirits ousted by the building's construction. Usually raised on a short column to set it at or above eye level, the spirit house must occupy an auspicious location – not, for example, in the shadow of the main building. It's generally about the size of a dolls' house and designed to look like a wat or a traditional Thai house, but its ornamentation is supposed to reflect the status of the humans' building, so if that building is enlarged or refurbished, the spirit house should be improved accordingly. And as architects become increasingly bold in their designs, so modernist spirit houses are also beginning to appear in Bangkok, where an eye-catching new skyscraper might be graced by a spirit house of glass or polished concrete. **Figurines** representing the relevant guardian spirit and his aides are sometimes put inside, and daily offerings of incense, lighted candles and garlands of jasmine are placed alongside them to keep the *phi* happy – a disgruntled spirit is a dangerous spirit, liable to cause sickness, accidents and even death. As with any religious building or icon in Thailand, an unwanted or crumbling spirit house should never be dismantled or destroyed, which is why you'll often see damaged spirit houses placed around the base of a sacred banyan tree, where they are able to rest in peace.

Art and architecture

Aside from pockets of Hindu-inspired statuary and architecture, the vast majority of Thailand's cultural monuments take their inspiration from Theravada Buddhism, and so it is temples and religious images that constitute Bangkok's main sights. Artists, sculptors and architects have tended to see their work as a way of making spiritual merit rather than as a means of self-expression or self-promotion, so pre-twentieth-century Thai art history is all about evolving styles rather than individual artists. This section is designed to help make sense of the most common aspects of Thai art and architecture at their various stages of development. Though Bangkok's temples nearly all date from the eighteenth century or later, many of them display features that originate from a much earlier time. The National Museum (see page 61) is a good place to see some of Thailand's more ancient Hindu and Buddhist statues, and a visit to the fourteenth- to eighteenth-century ruins at Ayutthaya (see page 116), less than two hours from Bangkok, is also recommended.

The wat

Buddhist temple complexes, or **wats**, are central to nearly every community in Thailand and, as the main expressions of public architecture and art over the centuries, are likely to loom large in visitors' experiences of Bangkok. Wat architecture has evolved in diverse ways, but the names and purposes of the main buildings have stayed constant in Thailand for some fifteen centuries.

Some **general design features** of Thai temples are also distinctive. The Khmers, who had ruled much of the country long before the Thais came onto the scene, built their temples to a cosmological plan, with concentric layers representing earth, oceans and heavens, rising to a central high point. Remnants of this layout persisted in Thai temples, including boundary walls – which are sometimes combined with a moat – and the multi-tiered roofs of so many wat buildings.

Furthermore, the Thais come from a tradition of building in wood rather than stone or brick, hence the leaning walls and long, curving roofs that give wats their elegant, tapering lines. On top of this, wat architects have long been preoccupied with light, the symbol of Buddhist wisdom and clarity, covering their buildings with gilt, filigree and vividly coloured glass mosaics.

The bot

The most important wat building is the **bot** (sometimes known as the *ubosot*), where monks are ordained. It usually stands at the heart of the compound, but lay people are rarely allowed inside. There's only one bot in any wat complex, and often the only way you'll be able to distinguish it from other temple buildings is by the eight **sema** or boundary stones which always surround it. Positioned at the four corners of the bot and at the cardinal points of the compass, these *sema* define the consecrated ground and usually look something like upright gravestones, though they can take many forms. They are often carved all over with symbolic Buddhist scenes or ideograms, and sometimes are even protected within miniature shrines of their own. There's a good *sema* collection in Bangkok's National Museum.

The viharn
Often almost identical in appearance to the bot, the **viharn** or assembly hall is the building you are most likely to enter, as it usually contains the wat's principal Buddha image, and sometimes two or three minor images as well. Large wats may have several viharns, while strict meditation wats, which don't deal with the laity, may not have one at all.

The chedi
Upon the Buddha's death, disciples from all over Asia laid claim to his relics, enshrining them in specially constructed towers, known as **chedis** in Thailand. In later centuries, chedis have also become repositories for the ashes of royalty or important monks – and anyone else who could afford to have one built. Each chedi's three main components reflect a traditional symbolism. In theory, the chedi base should be divided into three layers to represent hell, earth and heaven. Above this, the dome usually contains the cube-shaped reliquary, known as a *harmika* after the Sanskrit term for the Buddha's seat of meditation. Crowning the structure, the spire is graded into 33 rings, one for each of the 33 Buddhist heavens.

The mondop and ho trai
Less common wat buildings include the square **mondop**, usually built with a complex, cruciform roof, which houses either a Buddha statue or footprint, or holy texts.

The **ho trai**, or scripture library, is generally constructed on stilts, sometimes over a pond, to protect against termites and fire. You can see a particularly good example of a traditional *ho trai* at Wat Rakhang in Bangkok.

Buddhist iconography
In the early days of Buddhism, image-making was considered inadequate to convey the faith's abstract philosophies, so the only approved iconography comprised doctrinal **symbols** such as the Dharmachakra (Wheel of Law, also known as Wheel of Doctrine or Wheel of Life). Gradually these symbols were displaced by **images of the Buddha**, construed chiefly as physical embodiments of the Buddha's teachings rather than as portraits of the man. Sculptors took their guidance from the Pali texts, which ordained the Buddha's most common postures (*asanha*) and gestures (*mudra*).

All three-dimensional Buddha images are objects of reverence, but some are more esteemed than others. Some are alleged to have reacted in a particular way to unusual events, others have performed miracles, or are simply admired for their beauty, their phenomenal size or even their material value – if made of solid gold or jade, for example. Most Thais are familiar with these exceptional images, all of which have been given special names, always prefixed by the honorific "Phra", and many of which have spawned thousands of miniaturized copies in the form of amulets. Pilgrimages are made to see the most famous originals.

It was in the Sukhothai era that the craze for producing **Buddha footprints** really took off. Harking back to the time when images were allusive rather than representative, these footprints were generally moulded from stucco to depict the 108 auspicious signs or *lakshanas* (which included references to the sixteen Buddhist heavens, the traditional four great continents and seven great rivers and lakes) and housed in a special mondop. The feet of the famous Reclining Buddha in Bangkok's Wat Pho are also inscribed with the 108 *lakshanas*, beautifully depicted in mother-of-pearl inlay.

Hindu iconography
Hindu images tend to be a lot livelier than Buddhist ones; there are countless gods to choose from and many have mischievous personalities and multiple inventive

> ## POSTURES AND GESTURES OF THE BUDDHA
>
> Of the **four postures** – sitting, standing, walking and reclining – the **seated Buddha**, which represents him in meditation, is the most common in Thailand. A popular variation shows the Buddha seated on a coiled serpent, protected by the serpent's hood: a reference to the story about the Buddha meditating during the rainy season, when a serpent offered to raise him off the wet ground and shelter him from the storms. The **reclining** pose symbolizes the Buddha entering Nirvana at his death, while the **standing** and **walking** images both represent his descent from heaven.
>
> The most common **hand gestures** include:
>
> **Dhyana Mudra** (Meditation), in which the hands rest on the lap, palms upwards.
>
> **Bhumisparsa Mudra** (Calling the Earth to Witness, a reference to the Buddha resisting temptation), with the left hand upturned in the lap and the right-hand fingers resting on the right knee and pointing to the earth (see page 229).
>
> **Vitarkha Mudra** (Teaching), with one or both hands held at chest height with the thumb and forefinger touching.
>
> **Abhaya Mudra** (Dispelling Fear), showing the right hand (occasionally both hands) raised in a flat-palmed "stop" gesture.

incarnations. In Hindu philosophy any object can be viewed as the temporal residence, embodiment or symbol of the deity so you get abstract representations such as the phallic lingam (pillar) for Shiva, as well as figurative images. Though pure Hinduism receded from Thailand with the collapse of the Khmer empire, Buddhist Thais have incorporated some Hindu and Brahmin concepts into the national belief system and have continued to create statues of the three chief Hindu deities – Brahma, Vishnu and Shiva – as well as using many mythological creatures in modern designs.

The Hindu Trinity

Vishnu has always been a favourite god: in his role of "Preserver" he embodies the status quo, representing both stability and the notion of altruistic love. He is most often depicted as the deity, but has ten manifestations in all, of which **Rama** (number seven) is by far the most popular in Thailand. The epitome of ideal manhood, Rama is the superhero of the epic story the *Ramayana* – in Thai, the *Ramakien* (see page 55) – and appears in storytelling reliefs and murals in every Hindu temple in Thailand; in painted portraits you can usually recognize him by his green face. Manifestation number eight is **Krishna**, more widely known than Rama in the West, but slightly less common in Thailand. Krishna is usually characterized as a flirtatious, flute-playing, blue-skinned cowherd, but he is also a crucial moral figure in the lengthy moral epic poem, the *Mahabharata*. Confusingly, Vishnu's ninth avatar is the **Buddha** – a manifestation adopted many centuries ago to minimize defection to the Buddhist faith. When represented as **the deity**, Vishnu is generally shown sporting a crown and four arms, his hands holding a conch shell (whose music wards off demons), a discus (used as a weapon), a club (symbolizing the power of nature and time) and a lotus (symbol of joyful flowering and renewal). He is often depicted astride a **garuda**, a half-man, half-bird. Even without Vishnu on its back, the garuda is a very important beast: a symbol of strength, it's often shown "supporting" temple buildings.

Statues and representations of **Brahma** (the Creator) are rare. He too has four arms, but holds no objects; he has four faces (sometimes painted red), is generally borne by a goose-like creature called a *hamsa*, and is associated with the direction north.

Shiva (the Destroyer) is the most volatile member of the pantheon. He stands for extreme behaviour, for beginnings and endings, as enacted in his frenzied Dance of Destruction, and for fertility, and is a symbol of great energy and power. His godlike form typically has four, eight or ten arms, sometimes holding a trident (representing creation, protection and destruction) and a drum (to beat the rhythm of creation). In his most famous role, as **Nataraja**, or Lord of the Dance, he is usually shown in a stylized standing position with legs bent into a balletic position and the full complement of arms outstretched above his head. Three stripes on a figure's forehead also indicate Shiva, or one of his followers. In abstract form, he is represented by a **lingam** (once found at the heart of every Khmer temple in the northeast). Primarily a symbol of energy and godly power, the lingam also embodies fertility, particularly when set upright in a vulva-shaped vessel known as a **yoni**. The yoni doubles as a receptacle for the holy water that worshippers pour over the lingam.

Lesser gods
Close associates of Shiva include **Parvati**, his wife, and **Ganesh**, his elephant-headed son. As the god of knowledge and overcomer of obstacles (in the path of learning), Ganesh is used as the symbol of the Fine Arts Department, so his image features on all entrance tickets to national museums and historical parks.

The royal, three-headed elephant, **Erawan**, usually only appears as the favourite mount of the god **Indra**, the king of the gods, with specific power over the elements (particularly rain) and over the east. Other **Hindu gods of direction**, which are commonly found on the appropriate antefix in Khmer temples, include **Yama** on a buffalo (south); **Varuna** on a naga (mythical serpent) or a *hamsa* (west); Brahma (north); and **Isaana** on a bull (northeast).

Lesser mythological figures, which originated as Hindu symbols but feature frequently in wats and other Buddhist contexts, include the **yaksha** giants who ward off evil spirits (like the enormous freestanding ones guarding Bangkok's Wat Phra Kaeo); the graceful half-woman, half-bird **kinnari**; and the ubiquitous **naga**, or serpent king of the underworld, often with as many as seven heads, whose reptilian body most frequently appears as staircase balustrades in Hindu and Buddhist temples.

The schools
In the 1920s art historians and academics began compiling a classification system for Thai art and architecture that was modelled along the lines of the country's historical periods; these are the guidelines followed below. The following brief overview starts in the sixth century, when Buddhism began to take a hold on the country; few examples of art from before that time have survived, and there are no known, earlier architectural relics.

Dvaravati (sixth to eleventh centuries)
Centred around Nakhon Pathom, U Thong and Lopburi in the Chao Phraya basin and in the smaller northern enclave of Haripunjaya (modern-day Lamphun), the **Dvaravati** civilization was populated by Mon-speaking Theravada Buddhists who were strongly influenced by Indian culture.

In an effort to combat the defects inherent in the poor-quality limestone at their disposal, Dvaravati-era **sculptors** made their Buddhas quite stocky, cleverly dressing the figures in a sheet-like drape that dropped down to ankle level from each raised wrist, forming a U-shaped hemline – a style which they used when casting in bronze as well. Nonetheless many **statues** have cracked, leaving them headless or limbless. Where the faces have survived, Dvaravati statues display some of the most naturalistic features ever produced in Thailand, distinguished by their thick lips, flattened noses and wide cheekbones.

Nakhon Pathom, thought to have been a target of Buddhist missionaries from India since before the first century AD, has also yielded many **dharmachakra**, originating in the period when the Buddha could not be directly represented. These metre-high carved stone wheels symbolize the cycles of life and reincarnation, and in Dvaravati examples are often accompanied by a small statue of a deer, which refers to the Buddha preaching his first sermon in a deer park.

Srivijaya (eighth to thirteenth centuries)

While Dvaravati's Theravada Buddhists were influencing the central plains, southern Thailand was paying allegiance to the Mahayana Buddhists of the **Srivijayan** civilization. Mahayanists believe that those who have achieved enlightenment should postpone their entry into Nirvana in order to help others along the way. These stay-behinds, revered like saints both during and after life, are called **bodhisattva**, and statues of them were the mainstay of Srivijayan art.

The finest Srivijayan *bodhisattva* statues were cast in bronze and show such grace and sinuosity that they rank among the finest sculptures ever produced in the country. Many are lavishly adorned and some were even bedecked in real jewels when first made. By far the most popular *bodhisattva* subject was **Avalokitesvara**, worshipped as compassion incarnate. Generally shown with four or more arms and with an animal skin over the left shoulder or tied at the waist, Avalokitesvara is also sometimes depicted with his torso covered in tiny Buddha images. Bangkok's National Museum holds the most beautiful Avalokitesvara, the Bodhisattva Padmapani found in Chaiya, but there's a good sandstone example *in situ* at Prasat Muang Singh near Kanchanaburi.

Khmer and Lopburi (tenth to fourteenth centuries)

By the end of the ninth century the **Khmers** of Cambodia were starting to expand from their capital at Angkor into the Dvaravati states, bringing with them the Hindu faith and the cult of the god-king (*devaraja*). As lasting testaments to the sacred power of their kings, the Khmers built hundreds of imposing stone sanctuaries across their newly acquired territory.

Each magnificent castle-temple – known in Khmer as a **prasat** – was constructed primarily as a shrine for a Shiva lingam, the phallic representation of the god Shiva. They followed a similar pattern, centred on at least one pyramidal or corncob-shaped tower, or **prang**, which represented Mount Meru (the gods' heavenly abode) and housed the lingam. Prangs were surrounded by concentric rectangular **galleries**, whose **gopura** (entrance chambers) at the cardinal points were usually approached by staircases flanked with **naga balustrades**; in Khmer temples, nagas generally appear as symbolic bridges between the human world and that of the gods. Most compounds enclosed ponds between their outer and inner walls, and many were surrounded by a network of moats and **reservoirs**: historians attribute the Khmers' political success in part to their skill in designing highly efficient irrigation systems.

Exuberant **carvings** ornamented almost every surface of the prasat. Usually gouged from sandstone, but frequently moulded in stucco, they depict Hindu deities – notably Vishnu Reclining on the Milky Sea of Eternity in the National Museum (see page 61) – and stories, especially episodes from the *Ramayana*. Towards the end of the twelfth century, the Khmer leadership became Mahayana Buddhist, commissioning Buddhist carvings to be installed alongside the Hindu ones, and often replacing the Shiva lingam with a Buddha or *bodhisattva* image.

During the Khmer period the former Theravada Buddhist principality of Lopburi produced a distinctive style of Buddha statue. Broad-faced and muscular, the classic **Lopburi** Buddha wears a diadem or ornamental headband – a nod to the Khmers' ideological fusion of earthly and heavenly power – and the *ushnisha* (the sign of enlightenment) becomes distinctly conical rather than a mere bump on the head. Early Lopburi Buddhas also come garlanded with necklaces and ornamental belts.

Sukhothai (thirteenth to fifteenth centuries)

Capitalizing on the Khmers' weakening hold over central Thailand, two Thai generals established the first major Thai kingdom in 1238 in **Sukhothai** (some 400km north of modern-day Bangkok), and over the next two hundred years its citizens produced some of Thailand's most refined art.

Sukhothai's artistic reputation rests above all on its **sculpture**. More sinuous even than the Srivijayan images, Sukhothai Buddhas tend towards elegant androgyny, with slim oval faces and slender curvaceous bodies usually clad in a plain, skintight robe that fastens with a tassle close to the navel. The sculptors favoured the seated pose, with hands in the *Bhumisparsa Mudra*, most expertly executed in the Phra Buddha Chinnarat image in Phitsanulok (replicated at Bangkok's Wat Benjamabophit) and in the enormous Phra Sri Sakyamuni, now enshrined in Bangkok's Wat Suthat. They were also the first to represent the **walking Buddha**, a supremely graceful figure with his right leg poised to move forwards and his left arm in the *Vitarkha Mudra*, as seen at Sukhothai's Wat Sra Si.

Sukhothai-era architects also devised a new type of chedi, as elegant in its way as the images their sculptor colleagues were producing. This was the **lotus-bud chedi**, a slender tower topped with a tapered finial that was to become a hallmark of the Sukhothai era.

Ancient Sukhothai is also renowned for the skill of its potters, who produced a **ceramic ware** known as Sawankhalok, after the name of one of the nearby kiln towns. It is distinguished by its grey-green celadon glazes and by the fish and chrysanthemum motifs used to decorate bowls and plates.

Ayutthaya (fourteenth to eighteenth centuries)

From 1351 Thailand's central plains came under the thrall of a new power centred on **Ayutthaya**, and over the next four centuries, the Ayutthayan rulers commissioned some four hundred grand wats as symbols of their wealth and power. Though essentially Theravada Buddhists, the kings also adopted some Hindu and Brahmin beliefs from the Khmers – most significantly the concept of *devaraja* or god-kingship, whereby the monarch became a mediator between the people and the Hindu gods. The religious buildings and sculptures of this era reflected this new composite ideology, both by fusing the architectural styles inherited from the Khmers and from Sukhothai and by dressing their Buddhas to look like regents.

Retaining the concentric layout of the typical Khmer **temple complex**, Ayutthayan builders refined and elongated the prang into a **corncob-shaped tower**, rounding it off at the top and introducing vertical incisions around its circumference. As a spire they often added a bronze thunderbolt, and into niches within the prang walls they placed Buddha images. In Ayutthaya itself, the ruined complexes of Wat Phra Mahathat and Wat Ratburana both include these corncob prangs, but the most famous example is Bangkok's Wat Arun, which, though built during the subsequent Bangkok period, is a classic Ayutthayan structure.

Ayutthaya's architects also adapted the Sri Lankan **chedi** so favoured by their Sukhothai predecessors, stretching the bell-shaped base and tapering it into a very graceful conical spire, as at Wat Phra Sri Sanphet in Ayutthaya. The **viharns** of this era are characterized by walls pierced by slit-like windows, designed to foster a mysterious atmosphere by limiting the amount of light inside the building. As with all of Ayutthaya's buildings, few viharns survived the brutal 1767 sacking, with the notable exception of Wat Na Phra Mane; Wat Yai Suwannaram in Phetchaburi (see page 135) is also a fine example.

From Sukhothai's Buddha **sculptures** the Ayutthayans copied the soft oval face, adding an earthlier demeanour to the features and imbuing them with a hauteur in tune with the *devaraja* ideology. Like the Lopburi images, early Ayutthayan statues wear crowns to associate kingship with Buddhahood; as the court became ever more lavish, so these figures became increasingly adorned, until – as in the monumental bronze at Wat Na Phra Mane – they appeared in earrings, armlets, anklets, bandoliers and coronets. The artists justified these luscious portraits of the Buddha – who was, after all, supposed to have given up worldly possessions – by pointing to an episode when the Buddha transformed himself into a well-dressed nobleman to gain the ear of an emperor, whereupon he scolded the man into entering the monkhood.

While a couple of wats in Sukhothai show hints of painted decoration, religious **painting** in Thailand really dates from the Ayutthayan era. Unfortunately most of Ayutthaya's own paintings were destroyed in 1767, but several temples elsewhere have well-preserved murals, in particular Wat Yai Suwannaram in Phetchaburi. By all accounts typical of late seventeenth-century painting, the Phetchaburi murals depict rows of *thep*, or divinities, paying homage to the Buddha, in scenes presented without shadow or perspective, and mainly executed in dark reds and cream.

Ratanakosin (eighteenth century to the 1930s)

When **Bangkok** emerged as Ayutthaya's successor in 1782, the new capital's founder was determined to revive the old city's grandeur, and the **Ratanakosin** (or Bangkok) period began by aping what the Ayutthayans had done. Since then neither wat architecture nor religious sculpture has evolved much further.

The first **Ratanakosin building** was the bot of Bangkok's Wat Phra Kaeo, built to enshrine the Emerald Buddha. Designed to a typical Ayutthayan plan, it's coated in glittering mirrors and gold leaf, with roofs ranged in multiple tiers and tiled in green and orange. To this day, most newly built bots and viharns follow a more economical version of this paradigm, whitewashing the outside walls but decorating the pediment in gilded ornaments and mosaics of coloured glass. Tiered temple roofs still taper off into the slender bird-like finials called *chofa*, and naga staircases – a Khmer feature inherited by Ayutthaya – have become almost obligatory. The result is that modern wats are often almost indistinguishable from each other, though Bangkok does have a few exceptions, including Wat Benjamabophit, which uses marble cladding for its walls and incorporates Victorian-style stained-glass windows, and Wat Rajapobhit, which is covered all over in Chinese ceramics. The most dramatic chedi of the Ratanakosin era – one of the tallest in the world – was constructed in the mid-nineteenth century in Nakhon Pathom (see page 126), to the original Sri Lankan style.

Early Ratanakosin sculptors produced adorned **Buddha images** very much in the Ayutthayan vein, sometimes adding real jewels to the figures; more modern images are notable for their ugliness rather than for any radical departure from type. The obsession with size, first apparent in the Sukhothai period, has plumbed new depths, with graceless concrete statues up to 60m high becoming the norm (as in Bangkok's Wat Indraviharn), a monumentalism made worse by the routine application of browns and dull yellows. Most small images are cast from or patterned on older models, mostly Sukhothai or Ayutthayan in origin.

Painting has fared much better, with the *Ramayana* murals in Bangkok's Wat Phra Kaeo (see page 50) a shining example of how Ayutthayan techniques and traditional subject matters could be adapted into something fantastic, imaginative and beautiful.

Contemporary

Following the democratization of Thailand in the 1930s, artists increasingly became recognized as individuals and took to signing their work for the first time. In 1933 the first school of fine art (now Bangkok's Silpakorn University) was established under the Italian sculptor **Silpa Bhirasri**, designer of the capital's Democracy Monument and, as the new generation experimented with secular themes and styles adapted from the West, Thai art began to look a lot more **"modern"**. As for subject matter, the leading artistic preoccupation of the past eighty years has been Thailand's spiritual heritage and its role in contemporary society. Since 1985, a number of Thailand's more established contemporary artists have earned the title **National Artist**, an honour that's bestowed annually on notable artists working in all disciplines, including fine art, performing arts, film and literature.

ART GALLERIES AND EXHIBITIONS

Bangkok has a near-monopoly on Thailand's **art galleries**. While the permanent collections at the capital's **National Gallery** (see page 64) are disappointing, regular exhibitions of more challenging contemporary work appear at the huge, ambitious **Bangkok Art and Cultural Centre** (see page 95); at the two galleries of the main art school, **Silpakorn University, in Bangkok** (see page 61) and Nakhon Pathom (see page 128); the **Queen's Gallery** (see page 74); and at smaller gallery spaces around the city.

For a preview of works by Thailand's best modern artists, visit the virtual Rama IX Art Museum at ⓦrama9art.org.

The artists

One of the first modern artists to adapt traditional styles and themes was **Angkarn Kalayanapongsa** (1926–2012), an early recipient of the title National Artist. He was employed as a temple muralist and many of his paintings, some of which are on show in Bangkok's National Gallery, reflect this experience, typically featuring casts of two-dimensional Ayutthayan-style figures and flying *thep* in a surreal setting laced with Buddhist symbols and nods to contemporary culture.

Taking this fusion a step further, one-time cinema billboard artist **Chalermchai Kositpipat** (b. 1955) specializes in temple murals with a modern, controversial, twist. Outside Thailand his most famous work enlivens the interior walls of London's Wat Buddhapadipa with strong colours and startling imagery. At home his latest project is the unconventional and highly ornate all-white Wat Rong Khun in his native Chiang Rai province.

Aiming for the more secular environments of the gallery and the private home, National Artist **Pichai Nirand** (b. 1936) rejects the traditional mural style and makes more selective choices of Buddhist imagery, appropriating religious objects and icons and reinterpreting their significance. He's particularly well known for his fine-detail canvases of Buddha footprints, many of which can be seen in Bangkok galleries and public spaces.

National artist **Pratuang Emjaroen** (1935–2022) was famous for his social commentary, as epitomized by his huge and powerful canvas *Dharma and Adharma; The Days of Disaster*, which he painted in response to the vicious clashes between the military and students in 1973. The 5m x 2m picture depicts severed limbs, screaming faces and bloody gun barrels amid shadowy images of the Buddha's face, a spiked Dharmachakra and other religious symbols. Many of Pratuang's subsequent works addressed the issue of social injustice, using his trademark strong shafts of light and bold colour in a mix of Buddhist iconography and abstract imagery.

Prolific traditionalist **Chakrabhand Posayakrit** (b. 1943) is also inspired by Thailand's Buddhist culture; he is famously proud of his country's cultural heritage, which infuses much of his work and has led to him being honoured as a National Artist. He is best known for his series of 33 *Life of the Buddha* paintings, and for his portraits, including many of members of the Thai royal family.

More controversial, and more of a household name, especially since the opening of his Baan Dam museum in Chiang Rai, **Thawan Duchanee** (1939–2014) tended to examine the spiritual tensions of modern life. His surreal juxtaposition of religious icons with fantastical Bosch-like characters and explicitly sexual images prompted a group of outraged students to slash ten of his early paintings in 1971 – an unprecedented reaction to a work of Thai art. Nevertheless, Thawan continued to produce allegorical investigations into the individual's struggles against the obstacles that dog the Middle Way, prominent among them lust and violence, but after the 1980s his street cred waned as his saleability mushroomed. Critics questioned his integrity at accepting commissions from corporate clients, and his neo-conservative image cannot have been enhanced when he was honoured as a National Artist in 2001.

Complacency is not a criticism that could be levelled at **Vasan Sitthiket** (b. 1957), one of Thailand's most outspoken and iconoclastic artists, whose uncompromising pictures are shown at – and still occasionally banned from – large and small galleries around the capital. A persistent crusader against the hypocrisies of establishment figures such as monks, politicians, CEOs and military leaders, Vasan's is one of the loudest and most aggressive political voices on the contemporary art scene, expressed on canvas, in multimedia works and in performance art. His significance is well established and he was one of the seven artists to represent Thailand at the 2003 Venice Biennale, where Thailand had its own pavilion for the first time.

Equally confrontational is fellow Biennale exhibitor, the photographer, performance artist and social activist **Manit Sriwanichpoom** (b. 1961). Manit is best known for his "Pink Man" series of photographs in which he places a Thai man (his collaborator Sompong Thawee), dressed in a flashy pink suit and pushing a pink shopping trolley, into different scenes and situations in Thailand and elsewhere. The Pink Man represents thoughtless, dangerous consumerism and his backdrop might be an impoverished hill-tribe village (*Pink Man on Tour*; 1998), or black-and-white shots from the political violence of 1973, 1976 and 1992 (*Horror in Pink*; 2001).

Women artists tend to be less high profile in Thailand, but in 2007 **Pinaree Sanpitak** (b. 1961) became the first female recipient of the annual Silpathorn Awards for established artists, sharing the honour that year with, among others, notorious bad boy Vasan Sitthiket. Pinaree is known for her interest in gender issues and for her recurrent use of a female iconography in the form of vessels and mounds, often exploring the overlap with Buddhist stupa imagery. She works mainly in multimedia; her "Vessels and Mounds" show of 2001, for example, featured installations of huge, breast-shaped floor cushions, candles and bowls.

Among the younger faces on the Thai art scene, **Thaweesak Srithongdee** (b. 1970) blends surrealism and pop culture with the erotic and the figurative, to cartoon-like effect. He is preoccupied with popular culture, as is **Jirapat Tatsanasomboon** (b. 1971), whose work plays around with superheroes and cultural icons from East and West, pitting the *Ramayana*'s monkey king, Hanuman, against Spiderman in *Hanuman vs Spiderman*, and fusing mythologies in *The Transformation of Sita (after Botticelli)*. **Alex Face** (Patcharapol Tangruen; b. 1982) is one of Thailand's first collectable street artists, employing plenty of wit and humour in his usually indirect political commentary.

Books

We have included publishers' details for books that may be hard to find outside Thailand. Other titles should be available worldwide. Titles marked ★ are particularly recommended.

TRAVEL

James O'Reilly and Larry Habegger (eds) *Travelers' Tales: Thailand*. Absorbing anthology of contemporary writings about Thailand, by Thailand experts, social commentators, travel writers and first-time visitors.

Steve Van Beek *Slithering South* (Wind and Water, Hong Kong). An expat writer tells how he single-handedly paddled his wooden boat down the entire 1100km course of the Chao Phraya River, and reveals a side of Thailand that's rarely written about in English.

William Warren *Bangkok*. An engaging portrait of the unwieldy capital, weaving together anecdotes and character sketches from Bangkok's past and present.

CULTURE AND SOCIETY

Michael Carrithers *The Buddha: A Very Short Introduction*. Accessible account of the life of the Buddha, and the development and significance of his thought.

★ **Philip Cornwel-Smith and John Goss** *Very Thai*. Why do Thais decant their soft drinks into plastic bags, and how does one sniff-kiss? Answers and insights aplenty in this intriguingly observant, fully illustrated guide to contemporary Thai culture. In similar vein is Cornwel-Smith's *Very Bangkok, an Insider's View of the City covering its Full Ethnic Diversity*.

James Eckardt *Bangkok People*. The collected articles of a renowned expat journalist, whose encounters with a varied cast of Bangkok inhabitants – from construction-site workers and street vendors to boxers and political candidates – add texture and context to the city.

Sandra Gregory with Michael Tierney *Forget You Had A Daughter: Doing Time in the "Bangkok Hilton"* – Sandra Gregory's Story. The frank and shocking account of a young British woman's term in Bangkok's notorious Lard Yao prison after being caught trying to smuggle 89 grams of heroin out of Thailand.

Father Joe Maier *Welcome To The Bangkok Slaughterhouse: The Battle for Human Dignity in Bangkok's Bleakest Slums* and *The Open Gate of Mercy*. Catholic priest Father Joe shares the stories of some of the Bangkok street kids and slum-dwellers that his charitable foundation has been supporting since 1972 (see page 43).

Trilok Chandra Majupuria *Erawan Shrine and Brahma Worship in Thailand* (Tecpress, Bangkok). The most concise introduction to the complexities of Thai religion, with a much wider scope than the title implies.

Cleo Odzer *Patpong Sisters*. An American anthropologist's funny and touching account of her life with the prostitutes and bar girls of Bangkok's notorious red-light district.

★ **Phra Peter Pannapadipo** *Little Angels: The Real-Life Stories of Twelve Thai Novice Monks*. A dozen young boys, many of them from desperate backgrounds, tell the often-poignant stories of why they became novice monks. For some, funding from the Students Education Trust (see page 43) has changed their lives.

Phra Peter Pannapadipo *Phra Farang: An English Monk in Thailand*. Behind the scenes in a Thai monastery: the frank, funny and illuminating account of a UK-born former businessman's life as a Thai monk.

★ **Pasuk Phongpaichit and Sungsidh Piriyarangsan** *Corruption and Democracy in Thailand*. Fascinating academic study, revealing the nuts and bolts of corruption in Thailand and its links with all levels of political life, and suggesting a route to a stronger society. Their sequel, a study of Thailand's illegal economy, *Guns, Girls, Gambling, Ganja*, co-written with Nualnoi Treerat, makes equally eye-opening and depressing reading.

Denis Segaller *Thai Ways*. Fascinating collection of short pieces on Thai customs and traditions written by a long-term English resident of Bangkok.

Richard Totman *The Third Sex: Kathoey – Thailand's Ladyboys*. As several *kathoey* share their life stories with him, social scientist Totman examines their place in modern Thai society and explores the theory, supported by Buddhist philosophy, that *kathoey* are members of a third sex whose transgendered make-up is predetermined from birth.

Tom Vater and Aroon Thaewchatturat *Sacred Skin*. Fascinating, beautifully photographed exploration of Thailand's spirit tattoos, *sak yant*.

Daniel Ziv and Guy Sharett *Bangkok Inside Out*. This A–Z of Bangkok quirks and cultural substrates is full of slick photography and sparky observations but was deemed offensive by Thailand's Ministry of Culture and so some Thai bookshops won't stock it.

HISTORY

Anna Leonowens *The English Governess at the Siamese Court*. The mendacious memoirs of the nineteenth-century

English governess that inspired the infamous Yul Brynner film *The King and I*; low on accuracy, high on inside-palace gossip.

Chang Noi *Jungle Book: Thailand's Politics, Moral Panic and Plunder 1996–2008* (Silkworm Books, Chiang Mai). A fascinating, often humorous, selection of columns about Thailand's political and social jungle, by "Little Elephant", an anonymous foreign resident, which first appeared in *The Nation* newspaper.

Michael Smithies *Old Bangkok*. Brief, anecdotal history of the capital's early development, emphasizing what remains to be seen of bygone Bangkok.

William Stevenson *The Revolutionary King*. Interesting biography of the normally secretive King Bhumibol, written by a British journalist who was given unprecedented access to the monarch and his family. The overall approach is uncritical, but lots of revealing insights emerge along the way.

John Stewart *To the River Kwai: Two Journeys – 1943, 1979*. A survivor of the horrific World War II POW camps along the River Kwai returns to the region, interlacing his wartime reminiscences with observations on how he feels 36 years later.

William Warren *Jim Thompson: the Legendary American of Thailand*. The engrossing biography of the ex-intelligence agent, art collector and Thai silk magnate whose disappearance in Malaysia in 1967 has never been satisfactorily resolved.

Thongchai Winichakul *Siam Mapped*. Intriguing, seminal account of how Rama V, under pressure on his borders from Britain and France at the turn of the twentieth century, in effect colonized his own country, which was then a loose hierarchy of city-states.

★ **David K. Wyatt** *Thailand: A Short History*. An excellent treatment, scholarly but highly readable, with a good eye for witty, telling details. Good chapters on the story of the Thais before they reached what's now Thailand, and on more recent developments. The same author's *Siam in Mind* (Silkworm Books, Chiang Mai) is a wide-ranging and intriguing collection of sketches and short reflections that point towards an intellectual history of Thailand.

ART, ARCHITECTURE AND FILM

Jean Boisselier *The Heritage of Thai Sculpture*. Expensive but accessible, seminal tome by influential French art historian.

★ **Susan Conway** *Thai Textiles*. A fascinating, richly illustrated work which draws on sculptures and temple murals to trace the evolution of Thai weaving techniques and costume styles, and to examine the functional and ceremonial uses of textiles.

★ **Sumet Jumsai** *Naga: Cultural Origins in Siam and the West Pacific*. Wide-ranging discussion of water symbols in Thailand and other parts of Asia, offering a stimulating mix of art, architecture, mythology and cosmology.

Bastian Meiresonne (ed) *Thai Cinema* (wasiexpo.com). Anthology of twenty short essays on Thai cinema, published to accompany a film festival in France, including pieces on arthouse, shorts and censorship. In French and English.

Steven Pettifor *Flavours: Thai Contemporary Art*. Takes up the baton from Poshyananda (see below) to look at the newly invigorated art scene in Thailand from 1992 to 2004, with profiles of 23 leading lights, including painters, multimedia and performance artists.

★ **Apinan Poshyananda** *Modern Art In Thailand*. Excellent introduction which extends up to the early 1990s, with very readable discussions on dozens of individual artists, and lots of colour plates.

Dome Sukwong and Sawasdi Suwannapak *A Century of Thai Cinema*. Full-colour history of the Thai film industry and the promotional artwork (billboards, posters, magazines and cigarette cards) associated with it.

★ **Steve Van Beek** *The Arts of Thailand*. Lavishly produced and perfectly pitched introduction to the history of Thai architecture, sculpture and painting, with superb photographs by Luca Invernizzi Tettoni.

William Warren and Luca Invernizzi Tettoni *Arts and Crafts of Thailand*. Good-value large-format paperback, setting the wealth of Thai arts and crafts in cultural context, with plenty of attractive illustrations and colour photo-graphs.

LITERATURE

Alastair Dingwall (ed) *Traveller's Literary Companion: Southeast Asia*. A useful though rather dry reference, with a large section on Thailand, including a book list, well-chosen extracts, biographical details of authors and other literary notes.

M.L. Manich Jumsai *Thai Ramayana* (Chalermnit, Bangkok). Slightly stilted abridged prose translation of King Rama I's version of the epic Hindu narrative, full of gleeful descriptions of bizarre mythological characters and supernatural battles. Essential reading for a full appreciation of Thai painting, carving and classical dance.

★ **Chart Korbjitti** *The Judgement* (Howling Books). Sobering modern-day tragedy about a good-hearted Thai villager who is ostracized by his hypocritical neighbours. Contains lots of interesting details on village life and traditions and thought-provoking passages on the stifling conservatism of rural communities. Winner of the Southeast Asia Write Award in 1982.

★ **Rattawut Lapcharoensap** *Sightseeing*. This outstanding debut collection of short stories by a young Thai-born author now living overseas highlights big, pertinent themes – cruelty, corruption, racism, pride – in its neighbourhood tales of randy teenagers, bullyboys, a child's friendship with a Cambodian refugee, and a young man who uses family influence to dodge the draft.

Nitaya Masavisut (ed) *The S.E.A. Write Anthology of Thai Short Stories and Poems* (Silkworm Books, Chiang Mai). Interesting medley of short stories and poems by Thai writers who have won Southeast Asian Writers' Awards. The collection provides a good introduction to the contemporary literary scene.

Kukrit Pramoj *Si Phaendin: Four Reigns* (Silkworm Books, Chiang Mai). A kind of historical romance spanning the four reigns of Ramas V to VIII (1892–1946). Written by former prime minister Kukrit Pramoj, the story has become a modern classic in Thailand, made into films, plays and TV dramas, with heroine Ploi as the archetypal feminine role model.

S.P. Somtow *Jasmine Nights*. An engaging and humorous rites-of-passage tale of an upper-class boy learning what it is to be Thai. Another of his works, *Dragon's Fin Soup and Other Modern Siamese Fables*, is an imaginative and entertaining collection of often supernatural short stories, focusing on the collision of East and West.

★ **Khamsing Srinawk** *The Politician and Other Stories*. A collection of brilliantly satirical short stories, full of pithy moral observation and biting irony, which capture the vulnerability of peasant farmers in the north and northeast as they try to come to grips with the modern world. Written by an insider from a peasant family, who was educated at Chulalongkorn University, became a hero of the left, and joined the communist insurgents after the 1976 clampdown.

Klaus Wenk *Thai Literature – An Introduction* (White Lotus, Bangkok). Dry, but useful, short overview of the last seven hundred years by a noted German scholar, with plenty of extracts.

THAILAND IN FOREIGN LITERATURE

Dean Barrett *Kingdom of Make-Believe*. Despite the clichéd ingredients – the Patpong go-go bar scene, opium smuggling in the Golden Triangle, Vietnam veterans – this novel about a return to Thailand following a twenty-year absence turns out to be a rewardingly multi-dimensional take on the farang experience.

★ **Mischa Berlinski** *Fieldwork*. Anthropology versus evangelism, a battle played out over an imaginary hill tribe in the hills of northern Thailand by a fascinating cast of characters. Wryly and vividly told by an eponymous narrator.

Botan *Letters from Thailand*. Probably the best introduction to the Chinese community in Bangkok, presented in the form of letters written over a twenty-year period by a Chinese emigrant to his mother. Branded as both anti-Chinese and anti-Thai, this 1969 prizewinning book is now mandatory reading in school social studies' classes.

Pierre Boulle *The Bridge over the River Kwai*. The World War II novel that inspired the David Lean movie and kicked off the Kanchanaburi tourist industry.

John Burdett *Bangkok 8*. Riveting Bangkok thriller that takes in Buddhism, plastic surgery, police corruption, the *yaa baa* drugs trade, hookers, jade-smuggling and the spirit world.

Richard Flanagan *The Narrow Road to the Deep North*. Written by a Tasmanian whose father worked as a prisoner of war on the Death Railway in Kanchanaburi, the winner of 2014's Man Booker Prize deals with the railway during World War II and the harrowing later lives of survivors.

Alex Garland *The Beach*. Gripping cult thriller (later made into a film) that uses a Thai setting to explore the way in which travellers' ceaseless quests for "undiscovered" utopias inevitably lead to them despoiling the idyll.

Michel Houellebecq *Platform*. Sex tourism in Thailand provides the nucleus of this brilliantly provocative (some would say offensive) novel, in which Houellebecq presents a ferocious critique of Western decadence and cultural colonialism, and of radical Islam too.

Christopher G. Moore *God of Darkness*. Thailand's best-selling expat novelist sets his most intriguing thriller during the economic crisis of 1997 and includes plenty of meat on endemic corruption and the desperate struggle for power within family and society.

Darin Strauss *Chang & Eng*. An intriguing imagined autobiography of the famous nineteenth-century Siamese twins (see page 86), from their impoverished Thai childhood via the freak shows of New York and London to married life in smalltown North Carolina. Unfortunately marred by lazy research and a confused grasp of Thai geography and culture.

FOOD AND COOKERY

Vatcharin Bhumichitr *The Taste of Thailand*. Another glossy introduction to this eminently photogenic country, this time through its food. The author provides background colour as well as about 150 recipes adapted for Western kitchens.

Jacqueline M. Piper *Fruits of South-East Asia*. An exploration of the bounteous fruits of the region, tracing their role in cooking, medicine, handicrafts and rituals. Well illustrated with photos, watercolours and early botanical drawings.

★ **David Thompson** *Thai Food and Thai Street Food*. Comprehensive, impeccably researched celebrations of the cuisine, with hundreds of recipes, by the owner of the first Thai restaurant ever to earn a Michelin star.

Language

Thai belongs to one of the oldest families of languages in the world, Austro-Thai, and is radically different from most of the other tongues of Southeast Asia. Being tonal, Thai is very difficult for Westerners to master, but by building up from a small core of set phrases, you should soon have enough to get by. Most Thais who deal with tourists speak some English, but once you stray off the beaten track you'll probably need at least a little Thai. Anywhere you go, you'll impress and get better treatment if you at least make an effort to speak a few words.

Distinct dialects are spoken in the north, the northeast and the south, which can increase the difficulty of comprehending what's said to you. **Thai script** is even more of a problem to Westerners, with 44 consonants and 32 vowels. However, street signs in touristed areas are nearly always written in Roman script as well as Thai, and in other circumstances you're better off asking than trying to unscramble the swirling mess of letters and accents. For more information on transliteration into Roman script, see the box in this book's introduction (see page 4).

The best **teach-yourself course** is the expensive *Linguaphone Thai* (including choice of USB, eight CDs or online audio), which also has a shorter, cheaper beginner-level *PDQ* version (with CDs or MP3 files). *Thai for Beginners* by Benjawan Poomsan Becker (book with CDs or app; Paiboon Publishing) is a cheaper, more manageable textbook and is especially good for getting to grips with the Thai writing system. For a more traditional textbook, try Stuart Campbell and Chuan Shaweevongse's *The Fundamentals of the Thai Language*, which is comprehensive, though hard going. The **website** ⓦ thai-language.com is an amazing free resource, featuring a searchable dictionary with eighty thousand entries, complete with Thai script and audio clips, plus lessons and forums; you can also browse and buy Thai language books and learning materials. There are also plenty of **language classes** available in Thailand (see page 46).

Pronunciation

Mastering **tones** is probably the most difficult part of learning Thai. Five different tones are used – low, middle, high, falling, and rising – by which the meaning of a single syllable can be altered in five different ways. Thus, using four of the five tones, you can make a sentence from just one syllable: "mái mài mâi mǎi" meaning "New wood burns, doesn't it?" As well as the natural difficulty in becoming attuned to speaking and listening to these different tones, Western efforts are complicated by our habit of denoting the overall meaning of a sentence by modulating our tones – for example, turning a statement into a question through a shift of stress and tone. Listen to native Thai speakers and you'll soon begin to pick up the different approach to tone.

The pitch of each tone is gauged in relation to your vocal range when speaking, but they should all lie within a narrow band, separated by gaps just big enough to differentiate them. The **low tones** (syllables marked ˋ), **middle tones** (unmarked syllables), and **high tones** (syllables marked ´) should each be pronounced evenly and with no inflection. The **falling tone** (syllables marked ˆ) is spoken with an obvious drop in pitch, as if you were sharply emphasizing a word in English. The **rising tone** (marked ˇ) is pronounced as if you were asking an exaggerated question in English.

As well as the unfamiliar tones, you'll find that, despite the best efforts of the transliterators, there is no precise English equivalent to many **vowel and consonant sounds** in the Thai language. The lists below give a simplified idea of pronunciation.

VOWELS

a as in dad
aa has no precise equivalent, but is pronounced as it looks, with the vowel elongated
ae as in there
ai as in buy
ao as in now
aw as in awe
ay as in pay
e as in pen

eu as in sir, but heavily nasalized
i as in tip
ii as in feet
o as in knock
oe as in hurt, but more closed
oh as in toe
u as in loot
uu as in pool

CONSONANTS

r as in rip, but with the tongue flapped quickly against the palate – in everyday speech, it's often pronounced like "l"
kh as in keep
ph as in put

th as in time
k is unaspirated and unvoiced, and closer to "g"
p is also unaspirated and unvoiced, and closer to "b"
t is also unaspirated and unvoiced, and closer to "d"

GENERAL WORDS AND PHRASES

GREETINGS AND BASIC PHRASES

When you speak to a stranger in Thailand, you should generally end your sentence in *khráp* if you're a man, *khâ* if you're a woman – these untranslatable politening syllables will gain goodwill, and are nearly always used after *sawàt dii* (hello/goodbye) and *khàwp khun* (thank you). *Khráp* and *khâ* are also often used to answer "yes" to a question, though the most common way is to repeat the verb of the question (precede it with *mâi* for "no"). *Châi* (yes) and *mâi châi* (no) are less frequently used than their English equivalents.

Hello sawàt dii
Where are you going? pai năi? (not always meant literally, but used as a general greeting)
I'm out having fun/I'm travelling pai thîaw (answer to pai năi, almost indefinable pleasantry)
Goodbye sawàt dii/la kàwn
Good luck/cheers chôhk dii
Excuse me khăw thâwt
Thank you khàwp khun
It's nothing/it doesn't matter mâi pen rai
How are you? sabai dii reŭ?
I'm fine sabai dii
What's your name? khun chêu arai?
My name is... phŏm (men)/diichăn (women) chêu...
I come from... phŏm/diichăn maa jàak...
I don't understand mâi khâo jai
Do you speak English? khun phûut phasăa angkrìt dâi măi?
Do you have...? mii...măi?
Is...possible? ...dâi măi?
Can you help me? chûay phŏm/diichăn dâi măi?
(I) want... ao...
(I) would like to... yàak jà...
(I) like... châwp...
What is this called in Thai? níi phasăa thai rîak wâa arai?

GETTING AROUND

Where is the...? ...yùu thîi năi?
How far? klai thâo rai?
I would like to go to... yàak jà pai...
Where have you been? pai năi maa?
Where is this bus going? rót níi pai năi?
When will the bus leave? rót jà àwk mêua rai?
What time does the bus arrive in...? rót theŭng... kìi mohng?
Stop here jàwt thîi nîi
here thîi nîi
there/over there thîi nâan/thîi nôhn
right khwăa
left sái
straight trong
north neŭa
south tâi
east tawan àwk
west tawan tòk
near/far klâi/klai
street thanŏn
train station sathàanii rót fai

bus station sathàanii rót mae
airport sanăam bin
ticket tŭa
hotel rohng raem
post office praisanii
restaurant raan ahăan
shop raan
market talàat
hospital rohng pha-yaabaan
motorbike rót mohtoesai
taxi rót táksîi
boat reua
bicycle jàkràyaan

ACCOMMODATION AND SHOPPING

How much is…? …thâo rai/kìi bàat?
I don't want a plastic bag, thanks mâi ao thŭng khráp/khâ
How much is a room here per night? hâwng thîi nîi kheun lá thâo rai?
Do you have a cheaper room? mii hâwng thùuk kwàa măi?
Can I/we look at the room? duu hâwng dâi măi?
I/We'll stay two nights jà yùu săwng kheun
Can you reduce the price? lót raakhaa dâi măi?
Can I store my bag here? fàak krapăo wái thîi nîi dâi măi?
cheap/expensive thùuk/phaeng
air-con room hâwng ae
ordinary room hâwng thammadaa
telephone thohrásàp
laundry sák phâa
blanket phâa hòm
fan phát lom

GENERAL ADJECTIVES

alone khon diaw
another ìik…nèung
bad mâi dii
big yài
clean sa-àat
closed pìt
cold (object) yen
cold (person or weather) năo
delicious aròi
difficult yâak
dirty sokaprok
easy ngâi
fun sanùk
hot (temperature) ráwn
hot (spicy) phèt
hungry hĭu khâo
ill mâi sabai
open pòet
pretty sŭay
small lek
thirsty hĭu nám
tired nèu-ay
very mâak

GENERAL NOUNS

Nouns have no plurals or genders, and don't require an article.
bathroom/toilet hâwng nám
boyfriend or girlfriend faen
food ahăan
foreigner fàràng
friend phêuan
money ngoen
water/liquid nám

GENERAL VERBS

Thai verbs do not conjugate at all, and also often double up as nouns and adjectives, which means that foreigners' most unidiomatic attempts to construct sentences are often readily understood.
come maa
do tham
eat kin/thaan khâo
give hâi
go pai
sit nâng
sleep nawn làp
walk doen pai

NUMBERS

zero sŭun
one nèung
two săwng
three săam
four sìi
five hâa
six hòk
seven jèt
eight pàet
nine kâo
ten sìp
eleven sìp èt
twelve, thirteen… sìp săwng, sìp săam…
twenty yîi sìp/yiip
twenty-one yîi sìp èt
twenty-two, twenty-three… yîi sìp săwng, yîi sìp săam…
thirty, forty, etc săam sìp, sìi sìp…
one hundred, two hundred… nèung rói, săwng rói…
one thousand nèung phan
ten thousand nèung mèun
one hundred thousand nèung săen
one million nèung láan

TIME

The most common system for telling the time, as outlined below, is actually a confusing mix of several different systems. The State Railway and government officials use the 24-hour clock (9am is *kâo naalikaa*, 10am *sìp naalikaa*, and so on), which is always worth trying if you get stuck.

1–5am tii nèung–tii hâa
6–11am hòk mohng cháo–sìp èt mohng cháo
noon thîang
1pm bài mohng
2–4pm bài sǎwng mohng–bài sìi mohng
5–6pm hâa mohng yen–hòk mohng yen
7–11pm nèung thûm–hâa thûm
midnight thîang kheun
What time is it? kìi mohng láew?
How many hours? kìi chûa mohng?
How long? naan thâo rai?
minute naathii
hour chûa mohng
day wan
week aathít
month deuan
year pii
today wan níi
tomorrow phrûng níi
yesterday mêua wan níi
now diǎw níi
next week aathít nâa
last week aathít kàwn
morning cháo
afternoon bài
evening yen
night kheun

DAYS

Monday wan jan
Tuesday wan angkhaan
Wednesday wan phút
Thursday wan pháréuhàt
Friday wan sùk
Saturday wan sǎo
Sunday wan aathít

FOOD AND DRINK

BASIC INGREDIENTS

kài chicken
mǔu pork
néua beef, meat
pèt duck
ahǎan thalay seafood
plaa fish
plaa dùk catfish
plaa mèuk squid
kûng prawn, shrimp
hǒy shellfish
hǒy nang rom oyster
puu crab
khài egg
phàk vegetables

VEGETABLES

makěua aubergine
makěua thêt tomato
nàw mái bamboo shoots
tùa ngâwk bean sprouts
phrík chilli
man faràng potato
man faràng thâwt chips
taeng kwaa cucumber
phrík yùak green pepper
krathiam garlic
hèt mushroom
tùa peas, beans or lentils
tôn hǒrm spring onions

NOODLES

ba mìi egg noodles
kwáy tiǎw (sên yài/sên lék) white rice noodles (wide/thin)
khanǒm jiin nám yaa noodles topped with fish curry
kwáy tiǎw/ba mìi haêng rice noodle/egg noodles fried with egg, small pieces of meat and a few vegetables
kwáy tiǎw/ba mìi nám (mǔu) rice noodle/egg noodle soup, made with chicken broth (and pork balls)
kwáy tiǎw/ba mìi rât nâ (mǔu) rice noodles/egg noodles fried in gravy-like sauce with vegetables (and pork slices)
mìi kràwp crisp fried egg noodles with small pieces of meat and a few vegetables
phàt thai thin noodles fried with egg, bean sprouts and tofu, topped with ground peanuts
phàt siyú wide or thin noodles fried with soy sauce, egg and meat

RICE

khâo rice
khâo man kài slices of chicken served over marinated rice
khâo mǔu daeng red pork with rice
khâo nâ kài/pèt chicken/duck served with sauce over rice
khâo niǎw sticky rice
khâo phàt fried rice
khâo kaeng curry over rice
khâo tôm rice soup (usually for breakfast)

CURRIES AND SOUPS

kaeng phèt hot, red curry
kaeng phánaeng thick, savoury curry
kaeng khîaw wan green curry
kaeng mátsàman rich Muslim-style curry, usually with beef and potatoes
kaeng karìi mild, Indian-style curry
hàw mòk thalay seafood curry soufflé
kaeng liang peppery vegetable soup
kaeng sôm tamarind soup
tôm khà kài chicken, coconut and galangal soup
tôm yam kûng hot and sour prawn soup
kaeng jèut mild soup with vegetables and usually pork

SALADS

lâap spicy ground meat salad
nám tòk grilled beef or pork salad
sôm tam spicy papaya salad
yam hua plee banana flower salad
yam néua grilled beef salad
yam plaa mèuk squid salad
yam sôm oh pomelo salad
yam plaa dùk foo crispy fried catfish salad
yam thùa phuu wing-bean salad
yam wun sen noodle and pork salad

OTHER DISHES

hâwy thâwt omelette stuffed with mussels
kài phàt bai kraprao chicken fried with holy basil leaves
kài phàt nàw mái chicken with bamboo shoots
kài phàt mét mámûang chicken with cashew nuts
kài phàt khîng chicken with ginger
kài yâang grilled chicken
khài yát sài omelette with pork and vegetables
kûng chúp paêng thâwt prawns fried in batter
mǔu prîaw wǎan sweet and sour pork
néua phàt krathiam phrík thai beef fried with garlic and pepper
néua phàt nám man hâwy beef in oyster sauce
phàt phàk bûng fai daeng morning glory fried in garlic and bean sauce
phàt phàk ruam stir-fried vegetables
pàw pía spring rolls
plaa nêung páe sá whole fish steamed with vegetables and ginger
plaa rât phrík whole fish cooked with chillies
plaa thâwt fried whole fish
sàté satay
thâwt man plaa fish cake

THAI DESSERTS (KHANǑM)

khanǒm beuang small crispy pancake folded over with coconut cream and strands of sweet egg inside
khâo lǎam sticky rice, coconut cream and black beans cooked and served in bamboo tubes
khâo niǎw daeng sticky red rice mixed with coconut cream
khâo niǎw thúrian/mámûang sticky rice mixed with coconut cream and durian/mango
klûay khàek fried banana
lûk taan chêum sweet palm kernels served in syrup
sǎngkhayaa coconut custard
tàkôh squares of transparent jelly (jello) topped with coconut cream

DRINKS (KHREÛANG DEÙM)

bia beer
chaa ráwn hot tea
chaa yen iced tea
kaafae ráwn hot coffee
kâew glass
khúat bottle
mâekhǒng (or anglicized Mekong) Thai brand-name rice whisky
klûay pan banana shake
nám mánao/sôm fresh, bottled or fizzy lemon/orange juice
nám plào drinking water (boiled or filtered)
nám sǒdaa soda water
nám taan sugar
kleua salt
nám yen cold water
nom jeùd milk
ohlíang iced black coffee
thûay cup

ORDERING

I am vegetarian/vegan Phǒm (male)/diichǎn (female) kin ahǎan mangsàwirát/jeh
Can I see the menu? Khǎw duù menu nóy?
I would like… Khǎw…
with/without… Sài/mâi sài…
Can I have the bill please? Khǎw check bin?

Glossary

Amphoe District.
Amphoe muang Provincial capital.
Ao Bay.
Apsara Female deity.
Avalokitesvara Bodhisattva representing compassion.
Avatar Earthly manifestation of a deity.
Ban Village or house.
Bang Village by a river or the sea.
Bencharong Polychromatic ceramics made in China for the Thai market.
Bhumisparsa mudra Most common gesture of Buddha images; symbolizes the Buddha's victory over temptation.
Bodhisattva In Mahayana Buddhism, an enlightened being who postpones his or her entry into Nirvana.
Bot Main sanctuary of a Buddhist temple.
Brahma One of the Hindu trinity – "The Creator". Usually depicted with four faces and four arms.
Celadon Porcelain with grey-green glaze.
Changwat Province.
Chao ley/chao nam "Sea gypsies" – nomadic fisherfolk of south Thailand.
Chedi Reliquary tower in Buddhist temple.
Chofa Finial on temple roof.
Deva Mythical deity.
Devaraja God-king.
Dharma The teachings or doctrine of the Buddha.
Dharmachakra Buddhist Wheel of Law (also known as Wheel of Doctrine or Wheel of Life).
Doi Mountain.
Erawan Mythical three-headed elephant; Indra's vehicle.
Farang Foreigner/foreign.
Ganesh Hindu elephant-headed deity, remover of obstacles and god of knowledge.
Garuda Mythical Hindu creature – half man, half bird; Vishnu's vehicle.
Gopura Entrance pavilion to temple precinct (especially Khmer).
Hamsa Sacred mythical goose; Brahma's vehicle.
Hanuman Monkey god and chief of the monkey army in the *Ramayana*; ally of Rama.
Hat Beach.
Hin Stone.
Hinayana Pejorative term for Theravada school of Buddhism, literally "Lesser Vehicle".
Ho trai A scripture library.
Indra Hindu king of the gods and, in Buddhism, devotee of the Buddha; usually carries a thunderbolt.
Isaan Northeast Thailand.
Jataka Stories of the Buddha's five hundred lives.
Khaen Reed and wood pipe; the characteristic musical instrument of Isaan.
Khao Hill, mountain.
Khlong Canal.
Khon Classical dance-drama.
Kinnari Mythical creature – half woman, half bird.
Kirtimukha Very powerful deity depicted as a lion-head.
Ko Island.
Ku The Lao word for *prang*; a tower in a temple complex.
Laem Headland or cape.
Lakhon Classical dance-drama.
Lak muang City pillar; revered home for the city's guardian spirit.
Lakshaman/Phra Lak Rama's younger brother.
Lakshana Auspicious signs or "marks of greatness" displayed by the Buddha.
Lanna Northern Thai kingdom that lasted from the thirteenth to the sixteenth century.
Likay Popular folk theatre.
Longyi Burmese sarong.
Luang Pho Abbot or especially revered monk.
Maenam River.
Mahathat Chedi containing relics of the Buddha.
Mahayana School of Buddhism now practised mainly in China, Japan and Korea; literally "the Great Vehicle".
Mara The Evil One; tempter of the Buddha.
Mawn khwaan Traditional triangular or "axe-head" pillow.
Meru/Sineru Mythical mountain at the centre of Hindu and Buddhist cosmologies.
Mondop Small, square temple building to house minor images or religious texts.
Moo/muu Neighbourhood.
Muang City or town.
Muay thai Thai boxing.
Mudra Symbolic gesture of the Buddha.
Mut mee Tie-dyed cotton or silk.
Naga Mythical dragon-headed serpent in Buddhism and Hinduism.
Nakhon Honorific title for a city.
Nam Water.
Nam tok Waterfall.
Nang thalung Shadow-puppet entertainment, found in southern Thailand.
Nielloware Engraved metalwork.
Nirvana Final liberation from the cycle of rebirths; state of non-being to which Buddhists aspire.
Pak Tai Southern Thailand.
Pali Language of ancient India; the script of the original Buddhist scriptures.
Pha sin Woman's sarong.
Phi Animist spirit.

Phra Honorific term – literally "excellent".
Phu Mountain.
Prang Central tower in a Khmer temple.
Prasat Khmer temple complex or central shrine.
Rama/Phra Ram Human manifestation of Hindu deity Vishnu; hero of the *Ramayana*.
Ramakien Thai version of the *Ramayana*.
Ramayana Hindu epic of good versus evil: chief characters include Rama, Sita, Ravana and Hanuman.
Ravana see Totsagan.
Reua hang yao Longtail boat.
Rishi Ascetic hermit.
Rot ae/rot tua Air-conditioned bus.
Rot thammadaa Ordinary bus.
Sala Meeting hall, pavilion, bus stop – or any open-sided structure.
Samlor Three-wheeled passenger tricycle.
Sanskrit Sacred language of Hinduism; also used in Buddhism.
Sanuk Fun.
Sema Boundary stone to mark consecrated ground within temple complex.
Shiva One of the Hindu trinity – "The Destroyer".
Shiva lingam Phallic representation of Shiva.
Soi Lane or side road.
Songkran Thai New Year.
Songthaew Public transport pick-up vehicle; means "two rows", after its two facing benches.
Takraw Game played with a rattan ball.
Talat Market.
Talat nam Floating market.
Talat yen Night market.
Tambon Subdistrict.
Tavatimsa Buddhist heaven.
Tha Pier.
Thale Sea or lake.
Tham Cave.
Thanon Road.
That Chedi.
Thep A divinity.
Theravada Main school of Buddhist thought in Thailand; also known as Hinayana.
Totsagan Rama's evil rival in the *Ramayana*; also known as Ravana.
Tripitaka Buddhist scriptures.
Trok Alley.
Tuk-tuk Motorized three-wheeled taxi.
Uma Shiva's consort.
Ushnisha Cranial protuberance on Buddha images, signifying an enlightened being.
Viharn Temple assembly hall for the laity; usually contains the principal Buddha image.
Vipassana Buddhist meditation technique; literally "insight".
Vishnu One of the Hindu trinity – "The Preserver". Usually shown with four arms, holding a disc, a conch, a lotus and a club.
Wai Thai greeting expressed by a prayer-like gesture with the hands.
Wang Palace.
Wat Temple.
Wiang Fortified town.
Yaksha Mythical giant.
Yantra Magical combination of numbers and letters, used to ward off danger.

Small print and index

231 About the author
234 Small print
235 Index
239 Map symbols
239 City plan

ABOUT THE AUTHOR

A long-time resident of Thailand, Paul is author of *The Rough Guide to Thailand* and of *The Rough Guide to Thailand's Beaches and Islands*, as well as *The Rough Guide to Ireland*. He has edited and contributed to many other guidebooks, including an update of his native Northeast for *The Rough Guide to England*.

A ROUGH GUIDE TO ROUGH GUIDES

Published in 1982, the first Rough Guide – to Greece – was a student scheme that became a publishing phenomenon. Mark Ellingham, a recent graduate in English from Bristol University, had been travelling in Greece the previous summer and couldn't find the right guidebook. With a small group of friends he wrote his own guide, combining a contemporary, journalistic style with a thoroughly practical approach to travellers' needs.

The immediate success of the book spawned a series that rapidly covered dozens of destinations. And, in addition to impecunious backpackers, Rough Guides soon acquired a much broader readership that relished the guides' wit and inquisitiveness as much as their enthusiastic, critical approach and value-for-money ethos. These days, Rough Guides include recommendations from budget to luxury and cover more than 120 destinations around the globe, from Amsterdam to Zanzibar, all regularly updated by our team of roaming writers.

Browse all our latest guides, read inspirational features and book your trip at **roughguides.com**.

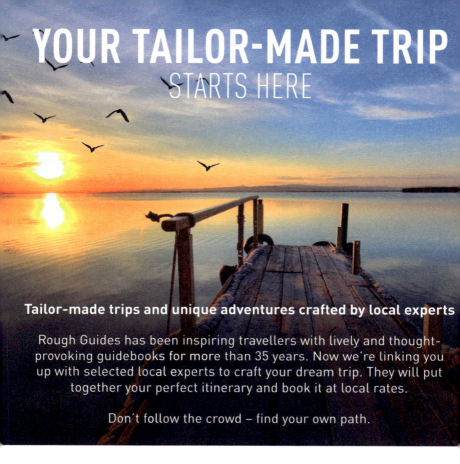

YOUR TAILOR-MADE TRIP
STARTS HERE

Tailor-made trips and unique adventures crafted by local experts

Rough Guides has been inspiring travellers with lively and thought-provoking guidebooks for more than 35 years. Now we're linking you up with selected local experts to craft your dream trip. They will put together your perfect itinerary and book it at local rates.

Don't follow the crowd – find your own path.

HOW ROUGHGUIDES.COM/TRIPS WORKS

STEP 1

Pick your dream destination, tell us what you want and submit an enquiry.

STEP 2

Fill in a short form to tell your local expert about your dream trip and preferences.

STEP 3

Our local expert will craft your tailor-made itinerary. You'll be able to tweak and refine it until you're completely satisfied.

STEP 4

Book online with ease, pack your bags and enjoy the trip! Our local expert will be on hand 24/7 while you're on the road.

BENEFITS OF PLANNING AND BOOKING AT ROUGHGUIDES.COM/TRIPS

PLAN YOUR ADVENTURE WITH LOCAL EXPERTS

Rough Guides' English-speaking local experts are hand-picked, based on their experience in the travel industry and their impeccable standards of customer service.

SAVE TIME AND GET ACCESS TO LOCAL KNOWLEDGE

When a local expert plans your trip, you save time and money when you book, even during high season. You won't be charged for using a credit card either.

MAKE TRAVEL A BREEZE: BOOK WITH PIECE OF MIND

Enjoy stress-free travel when you use Rough Guides' secure online booking platform. All bookings come with a money-back guarantee.

WHAT DO OTHER TRAVELLERS THINK ABOUT ROUGH GUIDES TRIPS?

Trip to Spain

This Spain tour company did a fantastic job to make our dream trip perfect. We gave them our travel budget, told them where we would like to go, and they did all of the planning. Our drivers and tour guides were always on time and very knowledgable. The hotel accommodations were better than we would have found on our own. Only one time did we end up in a location that we had not intended to be in. We called the 24 hour phone number, and they immediately fixed the situation.

Don A, USA

Trip to Morocco

Our trip was fantastic! Transportation, accommodations, guides – all were well chosen! The hotels were well situated, well appointed and had helpful, friendly staff. All of the guides we had were very knowledgeable, patient, and flexible with our varied interests in the different sites. We particularly enjoyed the side trip to Tangier! Well done! The itinerary you arranged for us allowed maximum coverage of the country with time in each city for seeing the important places.

Sharon, USA

PLAN AND BOOK YOUR TRIP AT
ROUGHGUIDES.COM/TRIPS

Rough Guide credits

Editor: Siobhan Warwicker
Cartography: Carte
Picture editor: Piotr Kala
Picture Manager: Tom Smyth
Layout: Ankur Guha
Publishing Technology Manager: Rebeka Davies
Production Operations Manager: Katie Bennett
Head of Publishing: Sarah Clark

Publishing information

Eighth edition 2025

Distribution

UK, Ireland and Europe
Apa Publications (UK) Ltd; mail@roughguides.com
United States and Canada
Two Rivers; ips@ingramcontent.com
Australia and New Zealand
Woodslane; info@woodslane.com.au
Worldwide
Apa Publications (UK) Ltd; mail@roughguides.com

Special Sales, Content Licensing and CoPublishing
Rough Guides can be purchased in bulk quantities at discounted prices. We can create special editions, personalized jackets and corporate imprints tailored to your needs. mail@roughguides.com.

roughguides.com

EU Representative
LOGOS EUROPE, 9 rue Nicolas Poussin, 17000, LA ROCHELLE, France; Contact@logoseurope.eu; +33 (0) 667937378

Printed by Elma Basim in Turkey

ISBN: 9781835292259

This book was produced using **Typefi** automated publishing software.

A catalogue record for this book is available from the British Library.

All rights reserved
© 2025 Apa Digital AG
License edition © Apa Publications Ltd UK

No part of this book may be reproduced, stored in a retrieval system, or transmitted in any form or by any means – electronic, mechanical, photocopying, recording, or otherwise – without prior written permission from Apa Publications.

Every effort has been made to ensure that this publication is accurate, free from safety risks, and provides accurate information. However, changes and errors are inevitable. The publisher is not responsible for any resulting loss, inconvenience, injury or safety concerns arising from the use of this book.

Help us update

We've gone to a lot of effort to ensure that this edition of **The Rough Guide to Bangkok** is accurate and up-to-date. However, things change – places get "discovered", transport routes are altered, restaurants and hotels raise prices or lower standards, and businesses cease trading. If you feel we've got it wrong or left something out, we'd like to know, and if you can direct us to the web address, so much the better.

Please send your comments with the subject line "**Rough Guide Bangkok Update**" to mail@roughguides.com. We'll send a copy of the next edition (or any other Rough Guide if you prefer) for the very best emails.

Photo credits

(Key: T-top; C-centre; B-bottom; L-left; R-right)

iStock 12, 14, 16C, 19BR, 20B, 49, 65, 111, 193
Jimmyfitness/Dreamstime.com 190
Martin Richardson/Rough Guides 18T, 180

Shutterstock 1, 2, 4, 5, 9, 11, 13T, 13B, 15TL, 15TR, 15C, 15B, 16B, 16T, 17T, 17B, 18B, 19T, 19BL, 21T, 21C, 21B, 22, 75, 81, 88, 91, 105, 149, 157, 169, 174, 176, 183
Yuna Yagi/Alexander Lamont 20T

Cover: Reclining buddha inside Wat Pho **iStock**

Index

A

accessible travel 42
accommodation 149
addresses 26
age of consent 40
age restrictions 39
AIDS 36
alcohol 40
Amphawa 132
amulets 72
antiques 44
antiques shops 189
aquarium 97
architecture 212
arrest, advice on 40
art galleries 219
    Ayutthaya National Art Museum 125
    Bangkok Art and Cultural Centre 95
    Jim Thompson Center for the Arts 94
    National Gallery 64
    Queen's Gallery 74
    Sanamchandra Art Gallery (Nakhon Pathom) 128
    Silpakorn University Art Centre 61
art, history of 212
ATMs 47
axe pillows 184
Ayutthaya 116
Ayutthaya, history of 195
Ayutthayan art 217
Ayutthaya tours and cruises 117

B

Bangkok Art and Cultural Centre 95
Bangkok Tourism Division 34
Banglamphu 27, 65
    nightlife 67
    transport to 66
Bang Pa-In 112
Ban Kamthieng 98
banks 46
bargaining 43
beer 172
Bhumibol, King 8
bike rental 33
boats 29
boat tours 82
    dinner and cocktail cruises 162
books 221
bookshops 188
boxing, Thai 177, 178
breastfeeding 191
Bridge over the River Kwai 138
Buddha images 44
Buddhaisawan chapel 63
Buddhism 8, 41, 206
buses, city 28, 115
buses, long-distance 24, 27
business hours 47

C

cabaret 178
calendar, Thai 47
Cambodia, travel to and from 24
car rental 33
Chao Phraya Express boats 29, 31
Chao Phraya River 27
Chao Phraya Tourist boats 30
charities 43
Chatuchak Weekend Market 105
children's Bangkok 190
Chinatown 27, 75
Chinese New Year 47
cinemas 179
City of Angels 10
climate 10
clinics 36
clothes shops 186
clothing 41
computers, buying 185
condoms 36
consulates in bangkok 45
consulates, Thai 45
contemporary art 218
cookery classes 164
costs 43
credit cards 46
crime 38
crocodiles 79
cuisine 158, 159
culture 40
culture shows 177
currency 46
customs regulations 44
cycle tours 82

D

Damnoen Saduak 128
dance-drama, traditional 178
dancing, Thai 177
Death Railway 140, 147
debit cards 46
Democracy Monument 70
dengue fever 35
dentists 36
department stores 185
diarrhoea 35
digestive problems 35
Don Muang airport 26
Downtown Bangkok 91
dress code 52
drinks 172
drugs 38, 40
durians 109
Dusit 27, 88
duty-free allowance 44
Dvaravati art 215

E

Eastern Bus Terminal 28
eating 157
e-cigarettes 40
electricity 44
elephants, white 58
embassies in bangkok 45
embassies, Thai 45
Emerald Buddha 50
emergency contacts 39
Eng and Chang 86
entry requirements 44
Erawan Shrine 97
etiquette 40, 41, 42
excursions from Bangkok 111

F

fact file 8
fashion shopping 186
ferries 30
festivals 37, 161
flights 23
    from Australasia 23
    from North America 23
    from South Africa 24
    from the UK and Ireland 23
floating markets 82, 129
floating vendors 82
flukes 36
food 158

INDEX

food courts 158
food etiquette 159
fruits 163

G

gambling 39
gay scene 175
gem scams 188
gem shops 189
Giant Swing 72
Golden Buddha 76
Golden Mount 74
Grand Palace 50

H

handicrafts 185
health 34
health hazards for children 191
Hellfire Pass 147
Hinduism 210
history 194
holidays, public 47
hospitals 36
hotels 149

I

immigration office 45
inoculations 35
international dialling codes 47
internet access 45
Islam 8

J

jewellery shops 189
Jim Thompson's House 94

K

Kamthieng House 98
Kanchanaburi 137
katoey 175
khanom 137
Khlong Padung Krung Kasem 31
khlongs 81
Khlong Saen Saeb 31
khlongs, travel along 29
Khmer art 216
khon 178
King Prajadhipok Museum 74
kite flying 60

Ko Kred 109

L

lak muang 60
language 224
   transliteration 4
language classes 46
Laos travel to and from 25
laundry 46
laws 38, 39
left luggage 46
lèse majesté laws 41
LGBTQ+ Bangkok 174
listings magazines 34
living in Bangkok 46
longtail boats 82
Lopburi art 216
Loy Krathong 38
Lumphini Park 100

M

magazines 36
Mahachulalong-korn Buddhist University 61
mail 46
malaria 35
Malaysia, travel to and from 25
maps 34
   Ayutthaya 118
   Bangkok 6
   Banglamphu and the Democracy Monument area 68
   Downtown: Around Siam Square and Thanon Ploenchit 96
   Downtown Bangkok 92
   Downtown: South of Thanon Rama IV 102
   Dusit 89
   Excursions from Bangkok 113
   Greater Bangkok 108
   Hualamphong, Chinatown and Pahurat 77
   Kanchanaburi 139
   Phetchaburi 134
   Ratanakosin 51
   Thanon Sukhumvit 99
   Thonburi 83
   Wat Pho 57
   Wat Phra Kaeo & the Grand Palace 53
Marble Temple 89
markets 184
   amulet markets 72
   Chatuchak Weekend Market 105
   Chinatown 76
   Damnoen Saduak 129
   floating markets 129

   Phrannok pierside market 85
   Pratunam 98
   Taling Chan floating market 82
   Tha Ka floating market 133
   Wat Sai floating market 82
massage, traditional 181
media 36
medical resources 34
medical treatment 36
meditation 182
Memorial Bridge 87
mobile phones 185
monarchy 8, 41, 198
money 46
monks 41, 208
mosquitoes 35
motorbike taxis 33
M.R. Kukrit's Heritage Home 103
Muang Boran Ancient City 112
Museum of Siam 59
museums
   Ban Kamthieng 98
   Chantharakasem Palace Museum (Ayutthaya) 122
   Chao Sam Phraya National Museum (Ayutthaya) 121
   Hellfire Pass Memorial Museum and Walk 147
   JEATH War Museum (Kanchanaburi) 141
   Jim Thompson's House 94
   King Prajadhipok Museum 74
   Million Toy Museum (Ayutthaya) 121
   Museum of Siam 59
   National Museum 61
   Phra Pathom Chedi Museum (Nakhon Pathom) 127
   Phra Pathom Chedi National Museum (Nakhon Pathom) 127
   Prasart Museum 107
   Rama VII Museum 74
   Royal Barge Museum 84
   Siriraj Bimuksthan Museum 85
   Siriraj museums 84
   Suan Pakkad Palace Museum 93
   Thailand–Burma Railway Centre (Kanchanaburi) 138
   Thailand Creative and Design Center (TCDC) 103
   Wat Phra Kaeo Museum 57
Myanmar, travel to and from 24

N

Nakhon Kasem 79
Nakhon Pathom 126
names, Thai 42
Nam Tok, Kanchanaburi 146
National Gallery 64

INDEX

National Museum 61
newspapers 36
nightlife 169
Nonthaburi 107
Northern and Northeastern Bus Terminal 27

O

October 14 Memorial 71
Old Siam Plaza 80
opening hours 47
orientation 27

P

Pahurat 27, 80
passports 39, 44
Patpong 100
pharmacies 34, 185
Phetchaburi 134
phones 47, 185
Phra Mahakhan Fortress community 73
Phu Khao Tong 74
Ploughing Ceremony 60
police 39, 40
population 5
post offices 46
Prasart Museum 107
Prasat Muang Singh 146
Pratunam Market 98
prostitution 101

Q

Queen Saovabha Memorial Institute 98
Queen's Gallery 74

R

rabies 35
radio 36
rail travel 27
Rama I 10, 49
Rama IX 8
Ramakien 178
Rama V 8
Rama VII Museum 74
Rama X 8
Ramayana 55
Ratanakosin 27, 49
Ratanakosin art 218
Reclining Buddha 59
religion 8, 41, 206

restaurant boats 162
restaurants 157
room prices 150
Royal Barge Museum 84
royal barge processions 84
royal tonsure ceremony 57
rum 172

S

safety 38
Sai Yok Noi Falls 146, 148
Sampeng Lane 78
Samut Songkhram 130
Sanam Luang 59
San Chao Poh Seua 71
Sao Ching Cha 72
scams 39, 50, 188
Sea Life Bangkok Ocean World 97
sex industry 39, 101
shopping 47, 91, 183
Siam 8
Siamese twins 86
Siam Square 27
Silpakorn University Art Centre 61
Siriraj Bimuksthan Museum 85
Siriraj museums 84
Skytrain 31
smoking 40. *See also* e-cigarettes
Snake Farm 98
social conventions 42
Soi Issaranuphap 78
Southern Bus Terminal 28
spas 180
spellings 4
Srivijaya art 216
street names 4
Suan Pakkad Palace Museum 93
subway 32
Sukhothai art 216
Sukhothai, history of 195
Suvarnabhumi airport 25

T

tailors 187
taxis 33
telephone codes 47
television 36
textiles 185
Thailand–Burma Railway 138, 140, 147
Thailand Creative and Design Center (TCDC) 103
Thai people 194
Tha Ka floating market 133

Thanon Bamrung Muang 71
Thanon Khao San 66
Thanon Phra Athit 67
Thanon Rama IV 27
Thanon Silom 103
Thanon Sukhumvit 27
Thanon Tanao 70
Thompson, Jim 95
Thonburi 27, 81
Thonburi by boat 82
time 48
tipping 48
tourism 8
Tourism Authority of Thailand 34
tourist information 34
tourist police 39
tour operators 24
tours of the city 30
trains 27, 114, 131
transport 114
transport, city 28
transport, to and from Bangkok 23
travel advisories, government 25, 40
travel agents 24
tuk-tuks 33

V

Vajiralongkorn, King 8
VAT refunds 43
Vegetarian Festival 161
vegetarian food 161
Victory Monument 93
Vipassana Meditation Centre 61
visas 24, 44
volunteer projects 43

W

wai 42
walking tours 30
Wat Arun 85
Wat Benjamabophit 89
Wat Chakrawat 79
Wat Chalerm Phra Kiat 109
Wat Chana Songkhram 67
Wat Ga Buang Kim 79
Wat Indraviharn 70
Wat Leng Noei Yee 78
Wat Mahathat 61
Wat Mangkon Kamalawat 78
Wat Paramaiyikawat 110
Wat Pho 57
Wat Phra Chetuphon 57
Wat Phra Kaeo 50
Wat Prayoon 87

Wat Rajabophit 71
Wat Rajnadda 72
Wat Rakhang 85
Wat Saket 73
Wat Suthat 72
Wat Traimit 76

weather 10
wheelchair access 43
wine 172
women travellers 38, 41
working in Bangkok 46
worms 36

Y

Yaowarat Chinatown Heritage Centre 78

Map symbols

The symbols below are used on maps throughout the book

	International boundary		Point of interest		Arch
	Chapter division boundary	@	Internet access		Cave
	Expressway	(i)	Tourist information		Statue
	Pedestrianized road	(C)	Telephone office		Boat stop
	Road	+	Hospital/clinic		Museum
	One-way street		Post office		Temple
	Path	E	Embassy/consulate		Hindu temple
	Railway		Airline office		Chinese temple/pagoda
	Ferry route	✈	Airport		Stadium
	River/canal	★	Transport stop		Church
	Wall	$	Bank/ATM		Building
	Cable car & station		Market		Christian cemetery
	Bridge		Gate		Park/forest
	Mountain				

City plan

The **city plan** on the pages that follow is divided as shown:

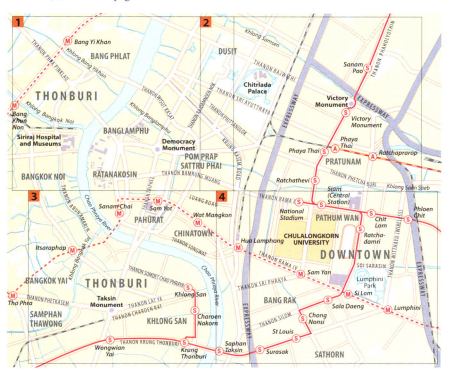

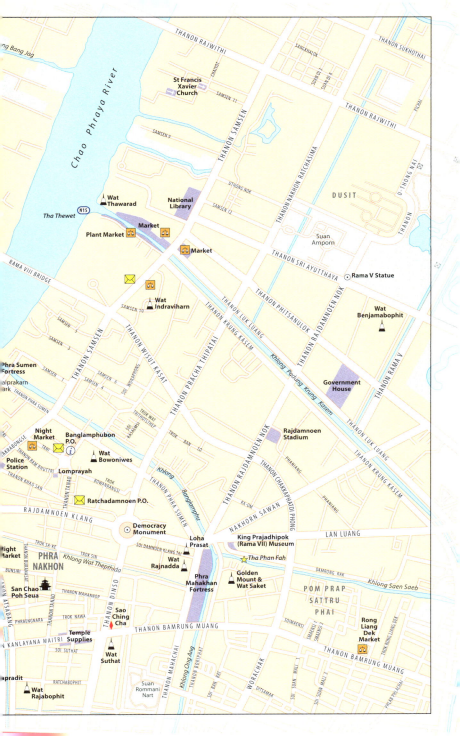

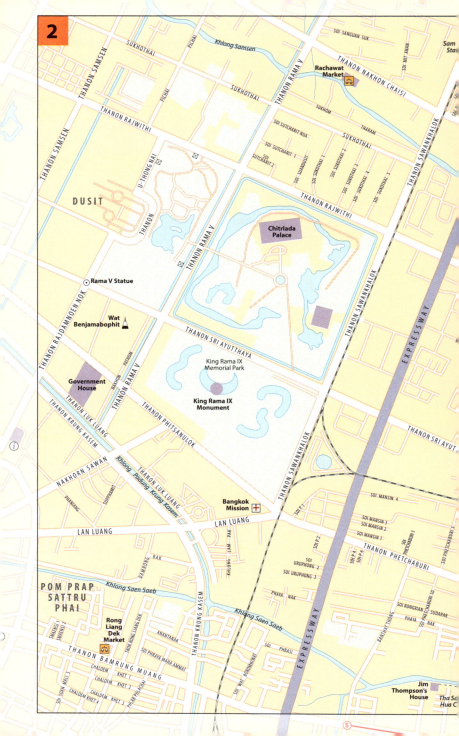

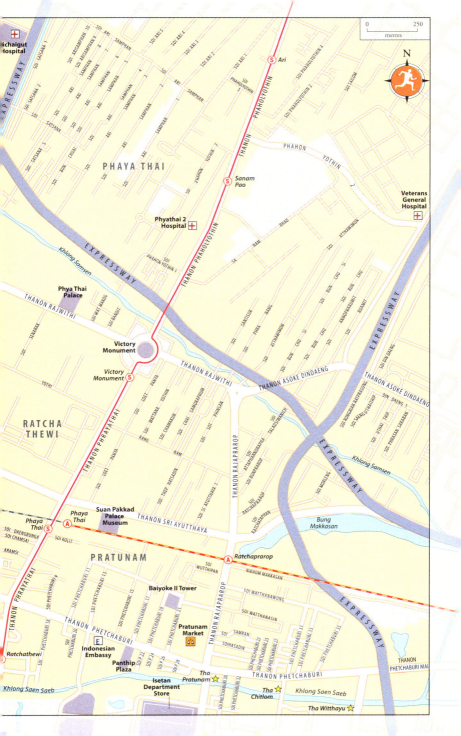

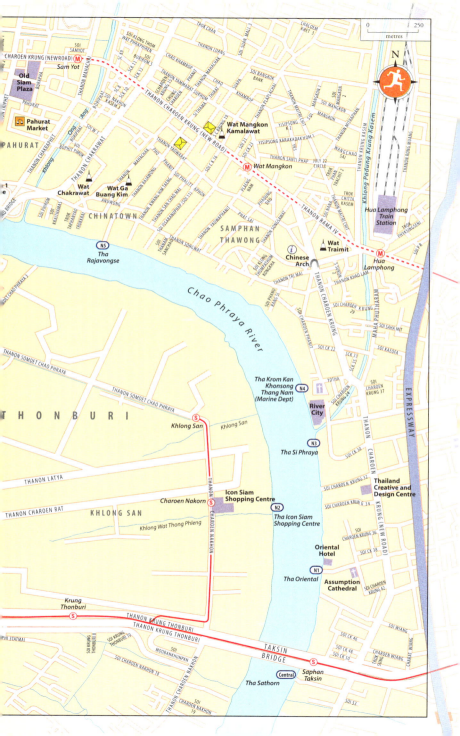

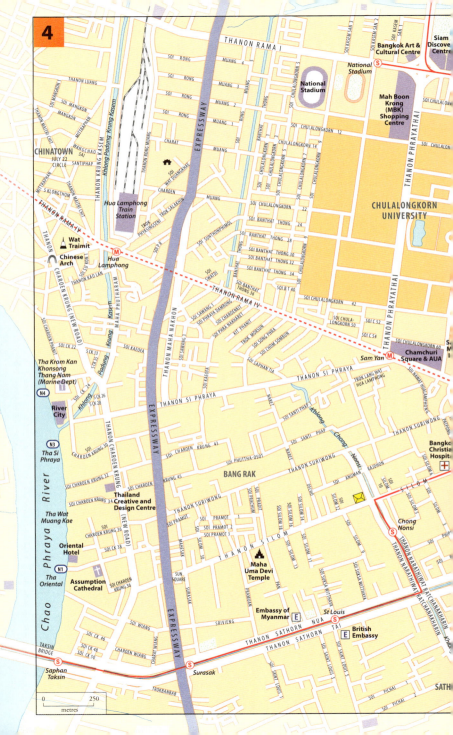